The Law and Special Education

MITCHELL L. YELL

University of South Carolina

Prentice Hall

Merrill,
an imprint of Prentice Hall
Upper Saddle River, New Jersey   Columbus, Ohio

Library of Congress Cataloging-in-Publication Data
Yell, Mitchell L.
    The law and special education / Mitchell L. Yell.
      p.   cm.
    Includes bibliographical references and index.
    ISBN 0-02-430872-2
    1. Handicapped children—Education—Law and legislation—United
States. 2. Special education—Law and legislation—United States.
I. Title.
KF4210.Y45   1998
344.73'0791—dc21
                          97-35699
                              CIP

Editor: Ann Castel Davis
Production Editor: Linda Hillis Bayma
Copy Editor: Jonathan Lawrence
Design Coordinator: Karrie M. Converse
Text Designer: Anne D. Flanagan
Cover Designer: Rod Harris
Production Manager: Laura Messerly
Electronic Text Management: Marilyn Wilson Phelps, Matthew Williams, Karen L. Bretz,
    Tracey B. Ward
Illustrations: Carlisle Communications, Ltd.
Director of Marketing: Kevin Flanagan
Marketing Manager: Suzanne Stanton
Advertising/Marketing Coordinator: Julie Shough

This book was set in ITC Century Light by Carlisle Communications, Ltd. and was printed and
bound by Phoenix Color Corp. The cover was printed by Phoenix Color Corp.

© 1998 by Prentice-Hall, Inc.
Upper Saddle River, New Jersey 07458

Printed in the United States of America

10   9   8

ISBN: 0-02-430872-2

Prentice-Hall International (UK) Limited, *London*
Prentice-Hall of Australia Pty. Limited, *Sydney*
Prentice-Hall of Canada, Inc., *Toronto*
Prentice-Hall Hispanoamericana, S. A., *Mexico*
Prentice-Hall of India Private Limited, *New Delhi*
Prentice-Hall of Japan, Inc., *Tokyo*
Prentice-Hall Asia Pte. Ltd., *Singapore*
Editora Prentice-Hall do Brasil, Ltda., *Rio de Janeiro*

This book is dedicated to the memory of my mother, Vonnet, and to my wife, Joy, and three sons, Nick, Eric, and Alex.

Mitchell L. Yell, Ph.D., is an Associate Professor in Special Education in the College of Education at the University of South Carolina in Columbia, South Carolina. Prior to working at USC, he taught for 16 years in elementary, middle, and secondary classrooms and in special schools for children with learning disabilities, emotional and behavioral disorders, and autism.

For the past eight years, Dr. Yell has conducted extensive research on legal issues in special education. His primary goal has been to extrapolate principles from legislation and litigation, communicate them to teachers and administrators in a clear, nonlegal manner, and assist school districts in the formation of legally sound, research-based policies. He has published 30 journal articles and 4 book chapters, and has conducted numerous workshops on special education law.

PREFACE

$\mathbf{F}$ederal laws mandating the provision of special education and related services to students with disabilities have been in effect for two decades. To understand the field of special education, it is important that we grasp the history and development of these laws. Furthermore, we live in a litigious society, and special education has become a highly litigated area. Thus it is important that special education teachers, administrators, and associated staff have a knowledge of the requirements of the laws. Moreover, the laws are in a constant state of development and refinement, so we need to be able to locate the necessary information to keep abreast of these changes. The purpose of this text is threefold: first, to acquaint readers with the legal development of special education; second, to expose readers to the current legal requirements in providing a free appropriate public education to students with disabilities; and third, to assist readers to understand the procedures involved in obtaining legal information in law libraries and on the Internet, and to conduct legal research using a variety of sources.

This textbook is written in the style of an educational textbook rather than a legal textbook. That is, rather than including passages from selected cases, legal principles from these cases will be presented. Exposure to the written opinions, however, is important, and readers are urged to locate and read them in a law library or on the Internet. References are presented in accordance with the format described in the *Publication Manual of the American Psychological Association* (4th edition) rather than in the standard legal format. Finally, legal terms are kept to a minimum, explained when used, and defined in the Glossary.

A unique feature of this textbook is its connection to a homepage on the World Wide Web titled *The Law and Special Education.* The homepage contains links to the text of the Individuals with Disabilities Education Act (IDEA), Section 504 of the Rehabilitation Act, the Americans with Disabilities Act (ADA), and the corresponding regulations. Links to legal resources on the Internet are also included on the homepage. The primary purpose of the homepage is to provide readers and instructors using the text with frequent updates regarding legal developments in special education. In a section titled "Chapters of the Law and Special Education," instructors and readers will be provided with updates on legal developments in special education. This section is organized by chapters of the text. Developments in legislation, regulations, or court cases are monitored on an ongoing basis and posted regularly and frequently on the homepage under the appropriate chapter title. For example, legal developments regarding the disciplining of students with disabilities will appear under Chapter 15. The URL of *The Law and Special Education* homepage is http://www.ed.sc.edu/spedlaw/lawpage.htm.

Acknowledgments

In writing this book I benefited from the help of many friends and colleagues. Thanks go to all of them. David Rogers and Elisabeth Lodge Rogers of the State University of New York at Geneseo contributed to Chapter 4. Bill Brown, Erik Drasgow, Jon and Stephanie Dubose, Chris Espin, Kathleen Marshall, Jim Shriner, J. David Smith, and Tom Zirpoli were very generous with their time and considerable editorial talents in commenting on drafts of the chapters. Thanks also to the reviewers of this text—Lyle E. Barton, Kent State University; Andrew R. Brulle, Northern Illinois University; Barbara C. Gartin, University of Alabama; Barbara Leary, Mounds View Public Schools, Minneapolis; Nikki L. Murdick, Southeast Missouri State University; and Mary Jane K. Rapport, University of Florida at Gainesville—for their timely and helpful comments. This is a better textbook because of their efforts. Delys Nast generously contributed her considerable talents in designing the homepage, and Cheryl Wissick provided assistance getting it up and running. Joseph Cross of the University of South Carolina law library was extremely helpful in the preparation of Chapter 2. Cheryl Cobb, administrative assistant in the special education program at the University of South Carolina, was, as always, a great help. I would like to thank Ann Davis at Merrill/Prentice Hall, who guided me through this new endeavor with enormous skill, patience, and sound advice. I also appreciate the help of Linda Bayma at Merrill/Prentice Hall, who directed the book through production, and of copyeditor Jonathan Lawrence. Thanks also go to the giants on whose shoulders I perched, Frank Wood and Stan Deno of the University of Minnesota. Finally, I want to thank my wife, Joy, and three sons, Nick, Eric, and Alex, for their love and our lives together.

CONTENTS

CHAPTER FOUR

The History of the Law and Children with Disabilities   53

CHAPTER FIVE

The Individuals with Disabilities Education Act   69

CHAPTER SIX

Section 504 of the Rehabilitation Act of 1973   95

CHAPTER TEN   **Related Services**   **195**

CHAPTER ELEVEN   **Identification, Assessment, and Evaluation**   **223**

CHAPTER TWELVE   **Least Restrictive Environment**   **243**

CHAPTER THIRTEEN   **Procedural Safeguards**   **269**

Introduction to the American Legal System

[Laws are] rules of civil conduct prescribed by the state . . . commanding what is right and prohibiting what is wrong.

Blackstone (1748)

Laws ensuring the provision of special education to students with disabilities are based on constitutional principles, written and enacted by legislatures and administrative agencies, and interpreted by the courts. It is through the interaction of the various components of the legal system, legislative and judicial, that special education law evolves. The purpose of this chapter is to examine the workings of the American legal system. Prior to examining the body of law on special education, an understanding of the workings of the American legal system, particularly federalism and the sources of law, is important.

Federalism

The American system is a federal system. That is, the government of the United States is comprised of a union of states joined under a central federal government. Federalism represents the linkage of the American people and the communities in which they live through a unique political arrangement. In this arrangement, the federal government protects the people's rights and liberties and acts to achieve certain ends for the common good while simultaneously sharing authority and power with the states (Elazar, 1984). The U.S. Constitution delineates the nature of this arrangement in the Tenth Amendment (see the Appendix for selected provisions of the U.S. Constitution). It does this by limiting excessive concentration of

1

power in the national government while simultaneously limiting full dispersal of power to the states. The national government, therefore, has specific powers granted to it in the Constitution; those powers not granted to the national government are the province of the states.

The Constitution does not contain any provisions regarding education. According to Alexander and Alexander (1992), this is not because the nation's founders had no strong beliefs regarding education. Rather, it is because they believed that the states should be sovereign in matters as important as education. Education, therefore, is governed by the laws of the fifty states.

Nevertheless, federal involvement has been an important factor in the progress and growth of education. The government's role provided under the authority given Congress by the general welfare clause of the Constitution has, however, been indirect. The earliest method of indirect federal involvement in education was through federal land grants in which the federal government made grants of land to the states for the purpose of creating and aiding the development of public schools. In addition to the land grants creating public schools, Congress, in the Morrill Act of 1862, provided grants of land to each state to be used for colleges. In the land grants, the federal government had no direct control of education in the public schools or colleges.

The federal government has continued the indirect assistance to education through categorical grants. The purposes of the categorical grants have been to provide supplementary assistance to the state systems of education and to shape educational policy in the states. States have the option of accepting or rejecting the categorical grants offered by the federal government. If states accept the categorical grants, the states must abide by the federal guidelines for the use of these funds. Examples of categorical grants include the National Defense Education Act of 1958, the Higher Education Facilities Act of 1963, the Vocational Education Act of 1963, the Elementary and Secondary Education Act of 1965, and the Education for All Handicapped Children Act of 1975 (now the Individuals with Disabilities Education Act). The role of the federal government in guiding educational policy has increased greatly through the categorical grants (Alexander & Alexander, 1992).

Sources of Law

There are four sources of law: constitutional law, statutory law, regulatory law, and case law. These sources exist on both the federal and state level. The supreme laws are contained in federal and state constitutions (i.e., constitutional law), and these constitutions empower legislatures to create law (i.e., statutory law). Legislatures in turn delegate lawmaking authority to regulatory agencies to create regulations that implement the law (i.e., regulatory law). Finally, courts interpret laws through cases, and these interpretations of law accumulate to form case law. Figure 1.1 illustrates the sources of law.

Figure 1.1
The Sources of Law

Figure 1.2
The Branches of Government

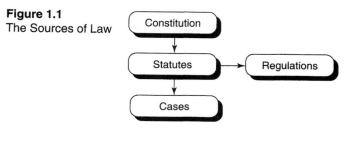

Constitutional Law

The United States Constitution

The Constitution of the United States is the basic source of law in our legal system. Article VI of the Constitution states that the Constitution, and laws derived from it, are to be the supreme law of the land. The Constitution defines the fundamental rules by which the American system functions, sets the parameters for governmental action, and allocates power and responsibility among the legislative, executive, and judicial branches of government (Cohen, Berring, & Olson, 1989). The Constitution further defines the separation of powers between the legislative, executive, and judicial branches. Figure 1.2 illustrates the branches of government and their powers as created by the Constitution.

Federal statutes are based on provisions of the Constitution. The specific section of the Constitution that is the basis for special education (e.g., the Individuals with Disabilities Education Act and Section 504 of the Rehabilitation Act of 1973) is the provision that allows spending money to provide for the general welfare (Article 1, Section 8).

The Constitution can be amended by Congress and the states. Thus far, the Constitution has been amended only 26 times. The first 10 amendments, known as the Bill of Rights, describe the basic rights of individuals.

The Fourteenth Amendment to the Constitution is important because of the major role it has played in the history of special education. This amendment has become the constitutional basis for special education. It holds that no state can deny equal protection of the law to any person within its jurisdiction. Essentially, the equal protection clause requires that states must treat all similarly situated persons alike (Tucker & Goldstein, 1992). The Fourteenth Amendment also states that persons may not be deprived of life, liberty, or property without due process of law. This amendment has played an important role in the right-to-education cases that will be explained in Chapter 4.

State Constitutions

All 50 states have their own constitutions. Like the U.S. Constitution, state constitutions establish the principle of separation of powers by establishing a lawmaking body (legislature), a chief executive officer (governor), and a court system. State constitutions tend to be more detailed than the federal Constitution. Often they address the day-to-day operations of the state government in addition to ensuring the rights of the state's citizens (Cohen et al., 1989). States cannot deny persons the rights found in the U.S. Constitution, but they can provide additional rights not found in the federal document. That is, they can provide additional rights, but they cannot provide fewer.

There is no constitutional mandate regarding the provision of education by the federal government and, therefore, no constitutional right to an education contained in the U.S. Constitution. The states, therefore, have the authority to mandate the provision of an education for their citizens. All states have educational mandates in their constitutions.

Statutory Law

The U.S. Constitution gives Congress the authority to make laws. The laws promulgated or created by Congress and state legislatures are referred to as statutes. The process of enacting laws is long and complicated. In Congress the formal process begins with the introduction of a bill in Congress by a senator or representative. The bill is assigned a number that reflects where it originated (House or Senate) and the order of introduction. The bill is then referred to the appropriate House or Senate committee. Most bills never pass this stage; some bills merely die, while some pass one house but not the other. If a bill passes both the House and the Senate but in different forms, a conference committee, comprised of House members and senators, is appointed to develop a compromise bill. The compromise bill is then voted on again. If both the House and the Senate initially pass the same bill, the conference committee is bypassed. The final version of the bill is sent to the president, who either signs or vetoes it. The House and Senate can override the veto with a two-thirds vote in each house. Figure 1.3 illustrates this process.

The enacted law (also called a statute or an act), if intended to apply generally, is designated as a public law (P.L.). In addition to a name given to the law (e.g., the Individuals with Disabilities Education Act, the Americans with Disabilities Act) the law is also given a number. The number reflects the number of the Congress in which it was passed and the number assigned to the bill. For example, P.L. 94-142 means that this public law was the 142nd law passed by the 94th Congress.

State statutes or laws may have different designations or names, but they are created and enacted in a manner very similar to federal statutes. Most statutes concerning matters of education are state rather than federal laws.

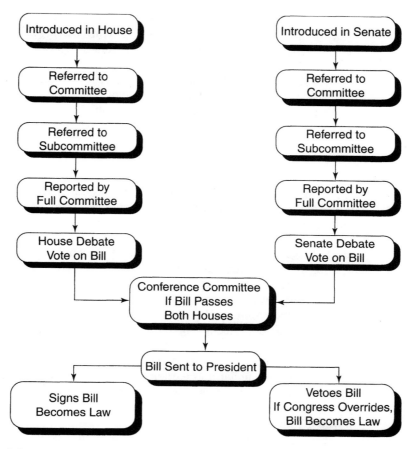

Figure 1.3
Creation of Law in the American Legal System

Regulatory Law

When Congress passes a law, it cannot possibly anticipate the multitude of situations that may arise under that law (Cohen et al., 1989). Members of Congress do not have expertise in all areas covered by the laws they pass. The statutes passed by Congress, therefore, tend to be broad and general in nature. Congress delegates power to the appropriate administrative agencies to create specific regulations to implement the laws. These agencies are part of the executive branch of government. The regulations (also called rules or guidelines) they create supply specifics to the general content of the law and provide procedures by which the law can be enforced. Regulations have the force of law. A violation of a regulation, therefore, is as serious as a violation of the law.

In addition to promulgating regulations, most administrative agencies have a quasi-judicial function that consists of making rulings on the law and regulations. These judgments may take the form of formal hearings or rulings on written inquiries. The agencies that often rule on special education matters are the Office of Special Education and Rehabilitative Services (OSERS) and the Office of Special Education Programs (OSEP). The Office of Civil Rights (OCR) of the Department of Education investigates and issues findings on claims of violation of Section 504 and, therefore, often investigates matters relating to special education.

Case Law

Case law refers to the published opinions of judges that interpret statutes, regulations, and constitutional provisions. The aggregate of published opinions forms a body of jurisprudence distinct from statutes and regulations (Black, Nolan, & Nolan-Haley, 1990). The American legal system relies heavily on the value of these decisions and the legal precedents they establish. Because only a small fraction of cases results in published opinions, these few cases take on a great deal of importance. If a judicial decision is not published, it has no precedential value.

The emphasis on case law comes to us from the English tradition known as common law, which refers to the legal tradition developed in England following the Battle of Hastings in 1066. According to Elias and Levinkind (1992), from this time forward the decisions of English juries, judges, and magistrates were written down and categorized according to the subject of the case. When courts heard cases, they reviewed the decisions in similar and earlier cases, often applying the legal principles developed in those cases. Thus, common law consists of court opinions in specific disputes. These decisions have led to the development of legal principles that are followed in later cases.

In the colonial period of America, the English common-law tradition was maintained. Judicial decisions, therefore, were of great importance. Over time, laws passed by Congress and regulations written by administrative agencies began to assume more significance (Elias & Levinkind, 1992). Courts, however, still follow the doctrine of *stare decisis*, a Latin phrase meaning "to stand by that which has been decided," in creating a body of case law.

There still are many areas of our law that consist largely of common law or case law. In special education, this is especially evident. For example, the laws involving the discipline of children with disabilities and the provision of extended school year services to special education students have been initiated by the courts.

Sources of Judicial Power

To understand the role of case law in the American legal system, it is necessary to become familiar with the sources of judicial power. Judicial power emanates from two sources; the first has been referred to as horizontal, the second vertical (Reynolds, 1991).

Horizontal Power.   There are essentially two types of horizontal power (Reynolds, 1991). The first is supreme power. In some areas of decision making, the power of the judiciary is virtually supreme. This is when the courts, especially the U.S. Supreme Court, act as the ultimate interpreter of the Constitution. The second type of horizontal power is limited power. Virtually all judicial decisions involve the interpretation of the laws of the legislative branch. The power is limited because the legislature has the final say as to the content of the law. If the legislature disagrees with the interpretation by a court, the legislature can change or alter the law or write another law. Figure 1.4 is a representation of the horizontal power of the courts.

An example of horizontal power was the passage of the Handicapped Children's Protection Act (1986) following the Supreme Court's decision in *Smith v. Robinson* (1984). The Education for All Handicapped Children Act (EAHCA) originally contained no mention of parents being able to collect attorneys' fees if they sued schools to obtain what they believed to be their rights under the law. Undaunted by this problem, attorneys for parents sued school districts for these rights and also brought suit under other federal statutes to collect attorneys' fees. In 1984, however, the U.S. Supreme Court held that attorneys could not collect fees under these statutes. According to the high court, because the EAHCA did not contain a provision for attorneys' fees, fees were not available. In a dissent, Justice Brennan argued that parents should not be required to pay when they had to go to court to obtain the rights given to them in the law. He further suggested that Congress revisit the issue and write attorneys' fees into the law. Congress did, and in 1986 passed the Handicapped Children's Protection Act (IDEA 20 U.S.C. § 1415(e)), which made possible the award of attorneys' fees under the EAHCA and overturned *Smith v. Robinson.*

Figure 1.4
The Horizontal Power of the
Courts

Supreme Power

| Judicial | → | Legislative |

When the courts act as the interpreter of the U.S.
Constituition, they are virtually supreme.

Limited Power

| Judicial | ← → | Legislative |

When the courts interpret the laws created by the
legislative branch, the legislature may change or alter
the law or write another law if it disagrees with the
court's interpretation.

Figure 1.5
The Vertical Power of the Courts

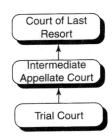

Vertical Power.   The vertical power of the courts lies in the hierarchical nature of the system. The hierarchy in most jurisdictions consists of a trial court, an intermediate appellate court, and a court of last resort. The vertical power of the courts is illustrated in Figure 1.5.

The first level of courts is the trial court level. Within the federal system, the trial courts are called district courts. The role of the trial court is essentially fact-finding. Litigants (i.e., participants in a lawsuit) may appeal the decision of the trial court to the next highest level of court, the intermediate appellate court. The decision of the appellate court is binding on all lower courts in its jurisdiction. The losing party in the appellate court may appeal the lower court's decision to the court of last resort. In most jurisdictions, the court of last resort (the highest level of court) is the supreme court. The decision of the supreme court is binding on all lower courts (trial and appellate).

There are 51 separate jurisdictions in the United States: the federal courts and the 50 state courts. While the names of the courts may differ, the equivalent of the generic system described above can be found in all 51 systems. A line of authority exists within the system, such that the inferior courts are expected to follow the decisions of courts superior to them. This line of authority is within a jurisdiction but does not cross jurisdictional lines. Therefore, a trial court in a certain jurisdiction is not obligated to follow the ruling of an appellate court in another jurisdiction. For example, a trial court in Minnesota is not obligated to adhere to an appellate court's ruling that is authority in South Carolina. A trial court in South Carolina, however, is obligated to follow a ruling of the appellate court with authority in South Carolina. Because lines of authority run only within a jurisdiction, it is important to know which jurisdiction a particular decision occurs in.

Court Structure

The generic model of the hierarchy of courts applies to both the federal system and the state jurisdictions. Figure 1.6 illustrates the generic model when applied to the federal judicial system.

In some states, the number of levels varies slightly, although the model is essentially the same. Questions involving state law are brought before the state courts, and questions involving federal law and constitutional issues are usually brought before the federal courts. The great majority of special education cases have been heard in the federal court system because most have concerned the application of federal law (e.g., the Individuals with Disabilities Education Act and Section 504).

Figure 1.6
The Federal Court System

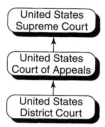

United States
Supreme Court

United States
Court of Appeals

United States
District Court

Trial Court.   The trial court is the first level in the court system. It is the level at which the fact-finding process takes place. Matters of dispute are heard by a judge or jury, and the issues of fact are determined. When the facts have been determined, they remain constant. This means that if the case goes to the appellate court or the court of last resort, the facts as determined by the trial court do not change, unless it is determined there was a procedural problem or bias in the fact-finding process. The facts of the case, once determined, cannot be appealed.

In addition to the facts of the case, issues of law arise at the trial court level. The judge makes determinations concerning the issue of law and applies them to the facts of the case. The rulings of the judge on the law, however, can be appealed to a higher court.

There are close to 100 trial courts in the federal judicial system. The federal trial courts are called U.S. District Courts. The geographic distribution of the district courts is based on state boundaries, with all states having between one and four district courts. All judicial districts have at least one and as many as three judges to share the federal district court caseload.

The role of the federal district court differs slightly in special education cases. Because the fact-finding process takes place at the administrative review process (i.e., the due process hearing or hearing by the state educational agency), the trial court takes on more of an appellate role and determines if the administrative agency or due process hearing officer correctly applied the law.

Intermediate Appellate Court.   Usually litigants have the right to an appeal of the decision of a trial court. The appeal will most often be to the intermediate appellate court. In an appeal, the appellate court reviews the decision of the trial court on the issues of law. The role of the appellate court is to ensure that the trial court did not err and to guide and develop the law within the jurisdiction (Reynolds, 1991). The appellate court determines whether the trial court's judgment should be affirmed, reversed, or modified. If the appellate court concludes that the lower court did not properly apply the law, the court may reverse the trial court's decision. If the appellate court determines that the law was not applied properly, but that the error was of a minor nature and did not affect the outcome, it may affirm the decision. Decisions of the appellate court develop law through the creation of precedents.

Because the facts are determined at the trial court level, the appellate court does not retry the case. The facts, therefore, are accepted as determined by the trial court.

The primary concern of the appellate court is whether the principles of law were correctly applied by the trial court.

There is no jury at the appellate level, only the justices. Typically, the attorneys for each party exchange written briefs. Oral argument may also be heard. An appellate court will usually consist of three or more judges who will then vote on the disposition of the dispute. Each federal appellate court is comprised of 12 judges, but typically cases will be heard by only 3 judges. By dividing judges in this manner, the courts can hear more cases. Occasionally the entire appellate court will hear a case (all 12 judges). A hearing by the full court is referred to as en banc.

There are 13 U.S. Courts of Appeals. The First through Eleventh Circuits cover three or more states each, a Twelfth covers the District of Columbia, and the Thirteenth, called the Federal Circuit, hears appeals from throughout the country on specialized matters (e.g., patents). The courts of appeal hear cases from trial courts in their jurisdictions. Their decisions become controlling authority in the court's jurisdiction.* Figure 1.7 shows the geographic jurisdictions of the federal appellate courts.

Court of Last Resort.   Litigants may file an appeal with the court of last resort. The court of last resort is the supreme court in a jurisdiction. Because the courts of last resort are extremely busy, they cannot hear every case that is appealed. The courts, therefore, have the power to determine which cases they will hear.

The court of last resort has an appellate function. That is, it reviews the decision of the intermediate appellate court to determine if the law has been correctly applied. As with the intermediate appellate court, the court of last resort is not a forum for retrying the case. The decision of the court of last resort will be binding on all lower courts (trial and appellate) in its jurisdiction. The decisions of a court of last resort, therefore, are important sources of law.

The U.S. Supreme Court is the highest court in the land. The Court has nine justices, one being designated as the Chief Justice. If a litigant decides to appeal a decision of an appellate court to the Supreme Court, the litigant files a petition for a writ of certiorari (usually called a petition for cert). This petition for cert essentially asks the Court to consider the case. The justices review the petitions, and if four of the nine justices decide to grant the petition, a writ of certiorari will be issued and the case will be heard. This is usually referred to as granting cert. If the Court decides not to hear the case, it will deny cert. When the Court denies cert, it does not have to explain why it is doing so. Because a denial can be for any of a number of reasons, it has no precedential value. If the high court denies cert, the lower court decision stands and may still exert controlling and persuasive authority.

---

*The U.S. Court of Appeals for the Eleventh Circuit was created in 1981 by taking Florida, Georgia, and Mississippi from the Fifth Circuit. Because there was no case law prior to that date, no controlling authority to guide court decisions (except decisions of the U.S. Supreme Court) was available in the Eleventh. To remedy this problem in the first case heard before the Eleventh Circuit Court, *Bonner v. Alabama* (1981), an en banc court ruled that all decisions of the U.S. Court of Appeals for the Fifth Circuit decided prior to September 30, 1981, would be controlling in the Eleventh Circuit.

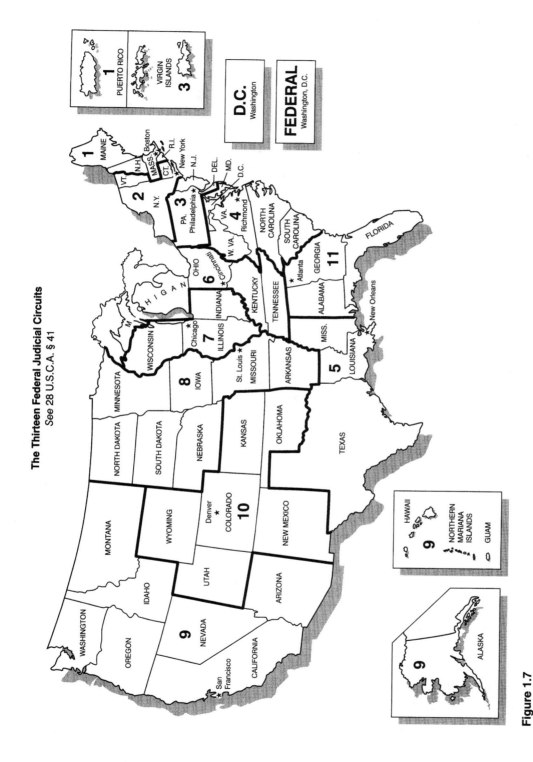

Figure 1.7

Jurisdictions of the U.S. Courts of Appeals

Reprinted by permission of the West Publishing Company.

11

The U.S. Supreme Court grants cert to only a very small number of cases, less than one percent. Cases that the Court hears will usually present an important question of constitutional or federal law or involve issues that have split the appellate courts. In the latter case the Supreme Court acts to resolve the conflict.

Precedence

The American system of law follows the doctrine of stare decisis. According to stare decisis, also referred to as precedence, courts are expected to follow the decisions of courts in similar cases. When a higher court applies the law to a specific set of facts, this decision controls decisions in similar cases in that and other courts. If the court does not follow the precedent, it must explain why that precedent does not apply or control in the particular case. Courts are not absolutely locked to every precedent, however, and can abandon earlier doctrines that are no longer useful (Valente, 1994). This doctrine helps to ensure uniformity, predictability, and fairness in court decisions (Reynolds, 1991).

A decision by a higher court controls the disposition of lower courts in the same jurisdiction. The lower court cannot make a decision contrary to decisions by the higher court. This is referred to as controlling authority. The decision of the supreme court in a jurisdiction controls the decisions of all lower courts.

Another type of authority may come from a court that is not controlling (e.g., a court in a different jurisdiction). This type of authority is called persuasive authority. A court is not bound to follow the precedent but does so because it is persuaded by the decision. For example, the decision of an appellate court in Minnesota will not control the decision of a court (even a lower court) in South Carolina, because they are in different jurisdictions. The court in South Carolina, may find the decision in the Minnesota court to be persuasive, however, and use similar reasoning in arriving at its decision. An example of a special education ruling that has been extremely persuasive is the decision of the U.S. Court of Appeals for the Fifth Circuit in *Daniel R.R. v. State Board of Education* (1989). The reasoning in the Fifth Circuit's decision regarding the determination of the least restrictive environment for children in special education has been accepted by the U.S. Courts of Appeals in the Third, Ninth, and Eleventh Circuits.

Only published cases can be used for precedence. Only a small percentage—less than 10%—of cases decided by the U.S. District Courts are published. Approximately 40% of the decisions of the U.S. Courts of Appeals are published. All of the decisions of the U.S. Supreme Court are published.

Holding and Dicta

The holding of the case is the portion of the decision that controls decisions of lower courts in the same jurisdiction. The holding of the case is the actual ruling on a point or points of law. It usually consists of one or two sentences. The rest of the decision, judicial comments, illustrations, speculations, and so on, are referred to as dicta (plural form of *dictum*). The dicta are everything in the opinion except the holding. Dicta are not controlling but can be very persuasive. They do not have value as precedent.

The Opinion

One of the judges of the appellate court or court of last resort will usually be appointed to write an opinion stating the ruling of the court and the court's reasoning for arriving at the decision. A written opinion usually contains a summary of the case, a statement of the facts, an explanation of the court's reasoning, and a record of the decision. The opinion of the court also lists the author's name and the names of justices who agree with it. A court's opinion may contain a concurring opinion or a dissent. A concurring opinion is written when a judge (or judges) agrees with the majority of the court on the ruling, but does not agree with the reasoning used to reach the ruling. A dissent is a statement of a judge (or judges) who does not agree with the results reached by the majority.

Dissents can be very important. Because dissents are typically circulated among the justices hearing a case prior to writing a final opinion, they can serve to dissuade the majority justices from judicial advocacy, encourage judicial responsibility, and appeal to outside audiences (e.g., Congress) for correction of perceived mistakes by the majority (Reynolds, 1991). They can also serve as general appeals or appeals to higher courts or legislators to correct a perceived judicial error. Although dissents carry no controlling authority, they can be very persuasive.

Dissents are sometimes used to appeal to a higher court or legislature to correct the court's action. An example of the latter is Justice Brennan's dissent in *Smith v. Robinson* (1984), discussed earlier. In his dissent, Justice Brennan disagreed with the Supreme Court's ruling that attorneys' fees were not available in special education cases, and appealed to Congress to revisit P.L. 94-142 and correct the Court's error. Congress did revisit the issue and passed the Handicapped Children's Protection Act in 1986.

The Law and Special Education

The four branches of law—constitutional, legislative, regulatory, and case law—often interact. Laws are sometimes made by one branch of government in response to developments in another branch. This can be seen clearly in the development of special education law.

Actions in the courts, such as *Mills v. Board of Education* (1972) and *Pennsylvania Association of Retarded Citizens (PARC) v. Commonwealth of Pennsylvania* (1972), created the right to a special education for children with disabilities under the Fourteenth Amendment to the Constitution. Congress reacted to this litigation by passing legislation to ensure the educational rights of children with disabilities (P.L. 94-142). Regulations were promulgated to implement and enforce the law by the then Department of Health, Education, and Welfare. In response to the federal law, all 50 states eventually passed state laws and created state regulations ensuring the provision of special education to qualified children. The inevitable disputes that arose concerning the special education rules and regulations led to a spate of federal litigation to interpret the special

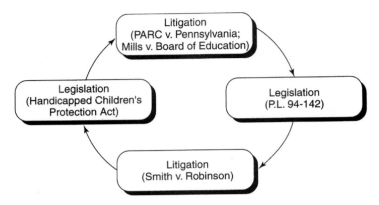

Figure 1.8
The Evolution of Law

education law. Some of this litigation, such as *Smith v. Robinson* (1984), has led to more legislation. In 1986, Congress passed new legislation (the Handicapped Children's Protection Act) to overturn the effects of *Smith v. Robinson*. This legislation, in turn, has led to more litigation to interpret it. Thus, the development of law is cyclical. Through the interaction of the various sources of law, special education law evolves. The interaction of the sources of law is depicted in Figure 1.8.

Summary

Special education is governed by an elaborate and extensive body of statutes, regulations, and court decisions. The U.S. Constitution and the state constitutions provide the foundations for special education. Congress and the state legislatures write statutes or laws that mandate and guide the provision of special education. These laws are implemented through the promulgation of regulations issued by administrative agencies such as the state and federal Departments of Education. Finally, laws and regulations are interpreted by the courts. The role of the courts is to apply the principles of the law to settle disputes. Although the courts do not initiate laws, their published decisions may result in judicially created principles known as case law. Legislation and litigation in special education have rapidly increased in the last decade. The effect of these judicial and legislative actions is that special education continues to evolve.

For Further Information

Davis, J. (1986). *Legislative law and process in a nutshell* (2nd ed.). St. Paul, MN: West Publishing Company.

Reynolds, W. L. (1991). *Judicial process in a nutshell* (2nd ed.). St. Paul, MN: West Publishing Company.

References

Alexander, K., & Alexander, M. D. (1992). *American public school law* (3rd ed.). St. Paul, MN: West Publishing Company.

Black, H. C., Nolan, J. R., & Nolan-Haley, J. M. (1990). *Black's law dictionary* (6th ed.). St. Paul, MN: West Publishing Company.

Bonner v. Alabama, 661 F.2d 1206 (11th Cir. 1981).

Cohen, M. L., Berring, R. C., & Olson, K. C. (1989). *How to find the law* (9th ed.). St. Paul, MN: West Publishing Company.

Daniel R.R. v. State Board of Education, 874 F.2d 1036 (5th Cir. 1989).

Elazar, D. J. (1984). Federalism. In *The guide to American law* (pp. 190–198). St. Paul, MN: West Publishing Company.

Elias, S., & Levinkind, S. (1992). *Legal research: How to find and understand the law* (3rd ed.). Berkeley: Nolo Press.

Handicapped Children's Protection Act of 1986, Pub. L. No. 99-372. 20 U.S.C. § 1415.

Individuals with Disabilities Education Act, 20 U.S.C. § 1415(e) (1986).

Mills v. Board of Education, 348 F. Supp. 866 (D.D.C. 1972).

Pennsylvania Association of Retarded Citizens v. Commonwealth of Pennsylvania, 343 F. Supp. 279 (E.D. Pa. 1972).

Reynolds, W. L. (1991). *Judicial process in a nutshell* (2nd ed.). St. Paul, MN: West Publishing Company.

Smith v. Robinson, 468 U.S. 992 (1984).

Tucker, B. P., & Goldstein, B. A. (1992). *Legal rights of persons with disabilities: An analysis of federal law.* Horsham, PA: LRP Publications.

Valente, W. D. (1994). *Law in the schools* (3rd ed.). Upper Saddle River, NJ: Merrill/Prentice Hall.

CHAPTER TWO

Legal Research

The material [on legal research] will not become meaningful or really useful to you . . . until you actually work through it. The great Zen koan of legal research is that you can't understand the materials without using them, and you can't use them very well without understanding them.

Johnson, Berring, & Woxland (1991, p. 126)

Legal research is the process of finding laws that govern activities in our society (Cohen & Olson, 1992). It involves finding statutes, regulations, and cases that interpret these laws. It also involves finding legal discussion and analyses of the laws. Special education is governed by a very specific set of rules and regulations on both a national and state level. It is also among the most frequently litigated areas in education. There is, therefore, an extensive body of cases interpreting these rules and regulations. By accessing the law through legal research, educators will have a better understanding of the principles of law, the facts giving rise to these principles, and the application of those facts to situations they may encounter.

Legal research requires the understanding of a variety of resources. These resources can be divided into three areas: primary sources, finding tools, and secondary materials. These resources differ in their legal authority. Some are controlling or binding, others are persuasive, and some are useful tools for finding still other controlling and persuasive materials.

Primary sources are actual statements of the law. There are three categories of primary source material: statutes or laws passed by either federal or state legislatures and signed into law; the regulations promulgated by administrative agencies to implement the statutes; and judicial decisions that interpret the statutes and regulations.

The enormous amounts of primary source materials available are issued chrono-logically rather than by subject. Resources used to locate the primary sources are referred to as finding tools. Finding tools include the annotated codes, West's digests, and Shepard's citators.

Finally, secondary materials analyze or discuss legal doctrines and principles. Because secondary materials are unofficial (i.e., not actual statements of law), they have no formal authority, although they may have a great deal of persuasive authority. They can be extremely useful in understanding the law.

Statutes and Regulations

Federal Statutes

Statutes are organized by topic and are published in a series of volumes called the *United States Code* (U.S.C.). There are 50 numbered titles in the U.S.C. The titles are divided into chapters and sections. Each title contains the statutes that cover a specific subject. For example, Title 20 contains education statutes, and the Individuals with Disabilities Act can be found in this title. Section 504 of the Rehabilitation Act can be found in Title 29, which contains labor statutes. The Americans with Disabilities Act (ADA) is in Title 42, which contains public health and welfare statutes. Some titles are published in one volume, while others have many volumes. The U.S.C. is issued every six years, and supplements are issued during the interim years. The U.S.C. is published by the U.S. Government Printing Office and is considered the official version of federal statutes.

There are two annotated versions of the *United States Code.* The first, published by West Publishing Company, is the *United States Code Annotated* (U.S.C.A.); the second is the *United States Code Service* (U.S.C.S.), published by Bancroft-Whitney/Lawyers' Cooperative. The annotated code versions are very useful because in addition to the actual text of the statutes, they contain information pertaining to each statute. For instance, the U.S.C.A. contains summaries of court cases that have interpreted the statute, notes and citations about the legislative history of the statute, cross-references to related statutes, and research guides to other relevant materials published by West. The U.S.C.S. reprints the statutes and, at the end of every section, examines relevant cases, provides citations to administrative materials, and gives other aids. Because the annotated versions of the U.S.C. have information that is more useful than just the text of the statute, many researchers prefer to use the U.S.C.A. or U.S.C.S. rather than the official government code. Annotated codes are also updated more frequently than the official code.

Because federal statutes are frequently amended, it is important that the researcher locates the most recent version. The codes are published in hardcover editions which are only reissued occasionally. In the back of each book, however, is a paper supplement called a pocket part which updates the hardcover book annually. It is important to check the pocket part to see if the statute being researched has been amended. When amendments and changes in federal statutes cannot be contained in only an annual pocket part, a separate softcover volume is issued (this volume sits next to the hardcover volume). The Individuals with Disabilities Education Act (1990) serves to illustrate the importance of the pocket part. The hardcover book containing the Education for All Handicapped Children Act (1975) has not been reissued recently and does not contain the 1990 amendments. To find these amendments it is necessary to refer to the pocket part of that volume. Pocket parts only reprint the sections of the statute that have been changed (i.e., amended or repealed). If a particular section has not been changed, the reader is referred to the hardcover volume for the text of that section.

If the statute being researched is very recent (e.g., four months old) or is currently pending in Congress, it will not be available in the pocket part. U.S.C.A has an advance legislative service called the *U.S.C.A. Quarterly Supplement* that publishes statutes within two months of their being passed by Congress. This service supplements the pocket part. Statutes are indexed by their public law number. The supplement also has a subject index if the public law number is unknown. Statutes that are currently pending before Congress can usually be obtained through representatives to Congress.

There are several methods that can be used to find federal statutes. The first method is to use the citation, the second is to use the popular name, and the third is to use the annotated code indexes when you only know the subject.

Finding a Statute by Citation

A reference to a primary law source is a citation. The citation tells where the law source is located. Citations are always written in standard form. Figure 2.1 is a citation for the Individuals with Disabilities Education Act (IDEA):

The first number, 20, is the title number. The letters following the title number refer to the particular code; in this case, U.S.C. refers to the *United States Code*. The numeral 1401 is the section number (§ is the symbol for section). In the U.S.C., the text of the IDEA begins at § 1400 and ends at § 1485. Title and section numbers will be constant in the three sources (e.g., the IDEA will appear in Title 20, §§ 1400–1485, in all three sources).

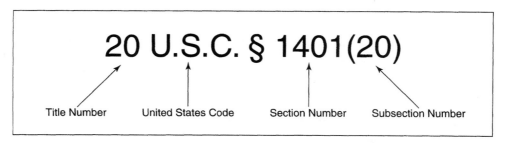

Figure 2.1
Citation for the Individuals with Disabilities Education Act (Statute)

To locate federal statutes, find the maroon set of books labeled U.S.C. or U.S.C.A. or the black set of hardcover books labeled U.S.C.S. On the spine of the volumes look for the title number (20). Under the title number are the section numbers contained in that volume. The table of contents contains the contents of the volume in chapters and subchapters. The chapter number of the IDEA is 33 (this number does not appear in the citation). The page number is listed for each chapter and subchapter. Turn to the page number for Chapter 33 and locate the section number on the upper left or right of the page. To find a citation with a particular section and subsection, such as 20 U.S.C.A. § 1412(1), locate the appropriate page for section 1412 and scan the page for subsection 1, which will be highlighted.

Finding a Statute by Popular Name

If the citation for a statute is not available but the popular name (e.g., Individuals with Disabilities Education Act) is known, the statute can be found in the *Popular Name Index*. In most law libraries, the *Popular Name Index* is placed after the codes. The index provides the following information: the popular name, statute number, date of passage, title, and section number. With this information, the researcher can locate the statute in U.S.C.A.

Finding a Statute Using the Annotated Code Index

If the researcher does not know the correct citation or popular name of the statute, but knows the subject of the statute, the annotated code indexes in each title may be used to locate the statute. For example, if the citation and popular name for the Individuals with Disabilities Education Act were unknown, the researcher knowing that the subject area was the education of children with disabilities would locate the index for Title 20 (education). Every title of the annotated codes has an index in the back of the final book in the series.

Federal Regulations

Regulations are published by the U.S. Government Printing Office in the *Federal Register* (issued daily) and the *Code of Federal Regulations* (C.F.R.) (issued annually). The C.F.R. is a multivolume set of paperbacks organized by subject. There are 50 titles in the C.F.R., with each title covering a general subject area. Titles in C.F.R. and U.S.C.A. do not always correspond. For example, the subject of Title 20 of the U.S.C.A. is education, but the subject of Title 20 of the C.F.R. is employee benefits. Regulations regarding education are found in Title 34. The C.F.R. provides, along with the text of the regulation, a reference to the statute that authorizes the regulation and the date of publication in the *Federal Register.*

Finding Regulations by Citation

Regulations, like statutes, also have citations. The citation tells where the regulation is located. Citations are always written in a standard form. Figure 2.2 is a citation for the IDEA regulations. The first number, 34, is the title number. C.F.R. stands for the

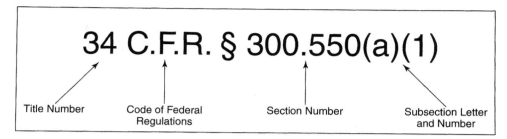

Figure 2.2
Citation for the Individuals with Disabilities Education Act (Regulations)

Code of Federal Regulations. The numerals 300.1–300.754 refer to the section numbers of the IDEA regulations.

To locate this federal regulation in a law library, find the paperbound set of books labeled *Code of Federal Regulations.* Every year the color of the C.F.R. volumes is changed. The title number (34) can be found on the spine of the volumes. Section numbers of regulations contained in the volume are listed under the title number.

Finding Regulations by Subject

If the citation for a federal regulation is unavailable, the general subject index of the C.F.R. should be consulted. If the title in which the regulation will appear is known (e.g., education is Title 34), the table of contents at the end of the title can be used to locate the regulation.

When the annual C.F.R. is published, the regulations in the volume are up-to-date. Like statutes, however, regulations are often changed in some way. It is important that current regulations be used. To determine if the regulation is up-to-date, consult the most recent issue of the monthly pamphlet titled "Code of Federal Regulations List of Sections Affected" (abbreviated C.F.R.–L.S.A.). In the pamphlet find the title and section number of the regulation of interest and see if there have been any recent changes. If changes have been made to the regulation, the affected sections will be noted.

State Statutes

State statutes are organized in three different ways. Some states organize state statutes in volumes according to subject (e.g., education, health). A number of states organize statutes by title number or chapter. Finally, in some states, statutes are not organized by subject but are numbered sequentially.

Most collections of state statutes have indexes for all laws as well as for each subject. Citations for state statutes typically refer to the volume and section number. State statutes, like federal statutes, are often changed. The hardcover volumes of state statutes will also have pocket parts inside the back cover that update the state statutes annually. If the statute has been recently amended, the change may not be reflected in the pocket part. Most states publish newly passed or amended statutes in update publications. The names of these publications vary by state. The statutes in the updates usually appear in numerical order.

State Regulations

State regulations can be difficult to locate. Many states have administrative codes, so locating appropriate regulations requires looking in the general index. Usually, special education regulations will be subsumed under the broader category of education regulations. This is because special education regulations are usually promulgated by the state's department of education. In many states, regulations are published in loose-leaf form by the promulgating agency. Law libraries will often only carry regulations for their own state.

Case Law

A very important part of legal research is finding cases that interpret statutes and regulations. Cases are published in volumes in accordance with the level of court at which the case was decided for federal courts, and by geographical regions and levels of courts for state courts. These volumes, called reporters, are available in all law libraries.

Federal Cases

There are no official case reporters published by the government for federal district or appellate courts. With the exception of computerized research, the only source of decisions of the lower federal courts are the reporters published by the West Publishing Company. West publishes federal cases in accordance with the level at which the case was decided. The published decisions of the U.S. District Courts are collected in a reporter called the *Federal Supplement* (abbreviated F. Supp.). There are currently over 950 hardcover volumes of the supplement, with more than 20 new volumes printed each year. Published decisions by the U.S. Courts of Appeals are collected in a series of hardcover volumes called the *Federal Reporter.* In 1924 the *Federal Reporter, Second Series,* began. This series (abbreviated F.2d) ran for 999 volumes. In 1994 volume one of the *Federal Reporter, Third Series* (abbreviated F.3d), was issued.

The complete decisions of the U.S. Supreme Court are published in three different sources. The *United States Supreme Court Reports* (abbreviated U.S.) is the official reporter because it is printed by the U.S. government. The reporter published by the West Publishing Company is called the *Supreme Court Reporter* (abbreviated S.Ct.). A third reporter, *Supreme Court Reports, Lawyers' Edition* (abbreviated L.Ed.), is published by Bancroft-Whitney/Lawyers' Cooperative. The three reporters contain the same cases, but the latter two have editorial enhancements (e.g., synopsis, related cases, historical information). S.Ct. is part of a complete legal reference system called the key system, and L.Ed. provides editorial comments about each case and annotations referring to other cases on the same subject. Table 2.1 lists abbreviations for the federal court reporters.

There is a lag between the date that the case is decided and the publication of the case in a hardcover reporter. During this lag period, new cases can be found in weekly updates called advance sheets. Advance sheets may be found next to the hardcover reporters, but often they are kept in the library's reference section.

State Cases

The published appellate court cases (intermediate and supreme court) for each state can be found in that state's official reporters published by the West Publishing Company (e.g., *West's Tennessee Reporter*).

The published appellate cases for each state and the District of Columbia can also be found in West's regional reporters. West divides the country into seven regions and publishes certain appellate decisions of states in particular regions together. Table 2.2 lists West's regional reporter system. Separate reporters are published for California and New York.

How to Find Cases

Cases are published chronologically, rather than according to subject. A typical law library may contain over 3 million cases, so without a means of accessing these cases, research would be a hopeless endeavor.

Table 2.1
Federal Court Reporters

Name	Coverage	Abbreviation
Federal Supplement	U.S. District Courts	F. Supp.
Federal Reporter, Second Series (1924–94)	U.S. Courts of Appeals	F.2d
Federal Reporter, Third Series (1994–present)	U.S. Courts of Appeals	F.3d
U.S. Supreme Court Reports	U.S. Supreme Court	U.S.
Supreme Court Reporter	U.S. Supreme Court	S.Ct
Supreme Court Reports, Lawyers' Edition	U.S. Supreme Court	L.Ed

Table 2.2
West's Regional Reporters

Reporter	States
Atlantic Reporter	CT, DE, DC, ME, MD, NH, NJ, PA, RI, VT
Northeastern Reporter	IL, IN, MA, NY, OH
Northwestern Reporter	IA, MI, MN, NE, ND, SD, WI
Pacific Reporter	AK, AZ, CA, CO, HI, ID, KS, MT, NV, NM, OK, OR, UT, WA, WY
Southeastern Reporter	GA, NC, SC, VA, WV
Southern Reporter	AL, FL, LA, MS
Southwestern Reporter	AR, KY, MO, TN, TX
New York Supplement	New York Supreme Court and Intermediate Appellate Courts
California Reporter	California Supreme Court and Intermediate Appellate Courts

Finding Cases by Citation

Every published case has a citation that makes it possible to locate the case in reporters. Case citations follow a standard format. Figure 2.3 is a citation to a special education case. The first item in the citation is the name of the case (*Daniel R.R. v. State Board of Education*). The name of the case will usually be two names separated by "v." (versus). The first name will be the plaintiff or the appellant. The plaintiff is the party that initially brought the suit seeking a remedy from the court. In the case of an appeal, the appellant is the party that appeals the decision of the lower court, whether the party was the original plaintiff or the defendant. The plaintiff in this case was Daniel R.R. The second name is that of the defendant (the party who has been sued and is responding to the complaint of the plaintiff). If the defendant appeals the ruling of the lower court, that party will become the appellant and be listed first. The defendant in this case was the State Board of Education of Texas. Cases sometimes only have a phrase and one name, such as *In Re Gary B.* The phrase *in re* is Latin and means "in the matter of." Usually this will mean that although there was a court proceeding, there was no opponent.

The second element in the citation is the volume number of the reporter in which the case appears. The volume number of the *Daniel R.R.* case is 874. Volumes in reporters are numbered consecutively.

The third element of the citation is the name of the reporter. The reporter in which *Daniel R.R.* can be found is the *Federal Reporter, Second Series,* written as F.2d (called "F second"). F.2d contains cases heard by the U.S. Courts of Appeals; therefore, *Daniel R.R.* was heard by an appellate court.

The fourth element of the citation will be the page number on which the case starts. Thus the *Daniel R.R.* decision can be found on page 1036 of volume 874 of F.2d.

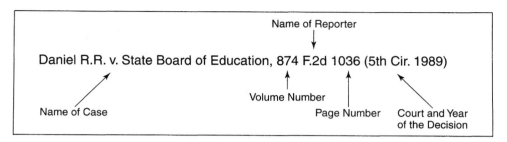

Figure 2.3
Case Citation

The final element of the citation is the year of the decision. In researching cases, it is important to choose the most recent ones. In federal cases, the level of court deciding the case will appear along with the year of the decision. *Daniel R.R.* was decided by the U.S. Court of Appeals for the Fifth Circuit in 1989. If the decision is from a federal district court, the state and judicial district of the case will often be included. For example, in the case *Hayes v. Unified School District,* 699 F. Supp. 1519 (D. Kan. 1987), the court was the U.S. District Court for the District of Kansas. In the case *Espino v. Besteiro,* 520 F. Supp. 905 (S.D. Tex. 1981), the court was the U.S. District Court for the Southern District of Texas. If cases can be found in more than one reporter, the names of all the reporters may be listed in this section of the citation. For example, a case decided by U.S. Supreme Court may appear in the three reporters (U.S., S.Ct., and L.Ed.). A citation, therefore, may list all three reporters. This is referred to as a parallel citation.

Finding Tools

There are a number of finding tools to help the researcher locate primary sources. Finding tools that can be used include annotated codes, digests, indexes, legal encyclopedias, and Shepard's citators. Because a comprehensive review of finding tools is beyond the scope of this chapter, only three such tools will be examined here: the annotated codes, West's key number digest system, and Shepard's citators.

The Annotated Codes

The annotated editions of the *United States Code—United States Code Annotated* (U.S.C.A.) and *United States Code Service* (U.S.C.S.)—are powerful research tools. In addition to the statutory language contained in the U.S.C., the annotated editions contain a wealth of information useful to the researcher. For example, West's U.S.C.A. contains information on legislative history; library references, including administrative law (i.e., regulations); references to the American Digest System topics and keynotes; *Corpus Juris Secundum* (i.e., West's legal encyclopedia); West's statutory treatises; law reviews; guides to finding pertinent information on Westlaw electronic research; and notes of relevant court decisions. The court decisions notes consist of abstracts of relevant cases that have interpreted the section. Because judicial interpretations are crucial in interpreting and understanding the law, the abstracts are the most useful part of the annotated codes (Cohen, Berring, & Olson, 1989).

When using an annotated code, the pocket part must be checked for recent developments. Between the issuance of the annual pocket parts, quarterly pamphlets are issued.

The West Digest System

Another useful tool for locating cases is West's digest system. For each set of West's reporters there is a corresponding digest. Table 2.3 contains a partial list of West's court digests and their coverage. West's digests are alphabetical indexes to case law, arranging headnotes of cases by topics and key numbers. To access the West digest system, the researcher must understand the headnote and key number system.

The West Headnote and Key Number System

A case published in a West reporter follows a standard format. The first item on the page is the title of the case. For example, on the first page of the *Daniel R.R. v. State Board of Education* written opinion, Daniel R.R. is listed as the plaintiff-appellant and the Board of Education is the defendant. Following the title is the docket number (No. 88-1279), the court in which the case was heard (U.S. Court of Appeals for the Fifth Circuit), and the date the court's decision was handed down (June 12, 1989). Following this information is the synopsis of the case, written by an editor at West.

Table 2.3
West's Digest System

Digest	Coverage
General Digest	List of every headnote, in every case, in every West reporter. Issued every 4 to 6 weeks.
Decennial Digest	10 years' cumulation of headnotes from the General Digest
Modern Federal Practice Digest	Cases prior to 1961
Federal Practice Digest 2d	Covers all federal cases between 1961 and 1975 (closed)
Federal Practice Digest 3d	Covers all federal cases between 1975 and 1992 (closed)
Federal Practice Digest 4th	Covers all federal cases after 1992
U.S. Supreme Court Digest	All U.S. Supreme Court cases

Next is the headnote section. A headnote is a one-sentence summary of a legal issue arising in a case. The headnotes are not part of the judicial opinion but are an editorial enhancement. Editors at West review judicial opinions and write the headnotes by isolating every individual issue of law that appears in the judicial opinion. Often cases contain a number of legal issues and will, therefore, have a number of headnotes. *Daniel R.R.* contained 16 headnotes. The headnote will appear as a boldface number (e.g., 1), followed by a topic (e.g., Federal Courts), an illustration of a key, and a number (e.g., 13.30).

The first numbers (e.g., the boldface 1) are in order and are used as a table of contents to the case. Numbers corresponding to the headnotes appear in the text of the case at the point where that legal issue was discussed. The term or phrase after the number (e.g., Federal Courts) is the topic where West has classified that legal issue. Following the key illustration is the key number (13.30), a subsection of the topic. To find out what the key number stands for, you must consult a digest.

The key number system was developed by John West, who founded West Publishing Company in the late 1800s. At the time, cases were being published with no systematic way of accessing information. West created a uniform classification system for legal issues raised in all published cases. Currently, the system consists of 414 topics and numerous subtopics, all classified under seven main divisions of law. Each of these topics is further broken down into subtopics, representing points of law. Each point of law is assigned a key number.

In the digests, every headnote, consisting of a topic phrase and number, is grouped with similar legal topics from every published case that deals with that issue. For example, number 2 of the 16 headnotes in *Daniel R.R.* is *Schools 148(2)*. Schools is a topic area (number 345 of West's 414 topic areas). The number 148 refers to a subtopic titled "Nature of Right to Instruction." The number in brackets refers to a subtopic of 148, in this case 2, which is titled "Handicapped children and special services therefore in general." Depending on which digest is used, every headnote numbered 148(2) from every published state or federal court can be located quickly. The key number before the headnote (e.g., *148(2)*) will enable the researcher to locate every published state or federal case on "handicapped children and special services."

Using the Digest System

To access the digest system, the researcher will need both topic and key number. In the digests, the headnotes are arranged by jurisdictions in chronological order, beginning with the most recent. The key number system is uniform in every digest West publishes.

There are a number of different digests published by West. Each is designed to fill a different need. The largest digests are the *Decennials* and the *General Digest*. This digest group, the American Digest System, contains headnotes from the published cases from all courts. The *Decennials* and the *General Digest* have been subdivided into smaller, more specific, digests.

When using the digests to find cases, it is preferable to start with the smallest digest first. For example, if the researcher is only interested in federal cases, the *Federal Practice Digests* should be consulted. The *Federal Practice Digests* also

Figure 2.4
Using West's Digest System

Step 1:	Locate the *Daniel R.R.* decision at 874 F.2d 1036 in the appropriate digest.
Step 2:	Read the headnotes and note the topic term and key numbers. If the researcher is interested in the issue of law raised in headnote 2, locate Schools 148(2).
Step 3:	Whenever possible use the smallest digest; therefore, locate the *Federal Practice Digest* in the library.
Step 4:	Because the case was decided in 1989, it can be found in the *Federal Practice Digest, Fourth Series*.
Step 5:	Locate the volume of the *Fourth Series* that contains the topic of Schools. The correct volume number is 84.
Step 6:	Turn to the page that begins with headnotes that are keyed 148(2). Headnotes with the key number 148(2) from all federal court cases will be listed by jurisdictions in reverse chronological order (most recent first).
Step 7:	Check pocket parts and white softcover supplements for the most recent cases.

contain U.S. Supreme Court cases. If the researcher is interested in U.S. Supreme Court cases, West's *U.S. Supreme Court Digest,* which contains only cases heard by the Supreme Court, should be consulted.

Cases can also be located by using the descriptive word index, the topic index, or table of cases in the digests. The digests also contain pocket parts and softcover supplements for very recent headnotes.

Special educators will usually be interested in federal special education cases, so the appropriate digest will be the *Federal Practice Digest.* It contains headnotes from every case appearing in West's *Supreme Court Reporter* (S.Ct.), *Federal Reporters* (F.2d and F.3d), and *Federal Supplement* (F. Supp.).

In Figure 2.4 the *Daniel R.R. v. State Board of Education* decision is used as an example to access West's digest system. Whatever case is used, the method of using the West digest system will be the same.

Shepard's Citators

Shepard's *Citations for Cases* is possibly the single most powerful legal research tool available (Elias & Levinkind, 1992). Once a case of interest has been located, it is critical that the case be currently valid. That is, does it still have legal authority, or has it been overturned or modified? An important function of Shepard's, therefore, is to help the researcher verify the case. A second function of Shepard's is to help researchers expand their research. A search of Shepard's will direct the researcher to other research materials such as cases, statutes, and secondary sources. The process of using Shepard's citators to find additional cases or to determine if a case has been reversed, overruled, or modified is called "shepardizing." Shepardizing is an essential part of legal research. Shepard's citators are available not only for cases but for virtually every primary or secondary source.

Once the citation for the case being shepardized is located in Shepard's, the citator lists every case that has referred to it. Shepard's also tells if the case was affirmed, modified, or reversed by a higher court, and helps the researcher find other cases that have dealt with similar issues. For example, if the researcher was interested in least restrictive environment cases and had the citation for *Daniel R.R. v. State Board of Education,* Shepard's could be used to locate other federal cases that cited *Daniel R.R.* in their decision.

Shepard's citators for federal cases list every case that has cited the particular case being researched. In this example, Shepard's cites every federal case that mentioned the *Daniel R.R.* decision by name. Because *Daniel R.R.* has proven to be a very persuasive case, every subsequent federal case on least restrictive environment has cited it. A difficulty with using Shepard's is that if a case on the same issue as the case being researched did not cite it, the case of interest will not be listed. Another difficulty in using Shepard's is that every case, important or unimportant, that cites the case being researched will be listed. This can result in numerous listings, especially for very important cases that are cited frequently. A third potential problem in using Shepard's is that it does not cumulate; that is, a volume of Shepard's will only cite cases covered by that particular volume year, so cases decided prior to that date will not be cited. A series of Shepard's citators, therefore, may be necessary for full coverage of a case.

Law libraries carry many volumes of Shepard's citators. They can be distinguished by their dark red bindings. Separate gold, white, or red softcover supplements update the hardcover volumes. Shepard's *Citations for Cases* are published for all state jurisdictions, for federal cases, and for U.S. Supreme Court cases. There are also Shepard's citators for regional reporters, state and federal statutes, federal administrative decisions, federal regulations, and law reviews. Shepard's case citators are organized according to the reporters that publish the cases. Table 2.4 is a partial listing of Shepard's citators.

The first page of each Shepard's citator identifies the specific court reporters covered in that volume. It is important that researchers look on the binding to see what years are covered in the volume.

Shepard's consists of page after page of columns of numbers and symbols. Figure 2.5 is a partial column of cases citing *Daniel R.R. v. State Board of Education* that appear in a 1994 supplement of Shepard's *Federal Citations—Part 1.*

When shepardizing cases, use the procedure shown in Figure 2.6, where *Daniel R.R. v. State Board of Education,* 874 F.2d 1036 (5th Cir. 1989), is used as an example. Additionally, Shepard's groups the citing cases according to the circuit in which they were decided. For example, in Figure 2.5 the following citation appears under the *Daniel R.R.* case: f995F2d1207. This particular citation (from the Third Circuit) is

Table 2.4
Shepard's Citators

Citator	Subject
Shepard's United States Citations	U.S. Supreme Court
Shepard's Federal Citations—Part 1	U.S. Courts of Appeals
Shepard's Federal Citations—Part 2	U.S. District Courts
Shepard's Administrative Law	Federal Administrative Decisions
Shepard's for Code of Federal Regulations	Code of Federal Regulations
Shepard's for Law Reviews	Selected Law Reviews
Statutory Shepard's	Coverage of every session statute for all 51 jurisdictions

Figure 2.5
Sample Page from Shepard's

```
         Vol. 874
         −1036−

         Cir 1
      807FS⁷864
      807FS¹⁴871
         Cir 2
      801FS¹1171
      801FS⁷1173
      801FS⁴1176
      801FS¹⁴1178
         Cir 3
      f995F2d1207
      995F2d1213
      995F2d1214
      995F2d1215
      995F2d1216
      d995F2d1207
      789FS1326
      789FS¹¹1327
      789FS¹⁵1333
      801FS1400
         Cir 5
      DK592-8427
      963F2d¹838
      999F2d131
      812FS672
```

Oberti v. Board of Education (1993). The citations in Shepard's have the volume number in which the case appears (e.g., 995), the reporter (e.g., F2d), and the page number of the citation (e.g., 1207). Shepard's citators may have numerous references to a particular citing case. In Figure 2.5 the *Oberti* decision (995F2d) is listed six times. This is because in the *Oberti* decision the *Daniel R.R.* case is cited six times.

Figure 2.6
Shepardizing a Case

Step 1:   Identify the citation of the case being shepardized. The citation for *Daniel R.R.* is 874 F.2d 1036 (5th Cir. 1989). The parts of the citation needed for shepardizing are the volume number (874), the reporter abbreviation (F.2d), and the page number (1036). The name of the case is not required when shepardizing.

Step 2:   Find the volume that covers the reporter listed in the citation. The reporter used in *Daniel R.R.* was F.2d; therefore the appropriate title will be Shepard's *Federal Citations—Part 1.*

Step 3:   Select the volume or volumes that contain citations for cases decided after the case being shepardized (1989). In addition to using the hardcover volumes, check the update supplements.

Step 4:   Using the volume number of the case (i.e., 874 for *Daniel R.R.*), find the number in Shepard's in bold type. Volume 874 will be listed in Shepard's as "Vol 874."

Step 5:   Under the volume, locate the page number of the case. The page number that is in the *Daniel R.R.* citation is 1036. Find 1036 in bold print. Page 1036 will be listed in Shepard's as "-1036-". Cases listed under -1036- have cited the *Daniel R.R.* decision.

Step 6:   For more specific information on whether the citation is worth reviewing, use the letters to the left of the citation.

Step 7:   Look up all potentially useful cases in the appropriate Shepard's.

The letters referred to in Step 6 in Figure 2.6 represent the code that Shepard's has developed to give the researcher additional information. The letters and their meanings can be found at the beginning of every Shepard's. These abbreviations indicate the history of the case and treatment of the case. A few of the notations are listed in Table 2.5. The use of these notations is important in determining if the case is still good authority.

In the 1990 volume of Shepard's *Federal Citations,* the following citing case appears under the *Daniel R.R.* case: f933F2d1290. The *f* means that the citing case followed the *Daniel R.R.* decision. If no letters are present it usually means that the case was cited but was not of importance to the decision of the citing case.

Shepard's gives the researcher the name of every case that has cited the case of interest. Cases, however, usually deal with more than one legal issue. In a West reporter, the text of the case is preceded by the headnotes. Some of the legal issues discussed in the case and written in a headnote may not be of interest to the researcher. For example, headnote 1 in *Daniel R.R.* concerns the issue of mootness, and headnote 16 concerns federal civil procedure. Headnote 4 deals with the court's interpretation of the continuum of alternative placements, and headnote 11 concerns the test the *Daniel R.R.* court used to determine if the school had complied with the IDEA's least restrictive environment principle. Cases that cite headnotes 4 and 11

Table 2.5
Shepard's Notations

Notation	Definition
A	Case affirmed on appeal
C	Soundness of decision criticized
F	Case cited as controlling (followed)
O	Holding in case overruled
R	Case reversed on appeal
US cert denied	Cert denied by U.S. Supreme Court

would be of greater interest to researchers investigating least restrictive environment cases than would cases that cite headnotes 1 and 16 of the *Daniel R.R.* decision. Shepard's identifies the specific legal issues discussed in the citing case. The superscript numbers to the right of the reporter (e.g., F2d) of the citing case refer to the headnotes of the case that is being cited. For example, the citation $933F2d^{12}1290$ means that the citing case discusses the 12th headnote of the *Daniel R.R.* decision on page 1290.

Computers and Legal Research

Legal research is rapidly becoming computerized. The two primary computer-assisted legal research (CALR) systems are West's Westlaw system and Mead Data Central's Lexis* service. The primary advantages of these systems are the enormous amounts of information they contain and the speed with which one can access that information. Research that might normally take hours in a law library may be accomplished in minutes at a computer terminal. Westlaw and Lexis are very current, and their databases are updated constantly. Both systems contain full libraries of information including cases from all jurisdictions, statutes, regulations, and administrative cases, as well as a variety of finding tools and secondary source materials. CALR, however, does not replace traditional legal research. Rather, CALR is used most effectively in combination with the printed resources available in the law library.

The Westlaw and Lexis CALR systems are organized into databases. In using either Westlaw or Lexis, researchers must specify the database they wish to search (e.g., U.S. Supreme Court decisions) and enter specific keywords to access the information required. The primary difference between traditional legal research and computerized research is keyword searching. In keyword searching, the researcher

---

*Mead Data Central also has a computer-assisted research system called Nexis, which primarily is a nonlegal research source. The Nexis system covers a wide variety of legal and nonlegal periodicals, trade publications, newspapers, government documents, and popular magazines.

determines the keywords that are likely to be used in the document (e.g., statute or case) needed and uses them to call up the information. Citations can also be used to retrieve information on CALR systems.

In using the Westlaw or Lexis system, it is first necessary to choose the appropriate database in which to conduct the search. For example, if a researcher is investigating all federal cases regarding least restrictive environment, the researcher might enter "federal courts" to access the appropriate database. The Westlaw and Lexis services provide the researcher with a menu of databases. If the researcher has a citation or knows which database is needed, the document or database can be accessed directly.

The second step in using a CALR system is to formulate a query. The researcher formulates a query by choosing keywords that are likely to be used in the documents needed. When the keyword is entered, the system will find all documents in the database that contain the keywords. For example, if the researcher searches the federal case law database and enters the keywords "special education" and "least restrictive environment," the computer will retrieve federal cases that contain these words. Both the Westlaw and Lexis systems allow the researcher to connect keywords using "and" or "or" so that only documents containing both keywords or either keyword will be retrieved from the database. Both systems also allow the researcher to specify the position of the keywords relative to each other (e.g., the two words must appear in the same paragraph), to restrict the scope of the search (e.g., court opinions issued after 1990), and to have the search conducted on certain segments of a database (e.g., search only the synopsis of the court's opinion rather than the entire opinion). Keywords that are more general will usually result in greater amounts of material, much of which may be irrelevant. When the keywords are more specific, the search will be more focused.

Currently these systems can be impractical to use unless the researcher is a law student or a member of a large law firm. Law schools often have both Westlaw and Lexis, but access is sometimes limited to law students and law faculty. Typically, only large law firms use the services because of their prohibitive expense. Additionally, unless the researcher is skilled in the CALR process, an hour of research might yield only a handful of relevant cases. Westlaw and Lexis terminals are available to the public in some libraries but often require large advance deposits to use.

Researchers with access to computers can obtain legal information without using either Westlaw or Lexis. An increasing amount of legal information of interest to special educators is available on the Internet. (For elaboration of legal resources on the Internet see Chapter 3.)

Secondary Sources

Secondary sources are materials that describe and explain the law. They analyze or discuss legal doctrines and principles. Because secondary materials are unofficial (i.e., not actual statements of law), they have no formal authority. They may, however, have a great deal of persuasive authority.

Secondary materials are useful in a number of ways. First, they introduce the researcher to an area of law; second, they provide the researcher with explanations of issues of law; and third, they serve as finding tools by providing citations to primary sources.

In conducting legal research, it is often easier to begin with secondary sources. Secondary sources have two primary functions: they provide citations to primary source material (in this function they serve as finding tools), and they explicate and analyze legal issues. There are many secondary sources of information available, including legal encyclopedias such as *Corpus Juris Secundum* and *American Jurisprudence 2d,* legal newspapers such as the *National Law Journal* and the *Legal Times,* law reviews, legal journals, law indexes, loose-leaf services, and resources on the Internet. The following discussion will center on the secondary source materials that may be of greatest use to the educator: legal journals, law reviews, and loose-leaf services.

Legal Journals

Legal journals are professional publications devoted to issues involving the law. Three primary legal journals that cover education law are West's *Education Law Reporter,* the *Journal of Law and Education,* and the publications of the National Organization on Legal Problems of Education (NOLPE).

Law Reviews

All accredited law schools in the United States produce law reviews. Law reviews are periodicals, usually published quarterly, that contain articles on legal developments, legal issues, historical research, and empirical studies. Law reviews typically follow a standardized format (Cohen et al., 1989). There are usually three sections in each issue. The first section contains the issue's lead articles. These articles are analyses of narrow legal topics or issues, and are usually written by law professors, scholars, or practitioners. They are extensively footnoted. It is not unusual to encounter pages in law review lead articles in which there may be only a paragraph of text or even just a few lines, with the remainder of the page being taken up by footnotes. Because of the extensive footnoting, lead articles may be used as case finding tools. Lead articles may often have great persuasive authority and are often cited by the courts as well as by legal scholars.

The second section is a commentary section. This section, which is written by students, is often similar to the lead articles (e.g., extensive footnoting, narrow focus) but tends to have less persuasive authority. A third section is composed of book reviews.

The H.W. Wilson Company publishes the *Index to Legal Periodicals* (ILP), which indexes several hundred legal periodicals. Articles are indexed by author and subject. Each volume also has an alphabetical table of cases. Since 1979, the ILP has been issued annually. The volumes are updated by softcover pamphlets issued every month except September.

H.W. Wilson also produces a CD-ROM version of the ILP as part of the WILSONDISC system. The CDs are updated quarterly. Only ILP information after 1981 can be accessed using the CD-ROM system. Information prior to 1981 is available only in the printed volumes.

The Information Access Company produces an index to legal materials called the *Current Law Index* (CLI). Articles are indexed by author and subject. Information Access began printing CLI in 1980, so it is not possible to do pre-1980 searches. The *Legal Resources Index* (LRI), also published by Information Access, is a companion publication to CLI. It is issued in microfilm. Cumulative indexes are issued monthly in the microfilm format. As with CLI, pre-1980 searches cannot be done on LRI. The LRI information is also available in CD-ROM format called LegalTrac. Discs are updated monthly.

Shepard's citators can also be used to find journal articles in which a case or statute is cited, and they can also be used to shepardize law review articles. The citators for each jurisdiction track select law reviews and include these journals as citing references. Shepard's also produces Shepard's *Federal Law Citations in Selected Law Reviews* and Shepard's *Law Review Citations*. The publication follows law review articles, published after 1973, that pertain to federal primary sources.

Loose-leaf Services

Loose-leaf services may contain not only analysis of legal issues but reprints of primary source material. A loose-leaf service, therefore, may serve as both a primary source and a secondary source.

A loose-leaf service is a publication that is issued in a binder with removable pages. The publisher monitors legal developments in the service's subject area and regularly issues new pages to keep the publication current. The primary advantages of loose-leaf services are that the information is current (with services that update frequently) and that much of the information needed to conduct research has already been compiled by the publishers of the service. There are two types of loose-leaf formats: the newsletter and the interfiled format.

Newsletter Loose-leaf Services

In the newsletter format, a newsletter is issued on a regular basis and is added to the end of the binder. Often the newsletter monitors current information from a variety of sources. Newly released material does not replace but rather supplements the older material in the newsletter format. Examples of special education loose-leaf services that use the newsletter format are the *Individuals with Disabilities Education Law Report* (IDELR); *The Special Educator* (TSE), published by LRP publications; *Special Education Law Update,* published by Data Research, Inc.; *Special Education Briefing Papers,* published by Legal Resources, Inc.; and *Special Education Report,* published by Capitol Publications.

Interfiled Loose-leaf Services

In the interfiled format, new pages are sent frequently for insertion into the binder. The new pages are interfiled and the old pages are discarded. The interfiled format, therefore, is constantly being edited to reflect legal developments. Interfiled special education loose-leaf services include *Legal Rights of Persons with Disabilities: An Analysis of Federal Law, Special Education Law and Litigation Treatise,* and *Section 504, the ADA and the Schools,* all published by LRP Publications.

Legal Research Strategies

The purpose of this chapter has been to introduce the essential tools of legal research: primary sources, finding tools, and secondary sources. In addition to this information, a method for conducting legal research is required. The following three-step model may be useful.

Step 1: Analyze the Problem

The first task of the researcher is to analyze the problem and determine the most efficient manner in which to proceed. In the problem-analysis phase, Johnson, Berring, and Woxland (1991) suggest that the researcher (a) think about the answer that is needed for the research problem; (b) determine what it is that the research is to accomplish; and (c) decide what the ideal final product will look like. After analyzing the problem, the researcher must decide what legal sources will be needed to answer that question. Will the research question require information from statutes, regulations, current cases, historical information, an analysis of the law, or some combination of these? Will primary source material (i.e., statements of the law), secondary sources (i.e., interpretations of the law), or both be required? Answers to these questions will help focus the research and indicate where to proceed in the research strategy.

Step 2: Conduct the Research

In the second step, the researcher must locate relevant primary source materials. If a statute citation is available, the researcher can find case citations by looking up the statute in the annotated codes (e.g., U.S.C.A.) and reading the abstracts of relevant cases. Regulations may also be found in this manner.

Perhaps the most important element of step 2 is the location of one good case on the subject being researched. Once the researcher has one good case, West's digests may be entered using the topic and key numbers in the case's headnotes. Additional cases may be located and researched. Shepard's citators may also be used to locate additional citations or secondary source materials. The researcher may take this information and go to the case reporters.

If a statute or relevant case citation is not available, the researcher should begin with secondary sources. For example, locate a law review article on the subject. Law review articles are replete with statutory, regulatory, and case citations. Using this information, the researcher can enter the primary source material. Loose-leaf services may also be used to locate the primary source material. In addition to references to primary sources, the secondary source materials contain opinions and analyses of the law.

The ability to move between the sources of law and pull together the relevant information is critical in this stage of research. Analysis of legal issues requires the integration of all the sources of law.

Step 3: Evaluate the Results

The final step of the process is evaluation of the results of the research. Has the researcher obtained enough information? Were the materials current? Was the analysis logically based on the legal sources located? Because the law is constantly changing, it is critically important that the research is current. Bringing the research up-to-date should be a continuous part of the process. Sources should be updated as they are being used. It is also a distinct final step in evaluating the results of the research (Cohen et al., 1989).

Summary

Law refers to the rules that govern activities in society. Legal research is the process of finding these laws. It involves locating actual statements of the law (i.e., primary sources) as well as explanations and analyses of the law (i.e., secondary sources).

The primary sources include statutes, regulations, and cases. To varying degrees, the primary sources are controlling authority; that is, these sources are the laws that govern the behavior of individuals and groups. These sources are available on both the federal and state level. Primary sources for federal laws, regulations, and cases are the *United States Code,* the *Code of Federal Regulations,* and the various court reporters.

Finding tools are resources for locating primary sources. The purpose of finding tools is to allow the legal researcher to access the enormous body of primary sources. Examples of finding tools include the annotated codes (i.e., U.S.C.A. and U.S.C.S.), West's digests, and Shepard's citators.

Secondary materials discuss and analyze the primary sources. Although secondary sources do not have controlling authority, they can be very influential and persuasive. Law reviews and loose-leaf services are examples of secondary sources.

Legal research requires the understanding of and ability to use primary sources, secondary sources, and finding tools. The researcher must also approach legal problems with a strategy. Although personal strategies vary, they will often include problem analysis, methods for systematically conducting the research endeavor, and an evaluation and updating phase.

For Further Information

The following texts are in-depth works:

Cohen, M. L., Berring, R. C., & Olson, K. C. (1989). *Finding the law: An abridged edition of* How to find the law (9th ed). St. Paul, MN: West Publishing Company.

Cohen, M. L., Berring, R. C., & Olson, K. C. (1989). *How to find the law* (9th ed.). St. Paul, MN: West Publishing Company.

Jacobstein, J. M., & Mersky, R. M. (1990). *Fundamentals of legal research* (5th ed.). Mineola, NY: Foundation Press.

Jacobstein, J. M., & Mersky, R. M. (1990). *Legal research illustrated: An abridgment of* Fundamentals of legal research (5th ed.). Mineola, NY: Foundation Press.

The following texts are nontechnical works:

Elias, S., & Levinkind, S. (1992). *How to find and understand the law* (3rd ed.). Berkeley, CA: Nolo Press

Johnson, N. P., Berring, R. C., & Woxland, T. A. (1991). *Winning research skills.* St. Paul, MN: West Publishing Company.

The following is a six-part videotape series:

Berring, R. C. (1989). *Commando legal research.* Los Angeles: Legal Star Communications.

For more information on Westlaw CALR write to:

West Publishing Company, 620 Opperman Drive, Eagan, MN 55123.

For more information on Lexis CALR write to:

Lexis, Mead Data General, 200 Park Ave., New York, NY 10017.

References

Cohen, M. L., Berring, R. C., & Olson, K. C. (1989). *How to find the law* (9th ed.). St. Paul, MN: West Publishing Company.

Cohen, M. L., & Olson, K. C. (1992). *Legal research in a nutshell.* St. Paul, MN: West Publishing Company.

Daniel R.R. v. State Board of Education, 874 F.2d 1036 (5th Cir. 1989).

Elias, S., & Levinkind, S. (1992). *How to find and understand the law* (3rd ed.). Berkeley, CA: Nolo Press.

Johnson, N. P., Berring, R. C., & Woxland, T. A. (1991). *Winning research skills.* St. Paul, MN: West Publishing Company.

CHAPTER THREE

Legal Research on the Internet

The first rule of legal research . . . is to find someone who has done the work for you.

Berring (1989, p. 82)

The Internet offers the legal researcher a wealth of information and can be a useful adjunct to the law library. In the preceding chapter, the fee-based online services of Westlaw and Lexis were introduced. There are many other legal sources on the Internet, some are them fee-based but most available at no charge to the researcher. Through these sources it is possible to monitor current legislation and regulations on a state and federal level, as well as developments in the courts.

Currently the Internet is most useful for researching volatile areas of information, that is, areas in which information changes very rapidly (Rowland & Kinnaman, 1995). This is because important changes can be made available instantly on the Internet, whereas there is a delay before the information becomes available on more traditional sources. For example, if the U.S. Court of Appeals for the Fourth Circuit announced a decision in an area of special education, it may be weeks before the final court opinion is available in a law library, and months before analyses of the decision appear in scholarly journals. Using the Internet, however, one could access the full opinion of the court within days, or sometimes hours, after it was announced. Analyses of the decision may be available almost as quickly.

The purpose of this chapter is to introduce the reader to legal research on the Internet. First, features of the Internet that are particularly useful to legal researchers will be examined. Second, a number of useful information sources on the Internet will be reviewed. Finally, a strategy for conducted legal research on the Internet will be offered.

Prior to a discussion of the Internet, a caveat is in order. Currently the Internet contains much of interest to the legal researcher, but it is not a substitute for the law library. It is best viewed as a useful supplement to the law library. Law libraries carry federal and state laws and regulations, volumes of cases from federal and state courts (dating back many years), and journals of peer-reviewed law articles. Recent federal circuit court decisions cases are on the Internet, although only dating from, at the earliest, 1994. Full texts of U.S. Supreme Court decisions are available, as are about 7,000 high court decisions dating from 1936 to 1995. State laws and regulations are available, but on a less consistent basis. Additionally, opinions and articles can be located easily; however, they have not been subjected to a rigorous peer review process, as have law review articles.

Internet Research Tools

E-Mail

Electronic mail, commonly referred to as e-mail, allows one user on the Internet to send messages to other users on the Internet. As such, it is an important tool because it allows communication with colleagues, researchers, and other Internet users. E-mail is also the foundation for discussion groups and newsgroups.

Discussion Groups

There are programs that will send your e-mail message to a group of individuals interested in similar information. To join a discussion group, you must send a message to the host computer. The list program then puts your e-mail address on the distribution list, and all e-mail sent to the list is automatically sent to you and the other list subscribers. Some lists are moderated, which means that the list sponsor or handler may control messages sent to participants. There are discussion groups on a large number and variety of topics. They can be tremendously useful to the researcher, as they provide a source of contacts and will keep one updated on current developments. The legal researcher will find that the law-related discussion groups are the places on the Internet most likely to contain analyses of legal developments.

Two sources that maintain a registry of law-related discussion groups are *The Legal List,* a book of law-related Internet resources compiled by Eric Heels and published by Lawyers Cooperative Publishing, and Gopher, a service maintained by Lyonette Louis-Jacques at the University of Chicago. The latter compilation can be found at Gopher://lawnet.uchicago.edu or by sending an e-mail message to llou@midway.uchicago.edu. The University of Chicago Gopher server can also be accessed through the World Wide Web.

Two discussion groups available to persons interested in disability-related law are ADA-Law, which is a discussion group primarily concerned with the Americans with Disabilities Act and other disability-related law, and EDLaw, a listserv that

Figure 3.1
Discussion Groups Related to Special Education Law

ADA-Law

Subscribe to: Listserv@vm1.nodak.edu
   Text of subscribe message: Subscribe ADA-Law *your name*
Post messages to: ADA-Law@vm1.nodak.edu
Unsubscribe: Listserv@vm1.nodak.edu
   Text of unsubscribe message: Signoff ADA-Law

EDLaw

Subscribe to: Listserv@lsv.uky.edu
   Text of subscribe message: Subscribe EDLaw
Post messages to: EDLaw@lsv.uky.edu
Unsubscribe to: Listserv@lsv.uky.edu
   Text of unsubscribe message: Signoff EDLaw

SpedTalk

Subscribe to: Majordomo@virginia.edu
   Text of subscribe message: Subscribe SpedTalk *your name*
Post messages to: SpedTalk@virginia.edu
Unsubscribe to: Majordomo@virginia.edu
   Text of unsubscribe message: Unsubscribe SpedTalk *your name*

involves discussion of many areas of education law including special education. A third discussion group that sometimes deals with legal issues in special education is SpedTalk, which covers special education in general. Figure 3.1 contains subscription and mailing instructions for ADA-Law, EDLaw, and SpedTalk.

Newsgroups

A resource very similar to discussion groups are newsgroups. The primary difference is that rather than sending multiple copies of messages, newsgroups let each host keep a single copy of a discussion. Individual participants can read through messages on the newsgroups and post replies. Rather than getting e-mail messages from the source computer, participants in the newsgroup may open and browse the discussions at their convenience. To access and participate in newsgroups, a news server and a newsreader program are required.

Gopher

Gopher is an extremely powerful Internet research tool that allows the researcher to search and access a vast amount of information. Gopher is a menu-driven software program that allows the user to choose from a series of menus. A Gopher service of interest to legal researchers is the Cornucopia of Disability Information (CODI). CODI's Internet address is Gopher://val-dor.cc.buffalo.edu/. As is the case with many, but not all, Gopher servers, CODI can now be accessed on the World Wide Web at http://codi.buffalo.edu.

World Wide Web

The World Wide Web (hereafter Web) has rapidly become the most flexible, commonly used, and rapidly growing component of the Internet. The Web is based on hypertext technology. Hypertext is essentially the presentation of text in which certain portions of the text, called links, are highlighted in some manner. When highlighted text is selected, the user is linked to another document. Because the Web uses hypermedia, the linked document may be any combination of text, graphics, audio, and video. These links allow the researcher to move to different sites, or different documents, on the Web.

In order to access documents on the Web, an individual user must have a Web browser. A Web browser is software that requests information from a server and displays it in the form of a document. The most commonly used Web browsers are Netscape Navigator, Microsoft's Internet Explorer, and Mosaic.

One of the more useful features of the most commonly used browsers is the one that allows users to keep a record of where they have been on the Internet as a bookmark. Bookmarks are essentially address books or directories of the Internet addresses of sites you have found useful. Once you have a site bookmarked or saved, you can return to it by merely selecting the bookmark. In conducting Internet research, you will likely find many sites you wish to bookmark. During a session you may find yourself going to a number of sites. If you forget to make a bookmark of a useful Web site and later decide you want to return to that site, the most popular browsers maintain a history list for each session. A history list is the Internet address of every site visited during a session. Unfortunately, when you end a session the history list will be erased. It is, therefore, important to use the bookmark feature as you conduct your search.

Law-Related Resources on the Internet

There is a tremendous amount of law-related resources and information available on the Internet. Unfortunately, there is not a great amount of material directly related to legal issues in special education, and some of what does exists tends to be updated rather sporadically. Nevertheless, there are some sources that are current and contain important material on the law and special education. This section will briefly review these sources. Figure 3.2 contains names and Internet addresses of these and other law- or education-related sites.

Figure 3.2
Web Sites Related to Special Education Law

Title: The Law and Special Education
URL: http://www.ed.sc.edu/spedlaw/lawpage.htm

Title: EDLaw
URL: http://www.access.digex.net/~edlawinc/

Title: Education Administration Online
URL: http://www.lrp.com/ed/

Title: Thomas Legislative Information
URL: http://thomas.loc.gov/

Title: U.S. Department of Education
URL: http://www.ed.gov/

Title: The Federal Court Locator
URL: http://www.law.vill.edu/Fed-Ct/fedcourt.html

Title: U.S. Supreme Court Decisions
URL: http://supct.law.cornell.edu/supct/

Title: The U.S. House of Representatives Internet Law Library
URL: http://law.house.gov/

Title: The Council for Exceptional Children
URL: http://cec.sped.org/home.htm

Title: The National Information Center for Children and Youth with Disabilities
URL: http://www.aed.org/nichy/

The Law and Special Education Homepage

The Law and Special Education is the homepage maintained by the author of this text. The purpose of the page is to (a) provide readers and instructors using the text with frequent updates regarding legal developments in special education; (b) provide links to legal resources on the Internet; and (c) provide access to special education statutes and regulations. The homepage is divided into three sections. The first section is "Chapters of the Law and Special Education." This section is organized by chapters of the text. Developments in legislation, regulations, or court cases are monitored regularly and posted on the page under the appropriate chapter title. For example, as this text went to press, two cases regarding public schools' responsibilities to students with disabilities enrolled in private schools were appealed to the U.S. Supreme Court (this topic is covered in Chapter 16 of the text). The progress of these cases will be monitored by the author, and when the high court decides whether either case will be heard, the information will be posted under Chapter 16, "Additional Issues." When and if the Supreme Court renders a decision, that also will be entered under the appropriate chapter. Only legal developments after the publication of the text will be included in this section of the Web page. Because of the constantly evolving nature of special education law, it is important that instructors and readers be updated on a regular basis.

The second section allows users to link to pertinent special education statutes and regulations. The third section will provide links to numerous law-related and special education resources on the Internet.

EDLaw

The homepage of EDLaw, Inc., was created, and is maintained, by S. James Rosenfeld, an attorney with 20 years of experience in special education law and the founder of Legal Resources, Inc. The purpose of the page is to provide basic legal information of use to special educators, parents, and attorneys in meeting state and federal requirements for special education services. The page contains texts of special education statutes and regulations, links to disability law on the Internet, analysis and commentary on legal issues affecting special education, and ordering information on EDLaw's products.

Education Administration Online

Education Administration Online (EAO), formerly LRPnet, is a fee-based page on the Web that is maintained by LRP Publications. Through this service, subscribers can access all of LRP's publications. EAO consists of three major components. The first, a section titled "What's New in Education," is available at no charge to users. This section contains brief summaries of legislative developments and court cases affecting education as well as access to federal education statutes and regulations. The second component of EAO is "Basic Services" and requires that the user subscribe to EAO and pay the basic services fee. The user then has access to a number of features, including twenty-four general and special education newsgroups; a full-text searchable database to the newsgroup archives; "DC Daily," a daily column of news from the federal government regarding educational matters; "Hot Law," a section devoted to daily briefings of new federal and state judicial decisions affecting education; and "Hot Docs," a compendium of recent federal documents regarding education. Basic services also has a link to the *Federal Register* and the *Congressional Record*. The third component of EAO is "Premium Services," which the subscriber may access by paying additional fees beyond those required to subscribe to "Basic Services." The user may subscribe to one or more of these packages. They include state law and policy pages, National Association of State Directors of Special Education (NASDE) Information Services, Special Education Library Package, General Education Library Package, *The Individuals with Disabilities Education Law Report* (IDELR), and the Education Research Library. Descriptions of EAO's various publications, Web packages, and information regarding subscriptions to the packages are available on the EAO homepage.

Figure 3.3
Thomas Legislative Information on the Internet Databases

Congress This Week

- Floor Activities—House and Senate

Bills

- Major Legislation

    105th Congress (by topic, popular/short title, bill number/type, enacted into law)
    104th Congress (by topic, popular/short title, bill number/type, enacted into law)

- Bill summary and status

    Congress: 105th (1997–98), 104th (1995–96), 103rd (1993–94)

- Bill text

    Congress 105th (1997–98), 104th (1995–96), 103rd (1993–94)

- Public laws by law number: Congress 105th (1997–98), 104th (1995–96)

Congressional Record

- *Congressional Record* text: 103rd to 105th Congress
- *Congressional Record* index: 103rd to 105th Congress

Committee Information

- Committee reports: 104th to 105th Congress
- Committee home pages: House and Senate

Historical Documents

- The Declaration of Independence, The Federalist Papers, early congressional documents (Constitutional Convention and Continental Congress), and the U.S. Constitution

The Legislative Process

- How our laws are made

U.S. Government Internet Resources

- *Congressional Internet Services*
- Library of Congress web links: legislative, executive, judicial, state/local

Thomas Legislative Information on the Internet

Thomas is a free Internet service designed to provide users with federal legislative information. Thomas, which is one of the most complete services on the Internet, is maintained by the Library of Congress. Figure 3.3 lists the databases available on

Thomas. Thomas uses a sophisticated searching system that is very easy to use. The service is updated several times a week, and frequently it is updated daily. The service is indispensable to researchers requiring federal legislative information.

The U.S. Department of Education

The U.S. Department of Education maintains a homepage that can be very useful to teachers, researchers, and students. It contains information on Education Department initiatives (e.g, Goals 2000, the IDEA), resources for teachers and researchers, grants and funding opportunities, and publications.

The Federal Court Locator

The federal court locator is a service of the Villanova Center for Information Law and Policy of the Villanova Law School. The purpose of the Federal Court Locator is to give users of the Internet a means to access information related to the federal judiciary. The page has links to the 13 U.S. Courts of Appeals (i.e., First through Eleventh Circuits, D.C. Circuit, and Federal Circuit). The links to the circuit courts contain decisions from 1994 to the present. Decisions are accessible through names and litigants as well as keywords. The service also contains links to a few district courts and related federal agencies.

U.S. Supreme Court Decisions

The U.S. Supreme Court homepage is a service of the Legal Information Institute at Cornell Law School. Recent decisions, from 1990 to the present, can be located by topic, date, party name, or keyword searching. The court calendar for the current high court term is also available. Additionally, selected historic decisions (e.g., *Brown v. Board of Education,* 1954) are available, as are approximately 7,000 decisions between 1937 and 1995. This is an extremely useful and user-friendly service. It is updated frequently.

The U.S. House of Representatives Internet Law Library

The U.S. House of Representatives Internet Law Library has a number of useful features for the legal researchers. Two of the most frequently resources are the fully searchable *Code of Federal Regulations* (C.F.R.) and *United States Code* (U.S.C.). The U.S.C. contains the text of current public laws enacted by Congress. Laws enacted by state legislatures are not included. Many states have their state laws on a section of the U.S. Internet Law Library called the U.S. State and Territorial Laws. The C.F.R. contains the text of public regulations issued by the agencies of the federal government. Currently, both the U.S.C. and the C.F.R. are somewhat out of date, so it is advisable that researchers double-check information with a local law library's U.S.C. pocket parts and current C.F.R.

The Council for Exceptional Children

The Council for Exceptional Children (CEC) is the largest international professional organization dedicated to the education of students with disabilities. The CEC home-page has links to a number of useful resources, including the ERIC Clearinghouse on Disabilities and Gifted Education, the National Clearinghouse for Professions in Special Education, and public policy and legislative information.

The National Information Center
for Children and Youth with Disabilities

The National Information Center for Children and Youth with Disabilities (NICHY) is a national information and referral center that provides information on disabilities and disability-related issues. Services offered through NICHY include specialists to answer specific questions; publications on a number of topics, including legal issues; and information searches.

Topical Searches on the Internet with LawCrawler

Although some of the fee-based services (e.g., Westlaw, EAO) have sophisticated topical search capabilities, it is currently not possible to conduct topical searches on special education law on the free Internet. Entering legal terms on the popular search engines or directories (e.g., Alta Vista, Yahoo) will generally yield many hits, but very few of them will be useful. One exception is LawCrawler, which searches legal documents.

LawCrawler is a legal search engine developed by Alta Vista. LawCrawler uses the Boolean search operators "and," "or," "near," and "not." LawCrawler searches Web sites with legal resources in accordance with the keywords entered. The Web index option is called FindLaw. It searches resources on the Web such as the legal subject index, U.S. statutes and laws, judicial opinions and case law, U.S. law schools, law reviews, legal associations, and more. Additional LawCrawler search options include USA LawCrawler, which searches government departments, the U.S.C., the C.F.R., U.S. Supreme Court decisions, and U.S. Appellate Court decisions.

LawCrawler is very user-friendly. Currently it does an excellent job of search-ing legal resources on the free Internet. Because there are not many resources de-voted specifically to special education law, there is not an abundance of informa-tion for LawCrawler to locate. Nevertheless, a submission of the term "least restrictive environment" resulted in a number of hits, some of which contained use-ful information. As greater amounts of special education legal information become available on the Internet, LawCrawler will become very useful to the special edu-cation law researcher.

A Strategy for Legal Research on the Internet

Research on the Internet demands an awareness of what you need and knowledge of where to look for it. Researching on the Internet is not the same as "surfing the net." Surfing the net brings to mind the image of persons sitting at their computers and jumping from link to link looking for anything that might pique their interest. Research, on the other hand, demands that users be focused, that they have a specific goal or question in mind, and that they proceed systematically to locate pertinent information on that question. It is also important that the legal researcher realize that the Internet does not replace the law library, but that it is a useful adjunct to it. The hard copies of reporters, books, journals, and texts that are available in libraries are not available on the Internet, nor are the peer-reviewed analyses and commentaries.

Preparing for Research

The first step in conducting research is to focus yourself by forming a goal or research question. Once the question is firmly in mind, determine what information is required to find your answer. Decide what research can be done on the Internet and what should be done in the law library. In regards to the research that can be done on the Internet, ask yourself what information will be needed and where it can be found.

Organizing Your Hard Drive or Data Disk

Prior to conducting research on the Internet, it is useful to organize your hard drive or a data disk so that you can download the information you locate and place it in an easily accessible location. For example, if you were conducting research on least restrictive environment and determined that you needed the pertinent statutes from the IDEA, regulatory information from the U.S.C., and the most recent cases from the U.S. Courts of Appeals, you might create a folder titled "LRE," with subfolders for statutes, regulations, and court cases. You can further divide the subfolders on cases into decisions in the appellate courts and Supreme Court. Subfolders may also be created for interviews and other pertinent information you find in discussion groups and newsgroups.

Remember to bookmark all places on the Internet where you find pertinent or potentially useful information. After a few sessions you may find that you have a tremendous amount of bookmarks. Fortunately, the popular browsers allow you to organize bookmarks into folders. Finally, remember to backup all your work.

Conducting the Research

Once you've determined what you need, begin a systematic search of the Internet. One final warning before you conduct your research: there is so much interesting information on the Internet that one can easily become overwhelmed and succumb to the temptation to explore. It is important to stay focused on your research. If you locate something of interest that is not pertinent to the task at hand, create a bookmark so that you may return to it at a later time and assess the importance of the information to your research.

Locating Information

One of the most common ways of locating information on the Internet is through the use of what computer users call the tree structure (Rowland & Kinnaman, 1995). Tree structures refer to the structure of data on computers where there is an initial or root directory and branches of directories and subdirectories. Whether you are using the Web, an FTP site, or a Gopher, they all use a system of tree-structured menus that can be used by the researcher to locate information. In addition, the Web uses hypertext links that allow the researcher to jump directly to related information at another location.

A good starting point for legal research is one of the Web pages listed in the text or the Law and Special Education homepage. Once you access the pages, the hypertext links may be followed to find the related information. Finding resources on the Internet can also be accomplished by using search engines and net directories.

Another way of locating legal information on the Internet is through visiting an online law library. Many universities with law schools have homepages on the Web. An advantage of using a local university law library is that often it will have information on state rules, regulations, and court decisions. Figure 3.4 contains the URLs of some useful Internet libraries.

Conducting an Internet Interview

Legal researchers often depend on the interview for information about a specific topic. The use of e-mail for conducting interviews is the latest and one of the most successful online research tools (Campbell & Campbell, 1995; Rowland & Kinnaman, 1995). The primary advantage of e-mail is that it allows asynchronous communications;

Figure 3.4
Internet Libraries

Title: The WWW Virtual Library
URL: http://www.w3.org/pub/DataSources/bySubject/Overview.html

Title: The WWW Virtual Law Library
URL: http://www.law.indiana.edu/law/v-lib/lawschools.html

Title: The House of Representatives Internet Law Library
URL: http://law.house.gov/

Title: Educational Research Resources
URL: gopher://gopher.cse.ucla.edu

that is, researchers can post their interview questions at their convenience and the persons being interviewed can answer the post at the most convenient time for them. Telephone tag, long-distance telephone bills, and the difficulties of arranging an interview time and place are eliminated with an online interview.

If you are doing research on an unfamiliar topic, finding a source for an interview on the Internet is not difficult. For example, you might subscribe to a discussion group (e.g., EDLaw, SpedTalk) or find an appropriate usenet group and monitor discussions to determine if your questions might be appropriate for posting. Prior to posting a question, have some basic information about your research area, which should have been developed through your research on the Web or in the library. This will help to ensure that your question is focused. When asking your question, clearly identify the purpose of your question and make certain it is tightly focused. Finally, suggest that the response can be made to your private e-mail. The advantage of getting a private response is that it will permit you to respond with follow-up questions or requests for more in-depth information.

Another method for locating contacts is through your library research. Perhaps you have come across the name of a university professor who has written an article in your research area, or in reading cases you found the name of a lawyer who has litigated in the area. Many universities and law firms have pages on the Web that list the e-mail addresses of the faculty members or of lawyers in the law firms. Locate the addresses of the persons you wish to interview and send them an e-mail asking if they would be willing to answer a few questions for you. Ask a few tightly focused questions in your initial e-mail, and wait for the professor or lawyer to respond.

The Internet is one of the best places to network with other researchers or persons knowledgeable about the area in which you are interested. When you have made contacts through discussion or usenet groups, save the addresses of the individuals in your e-mail address book. When using e-mail for interviews, however, be certain that you have done your research and that your questions are tightly focused and to the point. Questions that are unfocused or overly lengthy are sometimes met with silence and sometimes with negative responses.

Evaluating the Data

Knowing when to stop collecting data can be a problem with any type of research, but it is a particular problem when researching on the Internet. This is because there is such a vast amount of information on the Internet that is always a click away. It is far easier to keep collecting data when you only have to locate it and download it to your hard drive than when you have to go to the law library, copy it, and put your information in appropriate files for evaluation. Before getting on the Internet, do a thorough job of preliminary research so you know what you need. Go to the Internet, collect what you need while avoiding the fascinating sideroads, and then leave the Internet and evaluate your data. Keep what is useful and discard the irrelevant. As with any research, when evaluating data found on the Internet it is extremely important that you determine the recency, relevancy, authority, accuracy, and verifiability of the data you have collected.

Summary

The Internet offers the researcher a tremendous amount of easily accessible information. To access this data, the researcher needs a knowledge of the various tools the Internet has to offer and skill in using these tools. As is true of all research, a strategy must be followed to derive the maximum benefit from the Internet. Be focused, avoid the many fascinating sites that may not be immediately useful, and know when to stop. Above all, it is important to realize that the Internet is not a panacea, nor is it a substitute for the law library. It is, however, an extremely useful tool for the legal researcher.

For Further Information

Allison, G. B. (1995). *The lawyer's guide to the Internet.* Washington, DC: American Bar Association.

Campbell, D., & Campbell, M. (1995). *The student's guide to doing research on the Internet.* Reading, MA: Addison-Wesley.

Heels, E. J. (1995). *The legal list Internet desk reference: Law-related resources on the Internet and elsewhere.* Rochester, NY: Lawyer's Cooperative Publishing.

Rowland, R., & Kinnaman, D. (1995). *Researching on the Internet: The complete guide to finding, evaluating, and organizing information effectively.* Rocklin, CA: Prima.

References

Berring, B. (1989). *Research commando handbook.* Los Angeles: Legal Star Communications.

Brown v. Board of Education, 347 U.S. 483 (1954).

Campbell, D., & Campbell, M. (1995). *The student's guide to doing research on the Internet.* Reading, MA: Addison-Wesley.

Rowland, R., & Kinnaman, D. (1995). *Researching on the Internet: The complete guide to finding, evaluating, and organizing information effectively.* Rocklin, CA: Prima.

CHAPTER FOUR

The History of the Law and Children with Disabilities

In these days, it is doubtful that any child may reasonably be expected to succeed in life if he is denied the opportunity of an education. Such an opportunity, where the state has undertaken to provide it, is a right that must be made available to all on equal terms.

Chief Justice Earl Warren, *Brown v. Board of Education* (1954, p. 493)

The educational rights of children with disabilities were gained largely through the tireless efforts of parents and advocacy groups in the courts and legislatures of this country. The purpose of this chapter is to provide a brief chronology of these efforts. The history of special education law will be examined, as well as the historical development of special education from the initiation of compulsory attendance laws to the inclusion of children with disabilities. The effects of the civil rights movement on special education will be discussed, with particular attention paid to *Brown v. Board of Education* (1954), as well as the equal opportunity movement. Landmark cases of the equal opportunity movement and other significant cases related to special education will be presented as a part of this discussion. The manner in which these cases led inexorably to legislation will be explained. Finally, federal legislative mandates from Section 504 of the Rehabilitation Act of 1973 to P.L. 105-17, the Individuals with Disabilities Education Act of 1997, will be briefly examined.

This chapter was written by David Rogers and Elisabeth Lodge Rogers of the State University of New York at Geneseo, with assistance from Mitchell L. Yell.

Compulsory Attendance

In our country, public education is viewed as a birthright that leads to an educated electorate without which there would be no viable democracy (Levine & Wexler, 1981). A common misconception regarding public education is that it is guaranteed by the U.S. Constitution. In fact, education is the business of the states. The Tenth Amendment to the Constitution implies that education is the responsibility of state government.

Rhode Island was the first state to pass a compulsory education law, in 1840; Massachusetts passed the second, in 1852, with the other states following suit so that by 1918 compulsory education laws were in place in all states (Ysseldyke & Algozzine, 1984). Despite the enactment of compulsory education laws, however, children with disabilities were often excluded from public schools.

The Exclusion of Students with Disabilities

The continued exclusion of students with disabilities, notwithstanding the compulsory education laws enacted by the states, was upheld in the courts. For example, in 1893 the Massachusetts Supreme Judicial Court ruled that a child who was "weak in mind" and could not benefit from instruction, was troublesome to other children, and was unable to take "ordinary, decent, physical care of himself" could be expelled from public school (*Watson v. City of Cambridge,* 1893). Twenty-six years later, the Wisconsin Supreme Court, in *Beattie v. Board of Education* (1919), ruled that school officials could exclude a student with disabilities, even though that student had attended public school until the fifth grade. The student had a condition that caused him to drool and have facial contortions, as well as a related speech problem. School officials claimed this condition nauseated the teachers and other students, required too much teacher time, and negatively affected school discipline and progress. The school officials expelled the student from school and suggested he attend a day school for students who were deaf. In 1934, the Cuyahoga County Court of Appeals, in Ohio, ruled that the state statute mandating compulsory attendance for children ages 6 through 18 gave the State Department of Education the authority to exclude certain students (Winzer, 1993). This type of ruling indicates the internal contradiction frequently presented in legal rulings of the time on students with disabilities. The court stated that students have a right to attend, noting the importance of education as evidenced by the compulsory education statute. It acknowledged the conflict between compulsory education and the exclusionary provisions, but did not rule to resolve this conflict.

States continued to enact statutes that specifically authorized school officials to exclude students with disabilities. As recently as 1958 and 1969, the courts upheld legislation that excluded students whom school officials judged would not benefit from public education or who might be disruptive to other students. In 1958 the Supreme Court of Illinois, in *Department of Public Welfare v. Haas,* held that the state's existing compulsory attendance legislation did not require the state to provide a free public education for the "feeble minded" or to children who were "mentally deficient" and who, because of their limited intelligence, were unable to reap the benefits of a good education. In 1969 the State of North Carolina made it a crime for parents to persist in forcing the attendance of a child with disabilities after the child's exclusion from public school (Weber, 1992).

Six years later, the federal government decided to bring the various pieces of state and federal legislation into one comprehensive law regarding the education of students with disabilities. It enacted P.L. 94-142, the Education for All Handicapped Children Act of 1975 (EAHCA). This dramatic shift in the government's view on educating children with disabilities would not have been possible without the history of case law and legislation that preceded the EAHCA. One of the earlier precursors of the state and federal legislation and case law regarding the education of students with disabilities was the civil rights movement.

The Civil Rights Movement and *Brown v. Board of Education*

Every year hundreds of thousands of people immigrate to the United States. Many are escaping war or economic and political persecution. Many come not to avoid hardship, but to seek the promise of greater individual rights that are provided for the citizens of the United States under its Constitution. The civil rights that are protected under the Constitution and enforced by legislation, however, have not always been provided to all citizens on an equal basis.

In the 1950s and 1960s, the civil rights movement, which sought changes in society that would allow minorities, particularly African Americans, equality of opportunity led to litigation and changes in legislation. This legislation provided greater constitutional protection for minorities, and eventually for persons with disabilities. A landmark case, *Brown v. Board of Education* (1954; hereafter *Brown*), was a major victory for the civil rights movement and has been the major underpinning for further civil rights action. The *Brown* decision not only had a tremendous impact on societal rights for minorities, but also affected many aspects of educational law and procedure (Turnbull, 1993). Although it took time, the precedents set in *Brown* resulted in sweeping changes in the schools' policies and approaches to students with disabilities.

Central to *Brown* was the constitutional guarantee of equal protection under the law, found in the Fourteenth Amendment. This amendment stipulates that states may not deny any person within their jurisdiction equal protection under the law. If states have undertaken to provide an education to their citizenry, then they must do so for all their citizens.

State-mandated segregation of the races in the schools denied black students admission to schools attended by white students. The plaintiffs maintained that the practice of segregating schools was inherently damaging to the educational opportunities of minorities, that segregated public schools were not—and could not be made—equal, and that segregated public schools violated black students' constitutional rights under the Fourteenth Amendment. As an extension to this argument, the Court maintained that state-required or state-sanctioned segregation solely on the basis of a person's unalterable characteristics (e.g., race or disability) was unconstitutional. The high court also determined that segregation solely on the basis of race violated equal protections and denied minorities equal educational opportunity. This decision opened a number of legal avenues for those seeking redress for students with disabilities.

The Court reasoned that because of the importance of education in our society, the stigmatizing effects of racial segregation, and the negative consequences of racial segregation on the education of those against whom segregation was practiced, segregated public schools denied students equal educational opportunities. This basic truth was considered by many to be equally applicable to those denied equal opportunity to an education because of a disability.

Parental Advocacy

An outcome of the *Brown* case was that the equal protection doctrine was extended to a "class" of people, in this case racial minorities (Turnbull, 1993). Advocates for students with disabilities, citing *Brown,* claimed that students with disabilities had the same rights as students without disabilities. There were two key elements in their argument. First, they pointed out that there was an unacceptable level of differential treatment within the class of children with disabilities. Second, they argued that some students with disabilities were not furnished with an education, whereas all students without disabilities were provided an education. These crucially important inconsistencies gave rise to a series of court cases in which individuals both challenged and sought redress for similar inequities.

Parents led the way in seeking redress for the inequities in the educational programming for their children with disabilities. The parent movement had its genesis during a time of change in special education programs that reflected changes in the social climate of the turn of the century. The nation, having long ignored individuals with disabilities, focused on the need to humanely treat and educate these individuals, particularly children. In order to understand the impact parents had on legislation to protect the rights of children with disabilities, it is helpful to become aware of the evolution of special education in the first three decades of this century.

The White House Conference of 1910

National attention focused on the first White House Conference on Children in 1910. One goal of this conference was to define and establish remedial programs for children with disabilities or special needs. This goal reflected a broader societal shift in perspective on the treatment of children with disabilities. There was an increased interest, albeit limited, in educating these children in public school settings, rather than institutionalizing them. As children with disabilities were moved from institutions to public schools, permanent segregated classes were formed in public schools to meet their needs, resulting in a change from isolation to segregation (Winzer, 1993). Educators believed that the segregated classes were beneficial to the children because smaller class size would allow more individualized instruction, that homogeneous grouping would facilitate teaching, and finally, that the less competitive nature of these classes would do much for the self-esteem of the children. Thus, the number of special segregated classes and support services increased significantly from 1910 to 1930 (Winzer, 1993).

Despite the increase in the numbers of special education classrooms, many children with disabilities were struggling in regular classrooms and remained unidentified. Furthermore, many were beyond the reach of special education; they had dropped out of school, been expelled or excluded from school, or were considered unteachable (Winzer, 1993). In contrast with the growth seen in the previous two decades, the 1930s brought a decline in programs.

Many factors contributed to this decline in support for and provision of special education classes for students with disabilities. The country was in the midst of the Great Depression, and many, including public entities, were struggling with the resulting financial constraints. The public school system had been developed as an ideal for a democratic society. Compulsory education laws resulted in an increasingly heterogeneous student population, leading to a conflict between the democratic ideal and maintenance of order and high standards in public schools. The result of this conflict was to further separate children with special needs from the mainstream. Under increasingly grim conditions, the special classroom placements became as restrictive and custodial as placements in institutions had been (Winzer, 1993).

The Organization of Advocacy Groups

In response to the deplorable conditions that their children with special needs had to endure in school, as well as the increasing exclusion of children with disabilities from school, parents began to band together. They came together as a support for one another and in order to work for change. In 1933 the first such group formed in Cuyahoga County, Ohio. The Cuyahoga County Ohio Council for the Retarded Child consisted initially of five mothers of children with mental retardation who banded together to protest the exclusion of their children from school (Levine & Wexler, 1981; Turnbull & Turnbull, 1997; Winzer, 1993). This protest resulted in a special class established for the children, sponsored by the parents themselves. These types of local groups were established throughout the nation during the 1930s and 1940s, although they did not begin to band together at the national level until the 1950s. These local organizations served several purposes. They provided an avenue of support for parents, allowed for a venue to express frustration, offered a means to band together to make change locally, and ultimately set the stage for a national advocacy movement on behalf of individuals with disabilities.

The advocacy movement on behalf of individuals with disabilities was critical to the development of special education services as we know them today. The activities of interest groups were critical in terms of providing information, stimulus, and support to Congress when considering, developing, and acting on legislation. Congress cannot function without such interest groups (Levine & Wexler, 1981). What follows is a summary of the development of a few national advocacy groups that expanded the constituency of individuals with disabilities.

The National Association for Retarded Citizens

The National Association for Retarded Citizens (now ARC/USA—The Association for Retarded Citizens) was organized in Minneapolis, Minnesota, in September 1950. Forty-two parents and concerned individuals from thirteen local and state organizations met to establish what has become a powerful and significant organization of parents, families, and other persons with an interest in persons with mental retardation. ARC's mission is to provide information, monitor the quality of service given individuals with mental retardation, and serve as an advocate for the rights and interests of individuals with mental retardation.

The Council for Exceptional Children

The Council for Exceptional Children (CEC) is a professional organization concerned with the education of children with special needs. Based in Reston, Virginia, CEC was founded in 1922 by faculty and students at Teachers College, Columbia University, in New York. CEC is a longtime advocate for rights for individuals with disabilities and has been a leader in the movement to obtain these rights at the federal and state levels. CEC membership exceeds 60,000, and the organization remains a major force in the development of innovative programming, in teacher preparation, and in policy making for exceptional individuals.

The Association for Persons with Severe Handicaps

The Association for Persons with Severe Handicaps (TASH) is another organization that has provided strong support for individuals with disabilities. TASH was established in 1974 and is comprised of teachers, parents, administrators, and related service providers. TASH disseminates information on best practices, publishes research reports, and supports the rights and humane treatment of persons with severe and multiple disabilities through active involvement in court cases (Siegel-Causey, Guy, & Guess, 1995).

Additional Advocacy Groups

Other advocacy groups founded primarily by and for parents and families of individuals with disabilities include the United Cerebral Palsy Association, Inc. (founded in 1949); the National Society for Autistic Children (1961); the National Association for Down Syndrome (1961); and the Association for Children with Learning Disabilities (ACLD) (1964). More recently, the Federation of Families for Children's Mental Health was formed after a group of 60 parents and professionals interested in children and youth with emotional, behavioral, or mental disorders met in 1988 (Turnbull & Turnbull, 1997).

The progress made in special education can be attributed in great part to the success of parents as advocates for their children. Parents have worked together, and continue to do so, at the local level by pushing local school boards, administrators, and teachers to provide appropriate educational programming for their children. Parent groups such as ARC and ACLD banded together with professional organizations to challenge state and federal government in the courts, and ultimately to establish federal legislation that mandated a free and appropriate education for all children with disabilities.

The Equal Opportunity Movement

The *Brown* decision was important for students with disabilities because the concept of equal opportunity was applicable to them as well as to students of minority background. Sixteen years after the *Brown* decision, the concept of equal opportunity was applied to children with disabilities judicially in federal district court. Two landmark decisions in which action was sought against state statutes and policies that excluded students with disabilities were *Pennsylvania Association for Retarded Citizens v. Commonwealth of Pennsylvania* (1972), and *Mills v. Board of Education of the District of Columbia* (1972).

Pennsylvania Association for Retarded Citizens v. Pennsylvania (1972)

In January 1971, the Pennsylvania Association for Retarded Children brought a class-action suit against the Commonwealth of Pennsylvania (suit hereafter abbreviated *PARC*) in a federal district court. Specifically, the suit named the state's secretaries of Education and Public Welfare, the state Board of Education, and thirteen school districts. The plaintiffs argued that students with mental retardation were not receiving publicly supported education because the state was delaying or ignoring its constitutional obligations to provide a publicly supported education for these students, thus violating state statute and the students' rights under the Equal Protection of the Laws clause of the Fourteenth Amendment to the U.S. Constitution. Witnesses for the plaintiffs established four critical points. The first was that all children with mental retardation are capable of benefiting from a program of education and training. Second, education cannot be defined as only the provision of academic experiences for children (this legitimizes experiences such as learning to clothe and feed oneself as outcomes for public school programming). A third point was that, having undertaken to provide all children in the Commonwealth of Pennsylvania with a free public education, the state could not deny students with mental retardation access to free public education and training. Finally, it was stipulated that the earlier students with mental retardation were provided education, the greater the amount of learning that could be predicted, a point related to denying preschoolers with retardation access to preschool programs available to children without disabilities (Levine & Wexler, 1981, Zettel & Ballard, 1982).

PARC was resolved by consent agreement specifying that all children with mental retardation between the ages of 6 and 21 must be provided a free public education, and that it was most desirable to educate children with mental retardation in a program most like the programs provided for their peers without disabilities (Levine & Wexler; 1981; Zettel & Ballard, 1982). The decree, which was amended a year later, set the stage for continued developments regarding the educational rights of students with disabilities.

Mills v. Board of Education (1972)

Soon after the PARC decision, a class-action suit was filed in the Federal District Court for the District of Columbia. This suit, Mills v. Board of Education (1972; hereafter Mills), was filed against the District of Columbia's Board of Education on behalf of all out-of-school students with disabilities. The action was brought by the parents and guardians of seven children who presented a variety of disabilities, including behavior problems, hyperactivity, epilepsy, mental retardation, and physical impairments. These seven children were certified as a class, thereby representing over 18,000 students who were denied or excluded from public education in Washington, DC. The suit, which was based on the Fourteenth Amendment, charged that the students were improperly excluded from school without due process of law (Zettel & Ballard, 1982). Mills resulted in a judgment against the defendant school board which mandated that the board provide all children with disabilities a publicly supported education. In addition, the court ordered the district to provide due process safeguards. Moreover, the court clearly outlined due process procedures for labeling, placement, and exclusion of students with disabilities (Zettel & Ballard, 1982). The procedural safeguards included the following: the right to a hearing, with representation, a record, and an impartial hearing officer; the right to appeal; the right to have access to records; and the requirement of written notice at all stages of the process. These safeguards became the framework for the due process component of the EAHCA.

Additional Cases

The PARC and Mills decisions set precedent for similar cases to be filed across the country. In the two and a half years following the PARC and Mills decisions, 46 right-to-education cases were filed on behalf of children with disabilities in 28 states (Zettel & Ballard, 1982). The outcomes of these cases were consistent with those established in Mills and PARC. Notwithstanding the judicial success, many students with disabilities continued to be denied an appropriate public education (Zettel & Ballard, 1982). School districts continued to argue that sufficient funds did not exist, that facilities were inadequate, and that instructional materials and adequately trained teachers were unavailable. By the early 1970s, the majority of states had passed laws requiring that students with disabilities receive a public education. These laws, however, varied substantially and resulted in uneven attempts to provide education to these students. For these and other reasons, it became obvious to many that some degree of federal involvement was necessary.

Legislative Mandates

Early Federal Involvement

The first significant federal involvement in the education of students with disabilities came with the passage of the Expansion of Teaching in the Education of Mentally Retarded Children Act of 1958. In this statute, Congress appropriated funds for the training of teachers of children with mental retardation. The National Defense Education Act of 1958, passed in the same year, dramatically increased federal funding for the education of children in public schools. In 1965 the Elementary and Secondary Education Act provided additional federal funds to improve the education of certain categories of students, including those with disabilities. The following year an amendment to this act included Title VI, which added funding for grants for programs for children with disabilities. Title VI was replaced in 1970 by the Education of the Handicapped Act (EHA). This law became the basic framework for much of the legislation that was to follow.

Section 504 of the Rehabilitation Act of 1973

In 1973 Congress passed P.L. 93-112, the Rehabilitation Act of 1973. Section 504, a short provision of this act, was the first federal civil rights law to protect the rights of persons with disabilities. Section 504 states:

> No otherwise qualified handicapped individual in the United States . . . shall solely by reason of his handicap, be excluded from the participation in, be denied the benefits of, or be subject to discrimination under any activity receiving federal financial assistance. (Section 504, 29 U.S.C. § 794(a))

In both language and intent, Section 504 mirrored other federal civil rights laws that prohibited discrimination by federal recipients on the basis of race (Title VI of the Civil Rights Act of 1964) and sex (Title IX of the Education Amendments of 1972). A "handicapped" person was defined as any person who has a physical or mental impairment that substantially limits one or more of that person's major life activities, or a person who has a record of such an impairment, or who is regarded as having such an impairment.

The primary purpose of Section 504 was to prohibit discrimination against a person with a disability by any agency receiving federal funds. These agencies are any that receive funds, personnel services, and interests in property, whether receiving these benefits directly or through another recipient. Section 504 requires agencies that are the recipients of federal financial assistance to provide assurances of compliance, to take corrective steps when violations are found, and to make individualized modifications and accommodations to provide services that are comparable to those offered persons without disabilities.

P.L. 93-380, The Education Amendments of 1974

The Education Amendments of 1974, P.L. 93-380, were amendments to the Elementary and Secondary Education Act (ESEA). The ESEA provided funding for a variety of programs for children who were disadvantaged and for students with disabilities. The ESEA also authorized the creation of the Bureau of Education for the Handicapped as well as the establishment of the National Advisory Council on Handicapped Children. The purpose of the 1974 amendments was to require that each state receiving federal special education funding establish a goal of providing full educational opportunities for all children with disabilities.

P.L. 93-380 was a significant piece of legislation for both children with disabilities and children who are gifted and talented (Weintraub & Ballard, 1982). The amendment acknowledged students with disabilities' right to an education, provided funds for programs for the education of students with disabilities under Title IV-B, specified due process procedures, and addressed the issue of least restrictive environment. This amendment provided the first national initiative toward meeting the needs of students who are gifted and talented as well those with disabilities. The Act, however, was not sufficiently enforceable in the eyes of many advocates for students with disabilities (Weber, 1992).

P.L. 94-142, The Education for All Handicapped Children Act

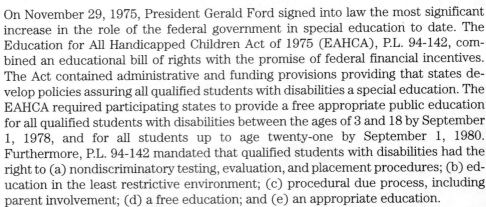

On November 29, 1975, President Gerald Ford signed into law the most significant increase in the role of the federal government in special education to date. The Education for All Handicapped Children Act of 1975 (EAHCA), P.L. 94-142, combined an educational bill of rights with the promise of federal financial incentives. The Act contained administrative and funding provisions providing that states develop policies assuring all qualified students with disabilities a special education. The EAHCA required participating states to provide a free appropriate public education for all qualified students with disabilities between the ages of 3 and 18 by September 1, 1978, and for all students up to age twenty-one by September 1, 1980. Furthermore, P.L. 94-142 mandated that qualified students with disabilities had the right to (a) nondiscriminatory testing, evaluation, and placement procedures; (b) education in the least restrictive environment; (c) procedural due process, including parent involvement; (d) a free education; and (e) an appropriate education.

The EAHCA delineated the educational rights of students with disabilities and also provided the promise of federal funding to the states. Funding would flow from the federal government to the state educational agencies (SEAs), and finally the local educational agencies (LEAs). To receive the funds, states had to submit plans meeting the federal requirements. Local school districts, in turn, had to have programs meeting the state requirements. Federal funding was to supplement state and local dollars and could not be used to supplant these funds. Additionally, 75% of the federal funds were to flow through the state to the local school districts. By 1985 all states had complied with the requirements of this act.

Legislation since 1975 has served to clarify and extend the requirements of the EAHCA. The Handicapped Children's Protection Act of 1986 was passed as an amendment to the EAHCA, providing for the award of reasonable attorneys' fees and costs to parents who are prevailing parties. In 1986 Congress passed an amendment to the EAHCA, P.L. 99-457, Education of the Handicapped Amendments, which added Part H to the law.

P.L. 101-476, The Individuals with Disabilities Education Act

The 1990 amendments to P.L. 94-142 renamed the EAHCA the Individuals with Disabilities Education Act (IDEA). The IDEA included the following major changes: (a) the language of the law was changed to emphasize the person first, including the renaming of the law to the Individuals with Disabilities Education Act, as well as changing the term "handicapped student" to "child/student/individual with a disability"; (b) students with autism and traumatic brain injury were identified as a separate and distinct class entitled to the law's benefits; and (c) a plan for transition was required to be included on every student's individualized education program (IEP) by age 16.

P.L. 101-336, The Americans with Disabilities Act

The Americans with Disabilities Act of 1990 (ADA) has been heralded both as the most sweeping civil rights legislation since the Civil Rights Act of 1964 and as the most comprehensive legislation for individuals with disabilities. The purpose of ADA was to provide comprehensive protection to individuals with disabilities similar to those provided to individuals on the basis of race, sex, national origin, age, and religion.

Persons protected under ADA are those individuals "with disabilities" as defined under Section 504 of the Rehabilitation Act: any person who has, has a history of having, or is regarded as having an impairment that significantly limits one or more of life's major functions. An individual with disabilities who is "otherwise qualified" to perform the essential functions of a job with or without reasonable accommodations is protected under the ADA. "Reasonable accommodation" may include making existing facilities accessible to and usable by individuals with disabilities. It should be noted that religious organizations and small businesses (after 1994, those with 15 or fewer employees) are exempt from the rules on employment discrimination.

ADA expanded the provisions of Section 504 of the Rehabilitation Act of 1973, which applied to a program or service receiving federal funds, to "all public services." This includes state or local government services such as recreational activities, public libraries, health services, and public transportation.

Furthermore, discrimination in public and private transportation based on disability was banned under ADA. Separate rules for complying with this ban were delineated along three categories of transportation systems: fixed-route systems, demand-response systems, and designated public transportation systems that provide the public with general or special services on a regular or continuing basis.

ADA prohibited discrimination by "public accommodations." The general rule stated that no individual shall be discriminated against on the basis of disability in the full and equal enjoyment of the goods, services, facilities, privileges, advantages, accommodations, or any place of public accommodation by any person who owns, leases (or leases to), or operates a place of public accommodation. Examples of public accommodations include restaurants, hotels, theaters, and grocery stores.

Finally, closed captioning of public service announcements and telecommunications services for hearing-impaired and speech-impaired individuals was required by the ADA. Telephone service companies must provide relay services to individuals who use telecommunication devices for the deaf (TDD). ADA also specified enforcement procedures and remedies for each of the areas addressed above. The law went into effect in 1992.

P.L. 105-17, The Individuals with Disabilities Education Act Amendments of 1997

The Individuals with Disabilities Education Act Amendments of 1997 were passed to reauthorize and make improvements to the IDEA. In passing the amendments, Congress noted that the IDEA had been very successful in ensuring access to a free appropriate public education and improving educational results for students with disabilities. Nevertheless, the implementation of the IDEA had been impeded by low expectations for students with disabilities, an insufficient focus on translating research into practice, and too great an emphasis on paperwork and legal requirements at the expense of teaching and learning. To improve the IDEA, Congress passed the most significant amendments to the law since original passage of P.L. 94-142 in 1975. The changes were seen as the next vital step in providing special education services by ensuring that students with disabilities received a quality public education through emphasizing the improvement of student performance.

The amendments restructured the IDEA by consolidating the law from eight parts to four, and made significant additions in the following areas: (a) strengthening the role of parents, ensuring access to the general education curriculum, and emphasizing student progress toward meaningful educational goals through changes in the IEP process; (b) encouraging parents and educators to resolve differences by using nonadversarial mediation and allowing school officials greater leeway in disciplining students with disabilities by altering aspects of the IDEA's procedural safeguards; and (c) funding formulas. (For elaborations on the IDEA Amendments of 1997 see Chapter 5.) Table 4.1 summarizes the rights found in case law and legislation for individuals with disabilities that are presented in this chapter.

State Education Statutes

As stated earlier in this chapter, education is the business of the states; however, with the passage of the EAHCA, special education became essentially federally controlled. States were not required to follow the EAHCA requirements, but by choosing not to they would forfeit federal funding for special education. All states have chosen to com-

Table 4.1
Case Law and Legislation Concerning Special Education

Date	Case Law and Legislation	Requirements
1954	Brown v. Board of Education	• Equal protection
1972	PARC v. Commonwealth of Pennsylvania	• Free appropriate public education (FAPE)
1972	Mills v. Board of Education of the District of Columbia	• FAPE • Procedural safeguards
1973	Section 504 of the Rehabilitation Act of 1973	• Prohibits discrimination in agencies receiving federal funds
1974	P.L. 93-380, Education Amendments of 1974	• FAPE • Procedural safeguards • Least restrictive environment (LRE) • Federal funds
1975	P.L. 94-142, Education for All Handicapped Children Act	• FAPE • Procedural safeguards • LRE • Nondiscriminatory evaluation • Individualized education program (IEP)
1986	P.L. 99-372, The Handicapped Children's Protection Act of 1986	• Recovery of attorneys' fees and costs to parents who prevail in suits
1986	P.L. 99-457, Education of the Handicapped Amendments of 1986	• Federal incentives to adopt infant/toddler programs
1990	P.L. 101-476, Individuals with Disabilities Education Act (IDEA)	• Changed language of law • Added students with autism and traumatic brain injury (TBI) • Required transition plan on IEP
1990	P.L. 101-336, Americans with Disabilities Act (ADA)	• Expands civil rights for individuals with disabilities in the public and private sector
1997	P.L. 105-17, Individuals with Disabilities Education Act Amendments of 1997	• Restructured the law • Changes in the IEP team and content of the IEP • States must establish a voluntary mediation system • Added language regarding the discipline of students

ply with the federal regulations based on the EAHCA. States who had special education programs in place were required to make the necessary changes to comply with the EAHCA, and states who were not providing special education programs for children with disabilities were required to develop them. Some states developed statutes and regulations that expanded the federal special education requirements. The inclusion of children who are gifted and talented as eligible for special education services is one such example of states (such as Kansas and New Mexico) going beyond the requirements of the EAHCA. States set their own regulations specifying teacher certification regulations, teacher-pupil ratios, transportation time, and age-span requirements in the classroom. In addition, states were allowed some flexibility in funding mechanisms. States were required to distribute 75% of the federal moneys to local educational agencies; however, they may exceed the 75% allocation if they so desired. As the examples indicate, state statutes and regulations must meet the federal requirements as outlined in the EAHCA, though they may go beyond these requirements.

Summary

This chapter has provided an examination of the historical development of special education as advanced through case law and legislation. By the early 1900s, all of the states had compulsory education laws, yet the exclusion of children with disabilities was still widely practiced. The educational rights of children with disabilities were gained largely through the efforts of parents and advocacy groups. The civil rights movement, and specifically the U.S. Supreme Court's decision in *Brown v. Board of Education* (1954), provided impetus for subsequent legislation and litigation granting students with disabilities the right to a free appropriate public education. Two seminal cases in securing these rights were *PARC v. Pennsylvania* (1972) and *Mills v. Board of Education* (1972). The early 1970s witnessed a number of federal legislative efforts to improve the education of students with disabilities. The major pieces of legislation to emerge in this decade were Section 504 of the Rehabilitation Act of 1973 and the Education for All Handicapped Children Act of 1975.

This chapter has traced the arduous struggle to equal opportunity for children with disabilities. Although tremendous progress has been made as we enter the 21st century, much remains to be accomplished. Individuals with disabilities, their advocates, and all persons who wish for a fair and equitable treatment must continue to work toward attaining the goal of an equal and just society for all.

For Further Information

Ballard, J., Ramirez, B., & Weintraub. F. (Eds.) *Special education in America: Its legal and governmental foundations.* Reston, VA: Council for Exceptional Children.

Levine, E. L., & Wexler, E. M. (1981). *P.L. 94-142: An Act of Congress.* New York: Macmillan.

Winzer, M. A. (1993). *History of special education from isolation to integration.* Washington, DC: Gallaudet Press.

References

Americans with Disabilities Act of 1990, 42 U.S.C.A. § 12101 *et seq.*

Beattie v. Board of Education, 172 N.W. 153 (Wis. 1919).

Brown v. Board of Education., 347 U.S. 483 (1954).

Civil Rights Act of 1964, 42 U.S.C. § 2000d.

Department of Public Welfare v. Haas, 154 N.E. 2nd 265 (Ill. 1958).

Education Amendments of 1972, 20 U.S.C. § 1681 *et seq.*

Education Amendments of 1974, Pub. L. No. 93-380, 88 Stat. 580.

Education for All Handicapped Children Act of 1975, 20 U.S.C. § 1401 *et seq.*

Education of the Handicapped Act of 1970, Pub. L. No. 91-230, § 601–662, 84 Stat. 175.

Education of the Handicapped Amendments of 1986, 20 U.S.C. § 1401 *et seq.*

Elementary and Secondary Education Act of 1965, Pub. L. No. 89-10, 79 Stat. 27.

Elementary and Secondary Education Act, amended by Pub. L. No. 89-750. § 161 [Title VI], 80 Stat. 1204 (1966).

Expansion of Teaching in the Education of Mentally Retarded Children Act of 1958, Pub. L. No. 85-864, 72 Stat. 1777.

Handicapped Children's Protection Act of 1986, 20 U.S.C. § 1401 *et seq.*

Individuals with Disabilities Education Act of 1990, 20 U.S.C. § 1401 *et seq.*

Individuals with Disabilities Education Act Amendments of 1997, Pub. L. No. 105-17, 105th Cong., 1st sess.

Levine, E. L., & Wexler, E. M. (1981). *P.L. 94-142: An act of Congress.* New York: Macmillan.

Mills v. Board of Education of the District of Columbia, 348 F. Supp. 866 (D.D.C. 1972).

National Defense Education Act of 1958, Pub. L. No. 85-864, 72 Stat. 1580.

Pennsylvania Association for Retarded Citizens (PARC) v. Commonwealth of Pennsylvania, 343 F. Supp. 279 (E.D. Pa. 1972).

Rehabilitation Act of 1973, Section 504, 29 U.S.C. § 794.

Siegel-Causey, E., Guy, B., & Guess, D. (1995). Severe and multiple disabilities. In E. L. Meyen and T. M. Skrtic (Eds.), *Special education and student disability, an introduction: Traditional, emerging, and alternative perspectives* (4th ed.) (pp. 415–448). Denver: Love Publishing Company.

Turnbull, A. P., & Turnbull, H. R. (1997). *Families, professionals, and exceptionality: A special partnership* (3rd ed.). Upper Saddle River, NJ: Merrill/Prentice Hall.

Turnbull, H. R. (1993). *Free appropriate public education: The law and children with disabilities* (4th ed.). Denver: Love Publishing Company.

Watson v. City of Cambridge, 32 N.E. 864 (Mass. 1893).

Weber, M. C. (1992). *Special education law and litigation treatise.* Horsham, PA: LRP Publications.

Weintraub, F. J., & Ballard, J. (1982). Introduction: Bridging the decades. In J. Ballard, B. Ramirez, and F. Weintraub (Eds.), *Special education in America: Its legal and governmental foundations* (pp. 1–10). Reston, VA: Council for Exceptional Children.

Winzer, M. A. (1993). *History of special education from isolation to integration.* Washington, DC: Gallaudet Press.

Ysseldyke, J. E., & Algozzine, B. (1984). *Introduction to special education.* Boston: Houghton Mifflin.

Zettel, J. J., & Ballard, J. (1982). The Education for All Handicapped Children Act of 1975 (P.L. 94-142): Its history, origins, and concepts. In J. Ballard, B. Ramirez, and F. Weintraub (Eds.), *Special education in America: Its legal and governmental foundations* (pp. 11–22). Reston, VA: Council for Exceptional Children.

CHAPTER FIVE

The Individuals with Disabilities Education Act

We must recognize our responsibility to provide education for all children [with disabilities] which meets their unique needs. The denial of the right to education and to equal opportunity within this nation for handicapped children— whether it be outright exclusion from school, the failure to provide an education which meets the needs of a single handicapped child, or the refusal to recognize the handicapped child's right to grow—is a travesty of justice and a denial of equal protection under the law.

Senator Harrison Williams, principal author of the Education for All
Handicapped Children Act, *Congressional Record* (1974, p. 15,272)

In 1975, P.L. 94-142, the Education for All Handicapped Children Act (EAHCA), was enacted to meet the educational needs of students with disabilities. Amendments to the EAHCA enacted in 1990, P.L. 101-476, changed the name of the Act to the Individuals with Disabilities Education Act (IDEA). Amendments to the IDEA added in 1997 further clarified, restructured, and extended the law.

The IDEA is codified at 20 U.S.C. §§ 1400–1485. Originally the law was divided into nine subchapters. In the IDEA Amendments of 1997, the law was restructured into four subchapters. Subchapters one and two are referred to as Parts A and B, respectively. Part A contains the general provisions of the law (e.g., definitions). Part B details the grant program that requires states receiving federal assistance under the IDEA to ensure a free appropriate public education to all qualified children and youth with disabilities residing in the state. Part B also contains the procedural safeguards designed to protect the interests of children and youth with disabilities. Parts C and D are discretionary or support programs. These subchapters have been enacted to address various concerns regarding the education of students with disabilities. Part C

Table 5.1
Subchapters of the IDEA

Subchapter	Title	Purpose and Contents
1—Part A	General Provisions	Purposes, definitions
2—Part B	Assistance for Education for All Children with Disabilities	State formula grant program, FAPE entitlements, and procedural safeguards
3—Part C	Infants and Toddlers with Disabilities	Requires that states serve preschool students with disabilities (3 to 5) and authorizes grants to states to provide early intervention services to infants and toddlers (birth to 3)
4—Part D	National Activities to Improve Education of Children with Disabilities	State improvement grants, technical assistance, dissemination of information, funding research and demonstration projects, and training personnel for educating students with disabilities

extends Part B protections to infants and toddlers with disabilities and strengthens incentives for states to provide services to infants and toddlers (birth to age 3). Part C (originally Part H) was added to the IDEA in 1986 with the passage of P.L. 99-457 (IDEA, 20 U.S.C. §§ 1471–1485). The subchapters are listed in Table 5.1.

In 1976 the Department of Health, Education, and Welfare promulgated regulations implementing the IDEA. The extensive regulations can be found at 34 C.F.R. §§ 300.1–300.754. Regulations implementing the original Part H—early intervention programs for infants and toddlers with disabilities—can be found at 34 C.F.R. §§ 303.1–303.670. Regulations are forthcoming to implement the requirements added in the IDEA Amendments of 1997.

Legislative History of the IDEA

The genesis of the IDEA can be found in the advocacy of various disability coalitions, litigation, and federal and state legislation of the 1950s and 1960s. Many of the principles eventually incorporated into the IDEA can be traced to these court decisions and this legislation. Advocacy groups played a major role in securing the principle of an equal educational opportunity for students with disabilities. The advocacy of these groups was aided through the support of national figures like President John F. Kennedy and Senator Hubert H. Humphrey.

Until 1965, the cost of educating students with disabilities was borne by state and local governments. Very few teachers were being trained to work with students with disabilities, and extremely small amounts of funds were available to universities to support research (Levine & Wexler, 1981).

By the early 1970s, many states had statutes and regulations regarding the education of students with disabilities. Nevertheless, the efforts across states were uneven, and many believed that additional federal standards were needed (Weber, 1992). In early 1973, four bills were before the Senate regarding the education of students with disabilities: S.896, introduced by Senator Jennings Randolph, to extend the life of the Education of the Handicapped Act for 3 years; S.34, introduced by Senator Ernest Hollings, to fund research in the problems of children with autism; S.808, introduced by Senator Mike Gravel, to provide federal funds for screening preschool children for the presence of learning disabilities; and S.6, introduced by Senator Harrison Williams, a comprehensive bill for the education of students with disabilities based on two landmark cases, *Pennsylvania Association for Retarded Citizens v. Commonwealth of Pennsylvania* (1972) and *Mills v. Board of Education* (1972). The purpose of the Williams bill was to mandate that a free appropriate public education be available to all students with disabilities by 1976. These four bills were the subject of Senate hearings held in 1973. Eventually, conference committees agreed on a bill that would be known as the Education of the Handicapped Amendments of 1974, P.L. 93-380. The 93rd Congress, however, failed to act on this bill before adjournment.

Because bills pending at the end of a final session of Congress die, Senator Williams had to reintroduce his bill, S.6, the Education for All Handicapped Children Act (EAHCA), in the next session. In April 1973 the Senate Subcommittee on the Handicapped held hearings on this bill in Newark, New Jersey; Boston, Massachusetts; Harrisburg, Pennsylvania; St. Paul, Minnesota; and Columbia, South Carolina. Even though the years since the passage of Title VI of the Elementary and Secondary Education Act (1966) had seen great progress in the education of students with disabilities, the hearings on Senator Williams's bill indicated that significant problems remained.

The Senate passed S.6, and the House passed a similar bill, H.7217. The conference committee resolved differences in the two bills and sent one bill, the EAHCA, to both houses of Congress. The Senate and the House approved the bill and sent it to the president for signing. On November 29, 1975, the 142nd bill passed by the 94th Congress, the EAHCA, was signed into law by President Gerald Ford.

The EAHCA, also called P.L. 94-142, provided federal funding to states to assist them in educating students with disabilities. States receiving federal funding were required to submit a state plan to the Bureau of Education for the Handicapped. The plan was to describe the state's policies and procedures to educate students with disabilities in accordance with the procedures contained in the EAHCA. If the plan was approved by the bureau, the state was obligated to guarantee a free appropriate public education to students with disabilities in return for the federal funding. Federal regulations implementing the law took effect on August 23, 1977.

All but one state, New Mexico, submitted a plan for federal funding under P.L. 94-142. New Mexico decided not to accept the funds or implement the Act. An advocacy group for citizens with disabilities, the New Mexico Association for Retarded Citizens, sued the state for failing to provide an appropriate education for students with disabilities under Section 504 of the Rehabilitation Act of 1973. Section 504 prevents entities that receive federal funds from discriminating against persons with disabilities by denying students an appropriate education. (For elaboration on Section 504 see Chapter 6.) The association, in *New Mexico Association for Retarded Citizens v. New Mexico* (1982), prevailed. The decision indicated that even though a state did not accept federal funding and the requirements attached to the funds (adherence to P.L. 94-142), it would still have to comply with Section 504, a civil rights law that contained no funding provisions. New Mexico, therefore, was required to provide a free appropriate public education to students with disabilities even though the state received no federal funding under the IDEA. New Mexico subsequently submitted a state plan to the Bureau of Education for the Handicapped, opting to implement the law and accept the federal funding. Following this action, all 50 states were participants in federal funding through the EAHCA.

The Purpose of the IDEA

The IDEA was enacted to assist states in meeting the educational needs of students with disabilities via federal funding of state efforts. According to the U.S. Supreme Court, however,

> Congress did not content itself with passage of a simple funding statute. Rather the [IDEA] confers upon disabled students an enforceable substantive right to public education . . . and conditions federal financial assistance upon states' compliance with substantive and procedural goals of the Act. (*Honig v. Doe,* 1988, p. 597)

The purpose of the IDEA is to

> assure that all children with disabilities have available to them . . . a free appropriate public education which emphasizes special education and related services designed to meet their unique needs, to assure that the rights of children with disabilities and their parents or guardians are protected, to assist states and localities to provide for the education of all children with disabilities, and to assess and assure the effectiveness of efforts to educate children with disabilities. (IDEA, 20 U.S.C. § 1400(c))

Rather than establishing substantive educational standards to ensure that the goal of the IDEA was fulfilled, Congress created an elaborate set of procedural safeguards. The purpose of these safeguards was to allow parental input into a school's decisions and to maximize the likelihood of providing an appropriate education for children and youth with disabilities.

Who Is Protected?

Students meeting the IDEA's definition of a student with disabilities receive the procedural protections of the law. Students with disabilities, determined to be eligible in accordance with the provisions of the IDEA, are entitled to receive special education and related services. The determination of eligibility is made on an individual basis by the multidisciplinary team in accordance with guidelines set forth in the law. The IDEA uses a categorical approach to define students with disabilities by setting forth categories of disabilities. Not all students with disabilities are protected, but only those students with disabilities included in the IDEA, and only if those disabilities have an adverse impact on their education and, therefore, require a special education. Additionally, the IDEA categories are exhaustive.

Categories of Disabilities

Categories of disabilities covered under the IDEA are listed in Figure 5.1. The categories of autism and traumatic brain injury were added to the IDEA in 1990. The IDEA disability categories and regulations defining them can be found at 20 U.S.C. § 1401(a) and 34 C.F.R. § 300.7(a)(1)–(b)(13). The Department of Education (DOE) also solicited public comments regarding the possible addition of a category for Attention Deficit Hyperactivity Disorder (ADHD) prior to the publication of the 1990 amendments to the IDEA. ADHD was not made a separate category. The DOE, however, did issue a joint policy memo stating that a student with ADHD could be eligible for special education and related services under the categories of specific learning disability, serious emotional disturbance, or other health impairment (Joint Policy Memo, 1991). Students with ADHD may also be eligible for services under Section 504 of the Rehabilitation Act of 1973.

Figure 5.1
Categories of Disabilities Under the IDEA

Autism
Deaf-blindness
Deafness
Hearing impairment
Mental retardation
Multiple disabilities
Orthopedic impairments
Other health impairment
Emotional disturbance
Specific learning disability
Speech or language impairment
Traumatic brain injury
Visual impairment, including blindness

In the IDEA Amendments of 1997 the terminology "serious emotional disturbance" was changed to "emotional disturbance." The reason for this change was to eliminate the pejorative connotation of the term "serious." The change was not intended to have substantive or legal significance (Senate Report, 1997).

States are required to provide services to students who meet the criteria in the IDEA. This does not mean that states have to adopt every category exactly as specified in the IDEA. States may combine categories (e.g., many states combine deaf and hearing impairment), divide categories (e.g., many states divide the category of mental retardation in two or more categories, such as mild, moderate, and severe), use different terminology (e.g., serious emotional disturbance goes by a number of different terms such as emotionally and behaviorally disordered or emotionally handicapped), or expand the definitions (e.g., Minnesota does not exclude students identified as socially maladjusted in their definition of emotional or behavioral disorders as does the federal definition). At a minimum, however, all students with disabilities who meet the appropriate criteria as defined in the IDEA categories must receive services.

Age Requirements

The IDEA requires that a program of special education and related services be provided to all eligible students with disabilities between the ages of 3 and 21. States are required to identify and evaluate children from birth to age 21, even if the state does not provide educational services to students with disabilities in the 3-to-5 and 18-to-21 age groups (IDEA Regulations, 34 C.F.R. § 300.300, comment 3). The duty to provide special education to qualified students with disabilities is absolute between the ages of 6 and 17 (Weber, 1992). If states do not require an education for students without disabilities between ages 3 to 5 and 18 to 21, they are not required to educate students in those age groups (IDEA, 20 U.S.C. § 1412(2)(B)).

If a special education student graduates with a diploma, successfully completes an appropriate individualized education program (IEP) leading to graduation, or voluntarily drops out of school, the school's obligation to the student ends (*Wexler v. Westfield*, 1986). If the graduation is merely used to terminate a school district's obligation, however, the district can be required to supply compensatory education, such as educational services beyond the age of 21 (*Helms v. Independent School District #3*, 1985).

Infants and Toddlers

An amendment to the IDEA was passed in 1986 (P.L. 99-457; The Infants and Toddlers with Disabilities Act). This amendment was originally added to the then EAHCA as Part H. Part H provided incentive grants to states that provide special education and related services to children with disabilities from birth through age 2. At age 3, a child with a disability is entitled to receive services under Part B. To ensure a smooth transition, when a child receiving early intervention services turns 3, the state is required to convene a transition meeting with the Part H lead agency, the local educational agency (LEA), and the parents.

This amendment, which became Part C when IDEA was restructured in the 1997 amendments, is codified at 20 U.S.C. §§ 1541–1585. Regulations implementing this section of the IDEA, adopted in 1989, are codified at 34 C.F.R. §§ 303.1–303.653. Part C requires that participating states develop a statewide system of multidisciplinary interagency programs to provide early intervention services. The populations targeted for this program are infants and toddlers who

(1) Are experiencing developmental delays . . . in one or more of the following areas:
  (i)   Cognitive development;
  (ii) Physical development, including vision and hearing;
  (iii) Language and speech development;
  (iv) Psychosocial development; or
  (v)   Self-help skills; or
(2) Have a diagnosed physical or mental condition that has a high probability of resulting in developmental delay. (IDEA Regulations, 34 C.F.R. § 303.16)

Infants and toddlers may be designated as developmentally delayed and receive special education services. It is not required that the children fit into a category of disabilities included in the IDEA to receive services.

States have an option of submitting plans to participate in Part C funding. To determine if a state has submitted a plan and is obligated under Part C, state statutes and regulations should be consulted.

Major Principles of the IDEA

The IDEA was enacted to address the failure of states to meet the educational needs of students with disabilities (Tucker & Goldstein, 1992). The method chosen to accomplish this goal was federal funding of states that submitted special education plans that met the IDEA's requirements. After the plan is approved, the state assumes the responsibility for meeting the provisions of the law. In addition to setting the formulas by which states can receive funds, the IDEA contains provisions to ensure that all qualifying students with disabilities receive a free appropriate education and that procedural protections are granted to students and their parents. These provisions are:

- Zero reject
- Free appropriate public education
- Least restrictive environment
- Identification and evaluation
- Confidentiality of information
- Procedural safeguards
- Technology-related assistance
- Personnel development
- Placements in private schools

Zero Reject

According to the zero reject principle, all students with disabilities eligible for services under the IDEA are entitled to a free appropriate public education. This principle applies regardless of the severity of the disability. According to the U.S. Court of Appeals for the First Circuit, public education is to be provided to all students with educational disabilities, unconditionally and without exception (*Timothy W. v. Rochester, New Hampshire, School District,* 1989).

The state must assure that all students with disabilities, from birth to age 21, residing in the state who are in need of special education and related services or are suspected of having disabilities and in need of special education are identified, located, and evaluated (IDEA Regulations, 34 C.F.R. § 300.220). These requirements include children with disabilities attending private schools. This requirement is called the child find system. States are free to develop their own child find systems (IDEA, 20 U.S.C. § 1414(a)(1)(A)). The state plan must identify the agency that will coordinate the child find tasks, the activities that it will use, and resources needed to accomplish the child find. School districts are usually responsible for conducting child find activities within their jurisdiction. The child find applies to all children and youth in the specified age range regardless of the severity of the disability. Furthermore, the child find requirement is an affirmative duty, because parents do not have to request that a school district identify and evaluate a student with disabilities. In fact, parents' failure to notify a school district will not relieve a school district of its obligations (Gorn, 1996). It is up to the school district to find these students. When students are identified in the child find, the school district is required to determine whether they have a disability under the IDEA.

A school district's child find system can take many forms. One method is the general public notice. School districts are obligated to notify the public as a means of locating children with disabilities. Additional methods that may be used to locate and identify children with disabilities include referrals, public meetings, door-to-door visits, home and community visits, brochures, speakers, contacting pediatricians, contacting day care providers, kindergarten screening, and public awareness efforts. If a school district becomes aware or suspects that a student may need special education, an evaluation is required.

Free Appropriate Public Education

The IDEA requires that states have policies that assure all students with disabilities the right to a free appropriate public education (FAPE). According to Guernsey and Klare (1993), the FAPE requirement has both procedural and substantive components. The procedural components are the extensive procedural protections afforded to students and their parents. These protections ensure the parents' right to meaningful participation in all decisions affecting their child's education. The substantive right to a FAPE consists of special education and related services which (A) have been provided at public expense, under public supervision and direction, and without charge, (B) meet standards of the state educational agency, (C) include an appropriate preschool, elementary, or secondary school education in the state involved, and (D) are provided in conformity with the Individualized Education Program. (IDEA 20 U.S.C. § 1401(18)(C))

Special education is defined in the statutory language as "specially designed instruction, at no charge to the parents or guardians, to meet the unique needs of a child with a disability" (IDEA, 20 U.S.C. § 1404(a)(16)). Related services are any developmental, corrective, or supportive services that students need to benefit from special education (IDEA, 20 U.S.C. § 1404(a)(17)).

Public schools must provide special education and related services to eligible students at no cost. If a student is placed out of the school district by a school district, the home district retains financial responsibility. This includes tuition fees and related services charges. The only fees that schools may collect from parents of children with disabilities are those fees that are also imposed on the parents of children without disabilities (e.g., physical education fees, lunch fees).

The IDEA also acknowledges the rights of states to set standards for a FAPE. The IDEA requires that local school districts meet states' special education standards. These standards may exceed the minimum level of educational services provided for in the IDEA. For example, Massachusetts requires that schools provide a FAPE that will assure a student's maximum possible development (Massachusetts General Law Annotated, 1978), a standard greater than that contained in the IDEA. State standards may not, however, set lower educational benefits than the IDEA.

One of the most crucial aspects of the substantive component is that the special education and related services must be provided in conformity with the IEP. An IEP must be developed for all students in special education. (See Chapter 9 for elaborations of IEP requirements.) The school district is responsible for providing the student's education as described in the IEP. The IEP must be in effect at the beginning of the school year and be reviewed at least annually (IDEA, 20 U.S.C. § 1414(a)(5)).

Least Restrictive Environment

The IDEA mandates that students with disabilities are educated with their peers without disabilities to the maximum extent appropriate (IDEA Regulations, 34 C.F.R. § 300.550(b)(1)). Students in special education can only be removed to separate classes or schools when the nature or severity of their disabilities is such that they cannot receive an appropriate education in a general education classroom with supplementary aids and services (IDEA Regulations, 34 C.F.R. § 300.550(b)(2)). When students are placed in segregated settings, schools must provide them with opportunities to interact with their peers without disabilities where appropriate (e.g., art class, physical education).

To ensure that students are educated in the least restrictive environment (LRE) that is appropriate for their needs, school districts must ensure that a complete continuum of alternative placements is available. This continuum consists of regular classes, resource rooms, special classes, special schools, homebound instruction, and instruction in hospitals and institutions (IDEA Regulations, 34 C.F.R. § 300.551).

Identification and Evaluation

In hearings on the original EAHCA, Congress heard testimony indicating that many schools were using tests inappropriately, and therefore were making improper placement decisions (Turnbull & Turnbull, 1990). Sometimes schools placed students in special education based on a single test, administered and placed students using tests that were not reliable or valid, or used tests that were discriminatory. To remedy these problems, the IDEA includes protection in evaluation procedures (PEP). A fair and accurate evaluation is extremely important to ensure proper placement and, therefore, an appropriate education. The PEP procedures were incorporated into the IDEA to address the abuses in the assessment process (Salvia & Ysseldyke, 1995). These provisions, listed in Figure 5.2, address the evaluation and assessment procedures used by schools in identifying and placing students with disabilities (IDEA Regulations, 34 C.F.R. § 300.530 *et seq.*).

Figure 5.2
Protection in Evaluation Procedures

- Tests are provided and administered in the child's native language or mode of communication.
- Standardized tests must have been validated for the specific purpose for which they are intended.
- Standardized tests are administered by trained personnel in conformity with the publisher's instructions.
- The evaluation will be tailored to assess the child's specific areas of educational need, including information provided by the parent that may assist in determining disability and the content of the IEP.
- Evaluators must use technically sound instruments that assess multiple areas and factors.
- No single procedure is used as the sole criterion for determining the presence of a disability, the student's program, or placement.
- The evaluation team is comprised of a multidisciplinary team or group of persons, at least one of whom has knowledge in the child's suspected area of disability.
- The child is assessed in all areas related to the suspected disability.

Confidentiality of Information

The confidentiality of student records is protected by the IDEA (IDEA Regulations, 34 C.F.R. § 300.560 *et seq.*). The privacy rights in the IDEA were largely adopted from the privacy rights in the Family Educational Rights and Privacy Act (1974). (For elaborations on the Family Educational Rights and Privacy Act see Chapter 16.)

The parents of students with disabilities are entitled to certain rights regarding information concerning their child that is collected, maintained, or used by the school. There are four areas of protection: parental access, parental amendment, protection from disclosure, and destruction of records.

First, parents have the right to inspect all educational records. If parents request to view the records, the school district must respond in a timely manner. Parents may also request copies of all records. Second, if upon viewing the records the parents believe certain information is not accurate, they may request that the school amend the information. The school can decline the request. If it does so, the parents can request a hearing. If the parents prevail in the hearing, the school must amend the records. If the school prevails, the parents may place a statement of challenge in the records.

Third, the records are to be confidential. Only school staff with a legitimate need to know the information in the records (e.g., the student's teacher, the school principal) may have access. Records are unavailable to third parties that do not have a legitimate need to access the information unless parents give their consent. Schools must keep a record of parties inspecting the educational records (with the exception of parents and authorized employees). These records of access must include the name of the inspecting party, the date of access, and the purpose of the inspection. A single party should be responsible for maintaining the records. Schools must also train staff with access to information about the obligations of the agency.

Finally, when the records are no longer needed to provide educational services, the parents must be notified and informed that they may have the records destroyed. If parents do not request destruction of records, the school may retain them indefinitely. The right of destruction of records applies to personally identifiable information that is no longer needed to provide educational services, but does not apply to permanent student records kept by the school (e.g., student name, address, age, attendance records, grade levels completed). Parents must also be informed that the information contained in special education records may be needed for social security benefits or for other reasons.

The case of *Sean R. v. Town of Woodbridge Board of Education* (1992) addressed schools' responsibility to ensure confidentiality of information. The court indicated that if a school violates confidentiality of information through an unauthorized release of student records, it may be exposed to a suit for damages.

Procedural Safeguards

The heart of the IDEA lies in the procedural safeguards designed to protect the interests of students with disabilities (Tucker & Goldstein, 1992). The IDEA utilizes an extensive system of procedural safeguards to ensure that parents are equal participants in the special education process (IDEA Regulations, 34 C.F.R. § 300.500 *et seq.*). These safeguards consist of four components: general safeguards, the independent educational evaluation, the appointment of surrogate parents, and dispute resolution (i.e., mediation and the due process hearing).

The general safeguards for parents and students consist of notice and consent requirements. Specifically, notice must be given to parents a reasonable amount of time prior to the school's initiating or changing or refusing to initiate or change the student's identification, evaluation, or educational placement (IDEA Regulations, 34 C.F.R. § 300.504(a) *et seq.*). Parental consent must be obtained prior to conducting a preplacement evaluation and again prior to initial placement in a special education program (IDEA Regulations, 34 C.F.R. 300.504(b) *et seq.*).

When the parents of a child with disabilities disagree with the educational evaluation of the school, they have a right to obtain an independent evaluation at public expense (IDEA Regulations, 34 C.F.R. § 300.503). The school has to supply the parents, on request, with information about where the independent educational evaluation may be obtained. When the parents decide to have the evaluation done independently, the district must pay for the cost of the evaluation or see that it is provided at no cost to the parents. If, however, the school believes its evaluation was appropriate, the school may initiate a due process hearing. If the result of the hearing is that the school's evaluation was appropriate, the parents do not have the right to receive the evaluation at public expense. Parent-initiated independent evaluations, when done at the parents' own expense, must be considered by the school. Results may also be presented as evidence at a due process hearing. Finally, a hearing officer can request an independent evaluation as part of a hearing; in this case the cost must be borne by the school.

When a child's parents cannot be located or the child is a ward of the state, the agency is responsible for appointing surrogate parents to protect the rights of the child. Employees of the school or persons with conflicts of interest cannot serve as surrogate parents. The method of selecting a surrogate parent must be in accordance with state law. The actual selection and appointment methods, therefore, are not determined by the IDEA. The IDEA does require that the surrogate parent must represent the child in all matters relating to the provision of special education to the child (IDEA Regulations, 34 C.F.R. § 300.514 *et seq.*).

When there is a disagreement between the school and the parents on matters concerning identification, evaluation, placement, or any matters pertaining to the FAPE, parents may request a due process hearing. Schools may also request a due process hearing. For example, if the parents refuse consent for evaluation or initial placement, the school may use the due process hearing to conduct an evaluation or place the child (IDEA Regulations, 34 C.F.R. § 300.504(b)(3)). The IDEA Amendments of 1997 require that states offer parents the option of resolving their disputes through the mediation process prior to going to a due process hearing. The mediation process is voluntary and must not be used to deny or delay parents' right to a due process hearing. The mediation process is conducted by a trained mediator who is knowledgeable about the laws and regulations regarding the provision of special education and related services. A mediator has no decision-making powers as do impartial due process hearing officers. Rather, the mediator attempts to facilitate an agreement between the parents and school officials regarding the matter in dispute. If attempts to mediate and reach agreement are not successful, either party may request an impartial due process hearing.

The due process hearing must be conducted by either the state educational agency (SEA) or the LEA responsible for the education of the student. A due process hearing is a forum in which both sides present their arguments to an impartial third party, the due process hearing officer. During the hearing, the student must remain in the program or placement in effect when the hearing was requested. A school district cannot unilaterally change placement or program during the pendency of the due process hearing or judicial action. The provision of the IDEA that mandates that the student's placement or program not be changed without the agreement of both parties is referred to as the stay-put provision (IDEA Regulations, 34 C.F.R. § 300.513). The stay-put provision may be abrogated in situations where a student with disabilities brings a weapon to school, uses or sells illegal drugs, or presents a danger to other students or to staff. (See Chapter 15 for elaborations on the stay-put provision and students with disabilities.)

Any party in the hearing has the right to be represented by counsel, present evidence, compel the attendance of witnesses, examine and cross-examine witnesses, prohibit the introduction of evidence not introduced five days prior to the hearing, obtain a written or electronic verbatim record of the hearing, and be provided with the written findings of fact by the hearing officer. Additionally, the parent may have the child present and may open the hearing to the public. Following the hearing, the hearing officer announces the decision. This decision is binding on both parties. Either party, however, may appeal the decision. In most states, the appeal is to the SEA. The decision of the agency can then be appealed to the state or federal court.

Technology-Related Assistance

The pervasive impact of technology on the lives of persons with disabilities was recognized in a report issued by the Federal Office of Technology Assessment in 1982 (Gibbons, 1982). The report concluded that there was a lack of comprehensive, responsive, and coordinated mechanisms to deliver and fund technology to improve the lives of persons with disabilities. In 1988, Congress passed the Technology-Related Assistance for Individuals with Disabilities Act (29 U.S.C. § 2201 *et seq.*). The purpose of the law was to establish a program of federal grants to states to promote technology-related assistance to individuals with disabilities. Assistive technology, as defined in the law, included both technological devices and services. Congress further recognized the importance of technology in the lives of children and youth with disabilities by incorporating the definitions of assistive technology devices and services from the Technology Act into the IDEA:

The term "assistive technology device" means any item, piece of equipment, or product system, whether acquired commercially off the shelf, modified, or customized, that is used to increase, maintain, or improve functional capabilities of [children] with disabilities.

The term "assistive technology service" means any service that directly assists a [child] with a disability in the selection, acquisition, or use of an assistive technology device. Such a term includes—

(A) the evaluation of the needs of a [child] with a disability including a functional evaluation of the [child] in the [child's] customary environment;

(B) purchasing, leasing, or otherwise providing for the acquisition of assistive technology devices by [children] with disabilities;

(C) selecting, designing, fitting, customizing, adapting, applying, retaining, repairing, or replacing of assistive technology devices;

(D) coordinating and using other therapies, interventions, or services with assistive technology devices;

(E) training or technical assistance for a [child] with disabilities or, where appropriate, the family of a [child] with disabilities; and

(F) training or technical assistance for professionals. (IDEA, 20 U.S.C. § 1401 {25} {26})

These definitions were included in the IDEA; however, nothing in the law mandated that participating states provide assistive technology devices or services to students. Julnes and Brown (1993) note that this was because assistive technology devices and services were implicitly required by the EAHCA prior to the inclusion of the assistive technology definitions in 1990. Regulations implementing these definitions support this contention. The regulations provide that:

Each public agency shall ensure that assistive technology or assistive technology services, or both . . . are made available to a child with a disability if required as part of the child's—

(a) Special education under § 300.17;

(b) Related services under § 300.16; or

(c) Supplementary aids and services under § 300.550(b)(2). (IDEA Regulations, 34 C.F.R. § 300.308)

The regulations indicate that assistive technology devices and services should be included in the IEP if necessary to provide a FAPE as a special education service or a related service or to maintain children and youth with disabilities in the LRE through the provision of supplementary aids and services.

The IDEA Amendments of 1997 added a requirement regarding technology and special education to the IEP. IEP teams are now required to consider whether students with disabilities, regardless of category, need assistive technology devices and services.

Personnel Development

States are required to submit a plan to the U.S. Department of Education that describes the kind and number of personnel needed in the state to meet the goals of the IDEA. To receive funding from the state, school districts must also provide a description of the personnel they will need to ensure a FAPE to all students with disabilities. Each state, therefore, is required to develop and implement a Comprehensive System of Personnel Development (CSPD) plan that ensures that an adequate supply of special education and related services personnel are available, and that these persons receive adequate and appropriate preparation (IDEA Regulations, 34 C.F.R. § 380). The IDEA Amendments of 1997 added the requirement that paraprofessionals working in special education be appropriately trained and supervised in accordance with state law.

To ensure that these requirements are met, states must delineate current and projected needs for special education and related services personnel, and coordinate efforts among school districts, colleges, and universities to see that personnel needs are met. Grants are also made available to colleges and universities to train special education teachers (IDEA Regulations, 34 C.F.R. § 381).

CSPD plans must also include a system that involves the continuing development of personnel in special education and general education. The states must also have procedures for adopting promising practices, materials, and technology (IDEA Regulations, 34 C.F.R. § 382). Furthermore, states must be able to disseminate knowledge derived from research and demonstration projects to special educators.

Finally, LEAs must provide a description of special education personnel to the state to receive special education funding. LEAs must also submit plans to make use of the state CSPD program.

Placements in Private Schools

The IDEA addresses the placement of students with disabilities in private schools. When the school district is unable to provide a FAPE and places the student in a private facility, the school district retains responsibility for the student (IDEA Regulations, 34 C.F.R. § 300.400 *et seq.*). Therefore, costs incurred in the student's education (e.g., tuition, transportation) are the responsibility of the home school district. The school district is also responsible for ensuring that the student receives a special education and related services in conformity with the IEP. Students with disabilities in private schools are entitled to a proportionate amount of IDEA funds.

When an IEP is developed for a student placed in a private school by the district, the home school district must include a representative of the private agency on the IEP team. Following placement, the private school may conduct subsequent IEP meetings at the home school's discretion. If the private school conducts these meetings, however, the home school retains responsibility for ensuring that the IEP meeting is conducted in conformity with the IDEA.

When the home school is able to provide an appropriate special education but the parents choose a private school placement, the home school retains certain responsibilities regarding the provision of a special education. These responsibilities include the following: to identify and evaluate; to initiate and conduct meetings; to develop, review, and revise the IEP; and to ensure that a representative of the private school attends these meetings. The home school district is responsible for making the appropriate special education and related services available. The home school, however, does not have an obligation to provide the education and will not be financially liable. A court or hearing officer, however, may require the school district to reimburse the parents for the cost of the private school enrollment if the school district did not make a FAPE available for a student. (For elaborations on private school placements see Chapter 16.)

The IDEA and the Reauthorization Process

When Congress passes statutes that appropriate money, it may fund the statute on either a permanent or a limited basis. If on a permanent basis, the funding will continue as long as the law remains unchanged—that is, unless the law is amended to remove funding or is repealed, the funding will continue. Part B, the section of the IDEA that creates the entitlement to a FAPE and provides federal funding to the states, is permanently authorized. Congress may also appropriate funds for a statute on a limited basis. In this case, the funding period will be designated in the statute. When this period of time expires, Congress has to reauthorize funding or else let funding expire. The discretionary or support programs of the IDEA—Parts C and D—are authorized on a limited basis. In the past, funding for these programs has been authorized for periods of 4 or 5 years. Approximately every 4 or 5 years, therefore, Congress has had to reauthorize the IDEA (with the exception of Part B).

Amendments to the IDEA

Since the passage of the original EAHCA (P.L. 94-142) in 1975, there have been numerous changes to the law. Some of these changes have been minor (e.g., P.L. 100-630 in 1988 altered some of the statute's language, and P.L. 102-119 in 1991 modified parts of the infants and toddlers program). Some of the amendments, however, have made important changes to the law. These changes have expanded the procedural and substantive rights of students with disabilities protected under IDEA. Four acts that made significant changes to the then EAHCA were the Handicapped Children's Protection Act (P.L. 99-372), the Infants and Toddlers with Disabilities Act (P.L. 99-457), the Individuals with Disabilities Education Act Amendments of 1990 (P.L. 101-476), and the Individuals with Disabilities Education Act Amendments of 1997 (P.L. 105-17). As amendments, the changes were incorporated into the Act and are not codified as separate laws.

The Handicapped Children's Protection Act

Prior to 1984, there was no provision regarding attorneys' fees in the IDEA. Attorneys bringing actions pursuant to IDEA typically alleged violations of other laws (e.g., 42 U.S.C. 1983 and Section 504) to recover fees (Guernsey & Klare, 1993). This practice was halted by the decision of the U.S. Supreme Court in *Smith v. Robinson*

(1984). The high court held that the IDEA was the sole source for relief in cases brought under IDEA, therefore attorneys could not sue under other laws to collect attorneys' fees. The decision effectively made the recovery of attorneys' fees impossible because the IDEA contained no attorneys' fees provision. Less than two years later, President Reagan signed the Handicapped Children's Protection Act of 1986 (HCPA; P.L. 99-372) into law. The HCPA amended 20 U.S.C. § 1415, thereby granting courts the authority to award attorneys' fees to parents or guardians if they prevailed in their actions pursuant to the IDEA. The HCPA also overturned the Court's decision that the IDEA was the sole source of legal relief and allowed the HCPA to be applied retroactively to cases pending or brought after the 1984 *Smith v. Robinson* decision. (For elaborations on attorneys' fees see Chapter 14.)

The Infants and Toddlers with Disabilities Act

Congress recognized the importance of early intervention for young children when it passed the Infants and Toddlers with Disabilities Act (ITDA) in 1986. This law, which became a subchapter of the IDEA (Part H), made categorical grants to states contingent on their adhering to the provisions of ITDA. The amendment required participating states to develop and implement statewide interagency programs of early intervention services for infants and toddlers with disabilities and their families (IDEA, 20 U.S.C. § 1471(B)(1)). With the consolidation of the IDEA in the amendments of 1997, Part H became Part C.

For purposes of the Act, infants and toddlers with disabilities are defined as children from birth through age 2 who need early intervention services because they are experiencing developmental delays or have a diagnosed physical or mental condition that puts them at risk of developing developmental delays.

Early intervention services are defined as developmental services provided at public expense and under public supervision which are designed to meet the physical, cognitive, communication, social or emotional, and adaptive needs of the child (IDEA, 20 U.S.C. § 1472(2)). Early intervention services may include family training, counseling, home visits, speech pathology, occupational therapy, physical therapy, psychological services, case management services, medical services (for diagnostic or evaluation purposes only), health services, social work services, vision services, assistive technology devices and services, and transportation, along with related costs (IDEA, 20 U.S.C. § 1472(2)(E)). To the maximum extent appropriate, these services must be provided in natural environments (e.g., home and community settings) in which children without disabilities participate.

The infants and toddlers program does not require that the SEA assume overall responsibility for the early intervention programs. The agency that assumes responsibility is referred to as the lead agency. The lead agency may be the SEA, the state welfare department, the health department, or any other unit of state government. Many states provide Part C services through multiple state agencies (Weber, 1992). In these cases, an interagency coordinating council is the primary planning body that works out the interagency agreements concerning jurisdiction and funding.

The centerpiece of the ITDA is the individualized family services plan (IFSP). In states that receive Part C funds, all infants or toddlers with disabilities must have an IFSP. The plan is developed by a multidisciplinary and interagency team that includes the parents, other family members, the case manager (i.e., coordinator of the process), the person or persons conducting the evaluation, and other persons who will be involved in providing services (IDEA Regulations, 34 C.F.R. § 303.340). The IFSP must be reviewed and evaluated every six months, and revised every year if necessary.

The IFSP must contain

(1) a statement of the infant's or toddler's present levels of physical development, cognitive development, communication development, social or emotional development, and adaptive development, based on acceptable objective criteria,

(2) a statement of the family's resources, priorities, and concerns related to enhancing the development of the family's infant with a disability,

(3) a statement of the major outcomes expected to be achieved for the infant or toddler and the family, and the criteria, procedures, and timelines used to determine the degree to which progress toward achieving the outcomes is being made and whether modifications or revisions of the outcomes or services are necessary,

(4) a statement of the specific early intervention services necessary to meet the unique needs of the infant or toddler and the family, including the frequency, intensity, and the method of delivering services,

(5) a statement of the natural environments in which the early intervention services shall appropriately be provided,

(6) the projected dates for initiation of services and the anticipated duration of such services,

(7) the name of the case manager . . . from the profession most immediately relevant to the infant's or toddler's or family's needs . . . who will be responsible for the implementation of the plan and coordination with other agencies and persons, and

(8) the steps to be taken supporting the transition of the toddler with a disability to [special education] services. (IDEA, 20 U.S.C. § 1477(d))

Written consent of the parents is required prior to providing the services contained in the IFSP. The infants and toddlers amendment contains procedural safeguards similar to those in Part B. The primary area of differences between Part C and the rest of the IDEA is that Part C has a more flexible definition of eligible children, focuses on the family, and provides for coordinated interagency efforts.

The 1986 infants and toddlers amendments also created financial incentives for states to make children with disabilities eligible for special education at age 3. If a state lowers the age of eligibility, children with disabilities from 3 to 5 will be entitled to receive all the procedural and substantive protections of Part B of the IDEA (Weber, 1992).

The Individuals with Disabilities Education Act Amendments of 1990

Amendments to the EAHCA, P.L. 101-476, enacted in 1990, changed the name of the Act to the Individuals with Disabilities Education Act (IDEA). The Act also changed terminology from *handicap* to *disability*, incorporated "people first" language (e.g., "student with a disability" rather than "disabled student"), and made some substantive changes to the law. The 1990 amendments added two disability categories, autism and traumatic brain injury; added and clarified types of related services, assistive technology and rehabilitation services; and mandated the development of individualized transition plans for students with disabilities by the time they reach the age of 16.

The provision of transition services was a significant addition to the IDEA. Transition services refer to a

> coordinated set of activities for a student, designed within an outcome-oriented process, that promotes movement from school to post-school activities, including postsecondary education, vocational training, [and] integrated employment (including supported employment, continuing and adult education, adult services, independent living, or community participation). (IDEA Regulations, 34 C.F.R. § 300.18 *et seq.*)

Transition activities must be based on students' individual needs and take into account their preferences and interests. Transition services include instruction, community experience, the development of employment and adult living objectives, and acquisition of daily living skills and a functional vocational evaluation. Transition services may be either special education or related services.

The Individuals with Disabilities Education Act Amendments of 1997

The IDEA Amendments of 1997 added a number of significant provisions to the law, as well as restructuring it. The number of subchapters of the original IDEA was nine, and the 1997 amendments consolidated these subchapters into four parts. The purpose of the restructuring was to simplify the IDEA, thus making it easier to understand and use (Senate Report, 1997).

The Individualized Education Program

Congress believed that the IDEA had been extremely successful in improving students' access to public schools, and the critical issue in 1997 was to improve the performance and educational achievement of students with disabilities in both the special education and general education curricula. To this end, Congress mandated a number of changes to the IEP and the inclusion of students with disabilities in state- and district-wide assessments. Regarding the IEP, changes include the requirement that a statement of measurable annual goals, including benchmarks or short-term objectives, that would enable parents and educators to accurately determine a student's progress be included in the IEP. The primary difference in the statement of goals from that of the original IDEA is the emphasis on accurately measuring and reporting a student's progress toward the annual goals. The core IEP team was expanded to include both a special education teacher and a general education teacher. The original IDEA mandated that the child's teacher be a member of the IEP team but did not specify if the teacher should be in special or general education. The 1997 amendments also required that students with disabilities be included in state- and district-wide assessments of student progress. The amendments also required that the IEP team be the forum to determine if modifications or accommodations were needed to allow a student to participate in these assessments. The IEP, therefore, requires a statement regarding a student's participation in these assessments and what, if any, modifications to the assessment are needed to allow participation.

Mediation

Congress also attempted to alleviate what was believed to be the overly adversarial nature of special education by encouraging parents and educators to resolve differences by using nonadversarial methods. Specifically, the 1997 amendments required states to offer mediation as a voluntary option to parents and educators as an initial process for dispute resolution. The mediator must be trained or qualified to conduct mediation sessions and knowledgeable regarding special education law. Furthermore, the mediator cannot be an employee of the LEA or SEA and must not have any personal or professional conflict of interest. The results of mediation sessions shall be put in writing and are confidential. If mediation is not successful, either party may request an impartial due process hearing.

Discipline of Students in Special Education

Another significant addition of the 1997 amendments was a section affecting the discipline of students with disabilities. Congress heard testimony regarding the lack of parity school officials faced when making decisions about disciplining students with and without disabilities who violated the same school rules (Senate Report, 1997). To address these concerns, Congress added a section to the IDEA in an attempt to balance school officials' obligation to ensure that schools are safe and orderly environments conducive to learning and the school's obligation to ensure that students with disabilities receive a FAPE.

To deal with behavioral problems in a proactive manner, the 1997 amendments require that if a student with disabilities has behavior problems (regardless of the student's disability category), the IEP team shall consider strategies—including positive behavioral interventions, strategies, and supports—to address these problems. In such situations a proactive behavior management plan, based on functional behavioral assessment, should be included in the student's IEP. Furthermore, if a student's placement is changed following a behavioral incident and the IEP does not contain a behavioral intervention plan, a functional behavioral assessment and a behavioral plan must be completed no later than 10 days after changing the placement.

School officials may discipline a student with disabilities in the same manner as they discipline students without disabilities, with a few notable exceptions. If necessary, school officials may unilaterally change the placement of a student for disciplinary purposes to an appropriate interim alternative setting, move the student to another setting, or suspend the student to the extent that these disciplinary methods are used with students without disabilities. The primary difference is that with students who have disabilities, the suspension or placement change may not exceed 10 school days. School officials may unilaterally place a student with disabilities in an appropriate interim alternative educational setting for up to 45 days if the student brings a weapon to school or a school function or knowingly possesses, uses, or sells illegal drugs or controlled substances at school or a school function. The interim alternative educational setting must be determined by the IEP team. Additionally, a hearing officer can order a 45-day change in placement if school officials have evidence indicating that maintaining the student with disabilities in the current placement is substantially likely to result in injury to the student or others and that school officials have made reasonable efforts to minimize this risk of harm.

The Manifestation Determination

If school officials seek a change of placement, suspension, or expulsion in excess of 10 school days, a review of the relationship between a student's disability and his or her misconduct must be conducted within 10 days. This review, called a manifestation determination, must be conducted by a student's IEP team and other qualified personnel. If a determination is made that no relationship exists between the misconduct and disability, the same disciplinary procedures as would be used with students without disabilities may be imposed on a student with disabilities. Educational services, however, must be continued. The parents of the student may request an expedited due process hearing if they disagree with the results of the manifestation determination. The student's placement during the hearing will be in the interim educational setting. (For elaborations on the manifestation determination see Chapter 15.)

Special Education and Adult Inmates

The 1997 amendments also provide that states may opt not to provide special education services to persons with disabilities in adult prisons if they were not identified as IDEA-eligible prior to their incarceration. If these persons had been identified and received special education services when attending school, however, states must continue their special education while they are in prison.

Attorneys' Fees

The 1997 amendments also limited the conditions under which attorneys can collect fees under the IDEA. Attorneys' fees for participation in IEP meetings have been eliminated unless the meeting is convened because of an administrative or judicial order. Similarly, attorneys' fees are not available for mediation sessions prior to filing for a due process hearing. Attorneys' fees can also be reduced if the parents' attorney does not provide the appropriate information to the school district regarding the possible action. Finally, parents must notify school district officials of the problem and proposed solutions prior to filing for a due process hearing if they intend to seek attorneys' fees.

Charter Schools

The 1997 amendments also require school districts to serve students with disabilities who attend charter schools just as they would serve students attending the district's schools. Charter schools may not be required to apply for IDEA funds jointly in LEAs. Finally, school districts must provide IDEA funds to charter schools in the same manner as they provide funds to other schools.

Funding

The federal government, through the IDEA, provides funding to assist states with special education costs. To receive IDEA funds, states must submit a state special education plan to the U.S. Department of Education. This plan must show that a state is providing free appropriate special education services to all students with disabilities residing in the state between the ages of 3 and 21 in accordance with the procedures set forth in the IDEA (this includes students with disabilities who have been suspended or expelled from school). States that meet the IDEA requirements receive federal funding. The IDEA funds are received by the SEA for distribution to the LEAs. The federal funds do not cover the entire cost of special education, but rather are intended to provide financial assistance to the states. Congress originally intended to fund 40% of states' costs in providing special education services through the IDEA. The actual level of funding to the states, however, has amounted to approximately 6% to 7% of total expenditures. The Omnibus Consolidated Appropriations Act Fiscal Year 1997, enacted in 1996, raised the federal contribution to close to 10%.

Federal expenditures are computed on a state-by-state basis in accordance with the number of students with disabilities served (no adjustments are made either for the category of disability or for the setting in which a student is served). This number is multiplied by 40% of the average per-student expenditure in public schools in the United States. The federal government caps the number of students in special education in each state that federal sources will fund. States cannot serve more than 12% of the total number of school-age students in the state through special education.

A major change in funding was included in the 1997 amendments. The funding formula remains based on the child count until federal appropriations reach $4.9 billion. Federal appropriations above that level will be allocated according to a population-based formula with an adjustment for poverty rates. When the trigger of $4.9 billion is reached, the new formula, based on the state's population (85%) and poverty level (15%), will apply to all excess appropriations. Congress capped the total increases a state could receive under this formula as no more than 1.5% over the federal funding from the previous year. Neither can states receive less than they did in fiscal 1997. The purpose of the caps and floors is to limit the increase in federal monies to states that gain from the formula change and to prevent large decreases in states that receive less under the new formula.

The federal money received by the states must not be used to supplant state funds but is to be used to supplement and increase funding of special education and related services. This requirement, often referred to as the nonsupplanting requirement of the IDEA, ensures that states will not use IDEA funds to relieve themselves of their financial obligations, but that the funds will increase the level of state expenditures on special education. The state is ultimately responsible for ensuring the appropriate use of funds. IDEA regulations also grant school districts the authority to use other sources of funding to pay for special education services (IDEA Regulations, 34 C.F.R. § 300.600(c)).

The IDEA also requires that 75% of the federal funds received by the states be directed to the local schools and that 25% may be used at the state level. The majority of federal funding, therefore, flows from the federal to the state government and in turn to the local school districts. To receive state funds, local school districts must have programs that meet the state requirements. States are required to establish management and auditing procedures to ensure that federal funds will be expended in accordance with the provisions of the IDEA. States must also set up systems of fund allocation. The amount of flow-through funds given to an LEA is in proportion to the district's contribution to the state total of students in special education.

The 25% of the federal monies that may be set aside for state agency activities may be used for administration and supervision, direct and supportive services for students with disabilities, and monitoring and complaint investigation (IDEA Regulations, 34 C.F.R. § 300.370(a)). States may, however, use only 5% of the 25% of federal funds for administrative purposes. The states' administrative activities may include technical assistance to local educational agencies, administering the state plan, approval and supervision of local activities, and leadership activities and consultative services (IDEA Regulations, 34 C.F.R. § 300.621). The IDEA Amendments of 1997 capped the actual dollar amount of the 5% that may be used for administrative purposes at the fiscal 1997 level. States will also be given increases equal to the inflation rate or the increase in federal expenditures, whichever is less. If inflation is lower than the percentage increase in federal appropriations, states are required to spend the difference on improvements in services to students with disabilities.

Enforcement of the IDEA

The Department of Education conducts audits of states to determine if IDEA funds are being spent in an appropriate manner. States may be forced to return funds that were spent improperly. Federal monies, once disbursed, can be withheld by the U.S. Department of Education if the state fails to comply with the provisions of the IDEA. If the department withholds funds, this decision is subject to judicial review. The department also has the power to issue an administrative complaint requesting a cease-and-desist order and may enter into compliance agreements with a state that the federal agency believes is violating the IDEA (Weber, 1992).

There is some legal precedent indicating that the federal government may be able to sue a state that fails to provide a FAPE to students with disabilities. A federal district court in *United States v. Tennessee* (1992) held that the federal government has standing to sue a state under the Civil Rights of Institutionalized Persons Act of 1980 if the state fails to provide a FAPE to children in state-operated residential facilities.

States are required to monitor local school districts' use of funds. If a school district has failed to comply with the IDEA or the state law mandating a FAPE, the state may withhold funds until the district comes into compliance. If the school district wishes to contest the decision, it may request a hearing.

States must also have procedures to receive and resolve complaints regarding possible violations of the IDEA. Complaints can be filed by organizations or individuals, and states must investigate these complaints. Written complaint procedures help to fulfill federal requirements that states ensure that all special education programs conform to federal law (Weber, 1992).

Summary

In 1975, President Gerald Ford signed P.L. 94-142, the Education for All Handicapped Children Act. The law, renamed the Individuals with Disabilities Education Act in 1990, provides funding to states to assist them in providing an appropriate education, consisting of special education and related services, to students with disabilities. The IDEA uses a categorical approach to delineate students covered by the law by setting forth 13 categories of disabilities covered by the Act. Not all students with disabilities are protected by the IDEA, only those students with disabilities covered by the IDEA. Additionally, the disability must adversely affect the student's education.

The IDEA sets forth a number of principles that states must follow in providing a special education to students with disabilities. The primary objective of the law is to ensure that all eligible students with disabilities receive a free appropriate public education specifically designed to meet their unique needs.

For Further Information

The following books contain analysis of special education law, including the IDEA and Section 504; Tucker and Goldstein and Weber are loose-leaf services that are updated annually (or more frequently):

Gorn, S. (1996). *What do I do when: The answer book on special education law.* Horsham, PA: LRP Publications.

Guernsey, T. F., & Klare, K. (1993). *Special education law.* Durham, NC: Carolina Academic Press.

Tucker, B. P., & Goldstein, B. A. (1992). *Legal rights of persons with disabilities: An analysis of federal law.* Horsham, PA: LRP Publications.

Weber, M. C. (1992). *Special education law and litigation treatise.* Horsham, PA: LRP Publications.

In the following books, Ballard et al. detail the beginnings of governmental involvement in special education, and Levine and Wexler offer an account of the IDEA from inception to passage, providing an interesting study of how a bill becomes law:

Ballard, J., Ramirez, B. A., & Weintraub, F. J. (Eds.). (1982). *Special education in America: Its legal and governmental foundations.* Reston, VA: Council for Exceptional Children.

Levine, E. L., & Wexler, E. M. (1981). *P.L. 94-142: An act of Congress.* New York: Macmillan.

References

Education Amendments of 1974, Pub. L. No. 93-380, 88 Stat. 580.

Education for All Handicapped Children Act of 1975, 20 U.S.C. § 1401 *et seq.*

Elementary and Secondary Education Act, amended by Pub. L. No. 89-750. § 161 [Title VI], 80 Stat. 1204 (1966).

Family Educational Rights and Privacy Act, 20 U.S.C. § 1232.

Gibbons, J. (1982). *Technology and handicapped people.* Washington, DC: Office of Technology Assessment.

Gorn, S. (1996). *What do I do when: The answer book on special education law.* Horsham, PA: LRP Publications.

Guernsey, T. F., & Klare, K. (1993). *Special education law.* Durham, NC: Carolina Academic Press.

Helms v. Independent School District #3, 750 F.2d 820 (10th Cir. 1985).

Honig v. Doe, 479 U.S. 1084 (1988).

Individuals with Disabilities Education Act Amendments of 1997, Pub. L. No. 105-17, 105th Cong., 1st sess.

Individuals with Disabilities Education Act of 1990, 20 U.S.C. § 1400 *et seq.*

Individuals with Disabilities Education Act Regulations, 34 C.F.R. § 300.1 *et seq.*

Joint Policy Memo, (1991) 18 IDELR 118.

Julnes, R. E., & Brown, S. E. (1993). The legal mandate to provide assistive technology in special education programming. *Education Law Reporter, 82,* 737–749.

Levine, E. L., & Wexler, E. M. (1981). *P.L. 94-142: An act of Congress.* New York: Macmillan.

Massachusetts General Law Annotated, Chapter 71B § 3 (West, 1978).

Mills v. Board of Education, 348 F. Supp. 866 (D.D.C. 1972).

New Mexico Association for Retarded Citizens v. New Mexico, 678 F.2d 847 (10th Cir. 1982).

Omnibus Consolidated Appropriations Act, FY97, Senate Joint Resolution, N. 63, 104th Cong., 2d sess., *Congressional Record,* S12327 (1996).

Pennsylvania Association of Retarded Citizens v. Commonwealth of Pennsylvania, 343 F. Supp. 279 (E.D. Pa. 1972).

Rehabilitation Act of 1973, Section 504, 29 U.S.C. § 794.

Salvia, J., & Ysseldyke, J. E. (1995). *Assessment* (6th ed.). Boston: Houghton Mifflin Company.

Sean R. v. Town of Woodbridge Board of Education, 794 F. Supp. 467 (D. Conn. 1992).

Senate Report of the Individuals with Disabilities Act Amendments of 1997, available at wais.access.gpo.gov.

Smith v. Robinson, 468 U.S. 992 (1984).

Technology-Related Assistance for Individuals with Disabilities Act, 29 U.S.C. § 2201 *et seq.*

Timothy W. v. Rochester, New Hampshire, School District, 875 F.2d 954 (1st Cir. 1989).

Tucker, B. P., & Goldstein, B. A. (1992). *Legal rights of persons with disabilities: An analysis of federal law.* Horsham, PA: LRP Publications.

Turnbull, A. P., & Turnbull, H. R. (1997). *Families, professionals, and exceptionality: A special partnership* (3rd ed.). Upper Saddle River, NJ: Merrill/Prentice Hall.

United States v. Tennessee, 798 F. Supp. 483 (W.D. Tenn. 1992).

Weber, M. C. (1992). *Special education law and litigation treatise.* Horsham, PA: LRP Publications.

Wexler v. Westfield, 784 F.2d 176 (3rd Cir. 1986).

CHAPTER SIX

Section 504 of the Rehabilitation Act of 1973

[Section 504] is the civil rights declaration of the handicapped. It was greeted with great hope and satisfaction by Americans who have had the distress of physical or mental handicaps compounded by thoughtless or callous discrimination. These Americans have identified [Section] 504 with access to vital public services, such as education . . . . they consider it their charter . . . it is a key to, and a symbol of, their entry as full participants in the mainstream of national life.

Senator Hubert H. Humphrey, principal Senate author of Section 504,
Congressional Record, April 26, 1977, p. 12,216.

Although Section 504 of the Rehabilitation Act of 1973 (hereafter Section 504) became law prior to the enactment of the IDEA, it has only been in the last few years that educators seemingly have taken notice of the statute. Champagne (1995) contends that the struggle of educators to stay abreast of rules and developments of the IDEA's many procedures made it difficult to enlarge their scope to Section 504. The increased activity of the Office of Civil Rights (OCR) of the Department of Education regarding school district compliance with Section 504, as well as increased litigation, has resulted in more educators recognizing the importance of the law.

Section 504 significantly affects public education on all levels. Additionally, it covers a broad spectrum of activities beyond education, such as employment. Section 504 is codified at 29 U.S.C. §§ 706(8), 794, and 794a. The law is divided into seven subchapters, which are listed in Table 6.1. The purpose of this chapter is to examine the effects of Section 504 on public elementary, secondary, postsecondary, and vocational schooling.

Table 6.1
Subchapters of Section 504 of the Rehabilitation Act of 1973

Subchapter	Purpose	Contents
1—Subpart A	General provisions	Purposes, definitions
2—Subpart B	Employment practices	Prohibits discrimination in employment practices
3—Subpart C	Program accessibility	Accessibility and usability of facilities
4—Subpart D	Preschool, elementary, and secondary education	Prohibits discrimination in preschool, elementary, and secondary programs receiving federal financial assistance
5—Subpart E	Postsecondary education	Prohibits discrimination in postsecondary programs receiving federal financial assistance
6—Subpart F	Health, welfare, and social services	Prohibits discrimination in health, welfare, and social services receiving federal financial assistance
7—Subpart G	Procedures	Procedures for ensuring compliance with Section 504

The History of Section 504

In 1973, the first major effort to protect persons with disabilities against discrimination based on their disabilities took place when Congress passed Section 504 of the Rehabilitation Act. President Nixon signed the Act into law on September 26, 1973. Section 504 was seemingly out of place, located in a labor statute, and it had a rocky start to its existence (Zirkel & Kincaid, 1995).

What was to become Section 504 was originally proposed in 1972 as an amendment to the Civil Rights Act of 1964 by Representative Vanik of Ohio and Senator Humphrey of Minnesota. Section 504 was passed later that year as an amendment to the revision of the Rehabilitation Act. The Rehabilitation Act provided for federally assisted rehabilitation programs for persons with disabilities. The law, however, was vetoed twice by President Nixon, primarily due to budgetary concerns. The following year it was rewritten and passed. This time it was signed by President Nixon.

Section 504 was originally written in the same antidiscrimination language as Title VI of the Civil Rights Act of 1964 (prohibiting discrimination based on race and national origin) and Title IX of the Education Amendments of 1972 (prohibiting discrimination based on gender). It was not clear, however, what protections were actually extended to persons with disabilities through the statute. Many believed the purpose of Section 504 was merely to correct problems in the rehabilitation of persons with disabilities, while others understood the law to be an extension of the Civil Rights Act of 1964. Because Congress failed to include any means to eliminate discrimination based on disability in Section 504, such as civil or criminal remedies, it seemed that the law was not a civil rights statute.

Amendments to Section 504 in 1974 and the Rehabilitation, Comprehensive Services, and Developmental Disabilities Act of 1978 clarified these ambiguities (Schoenfeld, 1980). The result of these clarifications was to extend civil rights protection to persons with disabilities by including all the remedies, procedures, and rights contained in the Civil Rights Act of 1964.

The issuance of regulations to implement and enforce Section 504 also took an interesting route. Because of confusion over the original intent of Congress in passing Section 504, as well as political concerns (e.g., coverage of alcoholics and drug addicts), there was a four-year delay in promulgating regulations to implement the law. A lawsuit was filed protesting the government's failure to issue the regulations under Section 504. In 1976, in *Cherry v. Matthews,* the Federal District Court of Washington, DC, held that the secretary of Health, Education, and Welfare (HEW)[*] was required to issue the regulations implementing the act. In the opinion, the court sarcastically noted that Section 504 was certainly not intended to be self-executing.

Because of the importance of Section 504, the HEW secretary for the Ford administration, David Matthews, felt that the incoming Carter administration should assume responsibility for the regulations implementing the law. Matthews, therefore, left HEW without issuing the Section 504 regulations. The secretary of HEW in the Carter administration, Joseph Califano, also appeared to some to be stalling on the issuance of the regulations for political reasons. Advocacy groups for persons with disabilities began to exert political pressure on the new secretary. Sit-ins at regional HEW offices were held, and advocacy groups blocked Secretary Califano's driveway and various regional HEW offices with their wheelchairs. The weight of litigation and political pressure finally led to the issuance of the Section 504 regulations. According to Gerry and Benton (1982), "on May 4, 1977 the political system finally gave life to the promise of equal opportunity made in September 1973" (p. 47).

The Purpose of Section 504

The purpose of Section 504 is to prohibit discrimination against persons with disabilities in programs receiving federal financial assistance. The statute holds that

> No otherwise qualified individual with a disability in the United States . . . shall, solely by reason of his or her disability, be excluded from the participation in, be denied the benefits of, or be subjected to discrimination under any program or any activity receiving Federal financial assistance. (Section 504, 29 U.S.C. § 794(a))

Section 504 protects students with disabilities from discrimination in schools receiving federal financial assistance, whether or not they are protected by the IDEA. Protection from discrimination includes, and extends beyond, the school's provision

---

*HEW was later divided into the Department of Health and Human Services (DHHS) and the Department of Education (DOE).

of an education to such areas as the provision of related services, participation in extracurricular activities, and architectural accessibility. In addition to covering students in preschool, elementary, secondary, and postsecondary schools and institutions, Section 504 also applies to school district noneducation programs such as day care, afterschool care, and summer recreation programs (OCR Senior Staff Memorandum, 1990). There are no federal funds available under Section 504 to help school districts meet the requirements of the law.

Section 504 extends these protections only in programs or services that receive federal financial assistance. The Department of Justice defines a program receiving federal financial assistance as a program that receives "any grants, loans, contracts or any other arrangement by which the [school] provides or otherwise makes available assistance in the form of (a) funds, (b) services of federal personnel, or (c) real and personal property or any interest in or use of such property" (Section 504 Regulations, 28 C.F.R. § 41.3(e)).

In addition to elementary, secondary, and postsecondary schools that receive direct federal financial assistance, schools or programs that receive indirect federal financial aid (e.g., colleges where students receive federal education grants) are also covered under the statute. Section 504 does not apply to schools that receive no direct or indirect federal financial assistance.

Who Is Protected?

The original definition of persons covered under Section 504 was extremely narrow. The statute defined persons covered as being those with the ability to benefit from rehabilitative services. Congress recognized that this definition was not appropriate for major civil rights legislation, and in the Rehabilitation Act Amendments of 1974 developed a definition to clarify who was protected under Section 504. This definition is as follows:

> any person who (i) has a physical or mental impairment which substantially limits one or more of such person's major life activities, (ii) has a record of such an impairment, or (iii) is regarded as having such an impairment. (Section 504, 29 U.S.C. § 706(7)(B))

The definition of a handicapping condition in Section 504 has three parts. The first part defines a person as disabled if that person has a physical or mental impairment that substantially limits one or more major life activities. This part has three components. The impairment must (a) be physical or mental, (b) affect a major life activity, and (c) be substantial. The second part covers persons who have a record of an impairment. The third part provides coverage to persons who are regarded as being disabled. When a person meets the qualifications under the three-part definition, there is a further requirement that the person be otherwise qualified.

The second and third parts of the definition cover persons regarded as having a disability and those who have a record of having a disability. These two parts of the definition are frequently misunderstood. They generally only apply in the areas of employment and, occasionally, postsecondary education. In fact, they rarely apply in elementary and secondary education. According to OCR, many school officials believe that if someone (e.g., a student's doctor or parent) regards a student as having a disability or if a student has a record of a disability, he or she is automatically entitled to protection under Section 504. This is an incorrect assumption. These parts of the definition are insufficient to trigger Section 504 protections, in and of themselves. It is only when a student is discriminated against based on the perception that he or she has a disability (i.e., "regarded as") or because he or she had a disability (i.e., "has a record of") that a student is entitled to the protections of Section 504.

Moreover, these parts of the definition cannot serve as the basis of a free appropriate public education (FAPE) under Section 504. This is because the student who is regarded as having a disability or who has a record of a disability "is not, in fact mentally or physically [disabled], [therefore] there can be need for special education or related aids and services" (OCR Memorandum, 1992). That is, only students with a current disability are entitled to receive a FAPE. Students who are discriminated against in schools because they are regarded as having a disability or have a record of having a disability, however, may bring a claim of discrimination if a school district discriminates against them because of these perceptions.

The definition of disability under Section 504 is clearly broader than that under the IDEA (Zirkel, 1996). Whereas the IDEA requires that students have disabilities covered by the law and, as a result of their disability, require special education and related services, Section 504 does not have such specific requirements for protection. Students must have a disability that limits a major life activity (e.g., learning).

Physical Impairment

Regulations written for Section 504 in 1989, define physical and mental impairments as

> (A) any psychological disorder or condition, cosmetic disfigurement, or anatomical loss affecting one or more of the following body systems: neurological; musculoskeletal; special sense organs, respiratory, including speech organs; cardiovascular; reproductive, digestive, genito-urinary; hemic and lymphatic; skin and endocrine; or (B) any mental or psychological disorder, such as mental retardation, organic brain syndrome, emotional or mental illness, and specific learning disabilities. (Section 504 Regulations, 34 C.F.R. § 104.3(j)(2)(i))

This list is not intended to be exhaustive. In *E.E. Black Ltd. v. Marshall* (1980), a federal district court commenting on the above definition stated that the term *impairment* meant "any condition which weakens, diminishes, restricts, or otherwise damages an individual's health or physical or mental activity" (p. 1098).

The scope of physical impairment has been recognized as including those disabilities that substantially impair physical performance. Physical conditions that have been recognized by courts as constituting a disability under Section 504 include arthritis, asthma, deafness, blindness, diabetes, Crohn's disease, multiple sclerosis, paralysis, cerebral palsy, epilepsy, cardiac problems, Ménière's disease, chronic fatigue syndrome, kidney disease, Tourette's syndrome, and hyperthyroidism (Tucker & Goldstein, 1992; Zirkel & Kincaid, 1995). Physical characteristics or conditions, temporary or permanent, such as left-handedness, height, weight, strength capabilities, strabismus, and pregnancy have generally not been considered to be under the purview of Section 504.

Mental Impairment

The scope of mental impairments includes mental illness, mental retardation, and learning disabilities. In considering whether certain persons with psychological conditions (e.g., depression) are protected under Section 504, courts and OCR have tended to answer in the affirmative if the conditions are recognized by medical authorities as constituting a mental impairment (Tucker & Goldstein, 1992). For example, students with Attention Deficit Hyperactivity Disorder (ADHD) are protected under Section 504 if the disorder substantially affects a major life activity.

Mental impairments, however, do not extend to undesirable personality traits. In an employment-related 504 case, *Daley v. Koch* (1986), an applicant for a position of police officer was not hired when a police department psychologist determined that the applicant exhibited personality traits of poor judgment, irresponsible behavior, and poor impulse control. The court held that because the applicant had not been diagnosed as having a psychological illness or disorder, he did not have a disability under Section 504.

In the Rehabilitation Act Amendments of 1992, Congress added exclusions to Section 504. The term *impairments* specifically excluded individuals on the basis of homosexuality, bisexuality, transvestitism, transsexualism, pedophilia, exhibitionism, voyeurism, gender identity disorders, sexual behavior disorders, compulsive gambling, kleptomania, pyromania, or psychoactive substance abuse disorder resulting from illegal use of drugs (Section 504, 29 U.S.C. § 706(8)(E–F)).

The Americans with Disabilities Act (1990; hereafter ADA) further amended the definition of persons with disabilities in the Rehabilitation Act of 1973. Essentially, the definition was narrowed to exclude persons currently engaging in the illegal use or possession of drugs or alcohol. Individuals undergoing drug or alcohol rehabilitation and those who are not engaged in the illegal use of drugs or alcohol may be considered disabled under Section 504 if they are otherwise qualified.

Substantial Limitation of a Major Life Activity

The second and third components of the first part of the definition state that the mental or physical impairment must substantially limit one or more major life activities. To ensure that only persons with significant physical and mental impairments were protected under Section 504, Congress added this qualification. The question of what constitutes a substantial limitation of a major life activity has been the subject of considerable litigation and numerous guidelines from the OCR.

The term *major life activity* means "functions such as caring for one's self, performing manual tasks, walking, seeing, hearing, breathing, learning, and working" (Section 504 Regulations, 34 C.F.R. § 104.3(j)(2)(ii)). This list is not intended to be exhaustive. From an educational perspective, the relevant life activity is learning. If a physical or mental impairment interferes with a student's ability to learn, the student will be protected under Section 504.

Having a Record of an Impairment

The second part of the definition of persons with disabilities protects individuals who once had a physical or mental impairment but no longer have the particular disability. Under this part of the definition, a student who once had a disability but no longer does may not be discriminated against because of the past disability. Students who at one time were covered by the IDEA but are no longer covered and, therefore, have a history of a disability are protected under Section 504. This part of the definition also protects students who have been incorrectly classified as disabled (Zirkel & Kincaid, 1995).

Regarded as Being Disabled

Persons may be protected under Section 504 even if they do not actually have a disability, but are regarded as having one. The DOE defines being regarded as having a disability as meaning that the person

> (1) has a physical or mental impairment that does not substantially limit major life activities but is treated by the [school] as constituting such a limitation; (2) has a physical or mental impairment that substantially limits major life activities only as a result of the attitudes of others towards such impairment; or (3) has none of the impairments [protected under 504] . . . but is treated by a [school] as having such impairment. (Section 504 Regulations, 34 C.F.R. § 104.3(j)(2)(iv))

The purpose of this rule is to protect persons who may have only minor disabilities or no disabilities at all from being discriminated against because of the stereotypical beliefs or negative reactions of others (Tucker & Goldstein, 1992).

Otherwise Qualified

Section 504 protects only otherwise qualified individuals with disabilities from discrimination based solely on their disability. Persons who are not otherwise qualified, therefore, are not protected. In the final regulations, OCR used the term "qualified handicapped person" rather than the statutory language "otherwise qualified handicapped person." This was done because OCR believed that the statute, if read literally, might be interpreted as meaning that "otherwise qualified handicapped persons" included persons who were qualified except for their handicap. The actual meaning, according to OCR, includes all persons who were qualified in spite of their handicap.

Elementary and Secondary Schools

With respect to elementary and secondary schools, students are qualified if they are

> (i) of an age during which nonhandicapped persons are provided such services, (ii) of any age during which it is mandatory under state law to provide such services to handicapped persons, or (iii) [persons] to whom the state is required to provide a free appropriate public education [students served under the IDEA]. (Section 504 Regulations, 34 C.F.R. § 104.3(k)(2) (1989))

A state is not required to provide services to students who do not meet the school's age requirements. All students of school age, however, are by definition qualified.

Postsecondary and Vocational Schools

With respect to postsecondary and vocational schools, students with disabilities must meet the academic and technical standards requisite to admission or to participation in the educational program (Section 504 Regulations, 34 C.F.R. § 104.3(K)(3)). In postsecondary education and employment, the statutory language "no otherwise qualified individual with a disability . . . shall, solely by reason of his or her disability . . ." becomes particularly important. A student who is otherwise qualified is one who can meet program requirements, academic and technical, if provided with reasonable accommodations (auxiliary aids or services). The term "otherwise qualified" is intertwined with the concept of reasonable accommodations. Tucker and Goldstein (1992) state the relationship between "reasonable accommodation" and "otherwise qualified" as follows: "An individual with a disability is protected from discrimination under Section 504 only if he or she is able to perform in the . . . program at issue under existing conditions or with the provision of reasonable accommodations" (p. 5:1). "Reasonable accommodations" refers to the modifications of educational programs and facilities to make them accessible to persons with disabilities. If reasonable accommodations cannot be fashioned to permit the person with disabilities to participate in the program in spite of their disability, that person is not otherwise qualified (Dagley & Evans, 1995). The provision of reasonable accommodations will be examined in a later section of this chapter.

Summary of Section 504 Coverage

Section 504 is expansive in its coverage. Figure 6.1 illustrates the coverage of Section 504 (Zirkel & Kincaid, 1995). Students in the inner circle are covered by the IDEA, thereby receiving double coverage under Section 504. By definition, students eligible for services under the IDEA are disabled and, therefore, are also protected under Section 504. The second ring is comprised of individuals who meet the definition of having an impairment under Section 504. All students with disabilities meeting this definition are protected from discrimination by Section 504. This may include students with disabilities even if they are not eligible under the IDEA. Such disabilities may include ADHD, Tourette's syndrome, asthma, diabetes, arthritis, allergies, and AIDS; technologically dependent children and those with alcohol or drug problems (if not currently engaging in the illegal use of drugs) may also be included. Students

Figure 6.1
Coverage of Section 504
Note. From *Section 504, the ADA and the Schools*
(chapter 1, p. 4), by P. A. Zirkel and J. M. Kincaid, 1995,
Horsham, PA: LRP Publications. Reprinted with per-
mission from LRP Publications.

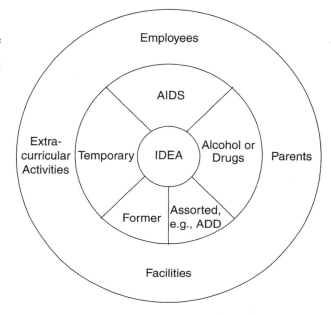

without disabilities who are treated as if they have disabilities are also protected.
Students (e.g., disruptive students) whose main problem is poor impulse control,
antisocial behavior, or poor judgment will not be covered if they do not have a physical or mental impairment that substantially limits their learning.

The final ring includes Section 504 coverage of facilities, extracurricular activities, parents, and employees. Section 504 also protects parents and employees who
are disabled from discrimination. As the final ring indicates, Section 504 protections
extend to extracurricular and nonacademic activities, (e.g., graduation ceremonies,
meals, recess, teams, clubs, sports activities). Finally, Section 504 requires that if a
school operates a facility for students with disabilities, the facility must be comparable to facilities used by students without disabilities. This comparability mandate
goes beyond the accessibility requirement. That is, even if a facility is accessible, it
must also be comparable to those facilities for students without disabilities.

Major Principles of Section 504

Congress made a commitment to citizens with disabilities that "to the maximum extent possible, [persons with disabilities] shall be fully integrated into American life"
(Senate Report, 1978). The regulations for Section 504 detail criteria for schools to
follow. The rules and regulations are not as complex and detailed as those contained
in the IDEA (Tucker & Goldstein, 1992; Zirkel & Kincaid, 1995). Section 504 regulations, however, are very specific with respect to postsecondary education.

Protection from Discrimination

All students with disabilities are protected from discrimination in elementary, secondary, and postsecondary schools. Discrimination refers to unequal treatment of qualified students with disabilities based solely on the basis of the disability. It is discriminatory for schools to provide services for students without disabilities and not provide such services to children with disabilities. Section 504 requires that individuals with disabilities have an equal opportunity to benefit from their education and that equivalent services or programs must be provided. The concept of equivalency does not mean that services and benefits must be identical. Neither does it mean that the benefits or services must produce identical results. The benefits and services, however, must be such as to allow a student with disabilities an equal opportunity. As such, Section 504 requires that to ensure equal opportunity, adjustments to regular programs or the provision of different, and sometimes separate, services may at times be necessary. Schools must make reasonable modifications to programs to ensure that discrimination does not occur.

Legitimate Considerations Regarding Disabilities

Protection from discrimination does not mean that the disabling condition cannot be considered by school administrators. In this respect, the definition of discrimination in Section 504 differs from the definition of discrimination in Titles VI (race) and VII (gender) of the Civil Rights Act of 1964. This is because disabilities may affect an individual's ability to perform in a program or job by impairing functioning, whereas race and gender virtually never tell anything about a person's ability to perform (Tucker & Goldstein, 1992). A school administrator, therefore, may consider a disability if it is a relevant factor. What is not permissible under Section 504 is discrimination against a person with a disability based solely on an illegitimate or unjustifiable consideration of the disability. For example, if school administrators denied a student with disabilities the right to participate in an academic or nonacademic program (e.g., extracurricular activities, recess, meals, field trips, transportation, groups or clubs) because of an erroneous conclusion that the disability would prevent the student from participating or because they failed to provide for reasonable modifications to allow participation, they may be guilty of discrimination. Additionally, schools will be seen as discriminating against persons with disabilities if they (a) deny opportunity to participate in or benefit from any program or service available to persons without a disability; (b) fail to provide aids and services that are provided to students without disabilities; or (c) provide different aids or services from those provided to students without disabilities unless those services are required to allow equal opportunity.

Avoiding Discrimination

Regulations to Section 504 (Section 504 Regulations, 34 C.F.R. § 104.22) list actions that may be taken by schools to avoid discriminating against students with disabilities. Such actions may include structural alterations, redesign of equipment, reassignment of classes, assignment of aides, regular classroom interventions, and modifications of classroom methods, materials, and procedures. (For a detailed list of potential modifications see Zirkel and Kincaid, 1995.)

An example of discrimination against students with disabilities based solely on the disability occurred in *Rice v. Jefferson County Board of Education* (1989). In this case, the Jefferson County Board of Education charged students with disabilities larger fees to attend after-school programs than they charged students without disabilities. The board justified the increased charges by maintaining that the school district had to provide care for the students with disabilities, and that the additional costs of this care had to be passed on to these students. The court held that the board's action was discrimination in violation of Section 504, because the district failed to show that students with disabilities' attendance at programs created substantial additional costs for the district.

Postsecondary Education and Section 504

Colleges, universities, and vocational or technical schools may not exclude a qualified person with a disability from any aspect of the educational program or activities conducted by the school. According to Zirkel and Kincaid (1995), Section 504 claims most likely to arise in postsecondary education are in admissions and access to nonacademic programs or activities.

With respect to admission in postsecondary education, regulations to Section 504 protect qualified students with disabilities from being denied admission or discriminated against solely because of their disability. To protect persons from discrimination, a postsecondary school cannot inquire if an applicant has a disability. An important distinction between the responsibilities of elementary and secondary schools and those of postsecondary schools is that elementary and secondary schools have an affirmative duty to find students with disabilities, while in postsecondary schools students must self-identify. After admission, however, the institution may make confidential inquiries about the disability to determine accommodations that may be required. Postsecondary institutions cannot limit the number of persons with disabilities that they accept.

Neither can postsecondary institutions administer tests for admission that may reflect adversely on students with disabilities unless the tests have been validated as predictors of success and alternative tests are not available. Admissions tests must be selected and administered to students with disabilities so as to reflect actual aptitude and achievement rather than reflecting the impaired skills.

Access to Nonacademic Programs and Services

Another aspect of Section 504 involves access to nonacademic programs and services. Postsecondary institutions that provide housing to students without disabilities must provide comparable housing for students with disabilities. The housing must also be accessible. The regulations also require that the cost of housing to students with and without disabilities must be the same.

In physical education, athletics, intramural activities, and clubs the postsecondary institution must provide qualified students with disabilities an equal opportunity to participate. If separate or different facilities or teams are required, they must be in the most integrated setting appropriate and only if no qualified students with disabilities are denied participation in the integrated activities.

Counseling, vocational, and placement services must be provided to students with disabilities to the same extent as provided to students without disabilities. Additionally, qualified students with disabilities must not be counseled to more restrictive career options than are students without disabilities.

Often postsecondary institutions provide assistance to fraternities, sororities, or other organizations. If they do so, they must ensure that these organizations do not discriminate against or permit discrimination based on a disability.

Finally, postsecondary institutions that provide financial assistance must not provide less assistance to students with disabilities than they provide to persons without disabilities. Neither can they limit the eligibility of students with disabilities.

Reasonable Accommodations

A program receiving federal financial assistance is required to provide reasonable accommodations to otherwise qualified persons with disabilities. An educational institution or place of employment, therefore, must make modifications to the existing environment to eliminate barriers for persons with disabilities. Section 504 regulations, however, only define reasonable accommodation as it applies to employment. Reasonable accommodation as applied specifically to preschool, elementary and secondary schools, and postsecondary institutions is not addressed. This had led to disagreement and confusion regarding the reasonable accommodation standard. Dagley and Evans (1995) argue that even though the regulations suggest that reasonable accommodations are only required in the employment context, the judiciary has used the standard in making decisions regarding school district and postsecondary institutions' responsibilities under Section 504. This standard requires school officials to examine the individual needs of students with disabilities and make a professional judgment about what can and cannot be done to accommodate their needs (Dagley & Evans, 1995).

In *Alexander v. Choate* (1985), the Supreme Court held that Section 504 does not require that programs make substantial modifications, only reasonable ones. Modifications are substantial, and not required, if they impose an undue hardship on the program. Relevant factors in determining if modifications are reasonable include size, type, and budget of the program, as well as the nature and cost of the accommodation. Determining what constitutes a reasonable accommodation, as opposed to substantial accommodation, is difficult and subjective. What is reasonable will vary given the specifics of a particular situation. The courts have offered some guidance, not so much by ruling what is reasonable but by ruling what is not reasonable.

Court Decisions Regarding Reasonable Accommodations

The Supreme Court, in *Southeastern Community College v. Davis* (1979), held that reasonable accommodations are those that do not impose excessive financial and administrative burdens or require a fundamental alteration in the program. Courts and OCR guidelines have held that Section 504 does not require that schools create new and special programs but that they make reasonable modifications to eliminate barriers in existing ones. A federal district court, in *Pinkerton v. Moye* (1981), held that a school district did not have to establish a self-contained program for students with learning disabilities because that would have required a substantial modification to the district's programs. In *William S. v. Gill* (1983), the court ruled that a school district was not required to send a student to a private residential school if the costs at the private school far exceeded the costs at the public school. The school district was not obligated under Section 504 to send the student to the private school, since it represented a service not available to students without disabilities. Some courts, in determining whether a change in a program required a substantial modification, have asked whether the modification violates the basic integrity of the program. If it does, the change would not be reasonable.

Reasonable Accommodations in Schools

The DOE's regulations to Section 504 suggest reasonable accommodations that might be made by postsecondary institutions to assist students with disabilities in obtaining an education (Section 504 Regulations, 34 C.F.R. § 104.44(a)). Although the regulations do not specifically address elementary or secondary schools, they do offer guidance for the modification of school programs to accommodate students at all levels. Figure 6.2 contains a list of potential classroom accommodations.

Academic adjustments are another category of accommodations. Accommodations needed to ensure that academic requirements do not discriminate on the basis of disability may include changes in the length of time needed to complete a degree, substitution of courses required to complete a degree, and adaptations in how courses are taught. Further, schools may not impose rules on students with disabilities, such as prohibiting tape recorders, that have the effect of limiting the students' ability to benefit from or participate in classes or programs. Academic adjustments that might be made include modifying methods of instruction, modifying materials, and altering environmental conditions.

Regulations also address the modification of examinations. Course examinations and evaluations should reflect students' achievement rather than their disability. Modifications, therefore, should be made to an examination if a student's disability will impair the student's performance on the test. Modifications to ensure that examinations do not discriminate might include giving tests orally, allowing the student to dictate answers, shortening the length of the test, allowing more time to take the test, altering the test format (e.g., multiple choice, essays), printing the test with enlarged text, and reducing the reading level of the test.

Figure 6.2
Reasonable Accommodations in Classrooms

Classroom Modifications

- Adjust placement of student (e.g., preferential seating)
- Alter physical setup of classroom
- Reduce distractions (e.g., study carrel)
- Provide increased lighting
- Schedule classes in accessible areas

Academic Adjustments

- Allow more time to complete assignments
- Adjust length of assignments
- Modify pace of instruction
- Use peer tutors
- Provide outline of lectures
- Use visual aids
- Use advance organizers
- Highlight texts and worksheets
- Tape lectures
- Adjust reading levels of materials
- Use specialized curricular materials

Modification of Tests

- Give tests orally or on tape
- Allow more time to complete tests
- Allow students to dictate answers
- Alter the test format
- Use enlarged type
- Reduce the reading level of the test

Auxiliary Aids and Devices

- Provide interpreters
- Provide assistive technology devices and services:
    Laptop computers
    Braille readers
    Text enlargement devices
    Alternative input devices

The fourth area involves the utilization of auxiliary aids. Auxiliary aids might include taped tests, interpreters, readers, and assistive technology such as laptop computers, braille readers, text enlargement devices, and alternative input devices.

Free Appropriate Public Education

Students with disabilities in elementary and secondary school are entitled to a free appropriate public education (FAPE) under Section 504. The Act provides that a public elementary or secondary school shall provide a FAPE to qualified students with disabilities regardless of the nature or severity of their disabilities. This applies to all students with disabilities in the school jurisdiction. Additionally, if a school district places a student in another school, even if the school is not in the district's boundaries, the home school district retains financial responsibility for the student. If students are placed in programs where they will be away from home, the school is also responsible for room, board, and nonmedical care (e.g., custodial and supervisory care). A FAPE applies to assessments, services, staffing, space, equipment, and materials as well as instruction. A FAPE is required to protect persons with disabilities from discrimination (Section 504 Regulations, 34 C.F.R. §§ 100.6–100.10).

The education and the related services required must be provided at no cost to students with disabilities or their parents/guardians. The only fees that can be charged to the parents of children with disabilities are those fees that are also charged to parents of children without disabilities.

Section 504 allows public agencies to use funds available from any public or private agency to assist them in meeting requirements. Furthermore, Section 504 regulations do not relieve a third-party payer or insurer from an otherwise valid obligation to provide or pay for services provided to persons with disabilities (Section 504 Regulations, 34 C.F.R. § 104.33(c)). If school districts use a third-party payer, it is important that they do not violate parental rights to secure payment.

An appropriate education must be individualized. It could consist of education in general education classes with supplementary aids and services, or special education and related services in a separate classroom. Special education may consist of specially designed instruction in a classroom, at home, or in a residential setting, and may be accompanied by related services (e.g., psychological counseling, speech therapy) that are necessary for a student's education. Section 504 also requires that related services be provided to students with disabilities in the general education classroom as well as to students in a special classroom when necessary. Related services in the classroom are required under Section 504 if they are necessary to provide an education comparable to that offered to students without disabilities.

The definition of appropriate education under Section 504 is one of equivalency. That is, the educational services designed to meet the needs of students with disabilities must do so as adequately as services designed to meet the needs of students without disabilities. To ensure this equivalency, Section 504 requires that the student's teachers must be trained in instruction of the student with the particular disability and that appropriate materials and equipment must be available. The equivalency requirement also applies to nonacademic activities. Regulations require that nonacademic and extracurricular activities be provided in such a manner as to afford students with disabilities an equal opportunity for participation. Nonacademic activities include counseling (personal, academic, and vocational), transportation, health services, special interest groups, clubs, and physical, recreational, and athletic activities.

To meet the appropriateness requirement, the educational program of a student with disabilities must be developed by a group of knowledgeable persons based on evaluation data. Section 504 requires that school districts design an individualized program to meet a student's needs. Moreover, school districts should document the provision of a FAPE. Section 504 regulations indicate that the development of an individualized education program (IEP) is one way to ensure that this requirement is met (Section 504 Regulations, 34 C.F.R. § 104.33(b)(2)). The IDEA requires IEPs for students in special education programs. Although IEPs are not required by Section 504, they may be used, because an IEP that meets the requirements of the IDEA will also meet the requirements for determining an appropriate education under Section 504.

When students are covered only by Section 504 and do not receive dual coverage under the IDEA, school officials still must develop an appropriate educational program. Furthermore, this program should be documented. Fossey, Hosie, Soniat, and Zirkel (1995) suggest that schools document the program provided by developing formalized intervention plans, called individualized accommodation plans. This plan should document (a) the nature of the student's disability and the major life activity it limits; (b) the basis for determining the disability; (c) the educational impact of the disability; (d) necessary accommodations; and (e) placement.

Questions regarding whether the standard for a FAPE under Section 504 requires less than does a FAPE under the IDEA remain largely unanswered (Dagley & Evans, 1995; Zirkel, 1996). For students with disabilities eligible for services under the IDEA, and thus also covered by Section 504, this question is not relevant because the FAPE standards for these students must conform to the standards of the IDEA. For students with disabilities who are eligible under Section 504 but not under the IDEA, the question is significant. Some court decisions have indicated that the standard for a FAPE involves the school making reasonable accommodations (*Southeastern Community College v. Davis,* 1979). OCR, however, seems to place a higher standard on school districts—to meet the FAPE standard of Section 504 based on a student's educational needs (Zirkel & Kincaid, 1995). Zirkel (1996) contends that the applicable FAPE standard may be higher than that of reasonable accommodations. This higher standard is based on the statutory language requiring that commensurate opportunity or educational equivalency for FAPE be provided to students with disabilities under Section 504.

Least Restrictive Environment

Regulations to Section 504 require that students with disabilities be educated along with students without disabilities to the maximum extent appropriate to the needs of the student. Additionally, the general education classroom is the preferred placement unless it is demonstrated that an education with supplementary aids and services in the general education classroom cannot be achieved satisfactorily and that the needs of the student would be better served by placement in another setting. OCR guidelines and rulings have specified that districts must document the reasons why more restrictive placements are needed when the student is removed from the general education classroom (or a less restrictive setting).

In making placement decisions to move students with disabilities to more restrictive settings, schools may take into account the effect of a student's behavior on students without disabilities if the effect is deleterious. In an analysis of final regulations, OCR stated that "where a handicapped child is so disruptive in a regular classroom that the education of other students is significantly impaired, the needs of the handicapped child cannot be met in that environment. Therefore, regular placement would not be appropriate to his or her needs and would not be required" (Section 504 Regulations, Appendix A, p. 384).

Section 504 also requires that when a student with disabilities is placed in a setting other than the general education classroom, the school must take into account the proximity of the alternative setting to the student's home. Schools, however, are not required to place students in schools closest to their homes. If a school does not offer an appropriate program or facilities, a student may be transferred to another school. The home school will still retain responsibility for the student and must provide transportation.

Schools must also ensure that in nonacademic and extracurricular services and activities, students with disabilities participate with students without disabilities to the maximum extent appropriate to their needs. This requirement is especially important when students' needs require that they are educated primarily in a segregated setting.

Evaluation and Placement Procedures

The purpose of the Section 504 evaluation and placement requirements is to prevent misclassification and misplacement. Students with disabilities who are believed to need special education or related services must be evaluated prior to placement. According to Zirkel and Kincaid (1995), the matter of evaluation has been the subject of more OCR investigations than any other requirement of 504.

Regulations to Section 504 regarding evaluations require that

(1) Tests and all evaluation materials have been validated for the specific purpose for which they are used and are administered by trained personnel in conformity with instructions provided by their producer;

(2) Tests and other evaluation materials include those tailored to assess specific areas of educational need and not merely those which are designed to provide a single intelligence quotient; and

(3) Tests are selected and administered so as best to ensure that, when a test is administered to a student with impaired sensory, manual, or speaking skills, the test results accurately reflect the student's aptitude or achievement level or whatever other factor the test purports to measure, rather than reflecting the student's impaired [abilities] (except

where those skills are the factors that the test purports to measure). (Section 504 Regulations, 34 C.F.R. § 104.35(b))

When determining placement for a student, the school must convene a group of persons knowledgeable about the student, the meaning of the evaluation data, and the placement options. Furthermore, the team must draw on information from a variety of sources. The group must establish procedures to ensure that all information gathered in the evaluation process is documented and considered.

The team must be aware of different options for placement. Moreover, team decisions must be based on a student's individual needs. If a school seeks a significant change of placement, a reevaluation must be completed prior to the placement change. Even in cases where a significant change of placement is not sought, schools must conduct periodic reevaluations of all students with disabilities.

Procedural Safeguards

Schools must establish a system of due process procedures to be afforded to parents or guardians prior to taking any action regarding the identification, evaluation, or educational placement of a student with a disability who is believed to need educational services. Notice must precede any identification, evaluation, or placement action taken by the school. Parents must also be notified of their right to examine educational records. If there is a disagreement concerning an evaluation or placement action, parents or guardians may request a due process hearing. Schools may also request due process hearings. Hearing officers must be impartial and must have no personal or professional conflicts or interest or connections with either school or student.

In the due process hearing, the parents have the opportunity to participate, present evidence, produce outside expert testimony, and be represented by counsel. Parents may have the student present at the hearing and may open the hearing to the public if they choose to do so. Following the hearing, the hearing officer reviews all relevant facts and renders a decision. The decision of the officer is binding on all parties but may be appealed to federal court.

The procedural rights of parents are listed in Figure 6.3. OCR recommends, but does not require, compliance with the procedural safeguards of IDEA as a way to ensure that the procedural safeguards of Section 504 are met.

Program Accessibility

School programs, academic and nonacademic, must be accessible to students with disabilities. Section 504 prohibits the exclusion of students with disabilities from programs because a school's facilities are inaccessible or unusable. Regulations state that "when viewed in its entirety," the program must be readily accessible and usable (Section 504 Regulations, 34 C.F.R. § 104.22). School districts are not required to make all of their schools, or every part of a school, accessible to and usable by students with disabilities if its programs as a whole are accessible. A school district, how-

Figure 6.3
Parental Rights Under Section 504

- Right to be notified of rights under Section 504
- Right to file a grievance with the school district
- Right to notification when eligibility is determined
- Right to an evaluation prior to making a significant change
- Right to be informed of proposed actions affecting the program
- Right to an evaluation that uses information from multiple sources
- Right to examine all relevant records and request changes
- Right to receive information in the parents' native language or primary mode of communication
- Right to periodic reevaluations
- Right to an impartial hearing when a disagreement occurs
- Right to be represented by counsel in the hearing
- Right to appeal the hearing officer's decision

ever, may not make only one school or a part of a school accessible when the result would be segregation of students with disabilities into one setting. For example, if a school district had a large high school campus with a number of buildings, only some of which were wheelchair accessible, the district would not have to make structural changes to all nonaccessible buildings. They could reassign classes to the accessible buildings to accommodate the students with disabilities. A district with only one wheelchair-accessible school, thereby requiring that all students needing wheelchairs attend only that school, would be in violation of Section 504 because students using wheelchairs would be segregated. School districts must meet the accessibility requirements of Section 504 even if they do not have students with mobility impairments.

The requirement of accessibility applies to all facilities within a school, such as classrooms, gyms, water fountains, and restrooms. There are various means to meet these obligations, including nonstructural alterations such as redesign of equipment, delivering services at alternate accessible sites, or assigning aides. Structural alterations are required only when there is no other feasible way to make facilities accessible. In determining which of these means will be chosen to meet the program accessibility requirements, schools are required to give priority consideration to methods that will allow the services to be provided in the most appropriate integrated setting. Districts must also inform persons with disabilities where they can obtain information regarding accessible facilities.

In school facilities that were built prior to 1977, programs and activities must be made accessible to and usable by persons with disabilities. Facilities constructed after 1977 must be in compliance with the American National Institute's accessibility standards. Schools constructed after January 1991 have to meet the Uniform Federal Accessibility Standards (1984).

Comparable Facilities

When a school operates a facility for students with disabilities, the facilities and services must be comparable to regular education facilities and services. This mandate goes beyond the accessibility requirement. OCR does not intend to encourage the creation or maintenance of separate facilities, but clearly states that when separate facilities are used, they must be comparable. This requirement is violated when schools provide separate facilities such as portables and classrooms specifically for students with disabilities that are inferior to those provided students without disabilities. For example, the placement of students with disabilities in portable units that were designated solely for use by students with disabilities would be a violation of Section 504. If, however, the portable units were used equally by all students, in both general and special education, there would be no violation of Section 504.

School District Responsibilities

School districts have a number of responsibilities under Section 504, including both general procedural duties and specific responsibilities:

- Procedural responsibilities
- Identification and evaluation
- Educational programming
- Placement
- Reevaluation
- Procedural safeguards

Procedural Responsibilities

School districts' procedural responsibilities include (a) appointment of a Section 504 coordinator, (b) public notification of the school's responsibilities under Section 504, (c) establishment of grievance procedures, (d) self-evaluation, and (e) staff training.

Appointment of a Section 504 Coordinator

School districts with 15 or more employees must appoint a Section 504 coordinator. It is the task of the coordinator to keep the school district in compliance with the mandates of Section 504. Because this individual has many duties, it is important that the school district ensure his or her thorough training. Although the special education director is frequently the Section 504 coordinator, Zirkel (1996) suggests that someone other than the special education director—preferably a general education administrator—be appointed to fill this position. This is because assigning the special education director could serve to reinforce the erroneous belief of many general educators that Section 504 is a special education law when, in fact, it is primarily a general education law.

Notification of School's Responsibilities Under Section 504

The coordinator must keep the public and internal staff notified that the district does not discriminate on the basis of disability in employment, educational services, or treatment. It is advisable that the coordinator head a multidisciplinary team whose responsibilities include the identification, evaluation, and placement of students with disabilities.

Establishment of Grievance Procedures

The coordinator is also responsible for procedural safeguards and grievance procedures for discrimination complaints. Regarding the grievance procedures, the coordinator must develop a formal mechanism for students, parents, or employees to file a grievance. Furthermore, the public must be notified regarding the grievance procedures. Zirkel and Kincaid (1995) suggested that a Section 504 grievance procedure include the following steps: (a) have an informal discussion with the Section 504 coordinator to attempt to resolve the dispute. If the complaint is not satisfactorily resolved, (b) file a written grievance with the coordinator, who will then conduct an investigation and issue a written report. If the complaint is not satisfactorily resolved, (c) appeal the decision to the school board. If the complaint is not satisfactorily resolved, (d) file a complaint with OCR.

Self-Evaluation

The coordinator should conduct periodic self-evaluations of the school district in order to ensure that all Section 504 mandates are followed. If the self-evaluation finds discrimination, the school district must take steps to correct the situation. If such remedial action is necessary, OCR has suggested that the agency seek the assistance of organizations representing persons with disabilities prior to undertaking the corrective procedures. The school district should also keep records of the self-evaluation process. The U.S. Department of Justice has published a technical assistance guide to conducting self-evaluations; it is available from the Coordination and Review Section, Civil Rights Division, U.S. Department of Justice, Washington, DC.

Staff Training

Another extremely important task of the Section 504 coordinator is the training of staff in the meaning and requirements of the law. Zirkel and Kincaid (1995) include the failure to conduct staff inservices on their "hit list" of Section 504 practices that school districts should avoid at all costs.

Identification and Evaluation

It is the responsibility of the school to identify and evaluate students who may qualify for special services under Section 504. Section 504 requires that schools annually take steps to identify and locate children with disabilities who are not receiving an appropriate education and to publicize parental and student rights under the law. These duties, referred to as child find, require that school district officials locate and identify eligible students who reside in the school district. This includes students transferring from other school districts, students in private schools, and homeless children. It is important that school districts realize that students may be eligible for services under Section 504 even if they do not qualify for special education under the IDEA. OCR has held that a blanket school district refusal to evaluate students who do not qualify under the IDEA is a violation of Section 504 (*Mesa Unified School District No. 4,* 1988). Referrals may be made by teachers, parents, school administrators, or other school personnel.

School district officials need to know and define what will "trigger" a referral for a Section 504 evaluation (Goldstein, 1994). Figure 6.4 lists suggestions of the Council of Administrators of Special Education (1992) regarding referral of students under Section 504. It is especially important that school personnel refer students when they have been evaluated and found to be ineligible for services under the IDEA.

Following a referral, evaluations must be completed in a timely manner (*Garden City Union Free School District,* 1990). Delays in completing student evaluations from 61 to 185 days were found to be in violation of Section 504 (*Philadelphia School District,* 1992). Similarly, a 7-month delay between referral and evaluation and a 9-month delay between evaluation and placement were violations of Section 504 (*Dade County School District,* 1993). There are, however, no specific timelines for conducting an evaluation.

Figure 6.4
When to Refer Students Under Section 504

- Suspension or expulsion is being considered
- Retention is being considered
- A student is not benefiting from instruction
- A student returns to school after a serious illness or injury
- A student is diagnosed by an outside source as having a disability
- A student exhibits a chronic health condition
- A student is identified as at risk
- A student is considered a potential dropout
- Substance abuse is an issue
- A disability is suspected

Educational Programming

If it is determined that a student is protected under Section 504, a multidisciplinary team should write an educational plan. This plan can involve general education and related services or special education and related services. Fossey et al. (1995) refer to this plan as an accommodation plan. The plan should include accommodations and modifications to a student's educational program. The plan details the "appropriate education" that a student will receive, and is the result of a multidisciplinary team planning process. Figure 6.5 is an example of a Section 504 accommodation plan.

School districts have a responsibility to provide a FAPE for each qualified child in the district's jurisdiction. This responsibility applies to all children, regardless of the nature or severity of their disabilities (Goldstein, 1994).

Placement

Schools must convene a multidisciplinary team to interpret evaluation data and make placement decisions. The team is to be composed of persons knowledgeable about the child, the evaluation, and the placement options. The multidisciplinary team that conducts evaluations and makes placement decisions under the IDEA may be used for evaluation and placement under Section 504.

Placement options may include regular classrooms, regular classrooms with related services, or special education and related services. Special education may be provided in regular classrooms, special classrooms, at home, or in private or public institutions, and may be accompanied by related services. If the school district cannot provide the appropriate placement, it must assume the cost of alternative placements. The placement must allow for contact with students without disabilities to the maximum extent appropriate. This applies to both academic and nonacademic settings.

Reevaluation

If a school proposes a significant change in placement, the student must be reevaluated in a manner similar to the initial evaluation. Regulations also state that reevaluations should be conducted periodically. No timeline for reevaluations is provided; however, regulations specify that conducting reevaluations in accordance with the more detailed requirements of the IDEA constitutes compliance with Section 504 requirements.

Procedural Safeguards

School districts must establish and implement a system of procedural safeguards. During the evaluation process, notification should be given when eligibility is determined, when an accommodation plan is developed, and before there is any significant modification of the student's program. Schools must establish grievance procedures for complaints that incorporate the appropriate procedural safeguards and

Figure 6.5
Sample Individualized Accommodation Plan

Section 504 Educational Plan

I. Personal Information

Student's name _____   Date of birth_____

Age_____   Grade_____

Referral by _____   Date of referral_____

Date and time of Section 504 conference _____

Reason for referral _____

_____

II. Multidisciplinary Team

504 Coordinator _____   Building Principal _____

Teacher(s)—General Ed. _____   _____

Teacher(s)—Special Ed. _____   _____

Parent(s)_____   _____

School Psychologist _____   Others _____

III. Evaluation Date

Results (include names of tests and instruments used) _____

_____

_____

Basis for determining disability under Section 504 _____

_____

Major life activity affected _____

Educational impact _____

Figure 6.5
Continued

IV. Educational Accommodations

Modifications _____

_____

Related Services _____

_____

Placement _____

V. Monitoring/evaluation procedures _____

_____

_____

VI. Substantiation of least restrictive environment _____

_____

VII. Review/Reevaluation date and location _____

Comments and observations

Date of implementation _____

Persons responsible _____

_____

_____

Parents/guardians notified of procedural rights   Yes   No

Parents' signatures _____

provide for prompt and equitable resolution (Fossey et al., 1995; Zirkel & Kincaid, 1995). Grievance procedures need not be exhausted before filing a complaint with OCR, although it is advisable to do so.

Enforcement of Section 504

Grievance Procedures

School districts are required to set up grievance procedures and notify parents and guardians of those procedures. Grievances are filed if a parent, student, community member, or staff member believes that discrimination based on a disability has occurred. The Section 504 coordinator is responsible for establishing grievance procedures, which must include appropriate procedural safeguards. There is no procedure set forth in Section 504 detailing the requirements of grievance procedures. The mechanics of the procedure are left to the agency.

Governmental Enforcement

Any person may file a grievance with OCR against a school district within 180 days of the alleged discriminatory action. All complaints filed with OCR are investigated as long as they have merit (OCR Complaint Resolution Manual, 1995). Prior to an investigation by OCR, it is advisable that a school attempt to make a settlement with the complainant (Zirkel & Kincaid, 1995). This is referred to as early complaint resolution (ECR).

The Pre-Determination Settlement Process

The first step in the OCR investigation process is the pre-determination settlement (PDS) process. OCR initiated the PDS process in an attempt to reduce its massive complaint load (Martin, 1993). Through this process the school can avoid an on-site investigation and essentially close the matter without admitting to a violation by agreeing to actions that resolve the complainant's issues to the satisfaction of OCR. If the complainant disagrees with the school district's actions, these actions can still be approved by OCR.

According to Martin (1993), the advantage of the PDS process is that it saves an enormous amount of time and expense for both the school district and OCR. The primary disadvantages are, first, that if the allegations are unfounded there is no opportunity to dispute them, and second, that the school must develop a reporting and monitoring timeline to assist OCR in determining if the school district is fulfilling its commitment. Martin (1993) suggests that if the complainant's case against the school is strong, the PDS process is a more favorable option than the OCR investigation and possible finding of violation.

On-Site Investigation

If the PDS process is not successful, OCR will then go to the on-site investigation option. In the investigative process, OCR will request pertinent documentation and conduct staff interviews. These investigations are time-consuming and uncomfortable for school district staff. Following the investigation, OCR will issue a verbal finding of violation or a finding of no violation. If the finding is no violation, the matter is closed. If a violation is found to exist, however, the focus shifts to correction of the violation. Martin (1993) warns school districts that at this stage of the process OCR is not interested in discussing their legal findings or school district objections, but only that the school district correct the problem. If the district voluntarily complies to correct the complaint, and does so to OCR's satisfaction, a letter-of-finding (LOF) violation corrected will be issued by OCR. If, however, the school does not comply to OCR's satisfaction, an LOF violation uncorrected will be issued. Following the issuance of this letter, OCR and the district attempt to negotiate appropriate corrective action. If there is no agreement, OCR can initiate enforcement proceedings to terminate federal funds to the school district. Terminations are unlikely to occur, however, and would only be imposed in the most egregious of cases. Any administrative decision, such as a decision to terminate, is subject to judicial review.

Private Right of Action

Although no private right of action is specifically mentioned in Section 504, there is case law that holds that such a right exists. This is especially significant if the student seeks reimbursement or monetary remedies. Sources of relief available to the individual include injunctions, attorneys' fees, and possibly damages. According to the U.S. Court of Appeals for the Eighth Circuit, punitive damages are only available in cases in which school districts act in bad faith or make gross errors in judgment (*Hoekstra v. Independent School District No. 283*, 1996). The U.S. Court of Appeals for the Sixth Circuit, however, ruled that punitive damages were not available under Section 504 (*Moreno v. Consolidated Rail Corporation*, 1996). Because Title II of the ADA, which applies to public schools, specifies the same remedies as Section 504, the Sixth Circuit decision implies that punitive damages are not available under either the ADA or Section 504.

Similarities Between the IDEA and Section 504

The IDEA and Section 504 form much of the legal foundation of special education. The IDEA, with its detailed rules and procedures, is often considered the more relevant of the two laws to educators. In fact, Section 504 has been viewed by many as the less detailed version of the IDEA (Champagne, 1995). Although there is a great deal of overlap between the two laws, there are also distinct differences. Table 6.2 compares and contrasts the two laws.

Table 6.2
Comparison of the IDEA and Section 504

Component	IDEA	Section 504
Purpose of law	• Provides federal funding to states to assist in education of students with disabilities • Substantive requirements attached to funding	• Civil rights law • Protects persons with disabilities from discrimination in programs or services that receive federal financial assistance • Requires reasonable accommodations to ensure nondiscrimination
Who is protected?	• Categorical approach • Thirteen disability categories • Disability must adversely impact educational performance	• Functional approach • Students (a) having a mental or physical impairment that affects a major life activity, (b) with a record of such an impairment, or (c) who are regarded as having such an impairment • Protects students in general and special education
FAPE	• Special education and related services that are provided at public expense, meet state requirements, and are provided in conformity with the IEP • Substantive standard is educational benefit	• General or special education and related aids and services • Requires a written education plan • Substantive standard is equivalency
LRE	• Student must be educated with peers without disabilities to the maximum extent appropriate • Removal from integrated settings only when supplementary aids and services are not successful • Districts must have a continuum of placement available	• School must ensure that the students are educated with their peers without disabilities
Evaluation and placement	• Protection in evaluation procedures • Requires consent prior to initial evaluation and placement • Evaluation and placement decisions have to be made by a multidisciplinary team • Requires evaluation of progress toward IEP goals annually and reevaluation at least every 3 years	• Does not require consent; requires notice only • Requires periodic reevaluation • Reevaluation is required before a significant change in placement

Table 6.2
Continued

Component	IDEA	Section 504
Procedural safeguards	• Comprehensive and detailed notice requirements • Provides for independent evaluations • No grievance procedure • Impartial due process hearing	• General notice requirements • Grievance procedure • Impartial due process hearing
Funding	• Provides for federal funding to assist in the education of students with disabilities	• No federal funding
Enforcement	• U.S. Office of Special Education Programs (OSEP) (can cut off IDEA funds) • Compliance monitoring by state educational agency (SEA)	• Complaint may be filed with Office of Civil Rights (OCR) (can cut off all federal funding) • Complaints can be filed with state's Department of Education

Summary

Section 504 of the Rehabilitation Act of 1973 is a civil rights statute that requires that no otherwise qualified person with disabilities be excluded from participation in, be denied the benefits of, or be subjected to discrimination in any program receiving federal financial assistance. Although there are no funds available through Section 504, it is illegal for schools receiving federal funds to discriminate based on a student's disability.

Section 504 defines disabilities very broadly. Students are protected under the statute if they have a physical or mental impairment that substantially limits a major life function, have a record of such an impairment, or are regarded as having such an impairment. The disability does not have to adversely affect educational performance, as is the case with the IDEA, and the student does not have to be in special education. Section 504 protects students with disabilities in both general and special education. All students protected under the IDEA are also protected under Section 504. The reverse, however, is not true.

In addition to offering protection from discrimination, Section 504 provides that schools must make reasonable accommodations—modifications to programs and services—if necessary to ensure that discrimination does not occur. Public schools are required to provide appropriate educational services to children protected by Section 504. The provision of general education and related services or special education and related services must be designed to meet the individual needs of students with disabilities as effectively as the education provided students without disabilities meets their needs. To provide an appropriate education, schools are required to follow a process to ensure equivalency. Schools are required to educate students with disabilities along with students without disabilities to the maximum extent appropriate.

Finally, Section 504 is enforced primarily by the Office of Civil Rights. When a discrimination complaint is filed, OCR will investigate. OCR can enforce compliance by terminating all federal funding.

For Further Information

Dagley, D. L., & Evans, C. W. (1995). The reasonable accommodation standard for Section 504–eligible students. *Education Law Reporter, 97,* 1–13.

Fossey, R., Hosie, T., Soniat, K., & Zirkel, P. A. (1995). Section 504 and "front line" educators: An expanded obligation to serve children with disabilities. *Preventing School Failure, 39*(2), 10–14.

Zirkel, P. A. (1996). The substandard for FAPE: Does Section 504 require less than the IDEA? *Education Law Reporter, 106,* 471–477.

Zirkel, P. A., & Kincaid, J. M. (1995). *Section 504, the ADA and the schools.* Horsham, PA: LRP Publications.

Zirkel and Kincaid (1995) is the most complete and thorough coverage of Section 504 available. It begins with the statute and regulations both in annotated and unannotated form. The annotated regulations include a comprehensive compilation of court decisions and administrative rulings on Section 504 and the schools. Sample forms and letters to help school districts comply with 504 are included. Supplements and updates are issued annually. (This book, first printed in 1993, was originally authored by Zirkel and titled Section 504 and the Schools.*)*

References

Alexander v. Choate, 469 U.S. 287 (1985).

Americans with Disabilities Act of 1990, 42 U.S.C. 12101 *et seq.*

Champagne, J. F. (1995). Preface. In P. A. Zirkel & J. M. Kincaid, *Section 504, the ADA and the schools.* Horsham, PA: LRP Publications.

Cherry v. Matthews, 419 F. Supp. 922 (D.D.C. 1976).

Civil Rights Act of 1964, 42 U.S.C. § 200d.

Congressional Record (1977, April 26, 1977), Remarks of Senator Hubert H. Humphrey, principal Senate author of Section 504, p. 12,216.

Council of Administrators of Special Education. (1992). *Student access: A resource guide for educators: Section 504 of the Rehabilitation Act of 1973.* Reston, VA: Author.

Dade County (FL) School District, 20 IDELR 267 (OCR 1993).

Dagley, D. L., & Evans, C. W. (1995). The reasonable accommodation standard for Section 504–eligible students. *Education Law Reporter, 97,* 1–13.

Daley v. Koch, 639 F. Supp. 289 (D.D.C. 1986).

E.E. Black v. Marshall, 497 F. Supp. 1088 (D.Hawaii, 1980).

Education Amendments of 1972, 20 U.S.C. § 1681 *et seq.*

Fossey, R., Hosie, T., Soniat, K., & Zirkel, P. A. (1995). Section 504 and "front line" educators: An expanded obligation to serve children with disabilities. *Preventing School Failure, 39*(2), 10–14

Garden City (NY) Union Free School District, EHLR 353;327 (OCR 1990).

Gerry, M. H., & Benton, J. M. (1982). Section 504: The larger umbrella. In J. Ballard, B. A. Ramirez, & F. J. Weintraub (Eds.), *Special education in America: Its legal and governmental foundations* (pp. 41–49). Reston, VA: Council for Exceptional Children.

Goldstein, B. A. (1994, May). *Legal and practical considerations in implementing Section 504 for students.* Paper presented at the National

Institute on Legal Issues of Educating Individuals with Disabilities, San Francisco, CA.

Hoekstra v. Independent School District, 25 IDELR 882 (8th Cir. 1996).

Martin, J. (1993, April). Section 504 of the Rehabilitation Act of 1973. Paper presented at the international conference of the Council for Exceptional Children, San Antonio, TX.

Mesa (AZ) Unified School District No. 4, EHLR 312:103 (OCR 1988).

Moreno v. Consolidated Rail Corporation, 25 IDELR, 7 (6th Cir. 1996).

OCR Complaint Resolution Manual (1995). In P. A. Zirkel & J. M. Kincaid, *Section 504, the ADA and the schools*. Horsham, PA: LRP Publications.

OCR Memorandum Re: Definition of a disability, 19 IDELR 894 (OCR 1992).

OCR Senior Staff Memorandum, 17 EHLR 1233 (OCR 1990).

Philadelphia (PA) School District, 18 IDELR 931 (OCR 1992).

Pinkerton v. Moye, 509 F. Supp. 107 (W.D. Va. 1981).

Rehabilitation Act of 1973, Section 504 Regulations, 34 C.F.R. § 104.1 *et seq.*

Rehabilitation, Comprehensive Services, and Developmental Disabilities Act of 1978, Pub. L. No. 95-062.

Rice v. Jefferson County Board of Education, 15 EHLR 441.632 (1989).

Schoenfeld, B. N. (1980). Section 504 of the Rehabilitation Act. *University of Cincinnati Law Review, 50,* 580–604.

Section 504 of the Rehabilitation Act of 1973, 29 U.S.C. § 794 *et seq.*

Senate Report No. 890, 95th Cong., 2nd Sess. 39 (1978).

Southeastern Community College v. Davis, 442 U.S. 397 (1979).

Tucker, B. P., & Goldstein, B. A. (1992). *Legal rights of persons with disabilities: An analysis of federal law.* Horsham, PA: LRP Publications.

Uniform Federal Accessibility Standards (1984), 49 31528.

William S. v. Gill, 572 F. Supp. 509 (E.D. Ill. 1983).

Zirkel, P. A. (1996). The substandard for FAPE: Does Section 504 require less than the IDEA? *Education Law Reporter, 106,* 471–477.

Zirkel, P. A., & Kincaid, J. M. (1995). *Section 504, the ADA and the schools.* Horsham, PA: LRP Publications.

CHAPTER SEVEN

The Americans with Disabilities Act

I now lift my pen to sign the Americans with Disabilities Act and say: Let the shameful walls of exclusion finally come tumbling down.

President George Bush, remarks on signing the Americans with Disabilities Act of 1990, July 26, 1990, *Weekly Compilation of Presidential Documents*, vol. 26, n. 30, p. 1165.

In 1990 President Bush signed P.L. 101-336, The Americans with Disabilities Act (ADA), into law. The ADA mandates protections for persons with disabilities against discrimination in a wide range of activities in both the public and private sector. The law focuses primarily on employment and public services. The impact of the ADA on special education services for students with disabilities in school districts is primarily limited to reinforcing and extending the requirements of Section 504 of the Rehabilitation Act of 1973 (Cline, 1994; Wenkart, 1993; Zirkel & Kincaid, 1995). The ADA will also affect public education as an employer of persons with disabilities. Furthermore, public education will also be affected in the areas of public access and in the preparation of students with disabilities to take advantage of the provisions of the law.

Court decisions regarding the ADA and students with disabilities have been inconclusive regarding schools' responsibilities under the law (Zirkel & Kincaid, 1995). The courts, however, have tended to rule that the ADA is to be interpreted consistent with Section 504. Therefore, case law under Section 504 may be used by courts for guidance in interpreting similar provisions of the ADA (Osborne, 1995). The ADA's effect on the provision of a free appropriate public education (FAPE) provided to students, especially when a school is in compliance with IDEA and Section 504, will be minimal (Wenkart, 1993). No student-specific rights are granted in the ADA beyond those of Section 504. Wenkart (1993) conjectures that because nothing in the legislative history suggests an intention to enlarge the substantive rights of children with disabilities, the ADA may not add to rights already existing.

One of the few courts to address the relationship between the IDEA and the ADA, the U.S. Court of Appeals for the Tenth Circuit, ruled in *Urban v. Jefferson County School District R-1* (1994) that the placement rights of a student with disabilities is no greater under the ADA than under the IDEA. Congress believed substantive rights of students with disabilities to be adequately protected under the IDEA and Section 504. This does not mean, however, that public education is unaffected by the ADA. Areas of public education that are affected include employment, general nondiscrimination (which parallels the requirements of Section 504), communications, and program accessibility (Kaesberg & Murray, 1994). Additionally, an important area of difference between Section 504, the IDEA, and the ADA is that the ADA applies to private schools.

Pitasky (1997) asserts that the special education community needs to be aware of how the courts will apply the ADA to the school setting. Furthermore, Zirkel and Kincaid (1995) contend that it would be a mistake for school officials to think that they will be in compliance with ADA because they adhere to the requirements of Section 504. School officials, therefore, should be aware of their responsibilities under both Section 504 and the ADA.

Finally, it is very important that administrators, counselors, and teachers working with students with disabilities are aware of the content of the ADA because of the law's implications for the lives of the students they serve. When students with disabilities leave school and enter the workforce, they will need to engage in self-advocacy (Osborne, 1995). A duty of educators, aptly stated by Marczely (1993), is to inform students with disabilities (and their parents) of the "power and promise the ADA gives them, and the ways in which that power and promise can be productively used" (p. 207).

The purpose of this chapter is to explicate the provisions of the ADA. Responsibilities of public schools under Title II and private schools under Title III will be emphasized.

The History of the ADA

Section 504 of the Rehabilitation Act of 1973 was the first federal effort to protect persons with disabilities from discrimination. Section 504 applied to the federal government, government contractors, and recipients of federal funds. Employers and public accommodations operated by the private sector and by state and local governments, however, were unaffected by the law. As a result, many persons with disabilities continued to suffer from discrimination in employment, education, housing, access to public services, and transportation. To rectify these continued inequities, President Reagan created the National Council on Disabilities, whose task was to recommend to Congress remedies for halting discrimination against persons with disabilities (Miles,

Russo, & Gordon, 1992). After three years of study, the council made recommendations to Congress that were to form the basis of the ADA. According to Miles et al. (1992), the bill, introduced in 1988, stalled in Congress because of congressional inaction, even though it enjoyed the strong support of President Bush and advocacy groups for persons with disabilities. In July 1990 the bill, recently arrived from the House-Senate Conference Committee, was passed by both houses of Congress. On July 26, 1990, the ADA was signed into law by President Bush on the White House lawn. The signing was witnessed by over 3,000 persons with disabilities, reportedly one of the largest ceremonies in White House history (Burnim & Patino, 1993).

The Purpose of the ADA

In the introduction to the ADA, Congress reported that 43 million Americans had physical or mental disabilities. Congress found that discrimination against persons with disabilities persisted in employment, housing, public accommodations, education, transportation, communication, recreation, institutionalization, health services, voting, and access to public services (ADA, 42 U.S.C. § 12101). Congressional findings also indicated that individuals with disabilities who had experienced discrimination based on disability had little or no recourse to redress such discrimination. Furthermore, this discrimination denied persons with disabilities the opportunity to compete on an equal basis, and severely disadvantaged them socially, vocationally, economically, and educationally. Stating that America's proper goals in this regard were to assure persons with disabilities equality of opportunity, full participation, independent living, and economic self-sufficiency, Congress passed the ADA. The primary purposes of the law were

> (1) To provide a clear and comprehensive national mandate for the elimination of discrimination against individuals with disabilities;
> (2) To provide clear, strong, consistent, enforceable standards addressing discrimination against individuals with disabilities;
> (3) To ensure that the federal government plays a central role in enforcing the standards established in the Act on behalf of individuals with disabilities; and
> (4) To invoke the sweep of Congressional authority, including the power to enforce the Fourteenth Amendment and to regulate commerce, in order to address the major areas of discrimination faced day-to-day by people with disabilities. (ADA, 42 U.S.C. § 12101)

The ADA extends the civil rights and antidiscrimination protections of Section 504 from the federal government, its contractors, and recipients of federal funds to employers, state and local governments or any instrumentality of the government, and any privately owned business or facility open to the public. The primary goal of the law, therefore, is that persons with disabilities will enjoy equal opportunity to fully participate in the life of the community and have an equal opportunity to live independently and enjoy economic self-sufficiency through the removal of the barriers that exclude them from the mainstream of American life (Turnbull, 1993).

Figure 7.1
The Americans with Disabilities Act

Title I—Employment
Title II—Public Services
    Subtitle A—General Prohibitions
    Subtitle B—Public Transportation
Title III—Public Accommodations and Services Operated by Private Entities
Title IV—Telecommunications
Title V—Miscellaneous Provisions

Figure 7.2
Discriminatory Practices

- Practices that deny a person with a disability the ability to participate in or cause a person to be denied the benefits from goods, services, facilities, or accommodations.

- Practices that provide an unequal benefit in goods, services, facilities, or accommodations on the basis of a disability.

- Practices that provide goods, services, facilities, or accommodations that, even though equal, are different or separate from those provided to persons without disabilities.

- Practices used in eligibility determinations for the use of goods, services, facilities, or accommodations that effectively exclude persons with disabilities through screening procedures.

- Practices that tend to segregate. Goods, services, and facilities shall be provided in settings in which persons with and without disabilities are integrated.

The ADA is codified at 42 U.S.C. §§ 12101–12213. The law consists of five titles or subchapters. These titles are listed in Figure 7.1. The sine qua non of the ADA is the protection of persons with disabilities from discrimination based on their disabilities. The ADA language that prohibits discrimination varies slightly in Titles I, II, and III. Differences between the titles also exist in definitions and enforcement. Figure 7.2 lists examples of discriminatory practices (ADA, 42 U.S.C. § 302(b) *et seq.*).

Who Is Protected?

The ADA follows Section 504 in defining those individuals protected by the law. The Section 504 definition of persons with disabilities, therefore, applies to the ADA as well as to Section 504. In the ADA, a person with a disability is defined as having

(i) a physical or mental impairment that substantially limits one or more of the major life activities of such individual;

(ii) a record of such an impairment; or

(iii) being regarded as having such an impairment. (ADA, 42 U.S.C. § 12102 (2))

Physical and Mental Impairments

The first part of the definition describes a disability very broadly. ADA regulations mirror the language in Section 504 in listing physical or mental impairments. Protected disabilities include any disorder affecting body systems, including neurological (including traumatic brain injury), physiological, musculoskeletal, sense, respiratory, cardiovascular, digestive, or psychological systems. Regulations to the ADA require that whether or not a person has a disability, an assessment should be conducted without regard to the availability of mitigating modifications or assistive devices (ADA Regulations, 28 C.F.R. § 38, Appendix A). For example, a person with epilepsy is covered under the first part of the definition even if the effects of the impairment are controlled by medication. Likewise, a person with a hearing loss is covered if the loss substantially limits the major life activity of hearing, even though the loss may be ameliorated through the use of a hearing aid.

Persons with HIV and Tuberculosis

The ADA includes persons with HIV (whether symptomatic or asymptomatic) and tuberculosis. If, however, a person with an infectious disease presents a "direct threat" (i.e., significant risk) of contagion or infection, he or she may be excluded from goods, services, facilities, privileges, advantages, and accommodations or denied a job if the threat cannot be eliminated by reasonable accommodations or modifications. The determination of a direct threat is made on an individual basis and relies on current medical or objective evidence to determine the nature, duration, and severity of the risk; the probability that injury will occur; and whether reasonable accommodations will alleviate the risk (ADA Regulations, 28 C.F.R. § 36.208).

For an individual to be covered under the ADA, the physical or mental disability must substantially limit one or more major life activities. These activities include caring for one's self, performing manual tasks, walking, seeing, hearing, speaking, breathing, learning, and working (ADA Regulations, 28 C.F.R. § 38, Appendix A). Persons are thus considered disabled under the first part of the definition when their "important life activities are restricted as to the conditions, manner, and duration under which they can be performed in comparison to most people" (ADA Regulations, 28 C.F.R. § 38, Appendix A).

Exclusions from Protection

Physical or mental disabilities do not include simple physical characteristics, nor do they include environmental, cultural, economic, or other disadvantages (e.g., prison record, being poor). Neither are the following conditions included as disabilities: (a) age (although medical conditions resulting from old age are disabilities); (b) temporary,* nonchronic impairments such as broken limbs; (c) pregnancy; and (d) obesity (except in rare circumstances). Environmental illnesses (e.g. multiple chemical sensitivity, allergy to smoke) are not considered disabilities under the ADA unless the impairment actually limits one or more major life activities.

The ADA specifically excludes certain individuals from its definition of a person with disability. Because courts had interpreted Section 504 as covering transsexuals and compulsive gamblers, Congress specifically excluded these individuals from coverage under the ADA (Tucker, 1992). Additionally, Congress acted to ensure that the ADA definition of disability would not include homosexuality, bisexuality, transvestitism, transsexualism, pedophilia, exhibitionism, voyeurism, gender identity disorders not resulting from physical impairments, or other sexual behavior disorders (ADA, 42 U.S.C. § 12211(a)(b)). The law also specifically excludes persons with compulsive gambling disorders, kleptomania, or pyromania (ADA, 42 U.S.C. § 12211(b)(2)).

Persons engaging in the illegal use of drugs, and any disorders resulting from current illegal drug use, are also excluded from protection under the ADA. Persons who have successfully completed or are participating in a supervised drug rehabilitation program and are no longer using illegal drugs are protected by the ADA. Persons who are discriminated against because they are erroneously believed to be engaged in illegal drug use are also protected. Furthermore, drug testing of employees is allowed under the law. The ADA effectively amends Section 504 to allow school districts to discipline students with disabilities for the use or possession of illegal drugs or alcohol in the same manner as students without disabilities would be disciplined (Staff memo, 1991).

Having a Record of a Disability or Being Regarded as Being Disabled

The second and third parts of the definition essentially protect individuals when a negative or discriminatory action is committed against them based on a record of a disability or because they are regarded as being disabled. Persons covered by these two parts either never were or are not currently disabled, but are treated in a discriminatory manner because they are perceived by others as being disabled. It is this manner of treatment, which is based on false assumptions, that entitles these persons to protection. Examples of persons having a record of a disability include persons with histories of cancer, heart disease, or mental or emotional illness. Examples of persons regarded as having a disability include persons misclassified as having an impairment and those discriminated against because of the fears and stereotypes of others.

---

*The word "temporary" was deleted from the final rules promulgated by the Equal Employment Opportunity Commission because it was not contained in the statute or the regulations. Whether a temporary impairment is a disability can only be determined on a case-by-case basis, taking into account both the impairment's duration and the extent to which the impairment actually limits a major life activity (ADA Regulations, 28 C.F.R. § 38, Appendix A).

Titles of the ADA

Title I: Employment

Title I of the ADA addresses employment. Employers, employment agencies, labor organizations, and labor-management committees are referred to in the law as "covered entities." These entities may not discriminate against any qualified individuals with disabilities, including employees or applicants for employment. Neither the U.S. government nor private membership clubs are covered entities. After July 1994, all employers with 15 or more employees are covered by Title I. Public school and private school employees are included under this title as long as the school employs 15 or more persons. Religious schools may give preference to applicants of the particular religion and may require that employees conform to its religious tenets (ADA Regulations, 29 C.F.R. § 1630.16(A)).

Title I defines a qualified individual with a disability as "an individual with a disability who, with or without reasonable accommodation, can perform the essential functions of the employment position that such individual holds or desires" (ADA, 42 U.S.C. § 12111(8)). To be protected by the ADA in employment, a person must not only have a disability but must also be qualified; that is, the person has to be able to perform the duties of the job with or without the provision of reasonable accommodations. The qualified individual with disabilities must satisfy the requisite skill, experience, education, and other job-related requirements of the employment position. In essence, he or she must be able to perform the essential elements of the job. The Equal Employment Opportunity Commission (1992) suggests that there should be two steps in determining if an individual with disabilities is qualified under the ADA. First, the employer should determine if the individual meets the necessary prerequisites of the job (e.g., education, work experience, training, skills, licenses, certificates, and other job-related requirements). If the individual with disabilities meets the necessary job requirements, the employer may go to the second step of the determination, which is assessing if the individual can perform the essential functions of the job with or without reasonable accommodations.

Reasonable Accommodations

A reasonable accommodation is a modification to the job or the work environment that will remove barriers and enable the individual with a disability to perform the job. Reasonable accommodations include:

> (A) making existing facilities used by employees readily accessible to and usable by individuals with disabilities; and
>
> (B) job restructuring, part-time or modified work schedules, reassignment to a vacant position, acquisition or modification of equipment or devices, appropriate adjustment or modifications of examination, training materials or policies, the provision of qualified readers or interpreters, and other similar accommodations for persons with disabilities. (ADA, 42 U.S.C. § 12111(9) *et seq.*)

When determining a reasonable accommodation, the employer should

(1) Analyze the particular job involved and determine its purpose and essential functions;

(2) Consult with the individual with a disability to ascertain the precise job related limitations imposed by the individual's disability and how those limitations could be overcome with a reasonable accommodation;

(3) In consultation with the individual to be accommodated, identify potential accommodations and assess the effectiveness each would have in enabling the individual to perform the essential functions of the position;

(4) Consider the preference of the individual to be accommodated that is the most appropriate for both the employee and the employer. (ADA Regulations, 29 C.F.R. § 1630.9)

The ADA differentiates between reasonable and unreasonable accommodations. Accommodations that impose "undue hardship" on the employer (i.e., require significant difficulty or significant expense) are not required. Only those accommodations that are reasonable are required. Factors to be considered in determining if an accommodation would impose an undue hardship include (a) the nature and cost of the accommodation; (b) the number of persons employed; (c) the effect on expenses and resources; (d) the overall financial resources of the covered entity; (e) the number, type, and location of the employer's facilities; and (f) the type of operation of the employer.

Prohibition Against Discrimination

Title I protects persons with disabilities from discrimination in "job application procedures, the hiring, advancement, or discharge of employees, employee compensation, job training, and other terms, conditions, or privileges of employment" (ADA, 42 U.S.C. § 12112(a)). Discrimination, according to the ADA, involves limiting or classifying applicants or employees in a way that adversely affects the employment status of that person, participating in contractual arrangements that indirectly discriminate against disabled persons, or following administrative procedures that have the effect of discriminating against persons with disabilities. Employers can also discriminate by not making reasonable accommodations for a qualified person with disabilities unless these accommodations would result in undue hardship. Neither may employees discriminate against associates of the persons with disabilities (e.g., relatives).

Title I is not an affirmative action mandate. That is, employers need not hire employees with disabilities to redress past discrimination. If two equally qualified people apply for a job or a promotion, one with a disability and one without, the employer may hire or promote the applicant without disabilities, as long as the employer's decision is not related to the applicant's disability (Tucker & Goldstein, 1992). Employers have no obligations regarding Title I, however, when an applicant or employee is currently using illegal drugs.

Enforcement of Title I

The ADA adopts the enforcement procedures in Title VII of the Civil Rights Act (ADA, 42 U.S.C. § 2000(e) *et seq.*). Powers of enforcement are given to the Equal Employment Opportunity Commission (EEOC), U.S. attorney general, and to persons with disabilities who are subjected to discrimination. Clearly the ADA allows both administrative and individual enforcement of its provisions. Individuals, however, must exhaust administrative remedies before taking judicial action. Disability discrimination claims must be filed within 180 days of the alleged discrimination. EEOC will investigate the claim and attempt to reach a settlement between the parties. If these attempts are not successful, the individual has the right to go to court. The remedies available under the ADA are injunctive relief (i.e., court orders to stop discrimination), reinstatement, and compensatory damages (e.g., back pay). Moreover, if an employer is found guilty of intentional discrimination "with malice or reckless indifference," a plaintiff may receive compensatory and punitive damages. The ADA contains damage caps on punitive damages that prevailing plaintiffs can collect. In cases where the employer has made good faith efforts to reasonably accommodate an individual but has not succeeded in doing so, damages will not be awarded (ADA Regulations, 28 C.F.R. § 36.504 *et seq.*). When plaintiffs seek damages, they may ask for a trial by jury. The court in which the complaint is heard may, at its discretion, award attorneys' fees.

Title II: Public Services

Title II contains two subtitles: Subtitle A prohibits discrimination by state and local governments, and Subtitle B covers discrimination in public transportation. Title II protects all qualified persons with disabilities from discrimination by public entities. Public entities are any state or local government or any department or instrumentality of the state or local government. According to the Department of Justice, an entity is considered "public" if it (a) operates using public funds; (b) has employees who are considered government employees; (c) receives significant assistance from the government in terms of property or equipment; or (d) is governed by an independent or elected board (Tucker & Goldstein, 1992). Public schools fall under the purview of Title II.

To be protected under Title II, the individual with disabilities must be qualified. That is, the individual,

> with or without reasonable modifications to rules, policies, or practices, the removal of architectural, communication, or transportation barriers, or the provision of auxiliary aids and services, meets the essential eligibility requirements for the receipt of services or the participation in programs or activities provided by a public entity. (ADA, 42 U.S.C. § 12131 (2))

Prohibition Against Discrimination

Discrimination on the basis of disability is prohibited. Specifically, Title II prohibits discrimination in employment, like Title I, and in accessibility, like Title III. Title II requires that a qualified person with disabilities cannot be excluded from participation in or be denied the benefits of the services, programs, or activities of a public entity or be subjected to discrimination by a public entity. Public schools and colleges, although not specifically mentioned in Title II, are public entities, so reasonable modifications* will be required in employee hiring as well as in student programs.

---

*Titles II and III use the term "reasonable modifications" rather than "reasonable accommodations." The terms, however, have similar meanings.

The statutory language and regulations concerning discrimination are very similar to those contained in Section 504 and provide similar protections. The ADA, unlike Section 504, contains no separate coverage for public schools, nor does it contain specific student requirements that schools must follow.

Subtitle B, concerning transportation, is a detailed compilation of accommodations that are required in making transportation accessible for persons with disabilities. Public school transportation is expressly omitted from Title II (49 C.F.R. § 37.27 Appendix). Subtitle B is made up of two parts. Part 1 covers public transportation provided by bus or rail (excluding commuter services) or other means of conveyance with the exception of air travel. Part 1 covers new vehicles, used vehicles, remanufactured vehicles, paratransit services, new and altered facilities used to provide public transportation, and light or rapid rail systems. Part 2 concerns public transportation by intercity and commuter rail services covering accessible cars, new cars, used cars, remanufactured cars, new stations for use in intercity transportation, existing stations, and altered stations. The provisions of both parts require that intercity and commuter rail services be made readily accessible to and usable by individuals with disabilities.

Public entities must conduct self-evaluations to determine if they are in compliance with Title II. Additionally, covered entities must have information regarding adherence to Title II. Entities with 50 or more employees must keep a record of the self-evaluation available to the public for 3 years following the self-evaluation. Furthermore, they must have an ADA coordinator and establish a complaint procedure. Finally, when they make structural changes to comply with the ADA, they must develop transition plans regarding the changes to be made.

Enforcement of Title II

Enforcement of Title II mirrors enforcement of Section 504, which incorporates similar remedies and procedures. The Department of Justice oversees compliance with Title II. Individuals may file a complaint with the appropriate agency within 180 days of the alleged discrimination or bring a private lawsuit to recover actual damages. Punitive damages, however, are not available against the government or a governmental agency. Under Title II the exhaustion of administrative remedies is not required before going to a court for relief.

Title III: Public Accommodations Operated by a Private Entity

The purpose of Title III of the ADA is to prohibit discrimination by private entities that own public accommodations by providing persons with disabilities an equal opportunity to receive the benefits of goods and services in the most integrated settings. All privately owned businesses, facilities open to the public, and commercial facilities (even if not open to the public) are subject to Title III. If a business is a place of public accommodation fitting into one of twelve categories, it is covered. The examples provided of public accommodations in the ADA are illustrative, not exhaustive (ADA, 42 U.S.C. § 12181(7)). Figure 7.3 lists these categories.

Figure 7.3
Public Accommodations

- Places of lodging
- Bars and restaurants
- Places of exhibition or entertainment (e.g., concert halls, movie theaters)
- Places of public gathering (e.g., conference centers, lecture halls)
- Stores and shopping centers
- Service establishments, including barber shops, laundromats, hospitals, professional offices, and others
- Terminals and depots
- Cultural institutions (e.g., museums, galleries)
- Places of recreation (e.g., amusement parks, zoos)
- Places of education (nurseries and all schools from preschool to university)
- Places where social services are offered (e.g., day care centers, homeless shelters, food banks)
- Places for exercise of recreation (e.g., golf courses, health clubs, gymnasiums)

Private schools from "nursery to postgraduate school" are specifically covered under Title III (ADA, 42 U.S.C. § 12181 (7)). Title III also applies to private entities that offer examinations or courses related to applications, licensing, certification, or credentialing for secondary or postsecondary education, professional, or trade purposes (ADA Regulations, 28 C.F.R. § 36.102(a)).

Commercial facilities are covered under Title III. Commercial facilities are defined as facilities "that are intended for nonresidential use and whose operations will affect commerce" (ADA, 42 U.S.C. § 12181(2) *et seq.*). Commerce is any means of travel, trade, transportation, or communication between states or between the United States and a foreign country.

Private residences, private clubs, religious entities, and public entities are exempt from the Title III mandates. Public schools, therefore, are exempt while private schools are not (Zirkel, 1993b). Private religious schools are also exempt under Title III.

Prohibition Against Discrimination

Title III forbids discrimination against persons with disabilities on the basis of their disabilities. Two types of discrimination are addressed: overtly discriminatory practices on the basis of disability, and practices and structures that effectively discriminate against persons with disabilities whether or not there was intention to discriminate (Coupe, Ness, & Sheetz, 1992).

Title III also prohibits discrimination in privately operated public transportation services. These entities do not have to be primarily engaged in the transportation of people. Examples include shuttle services, student transportation systems, and transportation provided within a recreational facility (e.g., amusement park). Discrimination involves the imposition of eligibility criteria that serve to screen out persons with disabilities from using the transportation systems, failure to make reasonable modifications to ensure nondiscrimination, or failure to remove barriers to accessibility.

Requirements of Title III

Businesses open to the public (i.e., public accommodations) must comply with the requirements regarding the provision of good and services, the prohibition against discrimination, the construction of new buildings, and the alteration of existing buildings. Commercial facilities are required to comply with the new construction and building alteration requirements only.

Public accommodations must modify their operations if they are discriminatory unless they can show that to do so would fundamentally alter the nature of the business. Businesses open to the public must also take steps to ensure effective communications with persons whose disabilities affect hearing, vision, or speech. Auxiliary aids and services, such as interpreters and readers, may be used. Businesses, however, are not required to provide personal devices (e.g., hearing aids, eyeglasses) or personal services (e.g., assistance in eating) to individuals.

Architectural Accessibility

Private entities operating public accommodations must remove architectural and structural barriers in existing facilities where the removal is "readily achievable" (i.e., easily accomplished and not unduly expensive or difficult). This obligation, however, does not extend to employee work areas within the public accommodations. If the removal of the barrier is not readily achievable, an obligation still exists to make goods and services available through alternative methods. Examples of alternatives to barrier removal include providing curb service or home delivery, retrieving merchandise from inaccessible shelves, and relocating activities to accessible locations (ADA Regulations, 28 C.F.R. § 36.305(b) *et seq.*). Figure 7.4 is a partial list of ways to remove architectural barriers. The list is not intended to be exhaustive.

The ADA provides no test for determining if the removal of these (or any other) barriers is readily achievable. The Department of Justice, and presumably the courts, will consider all claims that barrier removal is not readily achievable on a case-by-case basis. Factors in these determinations include the financial resources of the accommodation.

New Construction and Building Alterations

Public accommodations and commercial facilities are required to comply with ADA regulations regarding new construction and building alterations. All new construction must be accessible; however, alterations to existing facilities must only be made to the extent that they are readily achievable. The ADA contains detailed specifications on making new construction accessible.

Figure 7.4
Ways to Remove Architectural Barriers

- Installing ramps
- Making curb cuts in sidewalks and entrances
- Repositioning shelves
- Rearranging tables, chairs, and other furniture
- Repositioning telephones
- Adding raised markings on elevator control buttons
- Installing flashing alarm lights
- Widening doors and doorways
- Eliminating a turnstile or providing an accessible path
- Installing accessible door hardware
- Installing grab bars in toilet stalls
- Rearranging toilet partitions to increase maneuvering space
- Insulating lavatory pipes under sinks to prevent burns
- Installing a full-length bathroom mirror
- Repositioning the paper towel dispenser in the bathroom
- Creating designated accessible parking spaces
- Removing high-pile, low-density carpeting
- Installing vehicle hand controls

Enforcement of Title III

Under Title III, persons who believe they have been subjected to discrimination may file a complaint with the Department of Justice. An individual may seek a court order to prohibit discrimination. Courts may award injunctive relief. Punitive damages, however, are not available (ADA, 42 U.S.C. § 12188(b)(4)). In the area of transportation, claims may be filed with the Department of Transportation or with a court.

Title IV: Telecommunications

Title IV of the ADA involves the provision of telecommunication services for persons with hearing and speech impairments. Many individuals with these disabilities are unable to communicate by telephone, thereby cutting them off from an extremely important mode of communication. Title IV amends the Communications Act of 1934 (Communications Act, 47 U.S.C. § 151 *et seq.*) to require that phone companies (i.e., "common carriers") provide telecommunication services to allow persons with hearing and speech disabilities to communicate with persons without disabilities. To meet the ADA mandates, common carriers are required to establish systems of telephone relay services which connect telecommunication devices for the deaf to telephones. Title IV also requires that television public service announcements be close-captioned. Television broadcasters, however, are not required to close-caption television programs. Enforcement authority of Title IV was assumed by the Federal Communications Commission.

Title V: Miscellaneous

The final title of the ADA contains a number of miscellaneous provisions. The following are some of the more important ones:

1. States are not immune from actions under the ADA (ADA, 42 U.S.C. § 12202). This provision of the law allows states to be sued under the ADA. Generally, if a law does not specifically allow states to be sued under the law, states will be considered immune from lawsuits under the doctrine of sovereign immunity. (See Chapter 14 for elaborations on sovereign immunity.)

2. Courts and administrative agencies may award attorneys' fees to prevailing parties. Courts can also award expert witness fees (ADA, 42 U.S.C. § 12205). The award of attorneys' fees includes fees assessed against the plaintiff if the lawsuit is frivolous, unreasonable, or groundless (Tucker & Goldstein, 1992).

3. Retaliation and coercion against persons with disabilities seeking to enforce their rights under the ADA are prohibited. It is also illegal to coerce, intimidate, or threaten anyone attempting to help persons with disabilities exercise their rights under the ADA (ADA, 42 U.S.C. § 12203).

4. The ADA does not invalidate or limit remedies, rights, and procedures of any federal, state, or local law whose protection for persons with disabilities is equal to or greater than the ADA (ADA, 42 U.S.C. § 12201).

5. The ADA does not apply a lesser standard than Section 504 of the Rehabilitation Act of 1973 (ADA, 42 U.S.C. § 12201(a)).

6. Where appropriate, parties are encouraged to seek to resolve disputes through some alternative method of dispute resolution rather than through litigation (ADA, 42 U.S.C. § 12212). This provision is, however, completely voluntary.

7. An Access Board was convened to issue minimum guidelines for Titles II and III of the ADA. The board issues a volume of guidelines over 130 pages long (see 36 C.F.R. § 1191). These guidelines are intended to ensure that facilities are made accessible to persons with disabilities.

School District Responsibilities

There is nothing in the ADA that enlarges the right of students with disabilities to an appropriate education under either the IDEA or Section 504 (Wenkart, 1993). In fact, the ADA contains no specific student requirements such as the FAPE requirement

Figure 7.5
School District Responsibilities

1. Appoint an ADA compliance coordinator (if over 50 employees).
2. Conduct a self-evaluation which includes:
   - nondiscrimination provisions
   - employment
   - accessibility
   - communication
3. Develop transition plans to bring school into compliance with ADA.
4. Maintain a file of self-evaluation, available for public inspection, for 3 years following completion of the evaluation.
5. Provide notice regarding services, programs, or activities of the school.
6. Know which students are protected under the ADA or Section 504.
7. Recognize that the ADA covers employees with disabilities.
8. Ensure that new construction is readily accessible and usable by persons with disabilities.

of the IDEA and Section 504, or transition plans under the IDEA (Zirkel, 1993a). The ADA, however, will affect public education in other areas. In fact, schools may be liable for suits for remedies, possibly including monetary damages, when they violate the ADA (*Hoekstra v. Independent School District No. 283,* 1996). It is, therefore, important that school officials be aware of what constitutes compliance and noncompliance with the law. Figure 7.5 lists school district compliance requirements.

ADA Compliance Coordinator

School districts that employ 50 or more persons must have an ADA coordinator, as well as information available on how to reach that person. The duties of the coordinator include coordinating ADA compliance activities, informing and involving the community, coordinating the school district's self-evaluation and transition plan, establishing a grievance plan, and investigating grievances (ADA Regulations, 28 C.F.R. § 35.107 *et seq.*). The ADA coordinator should also be responsible for informing interested persons regarding the services, programs, and activities offered by the school district. The coordinator should conduct staff in-service training to make employees aware of ADA requirements (ADA, 42 U.S.C. § 84.7(b)).

Self-Evaluation

The ADA requires that school districts conduct a self-evaluation. If a school has already completed a Section 504 self-evaluation, then the ADA self-evaluation will apply only to those policies and practices not included in the previous self-evaluation

(28 C.F.R. § 35.105(d)). Provisions to ensure nondiscrimination, communication, employment, accessibility of programs and facilities, and staff training should be evaluated. Interested persons or organizations should be allowed to participate in the self-evaluation by submitting comments (ADA Regulations, 28 C.F.R. § 35.105 *et seq.*). The self-evaluation must be maintained for public inspection for three years. The description of the self-evaluation should include the names of interested persons consulted, a description of problems identified, and modifications to correct these problem areas.

Transition Plan

If areas of noncompliance with the ADA are identified, the school district must act to correct those deficiencies. If structural changes will be required to achieve program accessibility, a transition plan must be developed to guide completion of the necessary changes. This plan should identify accessibility problems and describe in detail methods to alleviate the problem.

The transition plan of the ADA is not to be confused with the transition plan required by the IDEA in the individualized education programs (IEPs) of students 16 or older. The ADA does not require transition plans for students with disabilities.

Prohibition Against Discrimination

The ADA's Title I requirements prohibiting discrimination against qualified persons with disabilities in employment applies to schools. School districts must also comply with the nondiscriminatory provisions of Title II. Additionally, private schools are covered by Title III of the ADA, which requires that (a) program, services, and activities should be provided in the most integrated setting feasible; (b) no written policies or procedures may exclude or discriminate; (c) school district contractors must not discriminate; (d) the use of criteria that screen out or have the effect of screening out eligible persons with disabilities are prohibited; and (e) modifications of policies, practices, and procedures that may discriminate must be made unless these changes will fundamentally alter the nature of the service, program, or activity.

Summary

In 1990, the Americans with Disabilities Act became law. The purpose of the law was to prohibit discrimination against persons with disabilities based on their disability. The ADA is similar to Section 504 of the Rehabilitation Act of 1973, but is larger in scope. Where Section 504 prohibits discrimination against persons with disabilities in programs receiving federal financial assistance, the ADA extends these protections to the private sector. The ADA prohibits discriminatory practices in employment, housing, and transportation. The ADA also legislates accommodations to facilities in order that they are free of barriers and accessible to persons with disabilities.

The ADA's effect on the provision of a free appropriate public education provided to students, especially when a school is in compliance with IDEA and Section 504, will be minimal. There are no additional student-specific rights beyond those contained in Section 504 and the IDEA granted by the ADA. This does not mean, however, that public education is unaffected by the ADA. Areas of public education that are affected include employment, general nondiscrimination (which parallels the requirements of Section 504), communications, and program accessibility. Additionally, administrators, counselors, and teachers working with students with disabilities need to become aware of the content of the ADA, because of the law's implications for the lives of the students they serve. When students with disabilities leave school and enter the workforce, they will need to engage in self-advocacy. A duty of educators is the responsibility to inform students with disabilities (and their parents) of their rights contained in the ADA.

For Further Information

Americans with Disabilities Act: Law, regulations, and interpretive guidance. (1992). Horsham, PA: LRP Publications.

Equal Employment Opportunity Commission. (1992). *A technical assistance manual on the employment (Title I) provisions of the Americans with Disabilities Act.* Washington, DC: Author (available from the EEOC, 189 L Street NW, Washington, DC 20507).

Kaesberg, M. A., & Murray, K. T. (1994). Americans with Disabilities Act. *Education Law Reporter, 90,* 11–21.

Marczely, B. (1993). The Americans with Disabilities Act: Confronting the shortcomings of Section 504 in public education. *Education Law Reporter, 78,* 199–207.

Miles, A. S., Russo, C. J., Gordon, W. M. (1992). The reasonable accommodations provisions of the Americans with Disabilities Act. *Education Law Reporter, 69,* 1–8.

Tucker, B. P. (1992). The Americans with Disabilities Act: An overview. *New Mexico Law Review, 22,* 3–112.

Wenkart, R. D. (1993). The Americans with Disabilities Act and its impact on public education. *Education Law Reporter, 82,* 291–302.

Zirkel, P. A., & Kincaid, J. M. (1995). *Section 504, the ADA and the schools.* Horsham, PA: LRP Publications.

References

Americans with Disabilities Act of 1990, 42 U.S.C. 12101 *et seq.*

Americans with Disabilities Act Regulations, 28 C.F.R. §§ Parts 36–38.

Burnim, I., & Patino, L. G. (1993). Employment issues under ADA and Section 504. *The Americans with Disabilities Act: New opportunities for children and families.* Horsham, PA: LRP Publications.

Cline, D. (1994). *Fundamentals of special education law: Emphasis on discipline.* Arden Hills, MN: Behavioral Institute for Children and Adolescents.

Communications Act, 47 U.S.C. § 611 *et seq.*

Coupe, B. W., Ness, A. D., & Sheetz, R. A. (1992). The Department of Justice's final regulations implementing Title III of the Americans with Disabilities Act. *Education Law Reporter, 71,* 353–359.

Equal Employment Opportunity Commission (1992). *A technical assistance manual on the employment (Title I) provisions of the Americans with Disabilities Act.* Washington, DC: Author.

Hoekstra v. Independent School District, 25 IDELR 882 (8th Cir. 1996).

Kaesberg, M. A., & Murray, K. T. (1994). Americans with Disabilities Act. *Education Law Reporter, 90,* 11–21.

Marczely, B. (1993). The Americans with Disabilities Act: Confronting the shortcomings of Section 504 in Public Education. *Education Law Reporter, 78,* 199–207.

Miles, A. S., Russo, C. J., & Gordon, W. M. (1992). The reasonable accommodations provisions of the Americans with Disabilities Act. *Education Law Reporter, 69,* 1–8.

OCR Staff Memorandum, 17 EHLR 609 (OCR, 1991).

Osborne, A. G. (1995). Court interpretations of the Americans with Disabilities Act and their effects on school districts. *Education Law Reporter, 95,* 489–498.

Pitasky, V. M. (1997). *The special education desk book.* Horsham, PA: LRP Publications.

Rehabilitation Act of 1973, Section 504, 29 U.S.C. § 794.

Tucker, B. P. (1992). The Americans with Disabilities Act: An overview. *New Mexico Law Review, 22,* 3–112.

Tucker, B. P., & Goldstein, B. A. (1992). *Legal rights of persons with disabilities: An analysis of federal law.* Horsham, PA: LRP Publications.

Turnbull, H. R. (1993). *Free appropriate education: The law and children with disabilities* (4th ed.). Denver: Love Publishing Company.

Urban v. Jefferson County School District R-1, 21 IDELR 985 (D. Col. 1994).

Wenkart, R. D. (1993). The Americans with Disabilities Act and its impact on public education. *Education Law Reporter, 82,* 291–302.

Zirkel, P. A. (1993a). The ADA and its impact on the schools. *Proceedings of the 14th National Institute on Legal Issues in Educating Individuals with Disabilities.* Horsham, PA: LRP Publications.

Zirkel, P. A. (1993b). Our "disability" with the ADA. *The Special Educator, 8*(17), 251–253.

Zirkel, P. A., & Kincaid, J. M. (1995). *Section 504, the ADA and the schools.* Horsham, PA: LRP Publications.

CHAPTER EIGHT

Free Appropriate Public Education

Free appropriate public education . . . evinces a congressional intent to bring previously excluded handicapped children into the public education systems of the states and to require the states to adopt procedures which would result in individualized consideration of and instruction for each child.

Justice Rehnquist, *Board of Education v. Rowley* (1982, p. 188)

Congressional hearings preceding passage of the Education for All Handicapped Children Act (EAHCA) in 1975 revealed that although a number of states had laws to improve the educational services afforded to students with disabilities, many did not. As a result, numerous students with disabilities were excluded from school entirely, and many others were offered an education not appropriate to their needs.

To correct these inequities, Congress passed the EAHCA (renamed the Individuals with Disabilities Education Act, or IDEA, in 1990). The law offered federal financial assistance to states to aid them in the development and improvement of educational programs for students who qualified for special education under the Act. To qualify for assistance, states were required to submit state plans that assured all students with disabilities the right to a free appropriate public education (FAPE).

Congress, however, did not provide a substantive definition of FAPE. Many have considered the unspecified nature of the mandate fitting because an appropriate education must take into account the individual needs of each child (Tucker & Goldstein, 1992). What constitutes an appropriate education, therefore, will vary from student to student.

The FAPE Mandate

The IDEA and Section 504 of the Rehabilitation Act of 1973 (hereafter Section 504) require that students with disabilities receive an appropriate education. The two statutes, however, vary somewhat in their procedural requirements, and significantly in the substantive requirements of a FAPE.

IDEA

The FAPE mandate of the IDEA includes substantive and procedural requirements. On a substantive level the IDEA defines FAPE as

special education and related services that—
(A) are provided at public expense, under public supervision and direction, and without charge,
(B) meet standards of the State educational agency,
(C) include an appropriate preschool, elementary, or secondary school education in the state involved, and
(D) are provided in conformity with the individualized education program. (IDEA, 20 U.S.C. § 1401(a)(18))

The IDEA defines special education as "specially designed instruction, at no cost to parents or guardians, to meet the unique needs of a child with a disability" (IDEA, 20 U.S.C. § 1401(a)(16)). Related services are defined as any services that "may be required to assist a child with disabilities to benefit from special education" (IDEA, 20 U.S.C. § 1401(a)(17)).

Procedural protections are the second component of the FAPE mandate. Congress was very specific in detailing the procedural requirements to be afforded parents. These safeguards include prior notice, parental consent, opportunity to examine records, independent educational evaluation, and the right to request an impartial due process hearing (IDEA Regulations, 34 C.F.R. § 300.500–515). (See Chapter 13 for an elaboration of procedural safeguards.) The purpose of these procedural safeguards is to ensure parental participation and consultation throughout the special education process.

Section 504

Under Section 504, FAPE refers to the provision of regular or special education and related aids and services that meet the needs of students with disabilities as adequately as the needs of a student without disabilities are met. Regulations implementing Section 504 state that

A recipient [of federal funds] that operates a public elementary or secondary education program shall provide a free appropriate public education to each qualified handicapped person who is in the recipient's jurisdiction regardless of the nature or severity of the person's handicap. (Section 504 Regulations, 34 C.F.R. § 104.33(a))

The regulations further define an appropriate education:

> the provision of an appropriate education is the provision of regular or special education and related aids and services that (i) are designed to meet individual educational needs of handicapped persons *as adequately* [emphasis added] as the needs of nonhandicapped persons are met and (ii) are based upon adherence to procedures. (Section 504 Regulations, 34 C.F.R. § 104.33(b)(1))

The FAPE standard of Section 504 is one of comparability. The definition also includes the provision of related aids and services to students in regular education as well as special education. No individualized education program (IEP) is required under Section 504, although implementation of an IEP developed in accordance with the IDEA procedures is one means of meeting the appropriate education requirement under Section 504 (Section 504 Regulations, 34 C.F.R. § 104.33(b)(2)). Another means to meet this requirement is through the development of a Section 504 plan (*Lunenberg School District,* 1994).

Section 504 also contains procedural mechanisms, albeit not as elaborate as those in the IDEA, to help ensure that schools meet their responsibilities to provide a FAPE to all students with disabilities (Section 504 Regulations, 34 C.F.R. § 104.36). The procedural safeguards are required in all school actions involving the identification, evaluation, or educational placements of students with disabilities. Specific requirements listed are notice, opportunity for parents to examine relevant records, an impartial hearing, and a review procedure. Compliance with the procedural safeguards of the IDEA is one means of meeting the Section 504 requirements.

Although the ADA does not specifically adopt a standard for FAPE, the law essentially establishes the right to a FAPE by extending the nondiscrimination requirements of Section 504 to all state and local government entities and to private school systems. According to the Office of Civil Rights (OCR) of the Department of Education, the Section 504 FAPE standard, therefore, is also a requirement under the ADA (*Waltham (MA) Public Schools,* 1993).

Components of a FAPE

Free Education

Special education and related services as delineated in an IEP or Section 504 plan must be provided at no charge to parents or guardians of students with disabilities. Furthermore, neither the IDEA nor Section 504 allows school districts to refuse to provide special education services because of the cost of those services. In enacting the IDEA, Congress specifically rejected limitations of federal funding as justification for denying a FAPE. The Office of Special Education Programs (OSEP) of the Department of Education has stated that schools are not precluded from charging "incidental" fees to the parents of students with disabilities for items such as art or lab supplies or field trips, provided that similar fees are also charged to students without disabilities as part of the educational program (OSEP Policy Letter, 1992).

Costs, however, may be considered in the decision-making process (*A.W. v. Northwest R-1 School District*, 1987; *Doe v. Brookline School Committee*, 1983; *Schuldt v. Mankato Independent School District*, 1991). The U.S. Court of Appeals for the Sixth Circuit, in *Clevenger v. Oak Ridge School Board* (1984), noted that "cost considerations are only relevant when choosing between several options, all of which offer an appropriate education. When only one is appropriate, then there is no choice" (p. 514). Guernsey and Klare (1993) cite an example of a school district choosing between a residential facility and a community group home option for providing an appropriate education. When both options will provide an appropriate education, the school district may choose the less expensive of the two placements. The U.S. Court of Appeals for the Ninth Circuit, in *Department of Education, State of Hawaii v. Katherine D.* (1984), noting that school officials were often confronted with limited financial resources, ruled that school officials were required to provide an appropriate education, not the best possible education. OSEP has stated that IEP teams may not make FAPE decisions solely on the basis of cost of services but must make decisions based on the individual needs of the child (*Greer*, 1992).

Similarly, a lack of funding cannot be used as a defense for choosing a less appropriate placement under Section 504. In a 1981 decision (*Bremen High School District*), the OCR stated that a Section 504 violation occurred when a school district refused to place a student in a residential facility based solely on cost.

Both the IDEA (IDEA Regulations, 34 C.F.R. § 300.301) and Section 504 (Section 504 Regulations, 34 C.F.R. § 104.33(c)) clearly indicate that the free service provision pertains only to the parents or guardians and does not relieve other governmental agencies, insurers, or third-party payers from valid obligations to pay for services. Title XIX of the Social Security Act, which established Medicare, was amended in 1988 to allow payment for covered services for eligible children and youth with disabilities, even if the services were incorporated into their special education programs (Social Security Act, 42 U.S.C. § 1396). Additionally, schools can often use private insurance companies as a funding source for costs related to a student's special education (Spaller & Thomas, 1994).

State Standards

The FAPE mandate of the IDEA includes the requirement that an appropriate education meet the standards of the state educational agency. This provision of FAPE acknowledges that providing an education to the citizens of a state is the responsibility of the state rather than the federal government. Provisions of the IDEA require states to submit state special education plans that assure qualified students with disabilities the right to a FAPE. These plans, at a minimum, have to meet the requirements set forth by the federal government. States, however, are free to impose more demanding standards than those contained in the IDEA. When a state standard is more demanding, that standard must be applied (Tucker & Goldstein, 1992). California, Massachusetts, Michigan, New Jersey, and North Carolina have FAPE standards considered by the courts to be more stringent than those of the federal government (Guernsey & Klare, 1993). Arkansas and Iowa had higher FAPE standards than the federal government in the IDEA, but the state legislatures amended the state statutes to bring them into line with the federal standards.

The state standards requirement of a FAPE also specifies that the education must meet any standards required by the state, including licensure and certification requirements for teachers (IDEA Regulations, 34 C.F.R. § 300.153). Any additional educational requirements enacted by state legislatures must also be followed.

The Individualized Education Program

A FAPE is realized through the development of an individualized education program. (See Chapter 9 for elaborations on the IEP.) The special education and related services a student receives are delineated in, and must be provided in conformity with, the student's IEP.

The school district in which the student resides is responsible for developing the IEP. Participants in the meeting must include, at a minimum, a representative of the public agency, the student's teacher, and the student's parents. Other individuals may be included at the request of the parent or school district. It is the task of this team to formulate the student's special education program. The IEP must include the following six components: (a) a statement of the student's present level of educational performance; (b) annual goals and short-term objectives; (c) a statement of the specific special education and related services required; (d) a statement of needed transition services; (e) the date the special education services will begin and the anticipated duration of these services; and (f) appropriate objective criteria and evaluation procedures.

The IEP does not guarantee that a student will achieve the goals, nor does it hold teachers or administrators liable if a student does not meet specified goals. The IEP, however, does commit the school to providing special education and related services and to making good faith efforts to achieve the goals. Additionally, if an IEP is designed to enable a student to achieve *meaningful* educational benefits, it is important that the goals be specific, sufficiently ambitious, and measurable.

Related Services

The provision of a FAPE requires special education and related services. Related services are defined in the IDEA as "supportive services . . . as may be required to assist a child with a disability to benefit from special education" (IDEA Regulations, 34 C.F.R. § 300.16(a)). (See Chapter 10 for elaborations on related services.) When related services are provided to a student with a disability, they must be included in the IEP and provided at no cost. The fact that a student has a disability under the definitions of the IDEA does not necessarily mean that the student is entitled to a specific related service (Guernsey & Klare, 1993). The school must provide the needed related service to students if the services are required to assist them to benefit from their education. Courts have ordered school districts to reimburse parents for the unilateral provision of related services when it has been determined that the service was necessary for educational benefit but was not provided by the school (*Max M. v. Illinois State Board of Education,* 1986; *Seals v. Loftis,* 1985).

Section 504 defines an appropriate education as "regular or special education and related aids or services . . . designed to meet individual education needs of handicapped persons as adequately as the needs of nonhandicapped persons are met" (Section 504 Regulations, 34 C.F.R. § 104.33(b)). The regulatory language indicates that Section 504 is broader than the IDEA regarding the aids and services it may require. Students with disabilities may be entitled to a related service under Section 504 even if they do not require a special education (*Elizabeth v. Gilhool,* 1987). The Section 504 language that mandates the provision of "related aids or services" seems to require the provision of equipment, whereas the language of the IDEA, which refers only to "related services," is less clear concerning equipment.

Litigation and FAPE

The lack of a substantive definition of FAPE in the IDEA has led to frequent disagreements between parents and schools regarding what constitutes an appropriate education for a particular student. State and federal courts, therefore, have often been required to define FAPE (Osborne, 1992).

Early court decisions set the standard of a FAPE as more than simple access to education but less than the best possible educational program (Osborne, 1992). In *Springdale School District v. Grace* (1981), the U.S. Court of Appeals for the Eighth Circuit held that FAPE did not require the state to provide the best education but instead required an appropriate education. The U.S. Court of Appeals for the Sixth Circuit, in *Age v. Bullitt County Public Schools* (1982), ruled that the existence of a better program did not make the school's proposed program inappropriate.

In 1982, a case from the U.S. Court of Appeals for the Second Circuit became the first special education case to be heard by the U.S. Supreme Court. In *Board of Education of the Hendrick Hudson School District v. Rowley* (hereafter *Rowley*), the high court considered the meaning of a FAPE.

Board of Education v. Rowley

Rowley was the Supreme Court's first opportunity to interpret the FAPE mandate. The case involved the education of Amy Rowley, a student at the Furnace Woods School in the Hendrick Hudson Central School District. Amy was deaf and was entitled to a FAPE under the IDEA. She had minimal residual hearing and was an excellent lip-reader. The year prior to Amy's attendance at Furnace Woods, a meeting was held between her parents and school officials to determine future placement and services. A decision was made to place Amy in the regular kindergarten class to determine what supplemental services she might need. Several school personnel learned sign language, and a teletype machine was placed in the school office to facilitate communication between Amy and her parents, who were also deaf. A sign language interpreter was also present in the classroom. Following a trial period in the kindergarten placement, a decision was made that Amy would remain in the class, with the school providing a hearing aid. Amy successfully completed her kindergarten year.

As required by law, an IEP was prepared for Amy prior to her entry into first grade. Her IEP provided for education in a general education classroom, continued use of the hearing aid, instruction from a tutor for deaf children for an hour daily, and speech therapy three hours a week. The Rowleys requested a qualified sign language interpreter in all of Amy's academic classes. Because Amy's kindergarten interpreter believed that Amy did not need the services at that time, the school officials concluded, after consulting with the school district's Committee on the Handicapped, that the interpreter was not necessary. The Rowleys requested a due process hearing. The hearing officer agreed with the school district, and the decision was affirmed on appeal by the New York Commissioner of Education. The Rowleys brought an action in federal district court, claiming that the district's refusal to provide a sign language interpreter denied Amy a FAPE.

The district court found Amy to be a well-adjusted child who was doing better than the average child. Nevertheless, the court ruled that Amy was not learning as much as she could without her handicap. The disparity between Amy's actual achievement and her potential convinced the district court that Amy had been denied a FAPE, which the court defined as "an opportunity to achieve [her] full potential commensurate with the opportunity provided to other children" (*Rowley*, p. 534). Moreover, because the requirements of a FAPE were unclear, the court stated that the responsibility for determining a FAPE had been left to the federal courts.

The U.S. Court of Appeals for the Second Circuit, in a divided decision, affirmed the lower court's ruling. The U.S. Supreme Court granted certiorari to the Board of Education's appeal. The high court considered two questions: What is a FAPE, and what is the role of state and federal courts in reviewing special education decisions?

Justice Rehnquist, writing for the majority, stated that a FAPE consisted of educational instruction designed to meet the unique needs of a student with disabilities, supported by such services as needed to permit the student to *benefit* from instruction. The court noted that the IDEA required that these educational services be provided at public expense, meet state standards, and comport with the student's IEP. Therefore, if individualized instruction allowed the child to benefit from educational services and was provided in conformity with the other requirements of the law, the student was receiving a FAPE. The court noted that any substantive standard prescribing the level of education to be accorded students with disabilities was conspicuously missing from the language of the IDEA.

Congress's primary objective in passing the law was to make public education available to students with disabilities. Therefore, "the intent of the Act was more to open the door of public education to handicapped children on appropriate terms than to guarantee any particular level of education once inside" (*Rowley*, p. 192). The Court disagreed with the Rowleys' contention that the goal of the IDEA was to provide each student with disabilities with an equal educational opportunity. The Court stated that the educational opportunities provided by our public school systems undoubtedly differ from student to student, depending upon a myriad of factors that might affect a particular student's ability to assimilate information presented in the classroom. The requirement that states provide "equal" educational opportunities would thus seem to present an entirely unworkable standard requiring impossible measurements and comparisons. Similarly, furnishing handicapped children with only such services as are available to non-handicapped children would in all probability fall short of the statutory requirement of "free appropriate public education"; to require, on the other hand, the furnishing of every special service necessary to maximize each handicapped child's potential is, we think, further than Congress intended to go. (pp. 198–199)

The high court, however, held that the education to which the IDEA provided access had to be "sufficient to confer some educational benefit upon the handicapped child" (p. 200). Therefore, the purpose of FAPE was to provide students with disabilities a "basic floor of opportunity" consisting of access to specialized instruction and related services individually designed to confer "educational benefit."

The *Rowley* Standard

The Supreme Court developed a two-part test to be used by courts in determining if a school has met its obligations under the IDEA to provide a FAPE. "First, has the [school] complied with the procedures of the Act? And second, is the individualized education program developed through the Act's procedures reasonably calculated to enable the child to receive educational benefits?" (*Rowley*, pp. 206–207). If these requirements were met, a school had complied with the requirements of a FAPE. The court cautioned the lower courts, however, that they were not establishing *any one test* for determining the adequacy of educational benefits.

Applying the two-part test to the *Rowley* case, the Supreme Court concluded that the circuit court had erred in affirming the decision of the district court. The school had complied with the procedures of the IDEA, and Amy had received an appropriate education because she was performing better than many children in her class and was advancing easily from grade to grade. In a footnote, the high court noted that the decision was a narrow one and that it should not be read too broadly. The Court stated that the ruling should not be interpreted to mean that every student with a disability who was advancing from grade to grade in a regular school was automatically receiving a FAPE. Rather, the FAPE standard can only be arrived at through a multifactorial evaluation conducted on a case-by-case basis. The high court also noted that in the case the sign language interpreter was not required to provide a FAPE to Amy Rowley. The decisions of the district and circuit court were reversed.

Regarding the role of the courts, Rehnquist wrote that

courts must be careful to avoid imposing their view of preferable educational methods upon the states. The primary responsibility for formulating the education to be accorded a handicapped child, and for choosing the educational method most suitable to the child's needs, was left by the Act to state and local educational agencies in cooperation with the parents or guardian of the child. (*Rowley*, p. 207)

In special education cases involving FAPE, therefore, the courts' role is (a) to determine if the procedural requirements are being met; (b) to examine the substantive requirements of FAPE; and (c) to determine if the special education is providing educational benefit. In making this determination, courts should not substitute their judgments for the judgments of educators, because courts lack the "specialized knowledge and experience necessary to resolve persistent and difficult questions of educational policy" (*San Antonio ISD v. Rodriquez*, 1973, p. 42).

The Supreme Court ruled that students with disabilities do not have an enforceable right to the best possible education or an education that allows them to achieve their maximum potential. Rather, they are entitled to an education that is reasonably calculated to confer educational benefit.

Post-*Rowley* Litigation

The first principle of the *Rowley* test establishes the importance of adherence to the procedural aspects of a FAPE. Clearly, a court could rule that a school district has denied a FAPE if the district has not adhered to the procedural safeguards in the IDEA. The second principle of the *Rowley* test is substantive. The principle requires courts to determine whether the IEP developed by the school is reasonably calculated to enable the child to receive educational benefits.

Procedural Violations of FAPE.   If a school fails to adhere to the required procedural mechanisms, and the failure results in harm to the student, the school could be found to be denying a FAPE on procedural grounds (Tucker & Goldstein, 1992). A number of post-*Rowley* decisions have ruled that based on procedural violations alone, schools had denied a FAPE. In *W.G. v. Board of Trustees* (1992), the U.S. Court of Appeals for the Ninth Circuit ruled that a school that had failed to include the classroom teacher or representative of a private school in developing an IEP had denied a FAPE to a student with disabilities. The court also noted, however, that procedural violations do not automatically require a finding of a denial of a FAPE. In *Tice v. Botetourt County School Board* (1990), the U.S. Court of Appeals for the Fourth Circuit ruled that a school had denied a FAPE because of a 6-month delay in evaluating a child and developing an IEP. Two decisions by the U.S. Court of Appeals for the Fourth Circuit also ruled that schools had denied students with disabilities a FAPE because of procedural violations. In *Spielberg v. Henrico County Public Schools* (1988), the school's determination to change a student's placement prior to developing an IEP violated the parents' right to participate in the development of the IEP and, therefore, violated the IDEA. In *Hall v. Vance County Board of Education* (1985), a school was found to have denied a FAPE because of its repeated failure to notify parents of their rights under IDEA.

A number of post-*Rowley* rulings, however, have held that technical violations of the IDEA, if they result in no harm to the student's education, do not warrant an adverse court ruling. For example, in *Doe v. Alabama Department of Education* (1990), the U.S. Court of Appeals for the Eleventh Circuit held that, because the parents had participated fully in the IEP process, a school's technical violation in failing to notify parents of their rights did not warrant relief. In *Doe v. Defendant 1* (1990), the U.S. Court of Appeals for the Sixth Circuit ruled that the failure of school officials to include a student's present level of educational performance and appropriate criteria for determining achievement of objectives did not invalidate the IEP when the parents were aware of this information. The school's procedural violations of inadequately notifying the parents of refusal to reimburse private tuition and failure to perform the 3-year evaluation in a timely manner were harmless errors because the parents had actual notice and their child's progress had not been harmed.

The crucial determinant in ruling a procedural violation a denial of FAPE is the degree of harm caused to the student's educational program. Procedural violations that have not caused significant difficulties in the delivery of a special education have not resulted in adverse court rulings.

Substantive Violations of FAPE.   The second principle of the *Rowley* test—the determination of whether the IEP was reasonably calculated to enable a student to receive educational benefits—has proven to be a more problematic determination than the first principle. Early post-*Rowley* rulings appeared to indicate that an IEP was appropriate if some educational benefit was obtained by a student (Osborne, 1992). In these early rulings, the courts seemingly regarded IEPs as appropriate if a school was able to show that the IEP was developed to provide some educational benefit, no matter how minimal it might be. Cases in which this line of judicial reasoning was followed include *Doe v. Lawson* (1984), *Karl v. Board of Education* (1984), and *Manual R. v. Ambach* (1986). Recent decisions, however, have indicated that minimal or trivial benefit may not be sufficient, and that special education services must confer meaningful benefit. The U.S. Court of Appeals for the Fourth Circuit, in *Hall v. Vance County Board of Education* (1985), held that the *Rowley* decision required courts to examine the IEP in order to determine what substantive standards meet the second principle of the *Rowley* test. Additionally, the court cited *Rowley* as stating that this could only be accomplished on a case-by-case basis. The appeals court affirmed the district court's ruling that because the plaintiff, who had a learning disability, had made no educational progress in the public school, and because the IEP was inadequate, the school district had to reimburse the parents for private school tuition. The court noted that Congress did not intend that schools offer educational programs that produce only trivial academic advancement.

The U.S. Court of Appeals for the Third Circuit provided a thorough discussion of *Rowley* and the IDEA's requirement to provide a "meaningful" education in *Polk v. Central Susquehanna Intermediate Unit 16* (1988). In the decision, the court noted that because *Rowley* involved a student who did very well in the general education class, the high court was able to avoid the substantive second principle of the *Rowley* test and concentrate on the procedural principle. In this case, however, the substantive question of how much benefit was required to meet the "meaningful" standard in educating the plaintiff, Christopher Polk, was inescapable.

Christopher Polk was a fourteen-year-old with severe mental and physical disabilities. The severity of his disabilities necessitated physical therapy, but the school's IEP provided only consultative services of a physical therapist. Christopher's parents brought action under the IDEA (then the EAHCA), claiming that the school had failed to provide an appropriate education. A federal district court held for the school district, finding that the *Rowley* standard held that the conferral of any degree of educational benefit, no matter how small, could qualify as an appropriate education. The circuit court reversed the district court, declaring that "just as Congress did not write a blank check, neither did it anticipate that states would engage in the idle gesture of providing special education designed to confer only trivial benefit. . . . Congress intended to afford children with special needs an education that would confer meaningful benefit" (*Polk*, p. 184). The court also stated that the type of education which constitutes a meaningful education can only be determined in the light of a student's potential. Courts in *Board of Education v. Diamond* (1986), *Doe v. Smith* (1988), and *Hall v. Vance County Board of Education* (1985) all reached a similar conclusion.

In *Carter v. Florence County School District Four* (1991), the U.S. Court of Appeals for the Fourth Circuit affirmed a district court's ruling that the school district's IEP had failed to satisfy the FAPE requirement of the IDEA. The IEP, which contained annual reading goals of 4 months' growth over a school year, did not, according to the district and circuit courts, represent meaningful growth, even if the goals were achieved. The case was later heard by the U.S. Supreme Court on a different issue. In *J.C. v. Central Regional School District* (1996), the U.S. Court of Appeals for the Third Circuit ruled that school districts must provide more than a de minimus or trivial education, and that districts are responsible for the adequacy of the IEP. In this case, the IEP developed for a student with severe disabilities failed to address important educational needs. Furthermore, the student had made little progress in the current program and had actually regressed in some areas.

The courts have not provided a precise definition to follow when determining whether the education offered is meaningful or trivial. This lack of precision appears appropriate because what constitutes a meaningful education to particular students can only be ascertained on a case-by-case basis. There can be no bright line formula (i.e, no clear standard) that will apply to all students. It is clear that courts, when determining if the substantive requirements of a FAPE have been met, will look to the school's IEP to determine if a meaningful education designed to confer benefit has been provided.

Methodology

In a few cases, courts have addressed the question of the school's choice of teaching methodologies in regards to FAPE. The plaintiffs in three cases—*Boughham v. Town of Yarmouth* (1993; hereafter *Boughham*), *Lachman v. Illinois State Board of Education* (1988; hereafter *Lachman*), and *Peterson v. Hastings Public Schools* (1993; hereafter *Peterson*)—brought actions against school districts, alleging a denial of a FAPE because the school districts had chosen particular educational methodologies not favored by the parents. The school districts prevailed in all three cases. The court in the *Lachman* decision stated that parents have no power under the IDEA to compel schools to choose a particular methodology over another.

Similarly, the court in *Peterson* held that in a methodology case the court would still only review the second principle of the *Rowley* test. The court stated that if the IEP developed by the school is reasonably calculated to provide educational benefits to the student, the courts can require no more. Finally, the *Boughham* court, in holding for the school district, cited the Supreme Court's admonition in *Rowley* that courts should not get involved in making decisions about educational theory and methodology and should take care to avoid imposing their view of preferential educational methods.

A federal district court in California, in *Adams v. Hansen* (1985; hereafter *Adams*), found that the plaintiff, a student with "dyslexia," had shown little progress in a public school program. The court found that the child had progressed 4 months in total reading achievement and 8 months in math achievement in 2 years of public school instruction. Consequently, the student's mother had placed him in a private school. Finding that the student did not make sufficient academic progress in his 2 years in public school, but did so in the private school, the court ruled that the mother was entitled to reimbursement from the school district for tuition and travel expenses. According to Huefner (1991), the court could have ended its analysis at this point. The court, however, went on to consider the educational methodology offered in the private school as opposed to the public school's educational methods. The court was impressed by testimony that the student had a "specific language disability [involving] all three learning modalities—auditory, visual, and sensory-motor" (*Adams*, p. 863)—but no relative strengths and weakness in all three modalities. Because of this "lack of relative strength" the court stated that the student needed an intensive "structured sequential simultaneous multi-sensory approach" (p. 864) that could not be provided in the public school. The *Adams* case, which was not appealed, seemingly went beyond the scope of judicial review as set forth in *Rowley*.

In *Wall v. Mattituck-Cutchogue School District* (1996), the parents of an elementary student with learning disabilities brought an action against a school district in New York. The parents wanted their child taught reading using the Orton-Gillingham instructional procedure. The student, who was educated in a public school's self-contained special education classroom, was unilaterally placed in a private school that used the reading procedure. At a hearing, the parents did not challenge the appropriateness of the IEP; rather, they contested the school district's failure to offer the Orton-Gillingham program. The hearing officer found that the school district's program was appropriate. The parents appealed to federal district court. The court, finding that the student had made progress in the school district's program, affirmed the ruling for the school district.

The cases reviewed seem to offer little encouragement to plaintiffs seeking to have the courts require schools to use favored educational procedures or methodologies. As held by the Supreme Court in *Rowley*, "once a court determines that the requirements of the [IDEA] have been met, questions of methodology are thus left for resolution by the states" (p. 207). The *Adams* case, however, indicates that courts may find it difficult to ignore comparisons between a public school's methodology and one used in a private school if only the latter results in significant progress.

Huefner (1991) contended that in such situations, if a student was making meaningful progress in the public school's program, the courts would uphold the placement even if it had been less effective than the alternative placement. Huefner's contention has proven prescient in a number of recent decisions involving a treatment for children with autism developed by Dr. O. Ivar Lovaas.

FAPE and Lovaas Treatment

The Lovaas treatment cases have been brought by parents of children with autism to obtain reimbursement for individual programs using Lovaas methods. Lovaas views autism as a constellation of behavioral deficits and excesses and has developed highly structured lessons to be taught in one-to-one training formats to children with autism by trained therapists. The system, based on the principles of applied behavior analysis, is an intensive program that focuses on changing a child's individual behavior excesses and deficits. Lovaas training is targeted toward preschoolers, preferably younger than 3, and can take as long as 2 or 3 years. It requires 40 hours per week of intensive one-to-one work with the child and usually is initially conducted in the child's home. Lovaas treatment is very expensive, generally ranging from $12,000 to $20,000 a year. In recent years many school districts have been confronted by parental demands to provide Lovaas treatment or to reimburse parents for their expenses in securing the therapy (Mandlawitz, 1996). A number of these cases have reached the due process level, and a few have been decided in the courts.

Administrative rulings by the state educational agencies (SEAs) of Maryland (*Frederick County Public Schools,* 1995), Connecticut (*In re Child with Disabilities,* 1995), and North Carolina (*Sherman v. Pitt County Board of Education,* 1995) awarded reimbursement for parents who had provided Lovaas programming in their homes. In all three cases the schools were found to have offered inappropriate programming, while the Lovaas educational programming was held to be appropriate.

In *Delaware County Intermediate Unit #25 v. Martin and Melinda K.* (1993), a federal district court ruled that a school-provided program for children with autism was inappropriate. The school had offered a 10-hour-a-week program based on the principles of the TEACCH method of educating students with autism, developed at the University of North Carolina by Dr. Eric Shopler. According to the court, the school district's program was inappropriate because it offered only 10 hours per week of TEACCH therapy, even though the program developers recommended 30 hours per week. The court also found that the Lovaas program was appropriate, and ordered that the school reimburse the parents for program costs and expenditures and pay for an additional year of the Lovaas program. The court noted that if the school district had increased the TEACCH program's intensity to recommended levels and provided a mainstreaming component to the program, the court would have been faced with a battle between the TEACCH and Lovaas programs, "a contest between two teaching methodologies, either of which would be appropriate under the IDEA. At that point, the Court will yield to the educational agency" (p. 1212).

In *Union City School District v. Smith* (1994), the U.S. Court of Appeals for the Ninth Circuit upheld a lower court ruling that the Union City School District had failed to provide a FAPE to a child with autism. The school district had placed the child in a classroom for students with communications disabilities with supplemental behavioral therapy counseling, even though the district had a program for children with autism. The parents removed their child from the public school program and placed him in a program at Lovaas's clinic at the University of California at Los Angeles. The court awarded the parents reimbursement for tuition and travel expenses. In its decision, the appellate court noted that had the school offered an appropriate special education in the program for autistic youngsters, the parents would not have won reimbursement.

A federal district court in New York awarded the parents of a child with autism reimbursement for 40 hours a week of Lovaas training weekly in *Malkentzos v. DeBuono* (1996). The case involved a 3-year-old child with autism. The New York Department of Health (DOH) had written an individualized family services plan (IFSP) that provided the child with 23 hours of structured play activities without a behavioral therapy component. The child's parents requested that the IFSP be revised to include 40 hours of weekly Lovaas programming. The DOH denied the request, stating that there was a lack of certified behavioral therapists. The parents provided the programming at their own expense and requested a due process hearing to challenge the appropriateness of the IFSP. The hearing officer ruled in favor of the DOH, stating that there was a shortage of qualified personnel to provide additional behavioral programming. The federal district court reversed the hearing officer's decision, holding that the New York DOH had failed to provide a FAPE under the IDEA. The court awarded the parents reimbursement for the amount expended in providing the Lovaas treatment and ordered the state to either fund continued training for 40 hours per week or reimburse the parents for securing the programming. Noting that the IDEA did not require that the DOH provide any particular program, provide the best possible program, or maximize the potential of the child, the court held that the IFSP had not adequately addressed the plaintiff's autism and was, therefore, inappropriate. The court found that the parents had provided convincing evidence that the DOH program was not reasonably calculated to provide educational benefit and that the child might have suffered imminent damage under the plan. The court also cited the Supreme Court's decision in *Florence County School District Four v. Carter* (1993) in holding that the parents were not required, as a prerequisite to being reimbursed, to employ certified therapists for the Lovaas programming. The case was appealed to the U.S. Court of Appeals for the Second Circuit. The circuit court held that the district court's order of reimbursement for the private therapy and prospective relief were improper. Because the child had aged out from Part H and was no longer eligible for services, the court declared the claim moot. That is, the case was legally insignificant because the court's decision would no longer have any practical effect on the controversy.

This decision is especially notable in that it was one of the first lawsuits brought under Part H (now Part C) of the IDEA. The court's decision in favor of the plaintiff seemingly indicated that a state's obligation to children with disabilities under Part H of the IDEA is the same as the obligation under Part B—that is, to provide free and appropriate programming to children with disabilities based on an individualized evaluation of their needs. The circuit court decision also demonstrated a problem with Part H (restructured as Part C in the IDEA Amendments of 1997). Because Part H covers such a short span in a child's life, by the time a case is litigated a child will often have aged out and no longer be eligible for services. In such situations, courts will declare such claims moot.

In an SEA decision, an administrative law judge determined that a school district's educational program for a student with autism was inappropriate and ordered the district to reimburse the parents for a program of home-based Lovaas therapy and rewrite the student's IEP (*Independent School District No. 318*, 1996). The district's program consisted of 8 hours per week of instruction in a classroom with a low student-teacher ratio, speech and language therapy, and occupational therapy. The home-based program consisted of 35 hours per week of Lovaas programming. The school district incorporated aspects of the Lovaas program in the school program and agreed to teach the student sign language. Additionally, the student was placed in a general education kindergarten with a full-time aide. The district, however, refused to have its teachers and staff trained in the Lovaas method and incorporate the method into the student's educational program, as the parents requested. The parents requested a due process hearing and reimbursement for the Lovaas programming. The hearing officer ruled for the parents. The hearing officer determined that the school's IEP was not appropriate because it failed to provide any educational benefit. The parents' home-based program, however, was appropriate. The ruling, in addition to requiring that the parents be reimbursed for the cost of Lovaas training, ordered the school to have the aide trained in the Lovaas method, and also ordered that the IEP be rewritten to include Lovaas programming, monthly consultation with Lovaas consultants, computer training, and extended school year services.

Despite the fact that the Lovaas programming prevailed in the decisions reviewed, the three courts noted that it was because the Lovaas programs were appropriate while the schools' and DOH's programming were inappropriate. The states' programming in the cases was found to be inappropriate because of the lack of intensity, the focus of the programs offered, and the lack of individualization. Additionally, there have been a number of decisions by SEAs to deny parents reimbursement for Lovaas programming when the school had offered appropriate programming, indicating that in contests of two appropriate programs, the SEA will prevail (*Central Susquehanna Intermediate Unit 16*, 1995; *Chester County Intermediate Unit 23*, 1995; *Fairfax County Public Schools*, 1995; *Tuscaloosa County Board of Education*, 1994). The SEA decision that ordered reimbursement for the Lovaas training also found the school district's programming inappropriate (*Independent School District No. 318*, 1996).

The case law on this issue is clear: as long as the school offers an appropriate program, the choice of educational methodology is up to the school district. In situations involving Lovaas therapy, however, the rulings indicate that when a school district's programming does not show results and is compared with the Lovaas method, which does collect evidence of progress, it is likely that judges will favor the Lovaas programming. To prevail in such situations, school districts need to provide a FAPE that results in meaningful educational benefit, and must have evaluation data to show that a student is progressing in the programming.

Extended School Year

Neither the IDEA nor regulations implementing the law specifically address the provision of special education programs that extend beyond the traditional school year of approximately 180 school days. Parents and advocates have contended, however, that extended breaks in educational programming can result in severe regression of skills and subsequent failure to recoup lost skills within a reasonable period of time. When lost skills are in areas necessary to self-sufficiency, extended school year (ESY) services may be needed to provide a FAPE. ESY services are only required when the lack of such a program will result in denial of a FAPE. ESY is not, therefore, required for all students with disabilities. When these services are provided to students with disabilities, there must be no cost to the parents. Additionally, ESY services must be offered, when necessary, even if the school district does not ordinarily provide summer school programming or other educational services outside of the regular school year (Gorn, 1996). The determination of whether a student with disabilities must be provided with ESY programming must be made on an individual basis.

Because the law and regulations are silent on ESY, courts have been called on to address the issue. The courts have clearly stated that if ESY services are required to ensure the provision of a FAPE, they must be provided (*Alamo Heights Independent School District v. State Board of Education,* 1986; *Cordrey v. Euckert,* 1990). SEA and local educational agency (LEA) policies that provide only the traditional number of school days have consistently been struck down by the courts (e.g., *Alamo Heights ISD v. Board of Education,* 1986; *Armstrong v. Kline,* 1979; *Bales v. Clark,* 1981; *Battle v. Commonwealth of Pennsylvania,* 1980; *Cordrey v. Euckert,* 1990; *Crawford v. Pittman,* 1983; *Georgia ARC v. McDaniel,* 1983; *Johnson v. Independent School District No. 4,* 1990; *Yaris v. Special School District of St. Louis County,* 1984). These policies have been overturned because the inflexibility of the traditional school year prohibits consideration of the rights of students to an individualized education or because the ESY services were determined to be necessary for students to receive a FAPE.

Many courts have based their decisions on the regression/recoupment problem (Boomer & Garrison-Harrell, 1995; Osborne, 1995; Tucker & Goldstein, 1992). In these cases, the students had regressed to such a degree on important skills during an extended break in educational programming that it took an inordinate amount of time to recoup the lost skills. Therefore, the student requires an ESY program to avoid the regression/recoupment problem. Courts have held that regression may be in a number of areas, including academics, emotional or behavioral status, physical skills, self-help skills, or communication (*Cremeans v. Fairland Local School District,*

1993; *Holmes v. Sobol,* 1991; *Johnson v. Lancaster-Lebanon Intermediate Unit 13,* 1991). Additionally, very young children (i.e., birth to 3 years of age), covered under Part H, must also receive ESY services if needed to provide a FAPE.

In the ESY cases, school districts have not been ordered to provide ESY services because students would benefit from such services but because they would be harmed by an interruption of special education services. It is important, however, that school districts be flexible in making ESY decisions and not rely solely on regression/recoupment considerations (Gorn, 1996). That is, criteria for determining extended school year should take into account individual factors and particular circumstances that may merit inclusion in an ESY program in addition to regression/recoupment.

In *Johnson v. Independent School District No. 4* (1990), the U.S. Court of Appeals for the Tenth Circuit gave some direction to school districts in making ESY determinations. According to the court, factors involved in determining if ESY is necessary to provide a FAPE may include the degree of impairment, the ability of parents to provide educational structure in the home, the availability of resources, whether the program is extraordinary as opposed to necessary, the student's skill level, and areas of the curriculum in which the child needed continuous attention. The court also noted that in using the regression/recoupment analysis, schools "should proceed by applying not only retrospective data, such as past regression and rate of recoupment, but also include predictive data, based on the opinion of professionals in consultation with the child's parents" (p. 1028).

Students who are determined to have disabilities under Section 504 but not under the IDEA must also be provided ESY services if it is a necessary element to a FAPE. A number of OCR rulings have indicated that ESY programming can be required under Section 504 (*Baltimore (MD) City Public Schools,* 1986; *Clark City (NV) School District,* 1989).

Katsiyannis (1991) recommends that SEAs and schools develop ESY policies. Included in his recommendations for developing ESY policies are the following: (a) clearly define the ESY program and objectives; (b) develop eligibility criteria; (c) generate a systematic referral process; and (d) construct a detailed plan for monitoring and data collection. He also suggests that LEAs provide in-service training on ESY programming for all administrators and teachers.

Placement Decisions and FAPE

One of the critical determinations in providing a FAPE to students with disabilities is placement, which refers to the setting in which a FAPE will be delivered. Prior to consideration of placement, students must have been evaluated and the IEP developed. The IDEA Amendments of 1997 require that placement decisions be made by the IEP team. Additionally, school districts must ensure that parents take part in all placement decisions. The IEP is often developed and the placement determined in the same team meeting; however, the IEP and the placement decision are actually two separate components of the special education decision-making process. The IEP delineates the special education and related services that will be provided, and the placement decision determines where these services will be delivered. Students' placements cannot be determined prior to writing their IEPs, since it is only after the IEP has been written that a team has a basis for determining where a particular student's needs can be met (Gorn, 1996). In *Spielberg v. Henrico County Public Schools* (1988), a decision to place a student prior to developing the IEP was held to be a violation of the IDEA.

Information for Determining FAPE

In determining the placement of students, schools must draw on a variety of informational sources, including aptitude and achievement tests, teacher recommendations, physical condition, social or cultural background, and adaptive behavior (IDEA Regulations, 34 C.F.R. § 300.533(a)(1)). Additionally, this information must be documented (IDEA Regulations, 34 C.F.R. § 300.533(a)(2)). According to OSEP, no single factor should dominate decision making regarding placement; rather, all factors are to be considered equally (OSEP Policy Letter, 1994).

Parental preference as to their child's placement is an important consideration in the decision, but according to the Office of Special Education and Related Services, it is not the most important factor (Burton, 1991). However, the U.S. Court of Appeals for the Seventh Circuit, in *Board of Education of Community Consolidated School District No. 21 v. Illinois State Board of Education* (1991), held that a court may consider parental hostility as a factor in making placement decisions. In this case the parents had objected with such hostility to the school's proposed placement that the court found that the proposed placement had been undermined. The lower court had held that the parents of a student with behavioral disorders had essentially "poisoned" the proposed placement in the mind of the youngster, thereby assuring failure in that setting. The court, therefore, ruled that the school district would be violating the IDEA by implementing a program that would not benefit the student. The appellate court affirmed the lower court's decision in a 2 to 1 ruling. The circuit court applied the *Rowley* test to the case. The court stated that the school had met the procedural principle but had not provided a FAPE because by not considering the negative effects of parental hostility, the school had failed to propose an education reasonably calculated to benefit the student. The dissenting judge stated that parental hostility to the proposed placement was not an appropriate factor to consider in applying the *Rowley* test and that the school district had fully satisfied the requirements of the *Rowley* test. According to the dissent, there was not the slightest evidence that the school district's proposed placement would not have provided educational benefit; further, the lower court's decision had improperly surrendered the school's educational authority to the parents. The decision was appealed to the U.S. Supreme Court, which decided not to hear the case. Although this decision was met with fears that the circuit court had given parents the absolute right to dictate the educational program for their child, Zirkel (1992) contends that the majority decision may not spread widely beyond the Seventh Circuit.

According to Zirkel, the dissent was strong and may be viewed as the correct decision by many, and the majority decision held that parental hostility was a factor to consider, but not the only factor.

Requirements in Determining Placement

There are essentially three requirements that the school must meet in determining placement:

1. The placement must be based on the student's IEP (IDEA Regulations, 34 C.F.R. § 300.552(a)(2)). The placement is designed to be the most appropriate setting in which the student's required special education and related services can be delivered.

2. The educational placement must be determined at least annually (IDEA Regulations, 34 C.F.R. § 300.552(a)(1)).

3. The placement must be in conformity with the least restrictive environment (LRE) rules (IDEA Regulations, 34 C.F.R. § 300.533(a)(4)). The LRE rules require that the student be educated to the maximum extent appropriate with students without disabilities and that removal of the student from the general education environment occurs only when education in general education classes with the use of supplementary aids and services cannot be achieved satisfactorily (IDEA Regulations, 34 C.F.R. § 300.550). To ensure that the LRE mandate is met, school districts are required to ensure the availability of a continuum of alternative placements from which to choose the LRE (IDEA Regulations, 34 C.F.R. § 300.551).

In addition, the placement should be as close to home as possible. Unless otherwise indicated in the IEP, students should be placed in schools they would be attending if they did not have a disability. This is not an absolute right so much as it is a preference. If placements in home schools will not provide a FAPE, schools may place students in more distant schools (*Hudson v. Bloomfield Hills School District*, 1995).

The FAPE and LRE requirements of the IDEA are interrelated. LRE refers to the relative restrictiveness of the setting in which students with disabilities are educated. The preferred environment is as close to the general education environment as is appropriate. Depending on what special education services an IEP team determines to be required for students to receive a FAPE, however, the LRE may be a more restrictive setting than the general education classroom. For example, a team could decide that a special school is the least restrictive and appropriate placement for a student. (See Chapter 12 for elaborations on the LRE requirements.)

Schools cannot unilaterally change students' placements. Placement decisions must be based on an existing IEP, so any change of placement must be supported either by that IEP or by a new, written IEP (Guernsey & Klare, 1993). If the school determines that a change in placement is necessary, the parents must be notified (IDEA Regulations, 34 C.F.R. § 300.504(a)(1)).

Summary

A free appropriate public education consists of special education and related services, provided at public expense, that meet the standards of the state educational agency and are provided in conformity with the IEP. The U.S. Supreme Court, in *Rowley* (1982), ruled that a FAPE does not require that schools maximize the potential of students with disabilities. Rather, a FAPE is a specially designed program that meets the individual needs of students and allows them to receive educational benefit. The Supreme Court provided lower courts with a two-part test for determining a school's compliance with the FAPE mandate. First, the court must determine whether the school has complied with the procedures of the Act. Second, the court will examine the IEP to ascertain if the IEP was reasonably calculated to enable the child to receive educational benefits. If these requirements are met, a school has complied with the requirements of a FAPE. Subsequent lower court rulings indicate that the schools must offer a meaningful level of educational benefits. According to the *Rowley* decision, courts are to give deference to educational determinations made by school officials. Educational procedures and methodology, therefore, are the responsibility of the schools. It is the responsibility of the courts to determine compliance with the IDEA.

FAPE is realized through the development of an IEP. In determining the special education and related services to be provided to students, a knowledgeable group of persons, which must include a representative of the school, the student's teacher, and the parents of the child, formulate the IEP. The IEP delineates the special education and related services to be provided by the school. Once the IEP has been developed, decisions concerning students placements are made. Placement decisions must be in conformity with the LRE rules of the IDEA, which require placements in general education settings when appropriate.

The courts have consistently struck down policies that do not consider students' individual needs when making educational programming decisions. An example of such policies are those which provide for school year lengths of only 180 days. If an IEP team determines that an extended school year is needed to provide a FAPE to a student, the school must make the services available.

For Further Information

Huefner, D. S. (1991). Judicial review of the special educational program requirements under the Education for All Handicapped Children Act: Where have we been and where should we be going? *Harvard Journal of Law and Public Policy, 14,* 483–516.

Katsiyannis, A. (1991). Extended school year: An established necessity. *Remedial and Special Education, 12,* 24–28.

O'Hara, J. (1985). Determinants of an appropriate education under P.L. 94-142. *Education Law Reporter, 27,* 1037–1045.

Osborne, A. G. (1992). Legal standards for an appropriate education in the post-*Rowley* era. *Exceptional Children, 58,* 488–494.

References

A.W. v. Northwest R-1 School District, 813 F.2d 158 (8th Cir. 1987).

Adams v. Hanson, 632 F. Supp. 858 (N.D. Cal. 1985).

Age v. Bullitt County Public Schools, 701 F.2d 233 (1st Cir. 1982).

Alamo Heights Independent School District v. State Board of Education, 790 F.2d 1153 (5th Cir. 1986).

Armstrong v. Kline, 476 F. Supp. 583 (E.D. Pa. 1979), aff'd. in part and remanded sub nom. Battle v. Commonwealth of Pennsylvania, 629 F.2d 269 (3rd Cir. 1980), cert. den. Scanlon v. Battle, 452 U.S. 968 (1980), further decision, 513 F. Supp. 425 (E.D. Pa. 1980).

Bales v. Clark, 523 F. Supp. 1366 (E.D. Va. 1981).

Baltimore (MD) City Public Schools, EHLR 311: 42 (OCR 1986).

Battle v. Commonwealth of Pennsylvania, 629 F.2d 269 (3rd Cir. 1980).

Board of Education of Community Consolidated School District No. 21 v. Illinois State Board of Education, 938 F.2d 712 (7th Cir. 1991).

Board of Education of the Hendrick Hudson School District v. Rowley, 458 U.S. 176 (1982).

Board of Education v. Diamond, 808 F.2d 987 (3rd Cir. 1986).

Boomer, L. W., & Garrison-Harrell, L. (1995). Legal issues concerning children with autism and pervasive developmental disorder. *Behavioral Disorder, 21,* 53–61.

Boughham v. Town of Yarmouth, 20 IDELR 12 (1993).

Bremen High School District No. 228, 257 EHLR 195 (OCR 1981).

Burton, Letter to, 17 EHLR 1182 (OSERS 1991).

Carter v. Florence County School District, 950 F.2d 156 (4th Cir. 1991).

Central Susquehanna Intermediate Unit 16, 2 ECLPR 109 (SEA PA 1995).

Chester County Intermediate Unit 23, 23 IDELR 723 (SEA PA 1995).

Clark City (NV) School District, 16 EHLR 311 (OCR 1989).

Clevenger v. Oak Ridge School Board, 744 F.2d 514 (6th Cir. 1984).

Cordrey v. Euckert, 917 F.2d 1460 (6th Cir. 1990).

Crawford v. Pittman, 708 F.2d 1028 (5th Cir. 1983).

Cremeans v. Fairland Local School District, 633 N.E. 2d 570 (OH App. 1993).

Delaware County Intermediate Unit #25 v. Martin and Melinda K., 831 F. Supp. 1206 (E.D. Pa. 1993).

Department of Education, State of Hawaii v. Katherine D., 531 F. Supp. 517 (D. Hawaii 1982), aff'd. 727 F.2d 809 (9th Cir. 1984).

Doe v. Alabama Department of Education, 915 F.2d 651 (11th Cir. 1990).

Doe v. Brookline School Committee, 1983, 722 F.2d 910 (1st Cir. 1983).

Doe v. Defendant 1, 898 F.2d 1186 (6th Cir. 1990).

Doe v. Lawson, 579 F. Supp. 1314 (D. Mass. 1984), aff'd. 745 F.2d 43 (1st Cir. 1984).

Doe v. Smith, EHLR 559:391 (N.D. Tenn. 1988).

Elizabeth v. Gilhool, 558 EHLR 461 (N.D. PA 1987).

Fairfax County Public Schools, 22 IDELR 80 (SEA VA 1995).

Florence County School District Four v. Carter, 114 S.Ct. 361 (1993).

Frederick County Public Schools, 2 ECLPR 145 (SEA MD 1995).

Georgia ARC v. McDaniel, 511 F. Supp. 1263 (N.D. Ga. 1981), aff'd. 716 F.2d 1565 (11th Cir. 1983), 740 F.2d 902 (11th Cir. 1984).

Gorn, S. (1996). *What do I do when . . . The answer book on special education law.* Horsham, PA: LRP Publications.

Greer, Letter to, 19 IDELR 348 (OSEP, 1992).

Guernsey, T. F., & Klare, K. (1993). *Special education law.* Durham, NC: Carolina Academic Press.

Hall v. Vance County Board of Education, 774 F.2d 629 (4th Cir. 1985).

Holmes v. Sobol, 18 IDELR 53 (W.D.N.Y. 1991).

Hudson v. Bloomfield Hills School District, 23 IDELR 612 (E.D. Mich. 1995).

Huefner, D. S. (1991). Judicial review of the special educational program requirements under the Education for All Handicapped Children Act: Where have we been and where should we be going? *Harvard Journal of Law and Public Policy, 14,* 483–516.

Independent School District No. 318, 24 IDELR 1096 (SEA MN 1996).

Individuals with Disabilities Education Act, 20 U.S.C. § 1400 *et seq.*

Individuals with Disabilities Education Act Regulations, 34 C.F.R. § 300.533 *et seq.*

In re Child with Disabilities, 23 IDELR 471 (SEA CT 1995).

J.C. v. Central Regional School District, 23 IDELR 1181 (3rd Cir. 1996).

Johnson v. Independent School District No. 4, 921 F.2d 1022 (10th Cir. 1990).

Johnson v. Lancaster-Lebanon Intermediate Unit 13, 757 F. Supp. 606 (E.D. Pa. 1991).

Karl v. Board of Education, 736 F.2d 873 (2nd Cir. 1984).

Katsiyannis, A., (1991). Extended school year policies: An established necessity. *Remedial and Special Education, 12,* 24–28.

Lachman v. Illinois State Board of Education, 852 F.2d 290 (7th Cir. 1988).

Lunenberg School District, 22 IDELR 290 (SEA VT 1994).

Malkentzos v. DeBuono, 923 F. Supp. 505 (S.D.N.Y. 1996).

Mandlawitz, M. (1996). Lovaas, TEACCH, and the public system: The court as referee. *Proceedings of the 17th National Institute on Legal Issues of Educating Individuals with Disabilities.* Alexandria, VA: LRP Publications Conference Division.

Manual R. v. Ambach, 635 F. Supp. 791 (E.D. N.Y. 1986).

Max M. v. Illinois State Board of Education, 684 F. Supp. 514 (N.D. Ill. 1986).

Osborne, A. G. (1992). Legal standards for an appropriate education in the post-Rowley era. *Exceptional Children, 58,* 488–494.

Osborne, A. G. (1995). When must a school district provide an extended school year program to students with disabilities? *Education Law Reporter, 99,* 1–9.

OSEP Policy Letter, 20 IDELR 1155 (OSEP, 1992).

OSEP Policy Letter, 21 IDELR 674 (OSEP, 1994).

Peterson v. Hastings Public Schools, 831 F. Supp. 742 (D. Neb. 1993).

Polk v. Central Susquehanna Intermediate Unit 16 (1988). No. 16, 853 F.2d 171 (3rd Cir. 1988).

San Antonio ISD v. Rodriquez, 411 U.S. 1 (1973).

Schuldt v. Mankato Independent School District, 1991, 937 F.2d 1357 (8th Cir. 1991).

Seals v. Loftis, 1985, 614 F. Supp. 302 (E.D. Tenn. 1985).

Section 504 Regulations, 34 C.F.R. § 104.33(a).

Sherman v. Pitt County Board of Education, 93 EDC 1617 (SEA NC 1995).

Social Security Act, 42 U.S.C. § 1396.

Spaller, K. D., & Thomas, S. B. (1994). A timely idea: Third party billing for related services. *Education Law Reporter, 86,* 581–592.

Spielberg v. Henrico County Public Schools (1988), EHLR 558:202 (E.D. Va. 1987).

Springdale School District v. Grace (1981), 494 F. Supp. 266 (W.D. Ark. 1980), aff'd., 656 F.2d 300, vacated, 73 L.Ed. 2d 1380, 102 S.Ct. 3504 (1982), on remand, 693 F.2d 41 (8th Cir. 1982), cert. den. 461 U.S. 927 (1983).

Tice v. Botetourt, 908 F.2d 1200 (4th Cir. 1990).

Tucker, B. P., & Goldstein, B. A. (1992). *Legal rights of persons with disabilities: An analysis of public law.* Horsham, PA: LRP Publications.

Tuscaloosa County Board of Education, 21 IDELR 826 (SEA AL 1994).

Union City School District v. Smith, 15 F.3d 1519 (9th Cir. 1994).

W.G. v. Board of Trustees of Target Range School District No. 23, 960 F.2d 1479 (9th Cir. 1992).

Wall v. Mattituck-Cutchogue School District, 24 IDELR 1162 (E.D.N.Y. 1996).

Waltham (MA) Public Schools, 20 IDELR 37 (OCR 1993).

Yaris v. Special School District of St. Louis County, 1984, 661 F. Supp. 996 (E.D. Mo. 1986).

Zirkel, P. A. (1992). A special education case of parental hostility. *Education Law Reporter, 73,* 1–10.

CHAPTER NINE

The Individualized Education Program

The importance of the IEP [should not] be understated . . . [it is] the fundamental prerequisite of any FAPE.

Justice Huntley, *Thorndock v. Boise Independent School District* (1988, p. 1246)

The individualized education program (IEP) is the centerpiece of the Individuals with Disabilities Education Act (IDEA) (*Honig v. Doe,* 1988). All aspects of the student's special education program are directed by the IEP and monitored throughout the IEP process (Smith, 1990). The goals and objectives of the student's program, as well as the educational placement, the length of the school year, and evaluation and measurement criteria that are developed in the IEP process, are contained in the document. It is this process that formalizes the free appropriate public education (FAPE) for a student with disabilities. The IEP is so important that the failure to properly develop and implement it may render a student's entire special education program invalid in the eyes of the courts (Horsnell & Kitch, 1996).

Purposes of the IEP

The development of the IEP is a collaborative effort between school personnel and parents to ensure that students' special education programs will meet their individual needs. The IEP also serves a number of other important purposes, including communication, management, accountability, compliance and monitoring, and evaluation (IDEA Regulations, 34 C.F.R. § 300 Appendix C:1).

Communication

The IEP meeting is a communication vehicle between parents and school personnel, who are equal participants in IEP planning. The process is an opportunity for collaboration in planning the student's education as well as a method for resolving any differences that may arise regarding the student's educational needs. If differences cannot be resolved at the IEP meeting, procedural safeguards are available to either party. (See Chapter 13 for elaborations on procedural safeguards.)

Management

The IEP is a management tool that sets forth the resources that the IEP team determines are necessary for the student to receive an appropriate education. The IEP is a written commitment delineating the special education and related services that will be provided by the school.

Accountability

The IEP is a legally constituted mechanism that commits the school to provide the student with an appropriate special education program. Schools can be held accountable for implementing the IEP. The school is also accountable for revising and rewriting the IEP when necessary. The IEP is not, however, a performance contract that imposes liability on a teacher, the IEP team members, or school officials if a student does not meet the IEP goals (IDEA Regulations, 34 C.F.R. § 300 Appendix C:60). That is, the IEP is not a guarantee that the student will accomplish all goals and objectives within the stated time period. The IEP does, however, commit the school district to providing the special education and related services and to making good faith efforts to carrying out its provisions. If parents believe that good faith efforts are not being made to properly implement the IEP, they may ask for revisions in the program or invoke due process procedures.

Compliance and Monitoring

The IEP may be used by governmental agencies in monitoring special education services delivered by the school, and the courts will use the IEP to assess compliance with the FAPE mandate of the IDEA. The IEP may be inspected to ensure that the student is receiving an appropriate special education and that the school is meeting all the legal requirements in delivering the special education.

Evaluation

Finally, the IEP is an evaluation tool. The goals and objectives are measured, using the criteria listed in the IEP, to determine the extent of the student's progress. To evaluate student progress toward meeting goals, the IEP must contain objective evaluation criteria and procedures.

The IEP Mandate

The IEP is defined in the IDEA as "a written statement for a child with a disability that is developed and implemented in accordance with [the requirements of the law]" (IDEA, 20 U.S.C. § 1401(a)(20)). An IEP must be developed for each student in special education. Furthermore, it must be in effect before special education and related services are provided to an eligible student (IDEA Regulations, 34 C.F.R. § 300.342(b)). The IEP is both a process in which an IEP team develops an appropriate program and a written document delineating the special education and related services to be provided to an eligible student. The IDEA contains extensive procedural and substantive requirements that schools must follow in developing IEPs.

Procedural Requirements

IEP planning takes place in a meeting of parents and school personnel. To ensure that the parents and school personnel develop an appropriate educational program, the IDEA mandates rigorous procedural requirements to be followed in planning the IEP. Strict adherence to these procedural requirements (e.g., notice, consent, participants) is extremely important, since major procedural errors on the part of a school district may render an IEP inappropriate (Bateman, 1996; Osborne, 1994). When procedural violations have been detected in the IEP process, courts have scrutinized the effects of the violations. If the violations interfered with the development of the IEP, the IEP may be ruled inappropriate.

The IEP Process

When students are suspected of having a disability, they are referred to a school's multidisciplinary team. The referral process is generally initiated by school personnel, although if parents of a student with disabilities believes educational progress is not satisfactory or they disagree with the current IEP, they may request the meeting (IDEA Regulations, 34 C.F.R. § 300 Appendix C:11). If the referral process is initiated by the school, the parents of the referred student must be notified. Because the IDEA provides no specific requirements regarding the referral process, states and local school districts are free to develop their own referral procedures.

Following referral, the school evaluates the student to determine the possible presence of a disability that adversely affects educational performance. The IEP team considers the results of the evaluation as well as the strengths of the student and the concerns of the parents for enhancing their child's education. Federal law contains no timeline for the period between initial referral and the actual evaluation; however, some states (e.g., New York) and many local school districts specify guidelines regarding the time within which an evaluation must be conducted following a referral. If a student is determined to be eligible for special education and related services, the school must convene an IEP team within 30 calendar days to develop the

IEP (IDEA Regulations, 34 C.F.R. § 300.343(c)). The purpose of the time limit is to ensure that there will not be a significant delay between when a student is evaluated and determined eligible and when the student begins to receive services (IDEA Regulations, 34 C.F.R. § 300 Appendix C:7).

In an IEP meeting, the participants discuss and develop a student's special education program. Regulations to the IDEA delineate the procedural requirements (including the required participants in the meeting and the actual content of the IEP) that must be followed in conducting the meeting and developing the IEP (IDEA Regulations, 34 C.F.R. §§ 300.340–300.350). During the meeting, participants review the results of the evaluation, the student's current records (including the current IEP if one exists), and other relevant information. The purpose of the meeting is to develop the student's educational program and document it in the IEP.

The actual format, procedures, and forms used in IEP meetings are not dictated by federal law but are the responsibility of the states or the schools. School districts, therefore, usually develop their own forms and procedures. A number of states have developed forms to be used by school districts. Federal statutes and regulations, however, mandate procedures that must be followed by schools in the IEP process.

The IDEA imposes no specific time limits within which the IEP must be implemented following its development, although the Office of Special Education Programs (OSEP) has indicated that generally no delay is permissible between the time the IEP is written and the provision of special education begins (OSEP Policy Letter, 1991b). Regulations specify only that the IEP must be implemented as soon as possible after the IEP meeting (IDEA Regulations, 34 C.F.R. § 300.342). There are two situations in which a delay in implementation is permitted: when the IEP meeting takes place during the summer or a vacation, and when circumstances, such as arranging transportation, require a short delay. In most situations, however, the school should provide services immediately following IEP finalization (IDEA Regulations, 34 C.F.R. § 300 Appendix C:4). Regulations require that the IEP be in place at the beginning of the school year (IDEA Regulations, 34 C.F.R. § 300.342(a)). To ensure that this requirement is met, the school may hold the IEP meeting at the end of the preceding school year or during the summer months (*Myles S. v. Montgomery County Board of Education*, 1993). The IEP must be reviewed—and, if necessary, revised—at least annually (IDEA Regulations, 34 C.F.R. § 300.343(d)).

The IEP Team

The IDEA delineates the persons who are to compose the IEP team as well as persons who are permitted, but not required, to attend (IDEA Regulations 34 C.F.R. § 300.344(A)(1)–(3)). Figure 9.1 lists the participants of the IEP team. It is the responsibility of the school district to have the required participants at the IEP meeting. IEPs have been invalidated by the courts and by administrative law judges when the required participants were not involved in the process and their absence affected the development of the document (*Girard School District*, 1992; *In re child with disabilities*, 1990; *New York City School District Board of Education*, 1992; OSEP Policy Letter, 1992; *W.G. v. Board of Trustees of Target Range School District No. 23*, 1992).

Figure 9.1
IEP Team Members

- A representative of the educational agency (e.g., principal)
- The student's special education teacher
- The student's general education teacher
- The student's parents or guardian
- A person who can interpret the instructional implications of the evaluation results
- The child, when appropriate (required for transition IEP)
- Related services personnel
- For a transition IEP, a representative of the agency that is likely to provide or pay for the transition services
- Other persons, at the discretion of parents or the educational agency

Generally the number of participants in the IEP meeting should be small because the meeting will tend to be more open and allow for more active parent involvement. Moreover, smaller team meetings may be less costly, easier to arrange and conduct, and more productive (IDEA Regulations, 34 C.F.R. § 300 Appendix C:20).

A Representative of the Local Educational Agency

A representative of the school or school district qualified to supervise the provision of the special education and to ensure that the educational services specified in the IEP will be provided must be in attendance. The representative of the agency must have knowledge regarding school district resources and the authority to commit them (IDEA Regulations, 34 C.F.R. § 300 Appendix C:13). If the representative can only commit resources within the school building, the IEP will not be valid (Martin, 1996). Moreover, the local educational agency (LEA) representative must be qualified to supervise the provision of special education and knowledgeable about the general education curriculum. This person cannot be the student's teacher, nor can this person represent the student's teacher (OSEP Policy Letter, 1992). This position may be filled by the school principal, the special education administrator, or any member of the school staff designated by the principal or administrator. It is the duty of the representative of the school or school district to ensure that the IEP is not vetoed by other administrators who are not part of the team. OSEP has consistently held that school officials, such as school board members, may not change decisions made by the IEP teams (OSEP Policy Letter, 1991b; OSEP Policy Letter, 1991c).

The Student's Special Education Teacher

Until the passage of the IDEA Amendments of 1997, the IEP did not specify if the teacher on the core IEP team should be a student's general education or special education teacher. In the 1997 amendments, both were added as required participants on the IEP team. The participation of the student's special education teacher or provider is required to ensure that the person who will implement the IEP will be involved in its development. If a teacher directly involved in educating the student is not a member of the IEP team, the IEP may not be valid (*Brimmer v. Traverse City,* 1994).

Many school districts appoint case managers to coordinate the IEP process, and some states (e.g., Minnesota) require the appointment of a case or IEP manager, although case managers are not mandated by the IDEA. The role of this person usually is to coordinate the evaluation process, collect and synthesize all reports and relevant information, communicate with parents, and participate in and conduct the IEP meeting (IDEA Regulations, 34 C.F.R. § 300 Appendix C:24). The case manager is often the student's special education teacher.

The Student's General Education Teacher

The IDEA Amendments of 1997 added the student's general education teacher to the core IEP team if the student is participating, or may participate, in general education. Congress, finding that the general education teacher often played a central role in the education of students with disabilities, stated that to the extent "appropriate," the general education teacher should participate in the development of the IEP, including the determination of appropriate behavioral interventions and strategies and supplementary aids and services, program modifications, and support for school personnel (IDEA Amendments of 1997). Congress, however, did not intend that the general education teacher participate in all aspects of the IEP team's work (Senate Report, 1997).

When a student (e.g., a middle school or high school student) has multiple teachers, only one teacher is required to attend the IEP meeting. The school, however, may allow the other teachers to attend. Administrators may not take the place of teachers in IEP meetings (OSEP Policy Letter, 1992). Although the number of participants at the IEP meeting should generally be kept to a minimum, there are instances when additional staff will be required.

The Student's Parents or Guardians

The IDEA clearly specifies that parents are to be equal partners in IEP development. Equal partnership includes the right to active participation in all discussions and decisions. To this end, parents are an integral part of the IEP process. This includes meaningful participation in all special education decision making, including IEP development and placement decisions. IEPs developed without parental input have been invalidated (*New York City School District Board of Education,* 1992).

The school is required to follow specific procedures to ensure that parents attend and fully participate in the IEP meeting (IDEA Regulations, 34 C.F.R. § 300.345). Figure 9.2 contains the requirements to ensure parental participation.

A Person Who Can Interpret the Instructional Implications of the Evaluation Results

In the IDEA Amendments of 1997, an individual who can interpret the instructional implications of the evaluation data was added to the core IEP team. This role could be filled by one of the above-mentioned team members or by an additional member. Often school psychologists fill this role.

Figure 9.2
Parental Participation in the IEP Meeting

The educational agency shall take steps to ensure parental participation:

1. Notifying parents of the meeting early enough to ensure participation
2. Scheduling the meeting at a mutually agreeable time and place
3. Content of notice

   • The notice must indicate the purpose, time, and location of the meeting and who will be in attendance
   • For a transition IEP, the notice must also include an invitation to the student and the name of the additional agencies that are invited

4. If neither parent can attend, the agency must use other methods to ensure parental participation (e.g., individual or conference telephone calls)
5. The school shall give the parents, on request, a copy of the IEP

The Student, When Appropriate

The school must inform the parents that the student may attend the meeting. The student, however, should only be present when appropriate. Additionally, if parents decide that their child's attendance will be helpful, the child must be allowed to attend. Whenever possible, the school and parents should discuss the appropriateness of having the student attend prior to making a decision. In cases where transition services are discussed, the student must be invited (IDEA Regulations, 34 C.F.R. § 300.344(c)(i)).

Related Services Personnel

When it is determined that the student will require related services, it is appropriate that related services personnel (e.g., social worker, school nurse, physical therapist) attend the IEP meeting and be involved in writing the IEP. The IDEA does not require that related services personnel attend the meeting; however, if related services personnel do not attend the IEP meeting, they should provide a written recommendation to the IEP committee regarding the nature, frequency, and amount of related services to be provided to the student (IDEA Regulations, 34 C.F.R. § 300 Appendix C:23). In the IDEA Amendments of 1997, Congress specifically noted that, whenever possible, a registered school nurse should be a member of the IEP team to help define and make decisions about a student's education-related health needs (Senate Report, 1997).

Transition Services Personnel

If transition services are to be considered at the IEP meeting, the school must invite the student and a representative of the agency likely to provide or pay for the transition services. If the student does not attend, the school must take steps to ensure that the student's interests and preferences are considered in designing the transition plan (IDEA Regulations, 34 C.F.R. § 300.344(c)(i)(2)).

Other Individuals at the Discretion of the Parent or School

Either the school or the parents may invite other persons to the meeting. Weber (1992) contends that confidentiality rules may prevent the attendance of persons who are not employed by the school district unless the parents give consent in writing. This rule would not apply to attorneys working for the school district or to related services personnel. It is inappropriate for representatives of teacher organizations to attend an IEP meeting (IDEA Regulations, 34 C.F.R. § 300 Appendix C:20). When the school does invite additional persons, it must inform the parents. Parents are not similarly required to inform the school districts of additional persons they will bring to the IEP meeting. It would be appropriate, however, for the school to inquire if the parents intend to bring other participants. Parents may also request the presence of school personnel at the IEP (Martin, 1996).

Parents may bring anyone who is familiar with education laws or the student's needs, including, for example, independent professionals (e.g., psychologists, therapists). The school district is required to consider recommendations that are offered by the additional participants; however, the district is not required to accept the recommendations.

Placement in Private Schools

When a school district places a student in a private setting, the IEP remains the responsibility of the district. Prior to placement, the school district should hold an IEP meeting that includes a representative of the private agency. In subsequent meetings the responsible school district may allow the private facility to conduct annual reviews, but the district retains responsibility for ensuring that the parents and a representative of the home school district participate and agree to any changes in the IEP (Weber, 1992). In situations where public schools provide special education services to students in private or parochial schools, the public school is responsible for the IEP. A representative of the private or parochial school must be in attendance at the meeting.

Individualization

Because the IEP is the foundation of a student's FAPE, it must be individualized; that is, the IEP must be developed to meet the unique needs of a student. Schools cannot use standard IEPs. The IDEA prohibits the designing of IEPs by disabling condition or any other categorical programming. The IEP must be based on the student's needs, not on the services available (IDEA Regulations, 34 C.F.R. § 300 Appendix C).

In writing the IEP, team members must consider (a) current records, if available; (b) whether the current IEP goals and objectives, if any, have been met, need to be revised, or can be maintained as written; (c) the results of evaluations and assessments; and (d) parents' concerns regarding the education to be provided. Meetings to review the IEP must be held at least annually. Additional meetings may be held as often as requested by either the parent or school personnel.

The parents' signatures are not required on the IEP; however, parental consent is required for the initial special education placement.* If the parents have been told and understand that a signature on the IEP constitutes consent for special education placement, the IEP can be used in this manner. Consent means that parents have been informed of all relevant aspects of the IEP, that they understand and agree in writing to the provision of a special education, and that they understand that the granting of consent is voluntary and can be revoked at any time. If the IEP is used to signify consent to placement in special education, language regarding the provision of consent should be included on the document. Furthermore, having the participants in the process sign the IEP is a way to document attendance.

Substantive Requirements

The crucial importance of the IEP was signified by the U.S. Supreme Court in *Board of Education of the Hendrick Hudson School District v. Rowley* (1982; hereafter *Rowley*). In part one of the two-part test developed to guide lower courts in determining compliance with the FAPE mandate of the IDEA, the high court directed the courts to examine the IEP. In the second part of the test, courts were directed to determine whether the IEP was "reasonably calculated to enable the [student with disabilities] to receive educational benefits" (*Rowley*, p. 207). (See Chapter 8 for elaborations of the *Rowley* test.) When courts are called on to determine whether a school district has offered an appropriate special education, the courts, acting on the directives from the *Rowley* decision, will often examine the content of the IEP.

Content of the IEP

The IDEA requires that, at a minimum, eight components be present in the IEP (IDEA, 20 U.S.C. § 1401(a)(20); IDEA Regulations, 34 C.F.R. § 300.346). States and local agencies, however, may require additional elements. Failure to include all of these elements in IEPs is a frequent source of litigation (Martin, 1996). In fact, IEPs have been invalidated by the courts when the required elements were not written into the IEP and their absence affected the development of the document (*Big Beaver Falls Area School District v. Jackson*, 1993; *Board of Education of the Casadaga Valley Central School District*, 1994; *Burlington School District*, 1994; *In re Child with Disabilities*, 1993; *New Haven Board of Education*, 1993; OSEP Policy Letter, 1991a; *School Administrative Unit #66*, 1993). It is crucial, therefore, that these elements be discussed at the IEP meeting and included in the document. Figure 9.3 lists the eight elements required in the IEP (IDEA Regulations, 34 C.F.R. § 300.346; IDEA Amendments of 1997). Figure 9.4 is an IEP form that meets the content requirements of the IDEA Amendments of 1997.

---

*The Office of Civil Rights (OCR) found that a school district was not at fault for failing to implement an initial IEP when the parents refused to sign a consent form which OCR stated was necessary for an initial placement in special education (*Davenport (IA) Community School District*, 1993).

Figure 9.3
Content of the IEP

The IEP for each student must include:

- The present levels of educational performance
- Measurable annual goals, including benchmarks or short-term instructional objectives
- The specific special education, related services, and supplementary aids and services to be provided to the student and the program modifications or supports for school personnel
- The extent to which the student will not participate with students without disabilities in general education
- Modifications in the administration of state- or district-wide assessment of student achievement
- The projected dates of initiation of services and the anticipated duration of the services
- If the student is age 14, a statement of needed transition services focusing on the appropriate course of study, and at age 16, the needed transition services
- A statement of how the student's progress toward annual goals will be measured and reported to the parents

The IDEA Amendments of 1997 added significant language and requirements to the IEP. One area of change was an emphasis on participation in the general education curriculum. According to Congress, the addition of this language was not intended to result in an increase in the size of the IEP document (e.g., a greater number of goals and objectives); rather, the new focus was intended to place attention on the accommodations and adjustments needed for the student with disabilities to successfully participate in the general education curriculum (Senate Report, 1997). The new focus was written by Congress into the 1997 amendments because the IDEA presumes "that children with disabilities are to be educated in regular classes" (Senate Report, 1997, p. 21).

Present Level of Educational Performance

The first component is a statement of the student's present level of educational performance, including how the student's disability affects his or her involvement and progress in the general education curriculum. For preschool children this statement should specify how the disability affects the child's participation in the appropriate activities. The purpose of the statement is to describe the problems that interfere with the student's education so that annual goals can be developed (Tucker & Goldstein, 1992). In effect, the statement of present level of

Figure 9.4
A Sample IEP

Individualized Education Program (IEP)
IEP TEAM MEMBERS

Position   *Name*

LEA Representative: _____   _____

General Education Teacher: _____   _____

Special Education Teacher: _____   _____

Evaluator: _____   _____

Parents: _____   _____

Others: _____   _____

STUDENT

Name: _____   Date of Birth: _____

Sex: _____   Grade: _____   Social Security/Identification #: _____

Primary Disability: _____

Secondary Disabilities: _____

Student's Strengths:

Parental Concerns:

LENGTH AND DURATION OF IEP

Date of IEP Meeting: _____   IEP Initiation Date: _____

Annual Review Date: _____   IEP Expiration Date: _____

Figure 9.4
Continued

PRESENT LEVELS OF EDUCATIONAL PERFORMANCE

Area of Need	Assessment Instruments	Date	Findings

How does the student's disability affect the student's involvement and progress in the general education curriculum or appropriate activities (if preschool)?

MEASURABLE ANNUAL GOALS/BENCHMARKS OR SHORT-TERM OBJECTIVES

Annual Goal:

Benchmarks or Short-Term Objectives:

Evaluation Method:

Review Dates and Results:

Method of Reporting Progress:

Figure 9.4
Continued

MEASURABLE ANNUAL GOALS/BENCHMARKS OR SHORT-TERM OBJECTIVES

Annual Goal:

Benchmarks or Short-Term Objectives:

Evaluation Method:

Review Dates and Results:

Method of Reporting Progress:

Annual Goal:

Benchmarks or Short-Term Objectives:

Evaluation Method:

Review Dates and Results:

Method of Reporting Progress:

Note: Attach as many goal pages as necessary.

Figure 9.4
Continued

SPECIAL EDUCATION AND RELATED SERVICES

Special Education Services   Location   Hours/Week

_____

_____

_____

_____

Related Services/Supplementary Aids and Services   Hours/Week

_____

_____

_____

_____

Modifications and Supports to General Education

_____

_____

_____

_____

LEAST RESTRICTIVE ENVIRONMENT

Extent to Which the Student Will Not Participate in General Education:

Rationale:

Figure 9.4
Continued

PARTICIPATION IN STATE- AND DISTRICT-WIDE ASSESSMENTS

Will the student participate in state- or district-wide assessments?   Yes ___ No ___

Will the student require modifications to participate in assessments? Yes ___ No ___

Modifications:

Rationale for modifications:

If the student will not participate in assessment, methods by which the student will be assessed:

Rationale for excluding the student from participation:

SPECIAL CONSIDERATIONS

Is the student age 14 or older?   Yes ___ No ___

If yes, attach a transition plan.

Does the student's behavior impede learning of self or others?   Yes ___ No ___

If yes, attach a behavior intervention plan.

Does the student require assistive technology devices or services? Yes ___ No ___

If yes, describe.

Other special considerations:

Note: One year before reaching the age of majority, the student must be informed of his or her rights under the IDEA.

performance is the starting point from which teams develop the IEP and measure its success. The statement should contain information on the student's academic performance; test scores and an explanation of those scores; physical, health, and sensory status; emotional development; social development; and prevocational and vocational skills. This statement should include nonacademic areas, such as behavioral problems, daily life activities, and mobility, as well as academic areas. Moreover, how these problems affect a student's performance in the general education curriculum should be specified. Labels (e.g., learning disabled, emotionally disturbed) are not appropriate substitutions for descriptions of educational performance.

The statement of current educational performance is a baseline from which the student's needs may be considered (Martin, 1979). The statement of needs should be written in objective terms using data from the multidisciplinary team's evaluation. When test scores are included in this section, an explanation of the results should be provided. The results of these scores should be understandable to all parties involved. Areas of educational performance in which the student has deficiencies should have corresponding goals and objectives, and any program or service must also relate to the current needs.

Measurable Annual Goals and Benchmarks or Short-Term Objectives

The IEP team determines annual goals and benchmarks or short-term objectives for students in special education. The goals are written to reflect what a student needs in order to become involved in and to make progress in the general education curriculum and in other educational areas related to the disability. These goals focus on remediation of academic or nonacademic problems and are based on the student's current level of educational performance. At least one goal should be written for each identified area of need. Failure to write goals for each need area can render an IEP inappropriate (*Board of Education of the St. Louis Central School District*, 1993; *Burlington School District*, 1994; *New Haven Board of Education*, 1993).

Annual goals are projections the team makes regarding the progress of the student in one school year. In writing the annual goals, IEP teams should consider the student's past achievement, current level of performance, practicality of goals, priority needs, and amount of instructional time devoted to reaching the goal (Strickland & Turnbull, 1990). While goals should be written for a level that the student has a reasonable chance of reaching, courts have indicated that when goals are so unambitious that achieving them will not result in meaningful improvements in performance, such goals may render the IEP inappropriate (*Adams v. Hansen*, 1985; *Carter v. Florence County School District Four*, 1991).

Benchmarks, or short-term objectives, are written for each annual goal. They describe expected student performance in terms that are measurable. The benchmarks are intermediate steps to be measured leading to the achievement of the annual goals (*Board of Education of the Whitesboro Central School District*, 1994). They are achievable components of the annual goal that allow monitoring of student progress on a short-term basis throughout the year. If a student achieves the short-term objectives, therefore, he or she should also achieve the annual goals (*Pocatello School District #25*, 1991). The benchmarks describe what a student is expected to accomplish in a given time period. The IDEA Amendments of 1997 changed the term "short-term objectives" to "benchmarks or short-term objectives" to emphasize the importance of using short-term objectives as benchmarks by which to measure a student's progress toward the annual goals.

The purpose of goals and objectives is to help determine whether a student is making educational progress and if the special education program is appropriate for meeting educational needs. Goals and objectives, correctly written, enable teachers and parents to monitor a student's progress in a special education program and make educational adjustments when necessary (Deno, 1992). In fact, Congress viewed the requirement of "measurable" annual goals and benchmarks as crucial to the success of the IEP (Senate Report, 1997).

Special Education and Related Services and Supplementary Aids and Services

The third requirement is a statement of the specific educational services to be provided by the school. This includes special education, related services, and supplementary aids and services that are required to assist a student in attaining the IEP goals and objectives. The statement of services must be unambiguous so that the school's commitment of resources is clear to parents and other members of the team (IDEA Regulations, 34 C.F.R. § 300 Appendix C:51).

Statements of related services discuss the services and equipment provided to help students benefit from special education; that is, the services provided to students should enable them (a) to advance appropriately toward attaining the annual goals; (b) to be involved in and progress in the general education curriculum and to participate in extracurricular and other nonacademic activities; and (c) to be educated with other children with and without disabilities. This requirement commits the school district to providing these services at no charge to the parents. The team must determine the special education and related services needs of a student based on the student's needs, not on the availability of services. In addition to enumerating the types of services, the IEP should also include the amount, frequency, and duration of services. If the required services are not available in the district but are determined by the IEP team to be necessary, they must be provided through contracts or arrangements with other agencies.

The supplementary aids and services that are provided as part of a student's special education must be included in the IEP (IDEA Regulations, 34 C.F.R. § 300 Appendix C:48). It is not necessary, however, to include components of a student's educational program that are not part of the special education and related services required by the student. In fact, Gorn (1996) contends that nonmandatory educational services should not be included in the IEP, because adding particular nonmandated services to the IEP may create an obligation on the part of the school district to provide the services while the IEP is in effect. Moreover, in a report on the IDEA Amendments of 1997, the Senate Committee on Labor and Human Resources noted that while teaching and related services methodologies are appropriate subjects to discuss in an IEP meeting, they should not be written into the IEP (Senate Report, 1997).

The Extent to Which Students Will Not Participate in the General Education Classroom

The IEP must also delineate the amount of time that the student will not participate in general education classes with students without disabilities. Students with disabilities must be allowed to interact with their peers to the maximum extent appropriate in both academic and nonacademic settings. When choosing the setting for a student's special education, the IEP team must place the student in the least restrictive environment (LRE) that is appropriate. A statement in the IEP regarding the extent of integration with students without disabilities is required to document the team's LRE decision (Strickland & Turnbull, 1990). A mere conclusionary statement that the multidisciplinary team has determined a particular setting to be the LRE would not pass legal scrutiny. According to the court in *Thorndock v. Boise Independent School District* (1988), a statement is required that describes a student's ability or inability to participate in a general education program and essentially provides justification for the team's decision.

If modifications in the general education classroom are necessary to ensure that the student participates in general education, the modifications must be incorporated into the IEP (OSEP Policy Letter, 1993). This applies to any general education programs in which a student participates (IDEA Regulations, 34 C.F.R. § 300 Appendix C:48).

A Student's Participation in the Administration of State- or District-Wide Assessments of Student Achievement

The IDEA Amendments of 1997 also require that all students with disabilities be included in state- and district-wide assessments of student progress. Because students with disabilities may need individual modifications and accommodations to participate in these assessments, the IEP must include a statement detailing all such modifications. If the IEP team determines that a student cannot be accurately assessed, even with modifications, the IEP must contain a statement indicating why the assessment is not appropriate, as well as alternative assessments that will be used in place of the state- or district-wide assessments.

The Projected Date of Initiation and Anticipated Duration of the IEP

The IEP must be initiated as soon as possible after it is written. The only exceptions are if the IEP is written during a vacation period, over the summer, or when circumstance requires a short delay (such as working out transportation arrangements). When a student moves from another district, the delay should not be more than a week. A student must not be placed in a special education program prior to the initiation date in the IEP.

Transition Services Needed

If a student is 16 years old or younger, if appropriate, the IEP must contain a statement of needed transition services. This requirement was added to the IDEA in 1990. Transition services are a coordinated set of activities for a student, designed within an outcome-oriented process, which promotes movement from school to post-school activities, including post-secondary education, vocational training, integrated employment (including supported employment), continuing and adult education, adult services, independent living, or community participation. The coordinated set of activities shall be based upon the individual student's needs, taking into account the student's preferences and interests, and shall include instruction, community experiences, the development of employment and other post-school adult living objectives, and, when appropriate, acquisition of daily living skills and functional vocational evaluation. (20 U.S.C. § 1401(a)(19))

The purpose of including transition services is to infuse a longer-range perspective into the IEP process and to help students better reach their potential as adults (Tucker & Goldstein, 1992). Most often the transition services will focus on the transition from school to work. An IEP that includes transition services must include the areas that are listed in the IDEA's definition (i.e., instruction, community services, and employment and other adult-living objectives). If any of these required services are not included in a student's transition plan, the IEP must include an explanatory note detailing the reasons for exclusion (Goldstein, 1993). The transition plan must also have measurable goals and objectives.

In the IDEA Amendments of 1997 an additional transition requirement was added mandating that certain transition services begin at age 14. This provision required the transition services statement to focus primarily on a student's courses of study (e.g., vocational education classes). Additionally, this statement must be updated annually.

Reporting Requirements and Measurement Criteria to Determine Progress Toward the Annual Goals

Finally, the IEP must include a statement of how a student's progress toward the annual goals will be measured. The measurement criteria and procedures must be appropriate for evaluating progress toward the particular goal. The purpose of this provision is to inform parents and educators how a student's progress toward his or her annual goals will be measured. Additionally, this statement must delineate how a student's parents will be regularly informed about their child's progress toward the annual goals. Parents of students with disabilities must be informed about their child's progress as regularly as are parents of children without disabilities (e.g., through regular report cards). Congress suggested providing an IEP report card along with a student's general education report card (Senate Report, 1997). Furthermore, Congress suggested that such a report card could list the IEP goals and rank each goal on a continuum (e.g., no progress, good progress, goal completed).

There is probably less substantive compliance with this component of the IEP than any other (Tucker & Goldstein, 1992). Appropriate evaluation of a student's progress toward meeting IEP goals and objectives is, however, absolutely essential. Without such evaluation, the goals and objectives are meaningless because it will be impossible to determine success or failure. If the goals and objectives of the IEP cannot be measured or evaluated, the IEP will not appropriately address the student's needs. The Idaho Supreme Court, in *Thorndock v. Boise Independent School*

District (1988), held that because a student's IEP goals and objectives lacked objective measurement criteria, the IEP was inappropriate. Similarly, in *Board of Education of the Casadaga Valley Central School District* (1994), the IEP of a student classified as other health impaired was invalidated because it failed to set forth objective criteria and evaluation procedures.

Special Considerations in IEP Development

The IDEA Amendments of 1997 added a section regarding five special considerations in developing the IEP. First, in the situation of a student with behavioral problems, regardless of the student's disability category, the IEP should include a behavior management plan. This plan should be based on a functional behavioral assessment and include positive behavioral interventions, strategies, and supports to address the behavior problems proactively. Second, when an IEP is developed for a student with limited English proficiency, the student's language needs that relate to the IEP must be considered. Third, in developing an IEP for a student who is blind or visually impaired, the IEP must provide for instruction in Braille and the use of Braille unless the team determines that instruction in Braille is not appropriate. Fourth, when a student is deaf or hard of hearing, the IEP team must consider the student's language and communication needs, opportunities for direct communications with peers and professionals in the student's language and communication mode, academic level, and full range of needs, including opportunities for direct instruction in the student's language and communication mode. Finally, the IEP team should consider whether the student requires assistive technology devices and services.

Placement Decisions

The IDEA Amendments of 1997 require that in most cases the placement decision should be made by the IEP team. Until the 1997 amendments, the IDEA only required that the placement decisions be made by a knowledgeable group of persons. The parents must participate in the placement decision.

Parental Participation

One of the most important of the IDEA mandates is that parents be equal partners in the IEP process. Parental participation is so crucial to the IEP process that the IDEA contains specific guidelines that schools must follow to ensure equal parental participation (IDEA Regulations, 34 C.F.R. § 300.345(a)–(f)). In fact, Congress considered strengthening the role of parents in the special education process one of the most important goals of the IDEA Amendments of 1997 (Senate Report, 1997).

The school must take steps to ensure that one or both parents are present at the IEP meeting or are afforded an opportunity to participate. The school must give parents or guardians sufficient notice of the IEP development meeting so that they have

Figure 9.5
Documentation when Parents Will Not Attend

The meeting may be conducted without the parents in attendance if the school is unable to convince the parents to attend. The school must have a record of its attempts to arrange a meeting. Examples of the documentation of these attempts include items such as:

- detailed records of telephone calls made or attempted, and the results of those calls

- copies of correspondence and any responses received

- detailed records of visits made to the parents' home or place of employment, and the results of those visits.

---

an opportunity to attend. The notice provided by the school must explain the purpose of the meeting, its time and location, and the persons to be in attendance. Participants in the meeting do not have to be identified by name; however, they must be identified by position (Livingston, 1994).

The IDEA does not specify how far in advance the school district must notify parents, but it does state that notification must be early enough to ensure that parents have the opportunity to attend the IEP meeting (IDEA Regulations, 34 C.F.R. § 300.345(a)). Furthermore, school personnel have to work with parents to hold a meeting at a mutually agreeable time and place. The school does not have to honor every parental request to schedule the meeting, but the district must make good faith efforts to mutually agree on scheduling. In determining the meeting time and place, however, school personnel are allowed to consider their own scheduling needs (OSEP Policy Letter, 1992). An IEP meeting can be held without parents in attendance if the school is unable to convince them that they should attend. In such cases, the school personnel must keep a record of their attempts to arrange the meeting. Figure 9.5 lists the types of documentation that should be kept by the educational agency in its attempts to arrange the meeting (IDEA Regulations, 34 C.F.R. § 300.345(2)(d)). If parents refuse to participate, the school district still has a responsibility to provide a FAPE to eligible students (Gorn, 1996).

The school must also make efforts to ensure that parents understand the proceedings, including arranging for an interpreter for parents who are deaf or whose native language is not English. If requested, the school must give the parents a copy of the IEP. The IEP meeting may be video or audiotaped at the discretion of either the parents or the school (Breecher, 1990; IDEA Regulations, 34 C.F.R. § 300 Appendix C:12). The party taping the proceedings may obtain the consent of the other party, but consent is not required. Recordings must be kept confidential.

When the parents cannot be located, surrogate parents must be appointed to represent the interests of the student. Surrogate parents have all the rights and responsibilities of the parent; they are entitled to participate in the IEP meeting, view the student's educational records, receive notice, provide consent, and invoke a due process hearing (IDEA Regulations, 34 C.F.R. § 300.514). (For elaborations on appointing surrogate parents see Chapter 13.) If the parents can be located but are unwilling to attend, the educational agency is not empowered to appoint a surrogate parent (Perryman, 1987). In such situations, the school should hold the meeting and document attempts to involve the parents.

Although parental participation is extremely important in the development of the IEP, parents do not have an absolute veto over the final results (*Buser v. Corpus Christi ISD,* 1994). When the parents and school personnel cannot reach agreement on an IEP, they should, when possible, agree to an interim special plan for serving the student until the disagreement is resolved (Boney, 1991; IDEA Regulations, 34 C.F.R. § 300 Appendix C:35). If no agreement is reached, the last IEP (if one exists) remains in effect until a final resolution. When the school and parents agree about basic IEP services but disagree about a related service, the IEP should be implemented in the areas of agreement. Additionally, the IEP should document the points of disagreement, and attempts to resolve the disagreement should be undertaken (IDEA Regulations, 34 C.F.R. § 300 Appendix C:35). If the disagreement concerns a fundamental issue, such as placement, the school should remind the parents of their right to call a due process hearing and attempt to develop an interim educational program. If agreements cannot be reached, the use of mediation or some informal means for resolving the disagreements prior to going to due process should be recommended (IDEA Regulations, 34 C.F.R. § 300 Appendix C:35). If a due process hearing is initiated, the school may not change the current educational placement unless the parents and school agree otherwise. For example, if the student is in a general education classroom and the parents cannot agree on a special education placement, even if they agree on the need for special education, the student must remain in the general education classroom unless the school and parents can agree on an interim placement. The same is true if the student is currently in a special education placement (IDEA Regulations, 34 C.F.R. § 300.513).

A completed IEP may not be presented to the parents in the IEP meeting. According to OSEP, presenting a completed document to the parents for review would minimize the parents' contributions, even if the document was to be used only as a basis for discussion (Helmuth, 1990). Schools may prepare a draft of an IEP, however, to present to the parents at the IEP meeting for discussion purposes. This draft may consist of evaluation findings, statements of present levels of performance, recommendations regarding goals and objectives, and the kinds of special education and related services recommended. This document may not be represented as the final IEP (Helmuth, 1990; IDEA Regulations, 34 C.F.R. § 300 Appendix C:55). At the beginning of a meeting in which the draft document is presented, it must be clarified that the document is only a working draft for review and discussion.

Reviewing and Revising the IEP

The IDEA mandates that the IEP be reviewed and, if necessary, revised annually. The review must be conducted under the following circumstances: (a) the student has shown a lack of progress toward the annual goals, and in the general education curriculum where appropriate; (b) the results of a reevaluation need to be considered; (c) the parents have provided additional information about the child; (d) the student's needs are anticipated to change; and (e) other considerations as deemed appropriate.

The timing of these meetings is to be left to the discretion of the school. The parents or the school, however, may initiate the IEP reviews as often as is deemed necessary (Sheridan, 1993). If either the school or parents decide that components of the IEP (e.g., annual goals or short-term objectives) need revision, a new IEP meeting must be called.

The IEP remains in effect until it is revised or until a new IEP is written. The IEP cannot be revised unless the parents are notified about the proposed change and the reasons for the change. When a student moves from one district to another, the student's former IEP is to be implemented until the new district evaluates the student and writes a new IEP (IDEA Regulations, 34 C.F.R. § 300 Appendix C:6). If the current IEP is not forwarded by the student's former school district or is inappropriate, the new district should conduct an IEP meeting as soon as possible. If the IEP is appropriate and can be implemented as written, however, the new district can use it without developing a new IEP.

If a school district proposes to change any aspect of the student's special education program, or refuses to change aspects of the student's program, it must issue prior notification to the parent. The notice must include a full explanation of proposed actions, justification for the changes, reasons for the rejection of alternatives, parental appeal rights, and other procedural safeguards. As long as the school provides adequate notice and conducts meetings in accordance with procedures set forth in the IDEA, parental consent is not required for review and revision of the IEP. If parents reject revisions, they have the option of calling a due process hearing (IDEA Regulations, 34 C.F.R. § 300.506).

Communicating the Requirements of the IEP

The IDEA requires that the IEP must be implemented as developed. This requirement applies to both special and general education. According to Martin (1996), some administrators misread the Family Educational Rights and Privacy Act (FERPA) as prohibiting release of IEP information to teachers because it is confidential. This is an incorrect understanding of the requirements of FERPA. (Chapter 16 elaborates the requirements of FERPA.) Teachers working with a student who has an IEP are entitled to review the information contained in the document. Schools have an affirmative duty to inform these teachers of any requirements in the IEP.

Furthermore, if a teacher is not implementing an IEP as required, the school must take steps to correct the situation. In *Doe v. Withers* (1993), an IEP required general education teachers to modify testing by giving oral examinations to a student with learning disabilities. The student's social studies teacher deliberately chose not to modify tests, even though it was required by the IEP. The parents prevailed in a lawsuit against the teacher. The court assessed the teacher compensatory and punitive damages in the amount of $15,000.

Section 504 and the IEP

Section 504 of the Rehabilitation Act of 1973 (hereafter Section 504) does not require the preparation of an IEP for students protected under the law. Regulations to Section 504, however, allow a school district to use an IEP to fulfill the requirements of the law, although this is only one method of meeting the requirements of the law (Section 504 Regulations, 34 C.F.R. § 104.33(b)(2)). Consequently, it is good practice to prepare a written individualized plan, in the manner of an IEP, to document educational services which the school district provides to a student under Section 504 (Fossey, Hosie, Soniat, & Zirkel, 1994; Gorn, 1996). Furthermore, Martin (1996) contends that when an IEP committee determines that a student is not eligible for services under the IDEA or that a student no longer requires services, the committee should automatically refer students for consideration for protection under Section 504. A student who does not qualify under the IDEA, or who no longer qualifies, might meet eligibility for services under Section 504.

Litigation

In *Rowley,* the U.S. Supreme Court directed lower courts to review schools' IEP process and written documents when determining compliance with the FAPE mandate of the IDEA. In using the high court's two-part test, lower courts are first to examine the procedural aspects of the IEP process; second, they must examine the IEP itself in order to determine whether the IEP is calculated to provide the student with educational benefit.

Cases reviewing procedural and substantive compliance with the FAPE mandate were summarized in Chapter 8 and will not be revisited here. It is instructive, however, to examine the FAPE cases for the specific attributes or defects in the IEPs that have led the courts to invalidate them.

The post-*Rowley* cases have indicated that procedural flaws may, but will not automatically, invalidate an IEP. Before a court will invalidate an IEP, the court must have reason to believe that the procedural error (a) compromised a student's right to an appropriate education; (b) resulted in the parents' being excluded from the IEP process; or (c) caused the student to be deprived of educational rights.

Substantively, the post-*Rowley* cases have held that the IEP must be reasonably calculated to produce educational benefit. An IEP that produces only trivial educational advancement or merely halts educational regression will not pass legal muster (Guernsey & Klare, 1993). To determine substantive compliance with the FAPE mandate courts and administrative law judges have examined the following factors:

- The IEP's goals and objectives (*Carter v. Florence County School District Four,* 1991; *Chris D. v. Montgomery County Board of Education,* 1990; *Straub v. Florida Union Free School District,* 1991; *Susquenita School District v. Raelee S.,* 1996; *Thorndock v. Boise Independent School*

District, 1988). For example, in *Carter v. Florence,* the U.S. Court of Appeals for the Fourth Circuit held that the school's IEP reading goal of 4 months' growth over a school year did not represent meaningful growth.

- The evaluation procedures used to measure a student's progress toward meeting IEP goals (*Board of Education of the Casadaga Valley Central School District,* 1994; *Chris D. v. Montgomery County Board of Education,* 1990; *Lewis v. School Board of Loudoun County,* 1992; *Susquenita School District v. Raelee S.,* 1996). In finding against the school district, the court in *Lewis v. School Board of Loudoun County* stated that, "significantly, the IEP also contained no evaluation procedures . . . to measure [the student's] progress towards meeting the goals and objectives of the IEP" (p. 528).

- Actual student progress in a school's special education program (*Adams v. Hansen,* 1985; *Hall v. Vance County Board of Education,* 1985; *Roland M. v. Concord School Committee,* 1990). In *Hall v. Vance County Board of Education,* the court invalidated a school's IEP, affirming the lower court's ruling that regardless of the goals and objectives in the IEP, the student had made no educational progress in 2 years. (For elaborations on court decisions regarding student progress see Chapter 8.)

The litigation regarding the appropriateness of IEPs indicates the importance of carefully adhering to the requirements set forth in the IEP. The case law puts a premium on involving parents in the IEP process and in developing an IEP that will result in educational benefit to the student. To assure that the IEP provides an appropriate education, school personnel must conduct thorough assessments, base goals on educational needs identified in these assessments, write meaningful goals and objectives, and measure student progress toward meeting these goals in ways that will allow educators to adjust educational procedures if they do not produce the desired outcomes within the time frame indicated in the IEP.

Summary

The IEP is the keystone of the IDEA, and special education is embodied in the IEP. The IEP is developed at a meeting that includes, at a minimum, a representative of the school or school district, the student's special education and general education teachers, the parents, and the student, when appropriate. Other persons may be invited at the discretion of the parent or school. If the student is being evaluated for the first time, a member of the evaluation team or a person familiar with the evaluation must be on the IEP team.

The IEP is developed in accordance with state and federal mandates. The program must include (a) the student's present level of educational performance; (b) annual goals and benchmarks or short-term objectives; (c) special education and related services to be provided; (d) the extent to which the student will not participate in the general education program; (e) student participation in state- or district-wide assessments and modifications if needed; (f) projected date of initiation and anticipated duration of the IEP;

(g) transition services for students 16 years of age, or, when determined appropriate, 14 years or older; and (h) appropriate objective criteria and evaluation procedures for determining, on at least an annual basis, whether the IEP goals are being met.

The IDEA Amendments of 1997 stress the importance of involving a student's parents in the IEP process. The law delineates specific procedures that schools must follow to ensure meaningful parental participation. Schools must communicate the requirements of the IEP to a student's general and special education teachers. Moreover, courts have stressed the importance of following proper procedures in IEP development, writing meaningful goals and objectives, evaluating a student's progress toward the goals, and communicating the results of this progress.

For Further Information

IEP development:

Bateman, B. (1996). *Better IEPs: How to develop legally correct and educationally useful programs.* Longmont, CO: Sopris West.

Chambers, A. C. (1997). Has technology been considered? A guide for IEP teams. In *CASE/TAM assistive technology policy and practice series.* Reston, VA: Council of Administrators of Special Education and the Technology and Media Division of the Council for Exceptional Children.

Smith, S. W. (1990). Individualized education programs (IEPs) in special education—From intent to acquiescence. *Exceptional Children, 57,* 6–14.

Strickland, B. B., & Turnbull, A. P. (1990). *Developing and implementing individualized education programs* (3rd. ed.). Upper Saddle River, NJ: Merrill/Prentice Hall.

Parental participation in IEP development:

Shea, T. M., & Bauer, A. M. (1991). *Parents and teachers of children with exceptionalities: A handbook for collaboration.* Boston: Allyn & Bacon.

Turnbull, A. P., & Turnbull, H. R. (1997). *Families, professionals and exceptionality: A special partnership* (3rd ed.). Upper Saddle River, NJ: Merrill/Prentice Hall.

References

Adams v. Hansen, 632 F. Supp. 858 (N.D. Cal. 1985).

Bateman, B. (1996). *Better IEPs: How to develop legally correct and educationally useful programs.* Longmont, CO: Sopris West.

Big Beaver Falls Area School District v. Jackson, 624 A.2d 806 (Pa. Cmwlth 1993).

Board of Education of the Casadaga Valley Central School District, 20 IDELR 1023 (SEA 1994).

Board of Education of the Hendrick Hudson Central School District v. Rowley, 458 U.S. 176 (1982).

Board of Education of the St. Louis Central School District, 20 IDELR 938 (SEA 1993).

Board of Education of the Whitesboro Central School District, 21 IDELR 895 (SEA NY 1994).

Boney, Letter to, 18 IDELR 537 (OSEP, 1991).

Breecher, Letter to, 17 EHLR 56 (OSEP, 1990).

Brimmer v. Traverse City, 872 F. Supp. 447 (W.D. Mich. 1994).

Burlington School District, 20 IDELR 1303 (SEA 1994).

Buser v. Corpus Christi ISD, 20 IDELR 981 (S.D. Tex. 1994).

Carter v. Florence County School District Four, 950 F.2d 156 (4th Cir. 1991).

Chris D. v. Montgomery County Board of Education, 753 F. Supp. 922 (M.D. Ala. 1990).

Davenport (IA) Community School District, 20 IDELR 1398 (OCR 1993).

Deno, S. L. (1992). The nature and development of curriculum-measurement. *Preventing School Failure, 36,* 5–11.

Doe v. Withers, 20 IDELR 442 (W.Va. Cir. Ct. 1993).

Family Educational Rights and Privacy Act (FERPA), 20 U.S.C. § 1232 *et seq.*

Fossey, R., Hosie, T., Soniat, K., & Zirkel, P. (1994). Section 504 and "front line" educators: An expanded obligation to serve children with disabilities. *Preventing School Failure, 39,* 10–14.

Girard School District, 18 IDELR 1048 (OCR 1992).

Goldstein, B. A. (1993). New regulations under Part B of the IDEA. In *Proceedings of the 14th National Institute on Legal Issues of Educating Individuals with Disabilities.* Horsham, PA: LRP Publications.

Gorn, S. (1996). *What do I do when . . . The answer book on special education law.* Horsham, PA: LRP Publications.

Guernsey, T. F., & Klare, K. (1994). *Special education law.* Durham, NC: Carolina Academic Press.

Hall v. Vance County Board of Education, 774 F.2d 629 (4th Cir. 1985).

Helmuth, Letter to, 16 EHLR 503 (OSEP 1990).

Honig v. Doe, 485 U.S. 305 (1988).

Horsnell, M., & Kitch, J. (1996). Bullet-proofing the IEP. In *Proceedings of the 15th National Institute on Legal Issues in Educating Individuals with Disabilities.* Alexandria, VA: LRP Publications.

Individuals with Disabilities Education Act, 20 U.S.C. § 1401 *et seq.*

Individuals with Disabilities Education Act Amendments of 1997, 105th Congress.

Individuals with Disabilities Education Act Regulations, 34 C.F.R. § 300.1 *et seq.*

Individuals with Disabilities Education Act Regulations, 34 C.F.R. § 300 Appendix C (1993).

In re Child with Disabilities, 16 EHLR 538 (SEA TN 1990).

In re Child with Disabilities, 20 IDELR 455 (1993).

Lewis v. School Board of Loudoun County, 808 F. Supp. 523 (E.D. 1992).

Livingston, Letter to, 21 IDELR 1060 (OSEP 1994).

Martin, R. (1979). *Educating handicapped children: The legal mandate.* Champaign, IL: Research Press.

Martin, R. (1996). Litigation over the IEP. In *Proceedings of the 16th National Institute on Legal Issues in Educating Individuals with Disabilities.* Alexandria, VA: LRP Publications.

Myles S. v. Montgomery County Board of Education, 20 IDELR 237 (M.D. Ala. 1993).

New Haven Board of Education, 20 IDELR 42 (SEA 1993).

New York City School District Board of Education, 19 IDELR 169 (SEA NY 1992).

Osborne, A. G. (1994). Procedural due process rights for parents under the IDEA. *Preventing School Failure, 39,* 22–26.

OSEP Policy Letter, 18 IDELR 530 (OSEP 1991a).

OSEP Policy Letter, 18 IDELR 627 (OSEP 1991b).

OSEP Policy Letter, 18 IDELR 969 (OSEP 1991c).

OSEP Policy Letter, 18 IDELR 1303 (OSEP 1992).

OSEP Policy Letter, 20 IDELR 541 (OSEP 1993).

Perryman, Letter to, EHLR 211:438 (OSEP, 1987).

Pocatello School District #25, 18 IDELR 83 (SEA Idaho 1991).

Roland M. v. Concord School Committee, 910 F. Supp. 983 (1st Cir. 1990).

School Administrative Unit #66, 20 IDELR 471 (1993).

Section 504 of the Rehabilitation Act Regulations, 34 C.F.R. § 104.33(b)(2).

Senate Report of the Individuals with Disabilities Act Amendments of 1997, available at wais.access.gpo.gov.

Sheridan, Letter to, 20 IDELR 1163 (OSEP 1993).

Smith, S. W. (1990). Individualized education programs (IEPs) in special education—From intent to acquiescence. *Exceptional Children, 57,* 6–14.

Straub v. Florida Union Free School District, 778 F. Supp. 774 (S.D.N.Y. 1991).

Strickland, B. P., & Turnbull, A. P. (1990). *Developing and implementing individualized education programs* (3rd. ed.). Upper Saddle River, NJ: Merrill/Prentice Hall.

Susquenita School District v. Raelee S., 25 IDELR 120 (M.D. Penn. 1996).

Thorndock v. Boise Independent School District, 767 P.2d 1241 (1988).

Tucker, B. P., & Goldstein, B. A. (1992). *Legal rights of persons with disabilities: An analysis of public law.* Horsham, PA: LRP Publications.

W.G. v. Board of Trustees of Target Range School District No. 23, 960 F.2d 1479 (9th Cir. 1992).

Weber, M. C. (1992). *Special education law and litigation treatise.* Horsham, PA: LRP Publications.

Related Services

. . . those services necessary to aid a handicapped child to benefit from special education must be provided.

Chief Justice Burger, *Irving Independent School District v. Tatro* (1984, p. 894).

To ensure that students with disabilities receive a free appropriate public service education (FAPE), it is often necessary to provide related services. Related services are supportive aids and services provided by a school to assist students with disabilities to benefit from the special education program. Usually, related services will be provided to students receiving a special education under the Individuals with Disabilities Education Act (IDEA). Even if students with disabilities are not receiving special education services, however, the school may be obligated to provide related services. If students qualify for protection under Section 504 of the Rehabilitation Act of 1973, related aids and services may be required to ensure that their educational needs are met as adequately as are the educational needs of students without disabilities.

Legislation

The IDEA

The IDEA defines related services as "services that may be required to assist the child with a disability to benefit from special education" (IDEA, 20 U.S.C. § 1401(a)(17)). Because the determination of the necessary related services can only be made on a case-by-case basis, the individualized education program (IEP) team's meeting is the proper forum to determine whether related services are required in order to provide a FAPE (Shelby, 1994). Congress enumerated a number of such services in the law. Related services may include

> Transportation and other such developmental, corrective, and other supportive services (including speech pathology and audiology, psychological services, physical and occupational therapy, recreation, including therapeutic recreation, social work services, counseling services, including rehabilitation counseling, and medical services, except that such medical services shall be for diagnostic or evaluation purposes only) as may be required to assist a child with a disability to benefit from special education, and includes the early identification and assessment of disabling conditions in children. (IDEA, 20 U.S.C. § 1401(a)(17))

IDEA regulations append additional related services to this list and provide definitions of these services (IDEA Regulations, 34 C.F.R. § 300.13). Related services and definitions from these regulations are provided in Table 10.1.

Comments to the regulations state that

> the list of related services is not exhaustive and may include other developmental, corrective, or supportive services (such as artistic and cultural programs, and art, music, and dance therapy), if they are required to assist a student with disabilities to benefit from special education. (IDEA Regulations, 34 C.F.R. § 300.13, comment)

In 1990, the list of related services was expanded to include assistive technology, social work services, rehabilitation counseling, and transition services. The IDEA Amendments of 1997 added orientation and mobility services to the list.

The particular type of related service necessary to assist a student to benefit from special education is determined by the IEP team based on an individualized assessment (Rainforth, 1990). The IEP team, in addition to listing the types of related services to be provided, must include the amount of services provided. This is required so that the commitment of needed resources will be clear to the parents and other IEP team members (IDEA Regulations, Notice of Interpretation on IEPs, Question 51).

According to Gorn (1996), an important term in the statutory and regulatory language is "assist." The standard required to assist a student to benefit is legally less rigorous than that required for a student to benefit. "Related services are not just those supportive services that are essential for a student to benefit from special education. Rather, they are services required to assist a student in benefiting from special education, a less rigorous standard" (Gorn, 1996, p. 6:4). This less rigorous standard gives IEP teams more flexibility in considering the provision of related services.

Section 504

Section 504 also includes related service in its definition of a FAPE: "the provision of regular or special education and related aids and services that are designed to meet individual educational needs of [students with disabilities] as adequately as the needs of [students without disabilities]" (Section 504 Regulations, 34 C.F.R. § 104.33(b)(1)). No specific definition of related services is included in the statute.

Table 10.1
Related Services

Related Service	Definition
Audiology	1. Identification of children with hearing loss. 2. Determination of the range, nature, and degree of hearing loss (including referral for medical or other professional attention). 3. Provision of habilitative activities, such as language habilitation, auditory training, speech reading (lip-reading), hearing evaluation, and speech conservation. 4. Creation and administration of programs for prevention of hearing loss. 5. Counseling and guidance of pupils, parents, and teachers regarding hearing loss. 6. Determination of the child's need for group and individual amplification, selecting and fitting an appropriate aid, and evaluating the effectiveness of amplification.
Counseling	Services provided by qualified social workers, psychologists, guidance counselors, or other qualified personnel.
Early identification and assessment	The implementation of a formal plan for identifying a disability as early as possible in a child's life.
Medical Services	Services provided by a licensed physician to determine a child's medically related disability that results in the child's need for special education and related services.
Occupational therapy	1. Improving, developing, or restoring functions impaired or lost through illness, injury, or deprivation. 2. Improving ability to perform tasks for independent functioning when functions are impaired or lost. 3. Preventing, through early intervention, initial or further impairment or loss of function.
Orientation and mobility services	Services provided to children who are blind or have visual impairments to assist them in traveling around their school or environment. This related service was added in 1997. The regulatory definition has not been promulgated.
Parent counseling and training	Assisting parents in understanding the special needs of their child and providing parents with information about child development.
Physical therapy	Services provided by a qualified physical therapist.

Table 10.1
Continued

Related Service	Definition
Psychological services	1. Administering psychological and educational tests and other assessment procedures. 2. Interpreting assessment results. 3. Obtaining, integrating, and interpreting information about child behavior and conditions related to learning. 4. Consulting with other staff members in planning school programs to meet the special needs of children as indicated by psychological tests, interviews, and behavioral evaluations. 5. Planning and managing a program of psychological services, including psychological counseling for children and parents.
Recreation	1. Assessment of leisure function. 2. Therapeutic recreation services. 3. Recreation programs in school and community agencies. 4. Leisure education.
Rehabilitation counseling services	Services provided by qualified personnel in individual or group sessions that focus specifically on career development, employment preparation, achieving independence, and integration in the workplace and community. This also includes vocation rehabilitation service provided under the Rehabilitation Act of 1973.
School health services	Services provided by a qualified school nurse or other qualified person.
Social work services in the schools	1. Preparing a social or developmental history. 2. Group and individual counseling with the child and family. 3. Working with those problems in a child's living situation (e.g., home, school, community) that affect the child's adjustment in school. 4. Mobilizing school and community resources to enable the child to learn as effectively as possible.
Speech pathology	1. Identification of children with speech or language impairments. 2. Diagnosis and appraisal. 3. Referral for medical or other professional attention. 4. Provision of speech and language services for the habilitation or prevention of communicative problems. 5. Counseling and guidance of parents, children, and teachers.
Transportation	1. Travel to and from schools and between schools. 2. Travel in and around school buildings. 3. Specialized equipment if required to provide special transportation (e.g., adapted buses, lifts, ramps).

The Section 504 definition indicates that related services must be provided if needed to ensure a FAPE, even if special education services are not provided (Zirkel, 1993). For example, the Pennsylvania Department of Education ruled that, under Section 504, a school had to provide related services to a student with a serious emotional disturbance, even though she did not qualify for special education. The educational agency stated that because her emotional disturbance substantially limited a major life activity (i.e., learning), she was entitled to receive the necessary related service to benefit from the regular education program (*West Chester Area School District,* 1992).

Section 504 is more specific than the IDEA in requiring schools to provide related services and equipment if necessary to provide a FAPE. Regulations to Section 504 refer to "related aids or services" (Section 504 Regulations, 34 C.F.R. § 104.33(b)(1)) and "supplementary aids and services" (Section 504 Regulations, 34 C.F.R. § 104.34(a)), while the IDEA regulations refer only to "related services" (IDEA Regulations, 34 C.F.R. § 300.16). Section 504, unlike the IDEA, does not provide a list of types of related services.

Related Services and Least Restrictive Environment

Both the IDEA and Section 504 require that, when appropriate, a student with disabilities shall be educated in the general education classroom. Regulations to the IDEA require that schools shall ensure "to the maximum extent appropriate [that] children with disabilities . . . are educated with children who are not disabled" (IDEA Regulations, 34 C.F.R. § 300.550(b)(1)). Similarly, Section 504 requires that students with disabilities be educated to the "maximum extent appropriate to the[ir] needs" (Section 504 Regulations, 34 C.F.R. § 104.34(a)). Education in the general education classroom, however, is not an absolute right. When the general education classroom is not an appropriate placement, a school must provide a student's special education in an appropriate setting, even when it is more restrictive. Nevertheless, the IDEA directs that schools move students to a more restrictive setting only when "education in regular classes with the use of supplementary aids and services cannot be achieved satisfactorily" (IDEA Regulations, 34 C.F.R. § 300.550(b)(2)). Section 504 also requires school officials to move a student from the general education environment only when it can be "demonstrated that the education of [a student] with the use of supplementary aids and services cannot be achieved satisfactorily (Section 504 Regulations, 34 C.F.R. § 104.34(a)). Both laws require schools to make good faith efforts to educate students with disabilities in less restrictive environments before proposing more restrictive placements. Such efforts must include the use of supplementary aids and services. For purposes of the law, supplementary aids and services are identical to related aids and services (Veir, 1993). Clearly, the law requires that related services must be used in an attempt to maintain a student in the general education classroom and other less restrictive settings.

Litigation

Irving Independent School District v. Tatro

The U.S. Supreme Court addressed the related services mandate in *Irving Independent School District v. Tatro* (1984; hereafter *Tatro*). The case involved an 8-year-old child, Amber Tatro, who had spina bifida and as a result had orthopedic disabilities and speech impairments. In addition, she had a neurogenic bladder and required catheterization every 3 or 4 hours to avoid damage to her kidneys. A relatively simple procedure, clean intermittent catheterization (CIC), was used to drain her bladder. In its decision, the high court noted that a trained layperson was capable of performing the procedure.

In 1979, the Irving Independent School District agreed to provide special education services to Amber. An IEP was written that included early childhood development classes and special services (e.g., physical and speech therapy). The IEP, however, contained no provisions to have school personnel administer CIC to Amber. The Tatros unsuccessfully pursued administrative remedies to have the school train personnel to provide these services. In an action brought by the Tatros in federal district court, the court ruled in favor of the school district, holding that CIC was not required by the IDEA. The court held that CIC was a medical service and thus excluded from the related services mandate. The Tatros filed an appeal with the U.S. Court of Appeals for the Fifth Circuit. The appellate court reversed the district court's ruling in holding that CIC was a supportive service, not a medical service, and thus had to be provided by the school. The school district then filed a petition of certiorari with the U.S. Supreme Court. The high court, finding the school district's contention that CIC was a medical service unpersuasive, affirmed the appellate court's ruling that required the school to provide CIC as a related service. The Court stated that the related services mandate requires that schools make "specific provisions for [related] services, like transportation, for example, that do no more than enable a child to be physically present in the class" (*Tatro,* p. 3376). The Court noted that CIC allowed Amber to go to school and, therefore, was as important as her special education services.

The *Tatro* Three-Part Test

In his opinion, Chief Justice Burger listed three criteria necessary for a service to qualify as a related service. First, to be entitled to related services under the IDEA, a student has to have a disability and be placed in special education. According to the Court, if a student was not entitled to special education, there would be no obligation to provide related services under the IDEA. The Court did not address obligations under Section 504. Second, only those services necessary to allow a student to benefit from special education were required. Third, related services were only required if they could be performed by a nurse or qualified person; thus services that could only be performed by a physician were not required. Figure 10.1 presents the *Tatro* three-part test.

Figure 10.1
The *Tatro* Three-Part Test

1. The student must be eligible for special education services under the IDEA.
2. The service must be necessary to assist the student to benefit from special education.
3. The service must be performed by a nonphysician.

Specific Related Services

Two primary concerns have arisen in parent–school disagreements regarding what constitutes a related service under the IDEA or Section 504: (a) the added costs of providing certain related services, and (b) the determination of whether particular related services are actually needed to provide a FAPE. Legal questions have often been raised, especially regarding the more expensive related services, such as transportation, occupational and physical therapy, psychological services, and health-related services.

Transportation

Transportation, which includes travel to and from school as well as travel within the school and between schools, is a related service enumerated in the IDEA (IDEA Regulations, 34 C.F.R. § 300.16). Transportation also includes "specialized equipment (such as special adapted buses, lifts, and ramps) if required to provide special transportation for a child with a disability" (IDEA Regulations, 34 C.F.R. § 300.16(iii)). The specialized equipment requirement was litigated in *Macomb County Intermediate School District v. Joshua S.* (1989), in which the district court ruled that the school district was required to provide transportation to a child in special education who needed suctioning of his tracheotomy tube and repositioning of his wheelchair during transit. According to the court, the service was not an excluded medical service because the services of the student's physician were not required to perform the suctioning and repositioning.

Reimbursement for Transportation

The IDEA provides no guidance regarding parental reimbursement for transportation costs. Nevertheless, in cases in which transportation was held to be a necessary related service but was not provided by the school, courts have required reimbursement for parents who had to arrange and pay for their child's transit (*Hurry v. Jones,* 1984; *Taylor v. Board of Education,* 1986). For example, in *Hurry v. Jones,* the court indicated that a parent be reimbursed for mileage, time, and effort in accordance with the market value for services provided. If a school district offers to provide appropriate transportation services but the parents refuse them, opting to provide their own transportation, the parents may not demand reimbursement.

The requirement to provide transportation includes, when necessary, transportation from a parochial school to a program in a public school (IDEA Regulations, 34 C.F.R. § 300.403). In *Felter v. Cape Girardeau School District* (1993), the court held that a student was entitled to transportation from her parochial school to the public school as a related service under the IDEA. The court further ruled that, because the service was provided to the student rather than to the school and because the action had a secular purpose, this transportation from a religious to a public school did not violate the establishment clause of the First Amendment to the Constitution (pertinent constitutional amendments are listed in the Appendix).

Student Time in Transit

The IDEA's transportation requirements do not address matters such as time in transit, distance of bus ride, types of assistance that must be provided, and location of bus stops. The Office of Civil Rights (OCR), however, ruled that special education bus routes that cost students as much as 70 minutes in lost instructional time per day were discriminatory because the students did not receive a school day comparable in length to that received by students in general education (*Lincoln County School District*, 1991). If the time of transit in special education transportation is greatly in excess of the length of regular school transportation, and if no reasonable accommodations are attempted by the school district, the district may be in violation of Section 504 (*Atlanta (GA) Public Schools*, 1989; *Lafayette (IN) School Corporation*, 1990; *San Bernardino (CA) Unified School District*, 1990; *Santa Rosa County (FL) School District*, 1991) or the IDEA (OSEP Policy Letter, 1993b). Additionally, excessive transportation time can result in the denial of a FAPE (*Bonadonna v. Cooperman*, 1985). Excessive daily commutes may suggest the need for a change of placement. Although no administrative guidance is provided regarding what constitutes an excessive length of time in commuting to and from school, the student's commute should not exceed 1 hour to or from school unless the school district is located in a rural area (*Covington Community School Corporation*, 1991).

Responsibility to Provide Transportation

If students in special education need transportation to assist them to benefit from their special education program, it is a related service and must be provided. In district and interdistrict programs, the district with the responsibility of providing a FAPE is obligated to provide transportation as a related service under both the IDEA and Section 504 (Lutjeharms, 1990). School districts must also ensure that the school buses used in the transportation of students in special education are accessible to children with physical disabilities (*Kanawha County (WV) Public Schools*, 1989).

A Pennsylvania state court, in *North Allegheny School District v. Gregory P.* (1996), ruled that although transportation would be a related service if it were required to assist a student to benefit from special education, it was not required to accommodate the parents' living arrangement. The case involved a custody arrangement in which the student lived part-time with his father, who lived out of the school district, and part-time with his mother, who lived in the school district. The student's father sought to have the student transported to his home when the student lived with him. The district refused, agreeing only to provide transportation to and from the student's mother's house. The court affirmed the position taken by the school district, ruling that the IDEA obligated the school district to provide only those transportation and related services needed to accommodate a student's needs and did not extend to lifestyle preferences or personal needs.

Occupational and Physical Therapy

Physical therapy (PT), which IDEA regulations define as services provided by a physical therapist (IDEA Regulations, 34 C.F.R. § 300.16(b)(7)), and occupational therapy (OT), which includes "improving, developing, or restoring functions, parent counseling and training" (IDEA Regulations, 34 C.F.R. § 300.16(b)(5)), can both be related services. A number of courts and administrative decisions have emphasized the necessity of the schools' providing such services when needed by students with disabilities. In *Polk v. Central Susquehanna Intermediate Unit 16* (1988), the U.S. Court of Appeals for the Third Circuit held that a placement offered by a school district was inappropriate and that the placement chosen by the parents was appropriate, largely because of the availability of OT and PT in the latter setting. In a similar decision, a federal district court in New York upheld a placement in a special school for students with cerebral palsy because the special school had a physical therapist (*Taylor v. Board of Education,* 1986). In *Pittsburgh Board of Education v. Commonwealth Department of Education* (1983), a state court finding against a school district's cessation of OT and PT for a student with physical disabilities, when the need was supported by substantial evidence, ordered the district to begin OT and PT programs and awarded compensatory OT and PT programs for 1 year. Similarly, courts have also ordered reimbursement for parents who purchased OT and PT when it was a required related service and should have been provided by the school (*Das v. McHenry School District No. 15,* 1994; *Rapid City School District v. Vahle,* 1990). Courts have also ordered OT and PT as part of extended school year programs (*Holmes v. Sobol,* 1988).

Interpreters

The services of sign language interpreters have been the subject of a number of court cases and administrative decisions. *Board of Education of Hendrick Hudson School District v. Rowley* (1982), the first special education case heard by the U.S. Supreme Court, involved a parental request for an interpreter. This case, however, was not strictly a related services case but rather a case involving the IDEA's FAPE mandate.

According to Weber (1992), the case law is mixed, with some courts rejecting requests for interpretive services and other courts granting them. The Office of Special Education Programs (OSEP) has ruled that an interpretive service may be a related service under the IDEA if it is a developmental, supportive, or other support service required to assist students to benefit from their special education (OSEP Policy Letter, 1993a). For example, the parents of a high school student with a profound hearing loss requested that the school provide a sign language interpreter in a private religious school. The student met the requirements to receive special education and related services under the IDEA. The school denied the interpreter, however, stating that to do so would violate constitutional prohibitions against the state establishment of a religion. The U.S. District Court and the U.S. Court of Appeals for the Ninth Circuit ruled in favor of the school district. The parents appealed to the U.S. Supreme Court. The high court, in *Zobrest v. Catalina Foothills School District* (1993), reversed the appellate court's decision, holding that the establishment clause did not bar placing a public employee at a religious institution. The Court, however, did not discuss the extent to which the IDEA requires that related services be provided in religious schools.

Sometimes related services may be provided to the parent of a child with disabilities. The U.S. Court of Appeals for the Second Circuit, in *Rothschild v. Grottenhaler* (1990), ruled that Section 504, which applies to all persons with disabilities, required that a school district provide the deaf parents of two hearing students with a sign language interpreter so that they could participate in school conferences.

School Health Services

School health services "provided by a qualified school nurse or other qualified person" are required under the IDEA (IDEA Regulations, 34 C.F.R. § 300.16). According to Lear (1995), the definition of school health services is extremely broad and may run the gamut from activities requiring almost no training (e.g., dispensing oral medication), to those requiring increased levels of training (e.g., catheterization), to those requiring extensive training and requiring a substantial amount of time (e.g., tracheotomy care and chest physiotherapy). When health care services must be provided by a physician, they are not required related services but are excluded medical services. Under some state health services laws, certain health care services can only be provided under physician supervision. If such supervision is indirect, and does not require that a physician be present, typically these services will be considered school health services covered under the IDEA (Gorn, 1996). Also recall that in *Tatro,* the Supreme Court held that catheterization was not an excluded medical service because it was required by the plaintiff in order to benefit from special education and because the services could easily be provided by a school nurse or other qualified person. Tracheotomy care was also held to be a related service when it could be performed by school personnel in *State of Hawaii Department of Education v. Katherine D.* (1983).

School districts, however, are not required to provide therapeutic or treatment services that are performed by physicians. For example, in *Laughlin III v. Central Bucks School District* (1994), a federal district court ruled that the school district was not required to have a physician on call to be able to respond to medical emergencies of a medically fragile student when the student was in school. Similarly, drug treatment programs have been held to be excludable medical services under the IDEA in *Haddonfield Board of Education* (1990) and *Field v. Haddonfield Board of Education* (1991). School districts, therefore, are not required to place students in drug treatment programs; neither have they been required to reimburse parents for the cost of such programs.

Medical Services

Medical services are specifically excluded as related services (IDEA Regulations, 34 C.F.R. § 300.16(b)(11)), but medical services strictly for diagnostic and evaluation purposes are allowable under the IDEA. The statute and implementing regulations give no further guidance as to what constitutes medical services.

The Supreme Court, in *Tatro,* indicated that related services do not include services that must be performed by a physician. Similarly, OSEP recommended that school districts conduct a three-part test to determine if services that are medical in nature are, in fact, required related services (Greer, 1991). First, the student must be eligible for special education services under the IDEA. Second, the service must be necessary to assist the student to benefit from special education services. Finally, the school is required to provide the service only if it can be provided by a nurse or other qualified professional. If services can only be provided by a physician, they are not required related services. Furthermore, if the service can be provided during non-school hours, the school is not required to provide the service. OSEP's three-part test was based on the Supreme Court's ruling in *Tatro.* By adopting the *Tatro* "bright-line test" (i.e., clear standard), OSEP indicated that the essential distinction between a required health service and an excluded health service was that the latter must be provided by a physician.

Complex Health Services

Controversy has arisen regarding whether certain health-related services are included school health services or excluded medical services, and regarding when school health services cross the line to become medical services (Osborne, 1988; Rapport, 1996). The distinction between school health services and medical services becomes especially problematic when it involves medically fragile students.

Court decisions regarding complex health services have been varied. Some courts have ruled that complex health services are required related services, while others have held that complex health services are excludable medical services. In these decisions, the courts have looked at the specific facts in each case.

Complex Health Services as Excluded Medical Services

A number of courts have held that complex health services, even when not provided by a licensed physician, are excludable medical services rather than related services. In such situations, the courts have focused on the nature and extent of the services to determine whether they are allowable health services or excluded medical services. Some courts have indicated that complex services provided to medically fragile children who are technology dependent (e.g., a child fed through a gastronomy tube) may go beyond the requirements of the IDEA and Section 504 (Weatherly, 1994).

In *Detsel v. Board of Education* (1987), a federal district court in New York ruled that a school district was not required to reimburse parents for in-school nursing. The court stated that the health services were complicated (e.g., monitoring, maintenance, and responding to emergencies), continuous, and costly, and that the school nurse lacked the skills to perform the services. According to the court, "extensive, therapeutic health services . . . more closely resemble the medical services specifically excluded from the [IDEA]" (p. 1027). The services were, therefore, held to be excludable medical services. The *Detsel* court explained that *Tatro* was not controlling because the student required multiple services that were complex and required the assistance of a trained nurse. Additionally, the services were required continuously during the day, and any difficulties could be life-threatening.

In a case in which a student breathed through a tracheostomy tube and needed to be fed and medicated through a gastrostomy tube (*Bevin H. v. Wright*, 1987), the court held that the required nursing services were excludable medical services. The student, Bevin H., required constant care, and her attendant would be unavailable to assist other children. The effect of the student's needs required that she essentially have a person attending only to her. The court read a "reasonableness" qualification into the IDEA, holding that the district was not required to provide private nursing care.

In *Granite School District v. Shannon M.* (1992), a federal district court stated that the *Tatro* decision did not require that all school health services performed by persons other than physicians be considered related services regardless of the amount, complexity, or cost of the required care. The court held that continuous nursing care was an excludable medical service and, therefore, was not a required related service.

Ellison v. Board of Education of Three Village Central School District (1993) involved the provision of a school nurse to attend to the needs of a student who was paraplegic and required use of a ventilator to breathe. The court ruled that the level of nursing care required, which would have cost between $25,000 and $40,000 per year, went beyond school health services and was an excludable medical service. Similarly, in *Fulginiti v. Roxbury Township Public School* (1996) a federal district court held that constant monitoring and suctioning of a tracheotomy tube, which would cost the school district $56,000 a year, was unduly burdensome. The decision has been appealed to the U.S. Court of Appeals for the Third Circuit.

A federal district court, in *Neely v. Rutherford County Schools* (1994), held that even costly or complex services for medically fragile students may be allowable school health services if they do not require the presence of a physician. In this case the services of a nurse who constantly monitored Neely, a medically fragile student who required suctioning and ventilation, was ruled to be a related service because it allowed the child to attend school. The school district appealed the decision to the U.S. Court of Appeals for the Sixth Circuit (*Neely v. Rutherford County Schools*, 1995). The circuit court reversed the lower court court's ruling, holding that certain complex health services were inherently burdensome and not required by the IDEA.

Complex Health Services as Required Related Services

Some federal courts, however, have arrived at the opposite conclusion regarding complex school health services as an excluded medical service. These courts have tended to stay closer to the bright-line test of the *Tatro* decision. For example, the reasoning used in the *Ellison* decision was criticized by the court in *Macomb County Intermediate School District v. Joshua S.* (1989). According to the court, decisions that held continuous or complex nursing care to be an excluded medical service departed from the *Tatro* ruling, which only excluded related services performed by a licensed physician. The court, in returning to the *Tatro* standard, held that a child who needed positioning and tracheotomy services from a trained aide during transportation was to receive these as related services at school expense. According to the court, such services were required by the IDEA unless a physician was needed.

In *Cedar Rapids Community School District v. Garret F. by Charlene F.* (1997), a 12-year-old medically fragile student required catheterization, suctioning of tracheostomy, ventilator setting checks, ambubag administrations, blood pressure monitoring, and observations to determine if he went into respiratory distress. In effect, the student required continuous nursing services. The school argued that the services were medical and, therefore, excluded under the IDEA. A due process hearing officer held that the district was required to provide the services under state law and the IDEA. The school appealed to the federal district court, which also held that the school district was required to provide complex health services for the student. Because the student's needs could be adequately met without the services of a physician, the court held that the services constituted required related services under the IDEA. The school district appealed to the U.S. Court of Appeals for the Eighth Circuit.

The circuit court adopted the *Tatro* bright-line test in ruling that a school district was required to provide a wide variety of health care services to a medically fragile child. In applying the three-part *Tatro* test, the circuit court held that the school district was required to provide the services because they did not need to be administered by a physician. The services, although complex and extensive, were not excludable medical services under the IDEA.

Summary of Litigation on Complex Health Services

The litigation regarding school health services and the IDEA is complex and diverse. Nevertheless, the increasing numbers of medically fragile students in schools make it likely that school officials will be confronted with requests to provide these complex and expensive health-related services under the IDEA. The court decisions regarding complex health services are case-sensitive and do not provide practitioners with rules that can be applied uniformly. These decisions do, however, provide some guidance to help schools with decisions regarding the provision of complex health service as related services. Schools and school districts should have policies to assist them in deciding whether a related service is a covered school health service or an excluded medical service. These policies, however, must not be blanket policies, and all such decisions must be made on a case-by-case basis. Moreover, the IEP team is the proper decision-making body to weigh such decisions. Finally, the team must determine if the procedure is required to assist the student in benefiting from his or her special education, ascertain the cost of providing the service, and judge the level of expertise needed to provide the service. In making these decisions, other factors the team should consider include state laws regarding the provision of complex health and medical services, the complexity of a procedure being considered, and the risk of providing the service (The Special Educator, 1996). Also, the makeup of the IEP team in such situations should include professionals familiar with the health-related needs of the student.

Assistive Technology

The 1990 amendments added definitions of assistive technology devices and assistive technology services to the IDEA. The IDEA incorporated definitions used in the Technology-Related Assistance for Individuals with Disabilities Act (1988). According to the law, an assistive technology device is

> any item, piece of equipment, or product system, whether acquired commercially off the shelf, modified, or customized, that is used to increase, maintain, or improve the functional capabilities of children with disabilities. (IDEA Regulations, 34 C.F.R. § 300.5)

An assistive technology service is

> any service that directly assists a child with a disability in the selection, acquisition, or use of an assistive technology device. (IDEA Regulations, 34 C.F.R. § 300.6)

Assistive technology services may include evaluation, purchasing or leasing equipment, selecting, customizing, designing, and training for users and service providers.

The IDEA requires that schools provide students with disabilities access to technology-related devices and services, if necessary, as a special education service, related service, or in the general education classroom as a supplementary aid or service (Goodman, 1990). If the assistive technology device or service is required to assist a student to benefit from his or her special education, therefore, the school district is obligated to provide it to the student.

These devices and services can be made available as part of the student's special education or related services or as supplementary aids and services. The IDEA regulations require that a district need only provide assistive technology when it is educationally relevant. According to Julnes and Brown (1993), although the definition of assistive technology is broad, a school district will not be obligated to provide assistive technology services or devices if they are for medical purposes. Additionally, if assistive technology might be required, it is necessary that a person qualified to conduct assistive technology evaluations be on the IEP team.

If the team determines that the child also requires access to the technology in his or her home, the district must provide for home use, although the district retains ownership of the devices (OSEP Policy letter, 1992a). Assistive technology devices that OSEP has stated must be provided if needed to ensure a FAPE include calculators (Lambert, 1992), FM auditory training systems (OSEP Policy Letter, 1992b), closed-circuit televisions (OSEP Policy Letter, 1992a), computers (*In re Mary H.,* 1986), and computerized communication systems (*San Francisco Unified School District,* 1986). The use of a Self-Injurious Behavior Inhibiting System (SIBS) device may be a related service for a student with autism when the disability includes self-injurious behavior (*Northville Public Schools,* 1990; *Salinas Union High School District,* 1995). A list of types of assistive technology devices developed by the RESNA Technical Assistance Project (RESNA, 1992) is given in Table 10.2.

The IEP team must make decisions regarding the provision of assistive technology as they would regarding the provision of any other related services, on a case-by-case basis. Cost may be considered in choosing the assistive technology device, because the school district is not required to choose the most expensive item if a less expensive one is appropriate. It would be a violation of the IDEA, however, for the school district to automatically deny an assistive technology device because of expense. OSEP has indicated that if an IEP team determines that a student requires assistive technology services or devices to receive a FAPE, the services and devices must be identified in a student's IEP (OSEP Policy Letter, 1996).

Table 10.2
Assistive Technology Services and Devices

Service	Definition
Positioning	Providing assistance in body positioning and appropriate equipment so the student can participate in schoolwork (e.g., sidelying frames, crawling assists).
Computer access	Providing the student specialized equipment access that enables him or her to access computers (e.g., alternative input, output, and electronic communication devices).
Mobility	Specialized equipment that allows students to move around the school building and participate in student activities (e.g., walkers, wheelchairs, electronic image sensors).
Computer-based instruction	Specialized software that allows enhanced instruction and enhanced participation in activities (e.g., software for writing, spelling, reading, calculation, reasoning).
Physical education, recreation, and leisure	Technological equipment that enables the student with disabilities to participate in recreational and leisure activities (e.g., drawing software, painting with head wand, interactive laser disks, computer games, beeping balls or goalposts, adapted swimming and exercise equipment).
Environmental control	Equipment that allows students some control over their environment (e.g., remote control switches, adaptations of off/on switches).
Augmentative communication	Communication devices (e.g., symbol systems, communication boards/electronic communication, speech synthesizers).
Assistive listening	Alternative means of getting verbal information (e.g., hearing aids, text telephones, closed-caption TV).
Visual aids	Methods for assisting with vision needs (e.g., optical or electronic magnifying devices, low vision aids, large-print books, Brailled materials).
Self-care	Assistance with self-care activities like feeding, dressing, and toileting (e.g., robotics, electric feeders, adapted utensils).

Julnes and Brown (1993) contend that in determining if assistive technology is required, the team should answer the following four questions:

1. Is an assistive technology service or device required for the student to receive a FAPE?
2. Is an assistive technology service or device a required related service?
3. Is an assistive technology service or device necessary to maintain a student in an integrated placement?
4. Is an assistive technology service or device necessary to permit the student with disabilities to receive an education equivalent to that provided students without disabilities, thereby avoiding discrimination under Section 504?

OSEP has ruled that schools may access alternative funding sources such as Medicaid, Maternal and Child Health (MCH), and private insurance proceeds in order to help defray the costs of assistive technology (Cohen, 1992). The use of alternative funding, however, may not result in a reduction of assistance or service.

Section 504 does not specifically mention assistive technology; however, it does require the provision of special education, related services, and supplementary aids and services if necessary to provide a FAPE to a student with disabilities. Title II of the Americans with Disabilities Act (ADA) addresses the requirement that assistive technology, called auxiliary aids and services, be provided when necessary to accommodate an individual with disabilities. Among the aids and services described in the ADA are qualified interpreters, notetakers, transcription services, telephone handset amplifiers, assistive listening devices and systems, closed-caption decoders, videotext displays, taped texts, audio recordings, and Brailled materials. The ADA, which also protects parents with disabilities, specifies that public entities are not obligated to provide assistive technology devices and services of a solely personal nature (e.g., eyeglasses). (For elaborations on the ADA see Chapter 7.)

Currently, little case law exists interpreting the new assistive technology requirements. It is certain, however, that the provision of assistive technology may be necessary under the IDEA, Section 504, and the ADA if required to provide a FAPE. All students who may require such devices should be evaluated, therefore, to determine their specific needs.

Counseling and Psychological Services

Related services enumerated in the IDEA include counseling and psychological services. Regulations implementing the IDEA define counseling services as "services provided by qualified social workers, psychologists, guidance counselors, or other qualified personnel" (IDEA Regulations, 34 C.F.R. § 300.16(2)). Furthermore, parent counseling and training means "assisting parents in understanding the special needs of their child and providing parents with information about child development" (IDEA Regulations, 34 C.F.R. § 300.13(b)(6)). Psychological services include

(i) Administering psychological and educational tests, and other assessment procedures;
(ii) Interpreting assessment results;

(iii) Obtaining, integrating, and interpreting information about child behavior and conditions related to learning;

(iv) Consulting with other staff members in planning school programs to meet the special needs of children as indicated by psychological tests, interviews, and behavioral evaluations; and

(v) Planning and managing a program of psychological services, including psychological counseling for children and parents. (IDEA Regulations, 34 C.F.R. § 300.13(b)(8))

Additionally, in 1990 rehabilitation counseling was added to the list of possible related services listed in the IDEA. Rehabilitation counseling services are counseling services that focus specifically on career development, employment preparation, the achievement of independence, and integration into the workplace and community (IDEA Regulations, 34 C.F.R. § 300.16(B)(10)).

The area of counseling and psychological services has been highly litigated, and a number of administration actions and lawsuits have been brought against school districts that have failed to provide such services. In these cases, courts have tended to adopt an expansive view regarding psychological services and the requirement that they be necessary to allow a student to benefit from special education.

In *Gary B. v. Cronin* (1980), an injunction was granted against a state rule that excluded counseling and therapy from being considered special education or a related service. In the frequently cited *North v. District of Columbia Board of Education* (1979), a federal district court stated that in some situations it may be possible to determine whether a student's social, medical, and educational needs are severable (can be separated from each other), but in many situations it is not. Moreover, the court stated that the school district had the responsibility to pay for the student's residential placement, which included educational and psychological services.

In a number of cases, courts have held that counseling (*Gary B v. Cronin*, 1980; *Papaconda v. State Board of Connecticut*, 1981) and psychological services (*In the Matter of "A" Family*, 1983; *T.G. and P.G. v. Board of Piscataway*, 1983) are related services if needed by a student to assist him or her to benefit from educational services, and do not constitute exempted medical services. When schools have refused to provide such services, and courts have determined that they were needed related services, school districts have had to reimburse parents for the expense of private psychotherapists and even private placements in residential treatment programs. For example, courts in *Gladys J. v. Pearland Independent School District* (1981) and *Kruelle v. New Castle County School District* (1981) held that an appropriate education for students with severe emotional disturbances included psychotherapy and residential treatment.

Federal district courts in *McKenzie v. Jefferson* (1983) and *Darlene L. v. Illinois State Board of Education* (1983) denied reimbursement when parent's placements of their children in residential schools for psychotherapy were seen as medical in nature. In *Max M. v. Thompson* (1984), however, psychotherapy provided by a psychiatrist was reimbursable because the court felt that even though the psychiatrist was a licensed medical doctor, similar services could have been provided by a nonmedical therapist. The court stated that if the service could have been provided only by a psychiatrist it would constitute a medical service and not be reimbursable. In *Doe v. Anrig* (1987), a federal district court rejected a school district's contention that a related service need only be provided when it was for direct educational benefit. In ruling that the district had to reimburse the student's parents for psychotherapy, the court held that the psychotherapy (or any related service) need only help students to benefit from their education.

Counseling and psychological services are related services and, if required to meet the standards of a FAPE, must be provided. If they are not provided, and a court determines that psychotherapy was a necessary related service, the school will have to pay for the services. If, however, the behavior for which students were receiving psychotherapy did not assist them to benefit from the special education, or if the psychotherapy was meant to correct behaviors occurring solely outside of school, the district would not be obligated to pay. Maag and Katsiyannis (1996) recommended that schools consider the ramifications of not including counseling as a related service in the IEPs of students with disabilities who may require such services, especially students with emotional or behavioral disorders. Given the possibility of school districts' having to reimburse parents for the services of private psychotherapists and residential placements, this is very sound advice.

Residential Placement

Mattison and Hakola (1993) and Weatherly (1994) assert that the language of the IDEA clearly intends that residential placements are related services when essential to the provision of a FAPE. Courts have required school districts to fund the placement of students in parent-chosen residential facilities as a related service under the IDEA (Weatherly, 1994). According to regulations implementing the IDEA,

> If placement in a public or private residential program is necessary to provide special education and related services to a child with a disability, the program, including non-medical care and room and board, must be at no cost to the parents of the child. (IDEA Regulations, 34 C.F.R. § 300.302)

Section 504 has a similar requirement:

> If placement in a public or private residential program is necessary to provide a free appropriate public education to a handicapped person because of his or her handicap, the program, including non-medical care and room and board, shall be provided at no cost to the person or his or her parents or guardian. (Section 504 Regulations, 34 C.F.R. § 104.33(c)(3))

Residential placement is typically the most expensive placement in special education. Litigation regarding residential placements has been resolved in any of three ways: the school district has been found liable for costs incurred in unilateral parental placements; the courts have not required reimbursement to parents for placement; or the courts have attempted to separate the educational costs out of the total costs and hold the school district liable for only that portion (McAndrews, 1996).

Litigation on Residential Placement

In a number of cases, courts have found that residential placements were necessary to provide a FAPE and, thus, have required school districts to pay expenses incurred by the plaintiffs in obtaining these placements. In *Christopher T. v. San Francisco Unified School District* (1982), the U.S. District Court for the Northern District of California held that a residential placement is a related service if it is necessary for a student to receive benefit from special education. In *Chris D. v. Montgomery County Board of Education* (1990), a school district had identified a student as having a serious emotional disturbance (SED). The district acknowledged that a residential placement would be the best placement; however, the school offered placement in an isolated room in the school district's administrative building or in a homebound placement. Stating that the least restrictive environment (LRE) mandate required a placement that would provide the plaintiff with an opportunity for reintegration, the federal district court ordered the residential placement because it was less restrictive.

Residential placement was also ordered by a Tennessee federal district court in *Brown v. Wilson County School Board* (1990). The plaintiffs argued that a residential program was needed to provide a FAPE to a student with a traumatic brain injury. The plaintiffs requested that the school district provide a program that consisted of education in basic living skills, socialization, and behavior therapy. The school district, countering that the residential placement was medical in nature, offered homebound instruction. The court ordered the residential placement, stating that the student's education must be broadly defined to include behavior therapy and rehabilitation.

A school district, however, will not be held liable for cost incurred in a residential program when an appropriate educational program exists in the public school system (Mattison & Hakola, 1993). For example, in *Martin v. School Board of Prince George County* (1986) the court determined that the school had offered an educational program that allowed a student with SED to benefit and, therefore, the school had met its obligation under the IDEA. The residential placement was not required. Similarly, in *Hall v. Shawnee Mission School District* (1994), a federal district court in Kansas held that a school district did not have to pay for a parent-chosen residential placement when the district's program provided a FAPE, even though the child had severe behavior problems in the home.

Litigation and Quasi-Psychiatric Services

Courts are split in cases where the residential placements primarily consist of psychiatric-like services. In *Clovis Unified School District v. California Office of Administrative Hearings* (1990), the school argued that although the plaintiff was in need of a residential program, the district should not be required for pay for the placement because it was in response to a medical need. The court ruled that the school was not responsible for reimbursement because the services provided by the residential program were primarily medical and psychiatric in nature, and thus were excluded medical services. The court also stated that services did not have to be provided solely by a physician to be considered excludable medical services. Courts that have reached similar conclusions include *Ciresoli v. M.S.A.D.* (1995), *Darlene L. v. Illinois State Board of Education* (1983), *Los Gatos Joint Union High School District v. Doe* (1984), and *Metropolitan Government v. Tennessee Department of Education* (1989). These cases emphasized the medical services component of the residential placements. Similarly, in *Field v. Haddonfield Board of Education* (1991) a federal district court held that the placement of a student with SED in a residential drug treatment facility was for medical reasons and, thus, excluded from coverage under the IDEA. The decision confirmed an OSEP policy letter (1988), which stated that

> if a child is addicted and handicapped, public agencies are only required to provide the aspects of the child's program that would enable the child to receive FAPE. If a service is required solely to treat the child's addiction and is not required to provide FAPE, then the public agency is not required to provide the service or provide it at no cost. (p. 133)

Some courts have attempted to separate educational costs from noneducational costs and to hold school districts liable only for the former. In *Tice v. Botetourt County School Board* (1990), the U.S. Court of Appeals for the Fourth Circuit refused to hold the school district liable for all the costs associated with psychiatric hospitalization of a student whose evaluation had been delayed by the school district. The district was required to reimburse the parents for education-related expenses as well as a portion of the counseling the child received that was related to the educational services. Similarly, in *Taylor v. Honig* (1990), the U.S. Court of Appeals for the Ninth Circuit held that a full-time residential placement in a hospital that offered both educational and psychiatric services was required. To determine if the services were excludable medical services, the court examined whether the educational services were required by the IEP or the medical team. In *Teague Independent School District v. Todd L.* (1993), the U.S. Court of Appeals for the Fifth Circuit ruled that a public school's special education program was a more appropriate placement than a residential placement at a psychiatric institution, and did not hold the school district liable for costs. Additionally, the court found that the school's placement allowed for a greater degree of integration and was, therefore, the LRE. The court also determined that some of the services provided had been medical in nature.

Finally, many courts have held that the social, emotional, and behavioral development of a child is such an integral part of the educational program that it is unrealistic to attempt to separate these three aspects. This is especially true in cases involving students with SED. In *Kruelle v. New Castle County School District* (1981), the court stated that placements for medical, social, emotional, and educational purposes, when not severable, are a basis for determining that such services are essential for learning and, therefore, mandated under the law.

In three cases from the U.S. Courts of Appeals for the Sixth Circuit, courts rejected school districts' assertions that parents' unilateral placement of children in private residential programs with a psychotherapeutic component constituted treatment rather than education and was thus not reimbursable. In *Clevenger v. Oak Ridge School Board* (1984) and *Tilton v. Jefferson County Board of Education* (1983), the courts held that the school districts had to reimburse parents for the expenses of the private program with a psychiatric component. In the *Tilton* case, the court stated that

> The concept of education under the Act clearly embodies both academic instruction and a broad range of associated services traditionally grouped under the general rubric of "treatment." Any attempt to distinguish academics from treatment when defining "educational placement" runs counter to the clear language of the Act. (p. 803)

The third case, *Babb v. Knox County School System* (1992), followed the *Clevenger* and *Tilton* decisions in ruling that the school system had incorrectly determined that the plaintiff did not have an emotional disability, thereby writing a deficient IEP and denying much-needed psychological related services. In this case, a student with a history of academic and behavioral problems was evaluated for an emotional disability. The school determined that the child was not SED and, therefore, was not entitled to special education. The student's mother agreed with the assessment. When she later found that her son would be expelled for his continuing behavior problems, she removed him from school and enrolled him in a private hospital with a special education program for students with SED. In the hospital, the boy was diagnosed as SED. The student's parents then requested a due process hearing to determine if their child was SED and to seek tuition reimbursement for the hospital placement. The hearing officer, and subsequently the federal district court, issued decisions against the parents. The parents appealed to the U.S. Court of Appeals for the Sixth Circuit. The appellate court held that the student was SED and was entitled to special education services, including psychological services. The court held, therefore, that the school had to reimburse the plaintiffs for placement in the private school and pay their attorneys' fees.

Similarly, the U.S. Court of Appeals for the Second Circuit, in *Mrs. B. v. Milford Board of Education* (1997), ruled that a school district had to fund a residential placement for a student with a learning disability and emotional problems. The court found that the student required the residential placement, which included an educational and therapeutic component, to make educational progress.

Clearly, school districts are required to pay for a residential placement if that placement is required to provide an appropriate education. If, however, an appropriate education can be provided in the school setting, the school will not be required to provide a residential placement, even if that placement would provide a better education. Additionally, if the residential facility is a medical treatment facility, the services received may be medical and, therefore, excludable as a related service. Residential placements are more likely to be required when a student is in need of intensive care. Such a situation is likely when a student has a severe and profound disability or a severe emotional or behavioral disorder and cannot be provided a FAPE in the school setting. In the case of such placements, courts will be likely to heed the advice of the court in *North v. District of Columbia Board of Education*

(1979) and determine that "all of the student's needs are so intimately intertwined that it is not possible for the court to perform the Solomon-like task of separating them" (p. 136). If a school places a student at a residential facility, however, the school retains responsibility for ensuring that the student receives a FAPE (Breecher, 1991).

Other Related Services

Administrative agencies' decisions and court rulings have examined a number of related services in addition to those reviewed above. Speech therapy has been held to be a related service when necessary to enable a student to benefit from a special education (*Baldwin County Board of Education,* 1994; *Hillsborough County Board of Education,* 1994; *Johnson v. Lancaster-Lebanon Intermediate Unit 23,* 1991). Vision therapy (*Westminister School District,* 1994), play therapy (*Mill Valley Elementary School District,* 1994), and private tutorial services (*School District of Philadelphia,* 1989) have also been ordered to be provided by schools as related services. If interscholastic sports or other extracurricular activities are determined by the IEP team to be related services, they must be provided by the school (OSEP Policy Letter, 1990).

In some situations, schools may be required to provide related services to parents of students with disabilities and to parents with disabilities. Section 504 requires that all persons with disabilities, parents and children, be provided necessary related services. The IDEA also requires that school districts provide training for parents in areas such as behavior management and sign language as related services if this training is required to enable their child to benefit from special education.

Although the types of services that may qualify as related services under the IDEA are many and varied, the South Dakota Supreme Court recently ruled that teacher training in particular educational methodologies did not constitute a related service under the IDEA. In *Sioux Falls School District v. Koupal* (1994), the parents of a child with autism sought to have the court require their child's school to train teachers in a particular educational methodology called the TEACCH method. According to the court, teacher training, over and above the state's teacher certification requirements, could not be required under the IDEA because questions of teacher competency and educational methodologies are the sole province of the states.

Third-Party Billing for Related Services

The IDEA requires that special education and related services required to provide a FAPE be provided at no charge to the parents of students in special education. Nothing in the IDEA, however, relieves an insurer or similar third-party payer from a valid obligation to provide or pay for services (IDEA Regulations, 34 C.F.R.

§ 300.301(b)). A 1988 amendment to the Social Security Act allows schools to collect payment for covered services under Medicaid for students with disabilities, even if the services are included in the IDEA. Medicaid covers persons receiving Aid to Families with Dependent Children (AFDC), low-income pregnant women and their children, qualified persons age 65 or older, and persons who are blind, disabled, or receiving Supplemental Security Income (SSI). Services which must be paid for by Medicaid include early and periodic screening, diagnosis, and treatment for children, and physician services. Other services that may be covered include physical and occupational therapy, speech and language pathology, audiology, and physiological services. It is not permissible, however, for a school to provide a related service based on the availability of Medicaid funding (Mattison, 1996).

Schools can also tap private insurance companies, nonprofit health corporations, and health maintenance organizations (HMOs) to help defray the costs of related services (Spaller & Thomas, 1994). If there is any financial loss to the parents if such third-party payers are used, parents cannot be forced to use the third-party payer. Such losses include (a) depletion or lessening of lifetime benefits or annual coverage; (b) interference with future insurability; (c) an increase in premiums; or (d) termination of coverage (Mattison, 1996; Spaller & Thomas, 1994).

School District Responsibilities

When a student with disabilities is eligible for special education under the IDEA, the IEP team must determine if the related service is necessary to assist the student to benefit from his or her education; that is, if the student requires the service(s) to make meaningful progress toward his or her IEP goals and objectives, these services must be provided at no cost to the student's parents. If the student does not have a disability under the IDEA, he or she is not eligible to receive related services under that law. The appropriate forum for determination of related services is the IEP team.

Students with disabilities who are not eligible for special education under the IDEA but are protected from discrimination by Section 504 may be eligible to receive related services. The appropriate test under Section 504 is comparability of educational programs to those provided students without disabilities. If a particular related service is needed by a student with disabilities to receive a comparable education, that service may be required as a reasonable accommodation. The appropriate forum for decision making is the group of persons in the school or district responsible for ensuring compliance with Section 504.

When determining specific related services to be provided, cost may be a consideration. Excessive cost may not be used as a reason to deny a related service, but it may be used as a deciding factor when choosing between several options when all would fulfill the requirements of the needed service.

Summary

Related services are those developmental, corrective, and supportive services that are required to assist students with disabilities to benefit from their special education. A student with disabilities, however, is not entitled to a related service simply because of the presence of a disability. Under the IDEA, the IEP team must determine if a particular related service will assist a student to benefit from special education. If determined to be an educational necessity, the related service must be made available to a student as part of the student's FAPE. Furthermore, school districts must provide the related service at no cost to parents. Although the IDEA provides a nonexhaustive list of related services, when and to what extent these services are provided is sometimes disputed. The provisions of transportation, health services, interpreters, counseling and psychological services, and residential placements have been the subjects of administrative and court disputes. Medical services, except for diagnostic or evaluative purposes, are excluded as related services.

Students with disabilities protected under Section 504, even those not in special education, may also require related services. These services would not be provided under the IDEA, but rather under the reasonable accommodations requirement of Section 504. The reasonable accommodations requirement applies to parents with disabilities as well as to students.

Finally, related services, especially those that involve assistive technology, can be extremely expensive. If a related service is necessary to provide the student with a FAPE, it will be the responsibility of the school district. To help defray some of the costs, the district may be able to tap into third-party payment plans. If the utilization of third-party payment results in any cost to the parents, however, the funding may be accessed by a school district only with parental permission.

For Further Information

Technology:

Julnes, R. E., & Brown, S. E. (1993). The legal mandate to provide assistive technology in special education programming. *Education Law Reporter, 82,* 737–748.

RESNA Technical Assistance Project. (1992). *Assistive technology and the individualized education program.* Available from RESNA Technical Assistance Project, 1101 Connecticut Ave. NW, Suite 700, Washington, DC 20036, 202-857-1140.

Virtual Assistive Technology Center, Internet access http://www.sped.ukans.edu/%7Edlance/atweb.html

Counseling:

Maag, J. W., & Katsiyannis, A. (1996). Counseling as a related service for students with emotional or behavioral disorders: Issues and recommendations. *Behavioral Disorders, 21,* 293–305.

Third-party payment:

Spaller, K. D., & Thomas, S. B. (1994). A timely idea: Third-party billing for related services. *Education Law Reporter, 86,* 581–592.

Complex health services:

Rapport, M. J. (1996). Legal guidelines for the delivery of special health care services in school. *Exceptional Children, 62,* 537–549.

References

Americans with Disabilities Act, 42 U.S.C. §§ 12101–12213.

Atlanta (GA) Public Schools, 16 EHLR 19 (OCR 1989).

Babb v. Knox County School System, 965 F.2d 104 (6th Cir. 1992).

Baldwin County Board of Education, 21 IDELR 237 (SEA AL 1994).

Bevin H. v. Wright, EHLR 559:122 (W.D. Pa. 1987).

Board of Education of Hendrick Hudson School District v. Rowley, 458 U.S. 176 (1982).

Bonadonna v. Cooperman, 1985–86 EHLR 557:178 (D.N.J. 1985).

Breecher, Letter to, 18 IDELR 625 (OSEP 1991).

Brown v. Wilson County School Board, 747 F. Supp. 436 (Tenn. 1990).

Cedar Rapids Community School District v. Garret F. by Charlene F., 25 IDELR (6th Cir. 1997).

Chris D. v. Montgomery County Board of Education, 753 F. Supp. 922 (M.D. Ala. 1990).

Christopher T. v. San Francisco Unified School District, 553 F. Supp. 1107 (N.D. Cal. 1982).

Ciresoli v. M.S.A.D., 901 F. Supp. 378 (D. Me. 1995).

Clevenger v. Oak Ridge School Board, 744 F.2d 514 (6th Cir. 1984).

Clovis Unified School District v. California Office of Administrative Hearings, 903 F.2d 625 (9th Cir. 1990).

Cohen, Letter to, 19 IDELR 278 (OSEP, 1992).

Covington Community School Corporation, 18 IDELR 180 (SEA Ind. 1991).

Darlene L. v. Illinois State Board of Education, 568 F. Supp. 1340 (1983).

Das v. McHenry School District No. 15, 20 IDELR 979 (N.D. Ill. 1994).

Detsel v. Board of Education, 820 F.2d 587 (2nd Cir. 1987).

Doe v. Anrig, 651 F. Supp. 424 (1987).

Ellison v. Board of Education of the Three Village Central School District, 19 IDELR 1027 (N.Y. App. Div. 1993).

Felter v. Cape Girardeau School District, 810 F. Supp. 1062 (E.D. Mo. 1993).

Field v. Haddonfield Board of Education, 769 F. Supp. 1142 (E.D. Mich. 1991).

Fulginiti v. Roxbury Township Public School, 24 IDELR 218 (D.N.J. 1996).

Gary B. v. Cronin, 542 F. Supp. 102 (1980).

Gladys J. v. Pearland Independent School District, 520 F. Supp. 869 (S.D. Tex. 1981).

Goodman, Letter to, 19 EHLR 1317 (OSEP 1990).

Gorn, S. (1996). *What do I do when . . . The answer book on special education law.* Horsham, PA: LRP Publications.

Granite School District v. Shannon M., 787 F. Supp. 1020 (D. Utah 1992).

Greer, Letter to, 19 IDELR 348 (OSEP 1992).

Haddonfield Board of Education, 16 EHLR 1293 (SEA N.J. 1990).

Hall v. Shawnee Mission School District, 21 IDELR 557 (Kan. 1994).

Hillsborough County Board of Education, 21 IDELR, 191 (SEA FL 1994).

Holmes v. Sobol, 690 F. Supp. 154 (W.D.N.Y. 1988).

Hurry v. Jones, 734 F.2d 879 (1st Cir. 1984).

Individuals with Disabilities Education Act (IDEA), 20 U.S.C. §§ 1400–1485.

Individuals with Disabilities Education Act (IDEA) Regulations, 34 C.F.R. §§ 300.1–300.653.

In re Mary H., EHLR 506:325 (1986).

In the Matter of "A" Family, 602 P.2d 157 (1983).

Irving Independent School District v. Tatro, 468 U.S. 883 (1984).

Johnson v. Lancaster-Lebanon Intermediate Unit 23, 17 EHLR 456 (ED PA 1991).

Julnes, R. E., & Brown, S. E. (1993). The legal mandate to provide assistive technology in special education programming. *Education Law Reporter, 82,* 737–748.

Kanawha County (WV) Public Schools, 16 EHLR 450 (OCR 1989).

Kruelle v. New Castle County School District, 642 F.2d 687 (3rd Cir. 1981).

Lafayette (IN) School Corporation, 16 EHLR 656 (OCR 1990).

Lambert, Letter to, 18 IDELR 1039 (OSEP, 1992).

Laughlin III v. Central Bucks School District, 20 IDELR 894 (E.D. Pa. 1994).

Lear, R. (1995). The extent of public schools' responsibility to provide health-related services. In *Proceedings of the 16th Annual Institute on Legal Issues of Educating Students with Disabilities.* Alexandria, VA: LRP Conference Division.

Lincoln County School District, 17 EHLR 313 (OCR 1991).

Los Gatos Joint Union High School District v. Doe, 1984-82 EHLR 556:281 (N.D. Cal. 1984).

Lutjeharms, Letter to, 16 EHLR 554 (OCR, 1990).

Maag, J. W., & Katsiyannis, A. (1996). Counseling as a related service for students with emotional or behavioral disorders: Issues and recommendations. *Behavioral Disorders, 21,* 293–305.

Macomb County Intermediate School District v. Joshua S., 715 F. Supp. 824 (E.D. Mich. 1989).

Martin v. School Board of Prince George County, 348 S.E. 2d 857 (Va. App. 1986).

Mattison, D. A. (1996). Related services. In *Proceedings of the 17th National Institute on Legal Issues in Educating Individuals with Disabilities.* Horsham, PA: LRP Publications.

Mattison, D. A., & Hakola, S. R. (1993). Related services under the IDEA. In *Proceedings of the 14th National Institute on Legal Issues in Educating Individuals with Disabilities.* Horsham, PA: LRP Publications.

Max M. v. Thompson, 592 F. Supp. 1450 (1984).

McAndrews, D. C. (1996). Psychiatric hospitalization: When is it the responsibility of school districts? In *Proceedings of the 16th National Institute on Legal Issues in Educating Individuals with Disabilities.* Alexandria, VA: LRP Publications.

McKenzie v. Jefferson, 556 F. Supp. 43 (1983).

Metropolitan Government v. Tennessee Department of Education, 771 S.W. 2d (Tenn. Ct. App. 1989).

Mill Valley Elementary School District, 21 IDELR 612 (SEA CA 1994).

Mrs. B. v. Milford Board of Education, 25 IDELR 217 (2nd Cir. 1997).

Neely v. Rutherford County Schools, 851 F. Supp. 888 (M.D. Tenn. 1994), 23 IDELR 334 (6th Cir. 1995).

North v. District of Columbia Board of Education, 471 F. Supp. 136 (D.D.C. 1979).

North Allegheny School District v. Gregory P., 25 IDELR (1996).

Northville Public Schools, 16 EHLR 847 (Mich. 1990).

Osborne, A. G. (1988). *Complete legal guide to special education services.* West Nyack, NY: Parker.

OSEP Policy Letter, EHLR 213:133 (OSEP 1988).

OSEP Policy Letter, 17 EHLR 180 (OSEP 1990).

OSEP Policy Letter, 18 IDELR 627 (OSEP 1992a).

OSEP Policy Letter, 18 IDELR 1037 (OSEP, 1992b).

OSEP Policy Letter, 20 IDELR 177 (OSEP 1993a).

OSEP Policy Letter, 20 IDELR 1155 (OSEP 1993b).

OSEP Policy Letter, 24 IDELR 854 (OSEP 1996).

Papaconda v. State Board of Connecticut, 528 F. Supp. 68 (1981).

Pittsburgh Board of Education v. Commonwealth Department of Education, 581 A.2d 683 (1983).

Polk v. Central Susquehanna Intermediate Unit 16, 853 F.2d 171 (3rd Cir. 1988).

Rainforth, Letter to, 17 EHLR 222 (OSEP 1990).

Rapid City School District v. Vahle, 922 F.2d 476 (8th Cir. 1990).

Rapport, M. J. (1996). Legal guidelines for the delivery of special health care services in school. *Exceptional Children, 62,* 537–549.

RESNA Technical Assistance Project. (1992). *Assistive technology and the individualized education program.* Washington, DC: Author.

Rothschild v. Grottenhaler, 907 F.2d 286 (2nd Cir. 1990).

Salinas Union High School District, 22 IDELR 301 (Cal. 1995).

San Bernardino (CA) Unified School District, 16 EHLR 656 (OCR 1990).

San Francisco Unified School District, EHLR 507:416 (OCR 1986).

Santa Rosa County (FL) School District, 18 IDELR 153 (OCR 1991).

School District of Philadelphia, 16 EHLR 119 (OCR 1989).

Section 504 Regulations, 34 C.F.R. § 104.33(a).

Senate Report of the Individuals with Disabilities Act Amendments of 1997, available at wais.access.gpo.gov.

Shelby, Letter to, 21 IDELR 61 (OSERS 1994).

Sioux Falls School District v. Koupal, 22 IDELR 26 (S.D. 1994).

Spaller, K. D., & Thomas, S. B. (1994). A timely idea: Third-party billing for related services. *Education Law Reporter, 86,* 581–592.

The Special Educator. (August 30, 1996). *Experts offer tips on evaluating related services.* Horsham, PA: LRP Publications.

State of Hawaii Department of Education v. Katherine D., 727 F.2d 809 (1983).

T.G. and P.G. v. Board of Piscataway, 576 F. Supp. 420 (1983).

Taylor v. Board of Education, 649 F. Supp. 1253 (N.D.N.Y. 1986).

Taylor v. Honig, 910 F.2d 627 (9th Cir. 1990).

Teague Independent School District v. Todd L., 999 F.2d 127 (5th Cir. 1993).

Technology-Related Assistance for Individuals with Disabilities Act, 29 U.S.C. § 2201, 2202 (1988).

Tice v. Botetourt County School District, 908 F.2d 1200 (4th Cir. 1990).

Tilton v. Jefferson County Board of Education, 705 F.2d 800 (6th Cir. 1983).

Veir, Letter to, 20 IDELR 864 (OCR 1993).

Weatherly, J. J. (1994). Recent developments concerning the provision of related services to children with disabilities. In *Proceedings of the 15th National Institute on Legal Issues in Educating Individuals with Disabilities.* Horsham, PA: LRP Publications.

Weber, M. C. (1992). *Special education law and litigation treatise.* Horsham, PA: LRP Publications.

West Chester Area School District, 18 IDELR 802 (SEA PA 1992).

Westminister School District 21 IDELR 398 (SEA CA 1994).

Zirkel, P. A. (1993). *Section 504 and the schools.* Horsham, PA: LRP Publications.

Zobrest v. Catalina Foothills School District, 113 S.Ct. 2462 (1993).

CHAPTER ELEVEN

Identification, Assessment, and Evaluation

The goal of all evaluations, whether district initiated or independent educational evaluation, is to aid the parties to develop an appropriate program to meet the child's needs.

Freedman (1996)

The individuals with Disabilities Education Act (IDEA) requires that before a student is placed in a special education program, he or she is evaluated or assessed to determine (a) whether a disability exists; (b) if, because of that disability, the student requires special education and related services; and (c) what educational needs the student has. The parents of the student must give consent prior to such an evaluation. Similarly, if a student has a disability under Section 504 of the Rehabilitation Act of 1973, an assessment must be conducted prior to developing an individualized accommodation plan. Under both laws, the evaluation is the key to determining whether a disability exists and what educational services or accommodations are required to meet the unique needs of the student.

The regulatory language of both of these federal laws covering evaluations is comprehensive and detailed. It is the responsibility of the schools to locate and evaluate students with special needs in accordance with these regulations. Deficiencies in a school's evaluation process and procedures are a very serious matter, especially if the school has reason to suspect the student may have a disability. Such deficiencies can lead to the deprivation of a free appropriate public education (FAPE), and possible court action (Gorn, 1996).

The purpose of this chapter is to examine federal statutes, regulations, and cases, as well as administrative rules and guidelines involving the identification, assessment, and evaluation of students with disabilities for determination of eligibility for and placement in special education. The issues of minimum-competency testing and the inclusion of students with disabilities in accountability efforts will also be discussed.

Definition of Assessment

According to Salvia and Ysseldyke (1995), assessment is the process of collecting information for the purpose of making decisions about students. The information collected may include test data, work samples, and the results of observations, interviews, and screenings. Assessment in special education involves decisions in a number of areas, including prereferral classroom decisions, entitlement decisions, post-entitlement decisions, and accountability/outcome decisions (Salvia & Ysseldyke, 1995).

Prereferral Decisions

Prereferral classroom decisions are made by the classroom teacher prior to formally referring a student for special education. Assessment tools may be used by teachers to assist them in making decisions regarding prereferral interventions. Prereferral interventions are used in the general education classroom to attempt to ameliorate the problem prior to referral to special education. Informal prereferral assessments may include classroom tests, daily observations, and interviews.

Entitlement Decisions

The second category of assessment decision involves so-called entitlement decisions. Entitlement decisions are those identification and classification decisions, based on individualized assessment, that are used to identify students as having disabilities and to determine if they require special education and related services. Salvia and Ysseldyke (1995) include screening, referral, and eligibility decisions under entitlement decisions.

Screening is the process of collecting data to determine whether more intensive assessment is necessary (Ysseldyke & Algozzine, 1995). Screenings are typically done with all students in a particular school or school district. Students scoring below a certain cutoff point on the screening instrument(s) are considered for further assessment. When screenings are conducted in this manner and not conducted selectively with individual students, they are not subject to the rules and regulations of the IDEA (IDEA Regulations, 34 C.F.R. § 300.500(3)(b)) or Section 504. If they are conducted with an individual or a small group of individuals to determine interventions or placements, however, they do require parental consent (Holmes, 1992).

Referral decisions usually involve a determination by a teacher or parent that a student may need special education. Usually a teacher completes a referral form that brings a student to the attention of a school's multidisciplinary team (MDT). The referral is a formal request made to the MDT to have a student evaluated for the presence of a disability. Although school districts may have procedures regarding referrals, referrals are not subject to the federal special education laws. Following a student referral, the MDT determines if the student requires further assessment to determine eligibility for special education. The final type of entitlement decision, therefore, is the determination of eligibility. Evaluations for eligibility are subject to the rules and regulations of the IDEA.

Post-Entitlement Decisions

Post-entitlement decisions are based on evaluations of students and are used in planning instruction, writing goals and objectives, and evaluating student progress. The post-entitlement decisions, such as writing the individualized education plan (IEP) and determining placement, are also subject to the strictures of the IDEA.

Accountability/Outcome Decisions

The final area of assessment decisions in special education, according to Salvia and Ysseldyke (1995), involves accountability/outcome decisions. Accountability/outcome decisions involve the collection of assessment data to evaluate curricula, specific programs, and the schoolwide, statewide, or national performance of students. Currently, the federal special education laws do not cover accountability and outcome data of this sort. A number of court cases, however, have addressed these macro assessments, especially as they involve minimum-competency testing.

Protection in Evaluation Procedures

Regulations to the IDEA and Section 504 require that schools evaluate students when a disability is suspected. According to Section 504, an evaluation or reevaluation that is in compliance with the procedural requirements of the IDEA will also be in compliance with the requirements of Section 504. Guernsey and Klare (1993), however, indicate that if a school is in compliance with either the IDEA or Section 504, this does not necessarily ensure compliance with the other law. It is, therefore, important that schools be aware of the procedural requirements of both laws.

Prereferral Evaluation

Prereferral evaluations have become an important component in the referral process (Salvia & Ysseldyke, 1995). Prereferral interventions are conducted in the general education classroom to attempt to ameliorate or remediate the problem prior to referral to special education. These interventions are typically based on informal prereferral evaluations such as classroom tests, daily observations, and interviews. Because of the informal nature of prereferral assessments and interventions, they are not subject to the strictures of the IDEA. It is important, however, that prereferral interventions not have the effect of delaying the referral of an eligible student (Bateman, 1995).

Preplacement Evaluation

A school's MDT determines the need for an evaluation based on referral or screening that indicates that a student may have a disability. Referrals from teachers or parents typically will lead to an evaluation by the school; in fact, according to Algozzine, Christenson, and Ysseldyke (1982), approximately 92% of all referrals lead to a full evaluation. Following consideration of the referral, the MDT may choose not to conduct an evaluation under either the IDEA or Section 504 if there is no reasonable basis to suspect that a disability exists (Gorn, 1996; Williams, 1993). If a school declines a parental request to evaluate a student, the district must notify the parents in writing of the refusal. The notification must include the reasons for the refusal and inform the parents of their due process options (OSEP Policy Letter, 1994). Although refusing a parental request to evaluate is an option, a school district invites court action and possible remedies for violation of the IDEA and Section 504 if it is later determined that a student did have a disability requiring services under either law.

Comprehensiveness of the Evaluation

The IDEA requires that prior to the initiation of special education placement or services, a comprehensive and individualized evaluation of the child's educational needs be conducted. The evaluation must include all suspected areas of need, including, when appropriate, health, vision, hearing, social and emotional status, general intelligence, academic performance, communicative status, and motor abilities (IDEA Regulations 34 C.F.R. § 300.532(f)). Additionally, a school district must conduct an assistive technology evaluation if needed (Fisher, 1995). Furthermore, once a child is identified during the screening or referral process as possibly having a disability, the MDT team must conduct the evaluation in a timely manner (Kelly, 1981). The federal statutes and regulations do not establish a specific time limit, although many states have chosen to do so (Guernsey & Klare, 1993). Typically, such time limits will be between 30 and 45 days. Delays in preplacement evaluations may result in due process hearings, court actions, and the possible imposition of remedies such as tuition reimbursement, attorneys' fees, or compensatory education (*Bartow (GA) County School District*, 1995; *Chicago Board of Education*, 1984; *Foster v. District of Columbia Board of Education*, 1982; Williams, 1993).

Section 504 Evaluation

Section 504 requires that preplacement evaluations be conducted of all students identified as possibly having a disability (Section 504 Regulations, 34 C.F.R. § 104.35). The Section 504 evaluation must be completed prior to placement and also must be completed in a timely manner once the school district becomes aware of the student's possible disability (Section 504 Regulations, 34. C.F.R. § 104.35(a)(b)(c)).

Parental Consent

A reasonable amount of time prior to conducting an evaluation, the school must notify the parents in writing of its intent to conduct an evaluation and obtain their consent to proceed. The notice must be understandable to the general public and must contain an explanation of the parents' due process rights as well as descriptions of what the school is proposing and the evaluation procedures to be used. If the parents refuse to consent to the evaluation, the school may use hearing procedures to determine if the child should be evaluated. The school district, however, is not required to request a hearing (Ackenhalt, 1994). Similarly, if the school refuses a parental request to conduct an evaluation, the parents may also challenge the refusal through the IDEA's hearing procedures. Section 504 also requires parental notice and consent for the initial evaluation. Unlike the IDEA, however, Section 504 does not require a due process hearing to override parental lack of consent (Zirkel, 1995).

Following parental consent for preplacement evaluation, the IDEA does not require that consent be obtained for subsequent evaluations, even when the school uses additional assessment procedures following the initial evaluation (*Carroll v. Capalbo,* 1983; Tinsley, 1990). This is because parental consent is for the entire evaluation process, not for individual parts of it (Graham, 1989).

Qualifications of Evaluators

The evaluation is conducted by members of the MDT. Moreover, the MDT must include at least one teacher or specialist in the area of the child's suspected disability. When a learning disability is suspected, the team must also include the student's general education teacher or a person qualified to teach students with learning disabilities, as well as a person qualified to conduct an individual diagnostic examination of the student, such as a school psychologist. The team's evaluators must be qualified in assessing and evaluating children with disabilities. Additionally, the Office of Special Education Programs (OSEP) has stated that evaluators must meet the qualification criteria established by the producer of the evaluation instrument (OSEP Policy Letter, 1995a).

Parental participation in the evaluation process is allowed, although it is not required (OSEP Policy Letter, 1993a). Parents may inquire about the qualifications of the examiner; therefore, OSEP recommends that school districts have written criteria for evaluators (OSEP Policy Letter, 1995a).

Section 504 also requires that the team be comprised of a knowledgeable and specialized group of persons; however, it does not specifically indicate the persons this team must include. The persons who actually conduct the evaluations must be trained in evaluation and must administer all assessment tools in accordance with the instructions provided by the test producers.

Evaluation Materials and Procedures

The IDEA details the specific requirements of the evaluation procedures and materials in a legally correct preplacement evaluation (IDEA Regulations, 34 C.F.R. § 300.532). Figure 11.1 lists the requirements of the IDEA regarding the selection of evaluation materials and procedures to follow in conducting the evaluation.

The evaluation materials must be provided and administered in the child's native language or other mode of communication unless it is not feasible to do so. This requirement is especially important when evaluating a student with limited English proficiency. According to the IDEA, a student's native language is the language normally used by the student's parents (IDEA Regulations 34 C.F.R. § 300.12). The reasoning behind this regulation is that the tests used must reflect a student's actual ability rather than his or her fluency in English. If a student is bilingual and shows age-appropriate English proficiency, however, the school district may test the student in English even though English may not be the student's native language. English may also be used in testing even when it is not the language used by the student's parents (*Greenfield Public School,* 1994; IDEA Regulations, 34 C.F.R. § 300.12, Note (1)). The term "mode of communication" refers to the means of communication normally used by individuals who are deaf, blind, or have no written language, and may include Braille, sign language, oral communication, or technologically enhanced communication (IDEA Regulations, 34 C.F.R. § 300.12, Note (2)).

Tests used for preplacement evaluation must be validated for the specific purpose for which they are being used. A valid test is one that measures what it purports to measure (Salvia & Ysseldyke, 1995). Neither the IDEA nor Section 504, however, sets forth rules or regulations regarding the determination of test validity. Presumably, tests validated by their publishers will fulfill this criterion (Gorn, 1996).

Figure 11.1
IDEA Evaluation Material and Procedures Requirements

1. Test and other evaluation materials must be
   - provided and administered in the student's native language or mode of communication unless not feasible to do so
   - validated for the specific purpose for which they are used
   - administered by trained personnel in conformity with instructions
2. The evaluation must be tailored to access specific areas of educational need.
3. The evaluation must be designed to reflect the student's aptitude or achievement level rather than reflecting the student's disabilities, unless intended to do so.
4. No single procedure is used as the sole criterion to determine FAPE.
5. Decisions are made by a multidisciplinary team including one person knowledgeable in the area of suspected disability.
6. The student is assessed in all areas of suspected disability.

Additionally, the evaluation must be designed to assess specific areas of educational need rather than merely providing a single intelligence score. Assessment instruments must be selected and administered to ensure that they accurately reflect the student's aptitude or achievement levels, rather than the student's impaired skills (unless they purport to measure the impaired skills). Finally, no single procedure can be used as the sole criterion for placement or determining the appropriate program.

The selection of the evaluation materials is left to the school district or state as long as the aforementioned criteria are met. The only exception is the evaluation of a student for a specific learning disability. The IDEA delineates a set of specific procedures that the MDT must follow when assessing a student for the presence of a learning disability (IDEA Regulations, 34 C.F.R. § 300.541). The additional requirements involve the determination of a "severe discrepancy" between achievement and ability. What exactly constitutes a severe discrepancy is not defined in the IDEA, but rather is left to the states. Quantitative formulas may be used, but MDTs must not use them in a mechanical matter. The MDT must be flexible in discrepancy determination and not depend solely on the formula in the decision-making process (Gorn, 1996). Furthermore, an observation of a student in the general education classroom and the preparation of a written report of the evaluation results are required (IDEA Regulations, 34 C.F.R. § 300.542–543). The additional criteria for determining the existence of a specific learning disability are listed in Figure 11.2. Figure 11.3 contains the IDEA's requirement for the written report.

Nondiscriminatory Evaluation

Both the IDEA and Section 504 require schools to select and administer tests that are not racially or culturally discriminatory. This requirement, however, is not specific and does not provide guidance to a school district in determining if an assessment measure is discriminatory or whether local norming to adjust for economic deprivation or discrimination is required (OSEP Policy Letter, 1992).

An area of particular concern in special education has been the overrepresentation of minority students. Much of this concern has focused on the selection of discriminatory evaluation materials and procedures, especially the use of tests that result in a global score indicating an intelligence quotient (IQ). The primary concern has been that IQ tests, when used for making placement decisions, may result in the overreferral of minority students or students from economically disadvantaged backgrounds.

Larry P. v. Riles

In *Larry P. v. Riles* (1979; hereafter *Larry P.*), a federal district court in California banned the use of standardized IQ instruments to evaluate African-American students for placement in classes for students with educable mental retardation (EMR). The court ruled that such tests contained racial and cultural bias and discriminated against students from racial minorities. The decision was affirmed by the U.S. Court of Appeals for the Ninth Circuit. In 1986, the *Larry P.* ban was expanded to include IQ testing of African-American students for all special education placements.

Figure 11.2
Criteria for Determining a Specific Learning Disability

1. The student does not achieve commensurate with age or ability level when provided with appropriate learning experiences.
2. The MDT finds that a student has a severe discrepancy between achievement and intellectual ability in one or more of the following:
   - oral expression
   - listening comprehension
   - written expression
   - basic reading skill
   - reading comprehension
   - mathematics calculation, or
   - mathematics reasoning
3. The MDT may not identify a student as having a learning disability if the discrepancy is primarily the result of
   - a visual, hearing, or motor impairment
   - mental retardation
   - emotional disturbance
   - environmental, cultural, or economic disadvantage

Figure 11.3
Written Report for Specific Learning Disability

1. The MDT shall prepare a written report of the evaluation results consisting of
   - whether the student has a specific learning disability
   - the basis for making the determination
   - the relevant behavior noted during the observation
   - the educationally relevant medical findings, if any
   - whether there is a severe discrepancy between achievement and ability that is not correctable without special education
   - the MDT's determination regarding the effects of environmental, cultural, or economic disadvantage
2. Team members shall certify in writing whether the report reflects their conclusions. If it does not, the member must submit a separate statement.

Parents in Action on Special Education v. Hannon

Shortly after the first *Larry P.* decision, a federal district court, in *Parents in Action on Special Education v. Hannon* (1980), arrived at a different conclusion regarding standardized IQ tests. According to the court, the Wechsler Intelligence Scale for Children (WISC), the WISC-R, and the Stanford-Binet IQ tests were not racially or culturally discriminatory. The court further held that they could be used in the special education placements of African-American children. The court also found that the school district had not used the IQ tests as the sole basis for special education placement, thereby complying with the IDEA.

Crawford v. Honig

The *Larry P.* ban on IQ testing for purposes of placing African-American students in special education classes was vacated in 1994 by the U.S. Court of Appeals for the Ninth Circuit in *Crawford v. Honig.* The action was brought by African-American students who sought to have standardized IQ tests administered in special education evaluations so that they could qualify for special education for students with learning disabilities. A federal district court consolidated the case with *Larry P.* and vacated the 1986 modification, which had prohibited IQ tests in all special education placements. The court, however, left the original ban against using IQ tests to place African-American students in EMR classes in effect. The *Larry P.* plaintiffs, the superintendent of public instruction, and the California State Board of Education appealed the decision to vacate the modification to the Ninth Circuit court. The appellate court affirmed the lower court's ruling, stating that the 1986 modification inappropriately expanded the scope of the original injunction because the modification was not supported by factual findings. The appellate court decision did not address the underlying facts of *Larry P.* but only examined the propriety of extending the original ban on IQ tests. In fact, the court indicated that the discriminatory nature of IQ tests was a disputed issue of fact to be addressed in future *Larry P.* proceedings.

Nevertheless, the decision of the appellate court seemed to indicate that neither the IDEA nor Section 504 prohibits the use of IQ tests per se in special education evaluations. This indication affirmed a position taken by the Office of Special Education and Rehabilitative Services (OSERS) a year earlier, that the appropriate use of IQ tests is not prohibited (Warrington, 1993). According to Gorn (1996), IQ tests can be a valuable part of the evaluation process as long as they are valid, are not racially or culturally discriminatory, and are not used as the sole criterion for placement.

Interpretation of Evaluation Data

When the evaluation is completed, the MDT must draw on the results of all the instruments used, as well as other information provided in the decision-making process. The law requires that professional judgment be relied on; sole reliance on formulas or quantitative guidelines is not permitted (Bateman, 1995).

Figure 11.4
Interpreting Evaluation Data

In interpreting evaluation data, the MDT must

- draw on information from a variety of sources, including aptitude and achievement tests, teacher recommendations, physical condition, social or cultural background, and adaptive behavior
- ensure that information is documented and carefully considered
- ensure that decisions are made by a team including a person knowledgeable about the student, the meaning of the evaluation data, and the placement options
- ensure that the placement decision is made in accordance with LRE requirements

Drawing on the information gathered during the evaluation process, the MDT first determines a student's eligibility; that is, does a student have a disability covered under the IDEA or Section 504? Second, the MDT determines whether, because of the disability, a student requires special education and related services. Regulatory guidelines for interpreting evaluation data are reported in Figure 11.4.

School districts have been cited for determining students were not eligible for services under IDEA but then failing to assess them for eligibility under Section 504. This problem has occurred frequently with students having Attention Deficit Disorder (ADD) or Attention Deficit Hyperactivity Disorder (ADHD) who were ineligible for services under the IDEA (*Anaheim School District,* 1993; *Calcasieu Parish (LA) Public School District,* 1992; *LaHonda-Pescadero (CA) Unified School District,* 1993; *Petaluma City (CA) Elementary School District,* 1995).

Both the IDEA (IDEA Regulations, 34 C.F.R. § 300.543) and Section 504 (Section 504 Regulations, 34 C.F.R. § 104.35(c)(2)) require that the decision of the MDT be documented in written form. The IDEA further states that the team members must certify that the final team decision reflects their conclusions. If team members disagree with the team decision, they may attach a separate report detailing their views. Finally, the IDEA does not address whether the decision must be by majority vote, although it does not have to be unanimous. In a policy letter, OSEP stated that the school district was required to comply with the decision made by the MDT as a whole (Greer, 1992). OSEP did not further elaborate on what "as a whole" meant, nor has it defined how many people, at a minimum, are required on the MDT.

Medical Diagnosis and Eligibility Determination

Multidisciplinary teams may use a medical diagnosis as part of the eligibility determination, when appropriate. It is clear, however, that a medical diagnosis cannot be used as the sole basis for eligibility determination (Joint Policy Memorandum, 1991). Furthermore, a medical diagnosis may not be required as part of an evaluation, although if an MDT believes a medical diagnosis is necessary, it must be provided at public expense (Parker, 1992; Veir, 1993). Although schools do not have to consult a physician when determining eligibility and services for a student with ADD or ADHD, the MDT must have someone on the committee with specific knowledge of how to identify and treat the disorder (Shrag, 1992).

Reevaluation

The educational needs of students with disabilities change over time. The IDEA, therefore, requires that students in special education be reevaluated every 3 years. A reevaluation is a comprehensive evaluation conducted on a student already in special education. The reevaluation is usually similar to the original preplacement evaluation, and it must meet the same procedural requirements under the IDEA as did the original evaluation (IDEA Regulations, 34 C.F.R. § 300.534). The reevaluation, however, does not have to be identical to the preplacement evaluation; it can consist of different assessment procedures so long as they address the student's current educational needs (Shaver, 1990).

The IDEA requires that eligible students be reevaluated more frequently than every 3 years if necessary or if requested by the student's parents or teacher (IDEA Regulations, 34 C.F.R. § 300.534). Regulatory language is unclear as to when it may be necessary to reevaluate more frequently than every 3 years. In *Corona-Norco Unified School District* (1995), it was determined that more frequent evaluations may be warranted when there is a substantial change in the student's academic performance or disability. Section 504 also requires that students receiving services under the law be reevaluated periodically (Section 504 Regulations, 34 C.F.R. § 104.35(d)). Reevaluations must also be conducted prior to any significant change in placement under Section 504, although the IDEA does not have a similar requirement. A federal district court, however, has used the Section 504 regulation (Section 504 Regulations, 34 C.F.R. § 104.35(a)) as authority for requiring a reevaluation under the IDEA when a school district made a significant change in placement (*Brimmer v. Traverse City Area Public Schools,* 1994). A reevaluation is also required when a school is contemplating the long-term suspension or expulsion of a student with disabilities. (For elaborations on suspension and expulsion see Chapter 15.)

If there is no need to conduct a full and complete reevaluation because there is no need to collect additional information, the reevaluation should focus on collecting information about how to teach the student in the most appropriate manner. If an IEP team determines that additional data are not needed, the team must notify the student's parents of the determination, the reasons for it, and the parents' right to still request a full evaluation.

Informed parental consent is required for a school to conduct a reevaluation. Until the IDEA Amendments of 1997, parental consent was not required. This requirement does not apply, however, if the school district can demonstrate that reasonable steps were taken to obtain consent but that the parents failed to respond. When a parent requests a reevaluation, the student must be reevaluated unless the district challenges the parents' request in a due process hearing (Tinsley, 1990). Section 504 contains no references to parent-requested reevaluations.

Independent Educational Evaluations

An independent educational evaluation (IEE) is an evaluation conducted by a qualified examiner who is not employed by the school district responsible for the education of the student in question (IDEA Regulations, 34 C.F.R. § 300.503). Parents have the right to request an IEE at any time during their child's education. On the parents' request, the school district must provide information about where the IEE may be obtained. Furthermore, although the school district is under no obligation to accept the results of the evaluation, it must consider the IEE as part of its decision-making process. School district responsibilities regarding the IEE are listed in Figure 11.5.

The IDEA allows parents to obtain one IEE at public expense if they disagree with the school district evaluation. Parents may also request an IEE if a school does not evaluate for assistive technology devices or services (Fisher, 1995). The school, however, may initiate a due process hearing if it believes the school district's evaluation is appropriate. If the hearing officer's decision is that the school had conducted an appropriate evaluation, the parent is not entitled to have the evaluation paid for by the district.

Apparently, the school district may choose whether it will fund the IEE in advance, pay the examiner directly, or reimburse the parent (Gorn, 1996). This issue is not addressed in the IDEA. However, if the refusal to fund the IEE in advance denies the parent the right to seek an IEE, the parent may seek relief (*Edna Independent School District*, 1994). In situations where the school district refuses to fund the

Figure 11.5
Independent Educational Evaluation Requirements

1. Schools must, on request, provide parents information on where to obtain an IEE.
2. If parents disagree with the schools evaluation, they have the right to an IEE at public expense.
3. If school personnel believe their evaluation is appropriate, they may initiate a hearing. If a hearing officer finds the evaluation appropriate, parents are still entitled to IEE, but not at public expense.
4. The results of the IEE, even if paid for by the parents, must be considered in the special education decision-making process.
5. The results of the IEE, even if paid for by the parents, may be presented as evidence at a hearing.
6. A hearing officer may request an IEE as part of a due process hearing. This IEE must be performed at public expense.

IEE, the parent must prevail at a due process hearing in order to secure the public funding.

Parents should notify the school district when they disagree with the school's evaluation, and plan to request an IEE at public expense. The school district must respond within a reasonable amount of time and either agree to fund the IEE or request a hearing to show that its evaluation was appropriate. Typically, school districts will challenge an IEE when they believe their evaluation was appropriate or when the IEE obtained by parents did not dispute the district's evaluation (Freedman, 1996). If parents have obtained the IEE to provide additional information or more meaningful information, they will not have a claim for public funding (*Millcreek Township School District*, 1995), nor will public funding be ordered if the findings of the independent evaluator are consistent with the district's findings (*Brandywine School District*, 1995). The criterion for public funding, therefore, involves the appropriateness of the district's evaluation. IEEs are typically funded when the district has been negligent in conducting the evaluation, when the evaluation was inadequate, when all sources of information were not considered, or when major procedural safeguards were not followed (*Carbondale Elementary School District 95*, 1996; *Douglas School District*, 1993; *Livingston Parish (LA) School Board*, 1993).

If the parents already have secured an IEE and requested payment, the district might contend in a hearing that the IEE was inappropriate, deficient, or conducted by an unqualified examiner. In a policy letter, OSEP stated that a district may disqualify an independent evaluator chosen by a parent, and may refuse to pay if the evaluator does not meet the district's criteria (OSEP Policy Letter, 1995b).

A school district may establish a fee structure for the IEE that the parents cannot exceed (OSEP Policy Letter, 1995b). The purpose of the maximum fee set by the school district is to eliminate unreasonable and excessive fees. School district limitations on the parents' choice of an independent examiner, the location of the IEE, and the fees for the evaluation will be upheld as long as they are reasonable (Gorn, 1996). The school district, however, must allow the parents the opportunity to demonstrate that unique circumstances justify an IEE that does not fall within the district's fee structure (OSEP Policy Letter, 1993b).

When parents initiate an IEE, the results of the evaluation must be considered by the school district in decisions regarding the education of the evaluated student. The district is not, however, obligated to accept or act on the recommendations made in the IEE. Although the IDEA does not detail what "consider" means in this context, the U.S. Court of Appeals for the Second Circuit, in *T.S. v. Board of Education of the Town of Ridgefield and State of Connecticut Department of Education* (1993), used the definition "to reflect on or think about with some degree of caution" (p. 89). The parents in this case argued that the school's MDT had not considered the IEE when only two members of the team had read the IEE prior to the meeting. The court rejected the argument, finding that nothing in the IDEA suggested that all team members had to read the IEE in order to consider it. The circuit court's decision indicated that it is important that a school district documents consideration of the IEE. According to Gorn (1996), school districts should (a) document how the

Figure 11.6
Freedman's Advice Regarding IEEs

- Remember that the goal of all evaluations, whether the school district's or an IEE, is to develop an appropriate program for the student.
- When an IEE is clearly and substantively wrong in its recommendations and facts, correct the record in writing.
- Consider all sources of information and attempt to find an appropriate balance between the district's recommendations and the IEE.
- Remember that IEEs are a pivotal part of the procedural safeguards granted to students with disabilities and their parents.
- Establish a cost structure for IEEs and notify parents in writing that if they believe a more costly IEE is warranted, they must inform the district of these unique circumstances.

From "Independent Educational Evaluations: Love 'em or Hate 'em, but Do 'em Right" by M. K. Freedman, 1996, in *Proceedings of the 16th Annual Conference on Special Education Law,* LRP Publications. Adapted with permission.

IEE was made available to the MDT or IEP team; (b) record the findings of the IEE and the team's review and discussion of the report; and (c) put any reasons for disagreement with the IEE in writing. OSEP has stated that the school does not need to document the results of the rejected IEE on the IEP (OSEP Policy Letter, 1993c), but that the school should review the IEE and discuss its results in all programming and placement decisions (OSEP Policy Letter, 1995b).

Finally, Section 504 regulations do not address the subject of IEEs. Gorn (1996) warns, however, that this does not mean that IEEs are unavailable to parents under Section 504. The Office of Civil Rights (OCR) of the Department of Education has stated that schools must consider IEEs under Section 504 and the Americans with Disabilities Act, but that they are not required to implement all information contained in the IEE (OCR Policy Letter, 1993).

Freedman (1996), stresses the importance of actively listening to and addressing parents' concerns when confronting parental requests for an IEE. Preventive actions and cooperative participation are crucial. Figure 11.6 presents Freedman's advice to schools regarding the IEE.

Accountability Efforts and Students with Disabilities

The early 1980s witnessed a series of reports that alerted the public to a crisis in American education and led to calls for improving the educational system. The publication of *A Nation at Risk* (National Commission on Excellence in Education, 1983) was especially influential in leading to calls for educational reform. The widespread criticism of the public school system and the perceived need to reform education led to efforts to increase accountability in our educational system. Two tools adopted to increase accountability in education are (a) the increased use of student assessments through the adoption of minimum-competency testing and (b) the development of standards and outcomes for America's students. Both have had an impact on the education of students with disabilities.

Minimum-Competency Tests

The purpose of minimum-competency tests (MCTs), or school exit exams, is to ensure that students attain minimum proficiency in tested academic areas before they graduate from high school. MCTs are seen as a means to restore meaning to the high school diploma, since students have to show a certain level of skill development and knowledge before receiving one. Advocates believe that these tests will help to establish educational standards, provide an incentive to learning, and give the public an opportunity to assess the effectiveness of schools. Critics raise concerns over the unsound psychometric properties of such tests, the narrowing of the curriculum caused by teachers teaching to the test, and the disproportionate impact of the use of these tests on students from economically disadvantaged backgrounds, racial minorities, and students with disabilities (Thomas & Russo, 1995).

Currently, 18 states require that students pass some form of exit examination before they can graduate from high school (Council of Chief State School Officers, 1996). (States that use these exit exams no longer call them minimum-competency tests, although the purpose remains the same.) Additionally, five more states are considering adopting some form of exit examination (M.L. Thurlow, personal communication, September 10, 1996). Litigative challenges to these examinations have shown that states clearly have the legal prerogative to require them. Courts are very reluctant to intervene in educational affairs, and both state and federal courts have overwhelmingly recognized the right of states to determine the effectiveness of their educational programs through methods such as exit examinations. For example, in an important court challenge to MCTs, the U.S. Court of Appeals for the Fifth Circuit, in *Debra P. v. Turlington* (1981), found that an MCT used in the state of Florida had been demonstrated to be instructionally valid, was not discriminatory, and could be used in the determination of diploma awards. The court praised Florida's efforts to improve the quality of education. The decision was affirmed by the U.S. Court of Appeals for the Eleventh Circuit in 1984 (*Debra P. v. Turlington*). In a case heard in the Seventh Circuit, *Brookhart v. Illinois State Board of Education* (1983), the court stated that the use of MCTs to ensure the value of the diploma was admirable and that the court would only interfere with educational policy decisions if needed to protect a student's individual statutory and constitutional rights. *Brookhart* was important in that it was the first case to address a state's decision to deny diplomas to students receiving special education who had failed to pass the state's MCT. The court, in analyzing the plaintiff's claims under the Education for All Handicapped Children Act (EAHCA), held that the denial of diplomas did not deny the student a FAPE and was, therefore, legal. The court also ruled that the use of MCTs did not violate Section 504 because the state, although required to provide reasonable accommodations, was not required to modify the test so substantially that the purpose of the test would be vitiated.

Thomas and Russo (1995) note that students with disabilities tend to perform more poorly on MCTs and, thus, be ineligible for a diploma more frequently than do students without disabilities. Claims of discrimination in violation of Section 504 and denial of a FAPE in violation of the IDEA, however, are unlikely to be successful. Thomas and Russo further contend that states giving MCTs are not required to establish separate standards or prepare individualized MCTs for students with disabilities. These authors conclude that parents should be made aware of the general use and content of MCTs. Moreover, the IEP team should consider including MCT content in the student's IEP.

Inclusion in Accountability Efforts

The last few years have seen a burst of activity in the area of developing standards and outcomes for students. Standards are statements of criteria against which comparisons can be made. The purpose of educational standards is to guide instruction regarding what students should know and be able to do. Standards and outcomes have been developed in all academic content areas, health and physical education, the arts, and vocational education (Shriner, Ysseldyke, & Thurlow, 1994). An area of concern in the development of standards has been how to include and address the needs of students with disabilities. Various options for including students with disabilities include setting separate standards, maintaining a single set of standards but allowing a range of performance relative to them, allowing standards to be demonstrated using alternative measures (e.g., portfolios), excluding students with disabilities from assessment, and using the IEP as a document and process in linking the student's program to the local, state, or national standards (Shriner et al., 1994). If the last option is used, the IEP team will be charged with preparing IEPs that are aligned to the these standards.

The IDEA Amendments of 1997 require that students with disabilities participate in state- and district-wide assessments of student progress, with or without accommodations, whichever is appropriate for individual students. Furthermore, states must report to the public on the assessment of students with disabilities with the same frequency and detail as they report on the assessment of students without disabilities. They must also report the number of students with disabilities participating in statewide regular assessments, and, eventually, the numbers participating in alternative assessments. The data on the performance of students with disabilities must be disaggregated when reporting to the federal government.

The IEP meeting is the proper forum for considering whether students with disabilities can appropriately participate in regular assessments or whether they need modifications in the administration of the state tests. According to Ysseldyke, Thurlow, McGrew, and Vanderwood (1994), the IEP should list any accommodations of the test or testing situation. Possible testing accommodations include altering the manner in which the assessment is presented (e.g., use of magnifying equipment, signing of directions), the manner of student response (e.g., using a computer for responding, giving responses orally), accommodations in setting (e.g., testing alone in a study carrel, testing with a small group), and time (e.g., more frequent breaks during testing, extending the testing session over several days). If an IEP team decides that a student will not participate in a particular state- or district-wide assessment of achievement, the IEP must include a statement of why the assessment is not appropriate and how the student will be assessed.

Summary

Before a student can be placed in special education or related services, the student must be identified as having a disability and needing special education services to meet his or her individual needs. The evaluation is not only important in identifying a student as eligible for special education, but it is crucial in the development of the student's FAPE.

Parents' written consent is required prior to conducting an initial evaluation. After permission is received, the evaluation must be conducted in a timely manner. The MDT must then make eligibility decisions based upon the evaluation data. If the parents refuse consent and the MDT believes the child needs special educational services, the school district may go to a due process hearing to obtain permission to conduct the evaluation.

The evaluation must be individualized and conducted in all areas related to the suspected disability. The MDT's charge is to use the results of the evaluation to determine if the student is eligible for services under the IDEA or Section 504 and to further determine if, because of the disability, the student needs special education and related services to meet his or her needs.

The IDEA Amendments of 1997 require that students with disabilities participate in state- and district-wide assessments. Furthermore, states are required to report on the assessments of students in special education as frequently as they report on assessments of students without disabilities. IEP teams must determine if students in special education can participate in such assessments or if they require modifications in administration of these assessments. The IEP must also list any testing modifications needed. If the team determines that a student cannot participate in such assessments, the IEP must include a statement of why the student cannot participate and how the student will be assessed.

For Further Information

Bateman, B. D. (1995). *Better IEPs: How to develop legally correct and educationally useful programs.* Longmont, CO: Sopris West.

Salvia, J., & Ysseldyke, J. E. (1995). *Assessment.* Boston: Houghton Mifflin.

Shriner, J. G., Ysseldyke, J. E., & Thurlow, M. L. (1994). Standards for all American students. *Focus on Exceptional Children, 26*(5), 1–19.

Shriner, J. S., & Spicuzza, R. J. (1995). Procedural considerations in the assessment of children at risk. *Preventing School Failure, 39,* 33–38.

References

Ackenhalt, Letter to, 22 IDELR 252 (OCR 1994).

Algozzine, B., Christenson, S., & Ysseldyke, J. E. (1982). Probabilities associated with the referral to placement process. *Teacher Education and Special Education, 5,* 19–23.

Anaheim School District, 20 IDELR 185 (OCR 1993).

Bartow (GA) County School District, 22 IDELR 508 (OCR 1995).

Bateman, B. D. (1995). *Better IEPs: How to develop legally correct and educationally useful programs.* Longmont, CO: Sopris West.

Brandywine School District, 22 IDELR 517 (SEA Del. 1995).

Brimmer v. Traverse City Area Public Schools, 22 IDELR 5 (W.D. Mich. 1994).

Brookhart v. Illinois State Board of Education, 697 F.2d 179 (7th Cir. 1983).

Calcasieu Parish (LA) Public School District, 20 IDELR 762 (OCR 1992).

Carbondale Elementary School District 95, 23 IDELR 766 (SEA Ill. 1996).

Carroll v. Capalbo, 563 F. Supp. 1053 (D.R.I. 1983).

Chicago Board of Education, EHLR 257:568 (OCR 1984).

Corona-Norco Unified School District, 22 IDELR 469 (Cal. 1995).

Council of Chief State School Officers. (1996). *Viewing the landscape: States' assessment practices.* Washington, DC: Author.

Crawford v. Honig, 37 F.3d 485 (9th Cir. 1994).

Debra P. v. Turlington, 644 F.2d 397 (5th Cir. 1981).

Debra P. v. Turlington, 730 F.2d 1405 (11th Cir. 1984).

Douglas School District, 20 IDELR 458 (SEA SD 1993).

Edna Independent School District, 21 IDELR 419 (SEA Tex. 1994).

Fisher, Letter to, 23 IDELR 565 (OSEP 1995).

Foster v. District of Columbia Board of Education, EHLR 553:520 (D.D.C. 1982).

Freedman, M. K. (1996). Independent educational evaluations: Love 'em or hate 'em, but do 'em right. In *Proceedings of the 16th Annual Conference on Special Education Law.* Horsham, PA: LRP Publications.

Gorn, S. (1996). *What do I do when . . . The answer book on special education law.* Horsham, PA: LRP Publications.

Graham, Letter to, 213 EHLR 212 (EHA 1989).

Greenfield Public School, 21 IDELR 345 (SEA Mass. 1994).

Greer, Letter to, 19 IDELR 348 (OSEP 1992).

Guernsey, T. F., & Klare, K. (1993). *Special education law.* Durham, NC: Carolina Academic Press.

Holmes, Letter to, 19 IDELR 350 (OSEP 1992).

Individuals with Disabilities Education Act (IDEA), 20 U.S.C. § 1400 *et seq.*

Individuals with Disabilities Education Act Amendments of 1997, 105th Congress.

Individuals with Disabilities Education Act Regulations, 34 C.F.R. § 300.1 *et seq.*

Joint Policy Memorandum, 18 IDELR 116 (OSERS 1991).

Kelly Inquiry, 211 EHLR (EHA 1981).

LaHonda-Pescadero (CA) Unified School District, 20 IDELR 833 (OCR 1993).

Larry P. v. Riles, 495 F. Supp. 926 (N.D. Cal. 1979), *aff'd in part, rev'd in part,* 793 F.2d 969 (9th Cir. 1986).

Livingston Parish (LA) School Board, 20 IDELR 1470 (OCR 1993).

Millcreek Township School District, 22 IDELR 1011 (SEA PA 1995).

National Commission on Excellence in Education. (1983). *A nation at risk: The imperative for educational reform.* Washington, DC: U.S. Government Printing Office.

OCR Policy Letter, 20 IDELR 1073 (OCR 1993).

OSEP Policy Letter, 18 IDELR 741 (OSEP 1992).

OSEP Policy Letter, 20 IDELR 1219 (OSEP 1993a).

OSEP Policy Letter, 20 IDELR 1222 (OSEP 1993b).

OSEP Policy Letter, 20 IDELR 1460 (OSEP 1993c).

OSEP Policy Letter, 21 IDELR 998 (OSEP 1994).

OSEP Policy Letter, 22 IDELR 563 (OSEP 1995a).

OSEP Policy Letter, 22 IDELR 637 (OSEP 1995b).

Parents in Action on Special Education v. Hannon, 506 F. Supp 831 (N.D. Ill. 1980).

Parker, Letter to, 19 IDELR 963 (OSEP 1992).

Petaluma City (CA) Elementary School District, 23 IDELR 245 (OCR 1995).

Salvia, J., & Ysseldyke, J. E. (1995). *Assessment.* Boston: Houghton Mifflin.

Section 504 of the Rehabilitation Act of 1973, 29 U.S.C. § 794 *et seq.*

Section 504 Regulations, 34 C.F.R. § 104.1 *et seq.*

Shaver, Letter to, 17 EHLR 356 (OSERS 1990).

Shrag, Letter to, 18 IDELR 1303 (OSEP 1992).

Shriner, J. G., Ysseldyke, J. E., & Thurlow, M. L. (1994). Standards for all American students. *Focus on Exceptional Children, 26*(5), 1–19.

T.S. v. Board of Education of the Town of Ridgefield and State of Connecticut Department of Education, 10 F.3d 87 (2nd Cir. 1993).

Thomas, S. B., & Russo, C. J. (1995). *Special education law: Issues & Implications for the '90s.*

Topeka, KS: National Organization on Legal Problems of Education.

Tinsley, Letter to, 16 EHLR (OSEP 1990).

Veir, Response to, 20 IDELR 864 (OCR 1993).

Warrington, Letter to, 20 IDELR 593 (OSERS, 1993).

Williams, Letter to, 20 IDELR 1210 (OSEP 1993).

Ysseldyke, J. E., Algozzine, B. (1995). *Special education: A practical approach for teachers* (3rd ed.). Boston: Houghton Mifflin.

Ysseldyke, J. E., Thurlow, M. L., McGrew, K., & Vanderwood, M. (1994). *Making decisions about the inclusion of students with disabilities in large-scale assessments* (Synthesis Report 13). Minneapolis, MN: University of Minnesota and National Center on Educational Outcomes.

Zirkel, Letter to, 22 IDELR 667 (OCR 1995).

CHAPTER TWELVE

Least Restrictive Environment

We are concerned that children with handicapping conditions be educated in the most normal possible and least restrictive setting, for how else will they adapt to the world beyond the educational environment, and how else will the nonhandicapped adapt to them?

Senator Robert T. Stafford, *Congressional Record*, May 20, 1974.

Justice Potter Stewart, writing for the U.S. Supreme Court in *Sheldon v. Tucker* (1960), stated that

> In a series of decisions this court has held, even though a governmental purpose be legitimate and substantial, that purpose cannot be pursued by means that broadly stifle fundamental personal liberties when the end can be more narrowly achieved. The breadth of legislative abridgment must be viewed in the light of less drastic means for achieving the same purpose. (p. 482)

Although this decision did not involve the education of students with disabilities, the Court set forth a principle that has had a profound effect on special education: that persons have a right to be free of unnecessary restrictions when the government undertakes actions that have consequences for those individuals, even though the actions are legitimate.

Champagne (1993) defines restrictiveness as "a gauge of the degree of opportunity a person has for proximity to, and communication with, the ordinary flow of persons in our society" (p. 5). In special education, this means that a student with disabilities has the right to be educated with students in the general education environment. The general education environment is considered the least restrictive setting because it is the placement in which there is the greatest measure of opportunity for proximity and communication with the "ordinary flow" of students in schools.

From this perspective, the less a placement resembles the general education environment, the more restrictive it is considered (Gorn, 1996). Specifically, a student with disabilities has the right to be educated in a setting that is not overly restrictive considering what is appropriate for that student. Appropriateness entails an education that will provide meaningful benefit for a student. When the educational program is appropriate, a student with disabilities should be placed in the general education environment, or as close to it as is feasible, so long as the appropriate program can be provided in that setting. (For elaborations on an appropriate education see Chapter 8.)

In 1954, the U.S. Supreme Court, in *Brown v. Board of Education,* declared that the practice of segregation could not be used in public education. Although the decision did not involve the education of students with disabilities, advocates argued that the principles in *Brown* were true for all persons, including those with disabilities. In *Hairston v. Drosick* (1976) the principles developed in *Brown* were used by the Court in a case involving the education of a child with spina bifida. The Court stated that

> A child's chance in this society is through the educational process. A major goal of this educational process is the socialization process that takes place in the regular classroom, with the resulting capability to interact in a social way with one's peers. It is, therefore, imperative that every child receive an education with his or her peers insofar as it is at all possible. (p. 184)

On May 20, 1974, Senator Robert Stafford of Vermont introduced an amendment to the Education of the Handicapped Act of 1974 that was intended to prevent the educational segregation of students with disabilities. The amendment required that school districts ensure that a student's placement be in the least restrictive appropriate educational setting (Stafford, 1978). This amendment was later incorporated into the Education for All Handicapped Children Act (EAHCA)* in what has become known as the least restrictive environment (LRE) mandate.

The LRE mandate has been the subject of considerable controversy and debate. The purpose of this chapter is to examine the legislative basis of the LRE mandate, as well as the major cases interpreting LRE. Finally a model for determining the LRE for students with disabilities will be presented.

LRE, Mainstreaming, and Inclusion

The terms *least restrictive environment, inclusion,* and *mainstreaming* are often used interchangeably. They are not, however, synonymous concepts. *Least restrictive environment* refers to the IDEA's mandate that students with disabilities should be educated to the maximum extent appropriate with peers without disabilities. An individualized education program (IEP) team could determine that a special

---

*The EAHCA was renamed the Individuals with Disabilities Education Act (IDEA) in 1990.

school, a setting considered to be quite restrictive, is the LRE for a particular student given that student's educational needs. The LRE is a method by which schools ensure the integration of students with and without disabilities to the maximum extent appropriate. It is not a particular setting.

Inclusion refers to placement of students with disabilities in the general education classroom with peers without disabilities. Inclusion generally connotes more comprehensive programming than the somewhat dated term *mainstreaming*. The courts, however, tend to use the terms synonymously. *Mainstreaming* and *inclusion* are narrower terms than *least restrictive environment* (McColl, 1992). Although placement in the general education classroom may be the LRE for some students with disabilities, it is not required in all cases. The IDEA requires mainstreaming or inclusion when the general education classroom setting can provide an appropriate education. This view was also expressed by the U.S. Court of Appeals for the Fourth Circuit in *Carter v. Florence County School District Four* (1991):

> Under the IDEA, mainstreaming is a policy to be pursued so long as it is consistent with the Act's primary goal of providing disabled students with an appropriate education. Where necessary for educational reasons, mainstreaming assumes a subordinate role in formulating an educational program. (p. 156)

The LRE Mandate

Both the IDEA and Section 504 of the Rehabilitation Act of 1973 require that, when appropriate, students with disabilities be educated in settings with children without disabilities.

IDEA

The IDEA provides that,

> to the maximum extent appropriate, children with disabilities, including children in public or private institutions or other care facilities, are educated with children who are not disabled, and that special classes, separate schooling, or other removal of children with disabilities from the regular educational environment occurs only when the nature or severity of the disability is such that education in regular classes with the use of supplementary aids and services cannot be achieved satisfactorily. (IDEA, 20 U.S.C. § 1412)

There are two parts to the LRE requirement of the IDEA. The first addresses the presumptive right of all students with disabilities to be educated with students without disabilities. Schools must make good faith efforts to place and maintain students in less restrictive settings. This presumptive right, however, is rebuttable; that is, the principle sets forth a general rule of conduct (i.e., integration) but allows it to be rebutted when integration is not appropriate for a student (Turnbull, 1993). The IDEA favors integration, but recognizes that for some students more restrictive or segregated settings may be appropriate. Clearly, the law anticipates that placements in more restrictive settings may sometimes be necessary to provide an appropriate education.

To ensure that schools make good faith efforts to educate students in less restrictive settings, the LRE mandate also requires that before students with disabilities are placed in more restrictive settings, efforts must first be made to maintain a student in less restrictive settings with the use of supplementary aids and services. It is only when an appropriate education cannot be provided, even with supplementary aids and services, that students with disabilities may be placed in more restrictive settings.

The IDEA further requires that state educational agencies ensure that the LRE requirement extends to students in public schools, private schools, and other care facilities. States are required to ensure that teachers and administrators in all public schools are fully informed about the requirements of the LRE provision and are provided with the technical assistance and training necessary to assist them in this effort.

Section 504

Section 504 also requires that students with disabilities be educated in less restrictive settings. According to regulations, schools

> shall educate, or shall provide for the education of, each qualified handicapped person in its jurisdiction with persons who are not handicapped to the maximum extent appropriate to the needs of the handicapped person. A [school] shall place a handicapped person in the regular educational environment . . . unless it is demonstrated . . . that the education of the person in the regular environment with the use of supplementary aids and services cannot be achieved satisfactorily. (Section 504 Regulations, 34 C.F.R. § 104.34(a))

Regulations to Section 504 further state that a school district maintaining a separate facility for students with disabilities "shall ensure that the facilities and the services and activities provided therein are comparable to other facilities" in the district (Section 504 Regulations, 34 C.F.R. § 104.34(c)).

Continuum of Alternative Placements

Senator Stafford (1978), an original sponsor of the IDEA, stated that Congress included the LRE principle in the law in recognition that for some students an education in the general education classroom would not be appropriate. For these students, placements in more restrictive settings would be required to provide an appropriate education. The U.S. Supreme Court, in *Board of Education of the Hendrick Hudson School District v. Rowley* (1982), interpreted congressional intent similarly:

> Despite this preference for "mainstreaming" handicapped children—educating them with nonhandicapped children—Congress recognized that regular education simply would not be a suitable setting for the education of many handicapped children . . . the act thus provides for the education of some handicapped children in separate classes or institutional settings. (p. 192)

The Office of Special Education and Rehabilitation Services (OSERS) of the U.S. Department of Education also recognized "that some children with disabilities may require placement in settings other than the general education classroom in order to be provided with an education designed to address their unique needs" (*Goodling*, 1991, p. 214).

To ensure that students with disabilities are educated in the LRE most appropriate for their individual needs, the IDEA requires that school districts have a range or continuum of alternative placement options to meet their needs. The continuum represents an entire spectrum of placements where a student's special education program can be implemented (Bartlett, 1993; Gorn, 1996). Regulations state that

> (a) Each [school district] shall ensure that a continuum of alternative placements is available to meet the needs of children with disabilities for special education and related services
> (b) The continuum required . . . must:
> (1) Include the alternative placements . . . (instruction in regular classes, special classes, special schools, home instruction, and instruction in hospitals and institutions); and
> (2) Make provision for supplementary services (such as resource room or itinerant instruction) to be provided in conjunction with regular class placement. (IDEA Regulations, 34 C.F.R. § 300.551)

The purpose of the continuum is to allow school personnel to choose from a number of options in determining the LRE that is appropriate for the student. OSERS has emphasized the importance of school districts' maintaining a continuum of placements "in order to be properly prepared to address the individual needs of all children with disabilities" (Frost, 1991, p. 594). If the local school district is unable to provide the appropriate placement, the state may bear the responsibility of ensuring the establishment and availability of a continuum of alternative placements (*Cordero v. Pennsylvania*, 1993). Figure 12.1 shows the continuum of placements (IDEA Regulations, 34 C.F.R. § 300.551).

A school district may not refuse to place a child in an LRE because it lacks the appropriate placement option (Tucker & Goldstein, 1992). Moreover, if gaps in the continuum exist within a school district, the district must fill them through whatever means are required (e.g., consortium-type arrangements). This does not mean that each school district must provide for a complete continuum within its own boundaries. When the educational needs of a student cannot be met in district programs, however, the district is obligated to provide a placement where the student's needs can be met. The regulations implementing the IDEA require that the various alternative placements in the continuum of placements "are to be available to the extent necessary to implement the individualized education program" (IDEA Regulations, 34 C.F.R. § 300.552(b)). This may necessitate the district's sending the student to another school (public or private) that provides the needed placement. In such cases, the neighborhood school district retains financial responsibility for the student's education.

Figure 12.1
Continuum of Alternative Placements

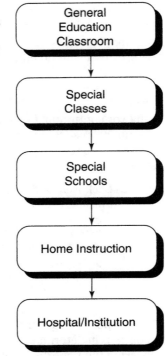

The IEP team determines the placement along this continuum that is the least restrictive setting in which a student will receive an appropriate education. Restrictiveness is defined, for purposes of the continuum, by proximity to the general education classroom. Education in the least restrictive setting (i.e., the general education classroom) is the preferred option so long as it is consistent with an appropriate education. If a student cannot receive a meaningful education in the general education classroom, another placement, in which the student will receive a meaningful education, is required.

Related Factors in Educational Placements

Placement in the Neighborhood School

Unless the IEP requires otherwise, students with disabilities should be educated in the school they would attend if they were not in special education (IDEA Regulations, 34 C.F.R. § 300.552(a) (3)). Moreover, the IDEA requires that if special education students cannot be placed in the neighborhood school, they must be placed as close to home as possible. Placement in the neighborhood school, however, is not an absolute right. The IEP team determines what constitutes an appropriate education for a student. If an appropriate education cannot be provided in the neighborhood school, the IEP team may choose a placement in a school that will provide an appropriate education.

The goal of educating a student with disabilities in the neighborhood school must be balanced with the requirement that a student's education be appropriate and individualized (Huefner, 1994). Courts have repeatedly held that the IDEA does not guarantee special education services in a student's neighborhood school (*Barnett v. Fairfax County School Board*, 1991; *Flour Bluff Independent School District v. Katherine M.*, 1996; *Hudson v. Bloomfield Hills School District*, 1995; *Lachman v. Illinois Board of Education*, 1988; *Murray v. Montrose County School District*, 1995; *Schuldt v. Mankato ISD*, 1991).

In *Schuldt v. Mankato ISD* (1991), the U.S. Court of Appeals for the Eighth Circuit ruled that a school district did not have to make the neighborhood school wheelchair-accessible for a student with spina bifida, since an elementary school only a few miles away was fully accessible. The court found that

> The school district satisfied its obligation under [IDEA] to provide [a student with disabilities] with a fully integrated public education by busing . . . the child to a nearby school, and therefore, did not violate the Act by refusing to modify neighborhood elementary school nearest to the child's home to make it accessible. (p. 1357)

If the neighborhood school cannot provide a free appropriate public education (FAPE), the school is not required to place a student with disabilities in that school. Schools retain the right to determine how to use their resources in the most efficient manner. If district administrators choose to concentrate resources at particular schools for particular needs and disabilities, it is allowed by the IDEA (Tucker & Goldstein, 1992).

The U.S. Court of Appeals for the Fifth Circuit, in *Flour Bluff Independent School District v. Katherine M.* (1996), ruled that the IDEA indicates a preference for placement in the neighborhood school but that this is not an entitlement. Furthermore, the court indicated that proximity is only one factor of many that the IEP team must consider in determining placement.

In *Murray v. Montrose County School District* (1995), the U.S. Court of Appeals for the Tenth Circuit held that although the IDEA gives a preference to education in the neighborhood school, the IDEA does not guarantee it. In *Urban v. Jefferson County School District R-1* (1994), the Tenth Circuit court reaffirmed this principle and extended it to Section 504 and the Americans with Disabilities Act (ADA) as well as the IDEA.

Nonacademic Programming

Both the IDEA and Section 504 extend LRE requirements to nonacademic settings. Regulations implementing the IDEA extend the LRE requirements to areas such as extracurricular services, meals, recess periods, counseling services, athletics, transportation, health services, recreational activities, and special interest groups or clubs sponsored by the school (IDEA Regulations, 34 C.F.R. § 300.553). For example, if a student requires a restrictive placement to receive an appropriate education, but will not have contact with students without disabilities in that placement, the LRE requirement extends to other settings and situations in which students with and without disabilities can be integrated. Recess periods, physical education classes, or student meal times might be used to provide for the necessary integrated experiences.

Section 504 also extends the LRE requirement to nonacademic settings that include extracurricular activities:

> In providing or arranging for the provision of nonacademic and extracurricular services and activities . . . a [school] shall ensure that handicapped persons participate with non-handicapped persons in such activities and services to the maximum extent appropriate to the needs of the handicapped person. (Section 504 Regulations, 34 C.F.R. § 104.34(b))

The Interests of Peers Without Disabilities

Both the IDEA and Section 504 indicate that a legitimate consideration in determining the LRE for a student with disabilities is the needs of the student's peers. According to the analysis in Section 504,

> it should be stressed that, where a [student with disabilities] is so disruptive in a regular classroom that the education of other students is significantly impaired, the needs of the [student with disabilities] cannot be met in that environment. Therefore regular placement would not be appropriate to his or her needs. (Section 504 Regulations, 34 C.F.R. § 104 Appendix, Paragraph 24)

The IDEA includes identical language in a comment to the LRE regulations (IDEA Regulations, comment following 34 C.F.R. § 300.552). The purpose of the comment is to provide guidance with respect to determining proper placement of the student with disabilities when the student is so disruptive that the education of other students is affected.

If the student has a health condition that poses an actual risk of contagion to other students, the student may be placed in a setting in which the risk is minimized. Such a placement would not violate the LRE mandate of either the IDEA or Section 504 (Zirkel, 1994).

Judicial Standards of Review

Few areas in special education law have been the subject of more debate and controversy than the LRE mandate. The issue of when an education in the general education environment constitutes the LRE for a given student with disabilities has proven to be a thorny legal issue (Huefner, 1994). Disagreements between parents and schools over LRE have led to a considerable amount of litigation. A number of these cases have made their way to the U.S. Courts of Appeals, but thus far the U.S. Supreme Court has not accepted a case interpreting the LRE mandate. Because the high court has not heard an LRE case, the LRE interpretations by the circuit courts are the highest authority available.

The results of these cases have been mixed, with some decisions favoring inclusive placements and others restrictive placements. The decisions of the circuit courts with respect to the proper standard of review to be used in determining a district's compliance with the LRE mandate, however, have begun to show some consistency. The following section will examine these cases and the methods they have adopted for determining a school district's compliance with the mainstreaming* requirement.

The *Roncker* Portability Test

One of the earliest LRE decisions was *Roncker v. Walter* (1983; hereafter *Roncker*). The decision is controlling in the Sixth Circuit, which covers the states of Kentucky, Ohio, Michigan, and Tennessee.

The case involved Neill Roncker, a 9-year-old classified as having moderate mental retardation. School personnel believed that the most appropriate placement for Neill was in a special school for children with disabilities. The parents objected, stating that their child would benefit from contact with his peers in a general education setting, brought suit against the school district, challenging the placement. The issue did not involve Neill's placement in a general education classroom; both sides agreed that he required special education. The Ronckers contended, however, that Neill could be provided the special education services in a setting that would allow greater integration and contact with students without disabilities.

The U.S. District Court for the Southern District of Ohio ruled in favor of the school district. The court stated that the mainstreaming requirement allowed schools broad discretion in the placement of students with disabilities. The court, finding that Neill had not made significant progress while in an integrated setting, ruled that the school district had acted properly in determining Neill's placement.

The Ronckers appealed to the U.S. Court of Appeals for the Sixth District. The circuit court reversed the decision of the district court, stating that

> The act (PL 94-142) does not require mainstreaming in every case but its requirement that mainstreaming be provided to the maximum extent appropriate indicates a very strong congressional preference. (p. 1063)

Although the court noted the importance of balancing the benefits of segregated special education services against the benefits of mainstreaming, the *Roncker* decision is best known for what has been referred to as the *Roncker* portability test (Huefner, 1994):

> In a case where the segregated facility is considered superior, the court should determine whether the services which make that placement superior could feasibly be provided in a nonsegregated setting. If they can, the placement in the segregated school would be inappropriate under the Act. (*Roncker*, p. 1063)

---

*The courts have tended to use the term *mainstreaming* in LRE cases. The term has been used to denote the practice in which children with disabilities are integrated into general education classrooms rather than a shorthand term for the LRE concept.

Figure 12.2
The *Roncker* Portability Test

> 1. Can the educational services that make a segregated placement superior be feasibly provided in a nonsegregated setting?
>
> 2. If so, the placement in the segregated setting is inappropriate.

Courts using this test must determine if the services that make the segregated setting more appropriate can be transported to the nonsegregated setting. If the services can be transported, the modification is required by the LRE mandate (Tucker & Goldstein, 1992). (See Figure 12.2 for the *Roncker* portability test.)

The *Daniel* Two-Part Test

Perhaps the seminal case regarding the LRE mandate came from the U.S. Court of Appeals for the Fifth Circuit in *Daniel R.R. v. State Board of Education* (1989; hereafter *Daniel*). The plaintiff in the case, Daniel, was a 6-year-old child with Down syndrome enrolled in the El Paso, Texas, Independent School District. At the request of his parents, Daniel was placed in a prekindergarten class for half of the school day and an early childhood special education class for the other half. Shortly after the beginning of the school year, Daniel's teacher informed the school placement committee that Daniel was not participating in class and was failing to master any of the skills taught, even with almost constant attention and instruction from the teacher and aide. The committee met and decided that the prekindergarten class was inappropriate for Daniel. Daniel was removed from the prekindergarten class, attended only the early childhood special education class, and interacted with children from the prekindergarten class at recess and lunch. The parents exercised their right to a due process hearing. The hearing officer agreed with the school in concluding that Daniel could not participate in the prekindergarten class without almost constant supervision from the teacher, that he was receiving little educational benefit, and that he was disrupting the class because his needs absorbed most of the teacher's time. The officer also noted that the teacher would have to modify the curriculum totally to meet Daniel's needs. The parents filed an action in the district and, eventually, the circuit court.

The circuit court stated that the imprecise nature of the IDEA's mandates were deliberate, and that Congress had chosen to leave the selection of educational policy and methods in the hands of local school officials. Congress, however, had created a statutory preference for mainstreaming while at the same time creating a tension between the appropriate education and mainstreaming provisions of the Act. By creating this tension, Congress recognized that the general education environment would not be suitable for all students with disabilities and, at times, a special setting or school may be necessary to provide an appropriate education. Essentially, the *Daniel* court said that when the provisions of FAPE and mainstreaming are in conflict, the mainstreaming mandate becomes secondary to the appropriate education mandate.

The *Daniel* court declined to follow the Sixth Circuit's analysis in *Roncker*, stating that the *Roncker* test necessitated "too intrusive an inquiry into educational policy choices that Congress deliberately left to state and local school districts" (p. 1046). Congress, according to the court, had left the choice of educational methods and policies to the schools. The court's task, therefore, was to determine if the school had complied with the IDEA's requirements.

The court believed that the statutory language of the LRE mandate provided a more appropriate test for determining a school's compliance with the mainstreaming requirement than did the *Roncker* inquiry. Relying on this language, the court developed a two-part test for determining compliance with the LRE requirement. (See Figure 12.3, the *Daniel* two-part test.)

First, the court must ask whether education in the general education classroom, with the use of supplementary aids and services, could be satisfactorily achieved. To make this determination, the court must decide whether the school has taken steps to accommodate a student with disabilities in the general education classroom. These attempts take the form of supplying supplementary aids and services and modifying the curriculum. In determining whether the school complied with this part of the test, the court must also decide if the student will receive benefit from the general education classroom and if the mainstreamed student will negatively affect the education of classroom peers. If the school has not attempted to mainstream the student to the maximum extent appropriate, the school will fail the first part of the test. The inquiry will thus end because the school district has violated the LRE mandate.

If the school passes the first part of the test, the court then moves to part two. Here the court asks whether the school has mainstreamed the student to the maximum extent appropriate; that is, by relying on the continuum of placements, the school must provide the student with as much exposure to students without disabilities as possible. The *Daniel* court suggested that students who are educated primarily in segregated settings should be placed in integrated settings outside the special education classroom when feasible (e.g., nonacademic classes, lunch, recess).

If the school meets both parts of the two-part test, then its obligation under the IDEA is fulfilled. After applying the two-part test in *Daniel*, the Fifth Circuit determined that Daniel's needs were so great and that he required so much of the teacher's

Figure 12.3
The *Daniel* Two-Part Test

1. Can education in the general education classroom with supplementary aids and services be achieved satisfactorily?
2. If a student is placed in a more restrictive setting, is the student integrated to the maximum extent appropriate?

time that it was affecting the education of the other students negatively. The court, finding that the school district had met the requirements of the two-part test, affirmed the decision of the district court that the school district has satisfied the LRE requirement of the IDEA.

In addition to the test, the *Daniel* court provided further direction for lower courts to follow in LRE cases in noting that the court's "task is not to second-guess state and local school officials; rather, it is the narrow one of determining whether state and local school officials have complied with the Act" (p. 1048).

The *Daniel* decision is the legal authority on LRE in the states that comprise the Fifth Circuit: Louisiana, Mississippi, and Texas. It has proven to be a very persuasive decision and has subsequently been adopted in the Third Circuit in *Oberti v. Board of Education of the Borough of Clementon School District* (1993), which is the legal authority in Delaware, New Jersey, and Pennsylvania; and in the Eleventh Circuit in *Greer v. Rome City School District* (1991), which is the legal authority in Alabama, Georgia, and Florida.

The *Rachel H.* Four-Factor Test

Sacramento City Unified School District v. Rachel H.

On January 24, 1994, the U.S. Court of Appeals for the Ninth Circuit affirmed a district court's decision in *Sacramento City Unified School District v. Rachel H.*[*] (1994; hereafter *Rachel H.*). This case is the legal authority for the Ninth Circuit, which covers Alaska, Arizona, California, Hawaii, Idaho, Montana, Nevada, Oregon, and Washington.

The case involved Rachel Holland, an 11-year-old girl with moderate mental retardation. From 1985 to 1989, Rachel attended a number of special education programs in the Sacramento School District. In the fall of 1989, Rachel's parents requested that she be placed in a general education classroom during the entire school day. The district contended that Rachel's disability was too severe for her to benefit from being in a general education class and proposed that she be placed in special education for academic subjects, attending the general education class only for nonacademic activities (e.g., art, music, lunch, recess). The parents removed Rachel from the school and placed her in a private school. The parents also requested a due process hearing. The hearing officer held for the parents, stating that the school district had failed to make an adequate effort to educate Rachel in the general education classroom. The school appealed the decision to the district court. The court, relying on the decisions in *Daniel* and *Greer v. Rome City School District,* considered four factors in making its decision. (See Figure 12.4 for the *Rachel H.* four-factor test.)

The first factor concerned the educational benefits available to Rachel in the general education classroom with supplementary aids and services as compared with

---

*Because the child was a minor, the circuit court used Rachel H. rather than her full name, Rachel Holland. At the district level the case was *Sacramento City Unified School District v. Holland.*

Figure 12.4
The *Rachel H.* Four-Factor Test

1. The educational benefits of the general education classroom with supplementary aids and services as compared with the educational benefits of the special classroom.
2. The nonacademic benefits of interaction with students without disabilities.
3. The effect of the student's presence on the teacher and on other students in the classroom.
4. The cost of mainstreaming.

the educational benefits of the special education classroom. The court found that the district, in presenting evidence, had failed to establish that the educational benefits of the special education classroom were better than or even equal to the benefits of the general education classroom.

The second factor the court considered was the nonacademic benefits of each classroom. The court decided that the Hollands' testimony, that Rachel was developing social and communication skills as well as self-esteem, was more credible than the district's testimony that Rachel was not learning from exposure to other children and that she was becoming isolated from her peers. The second factor, therefore, was decided in favor of the Hollands.

Third, the district court examined the impact of Rachel's presence on others in the general education classroom—specifically, whether Rachel's presence was a detriment to others because she was disruptive or distracting, and if she would take up so much of the teacher's time that the other students would suffer. Both parties agreed that Rachel followed directions and was not disruptive. Also, the court found that Rachel did not interfere with the teacher's ability to teach the other children. The court ruled that the third factor was in favor of placement in the general education class.

The final factor in the court's decision involved evaluating the cost of placement in the general education classroom. The court found that the school district had not offered persuasive evidence to support its claim that educating Rachel in the general education class would be far more expensive than educating her in the combined general education and special education placement. Thus, the cost factor did not provide an impediment to educating Rachel in general education. Weighing the four factors, the district court determined that the appropriate placement for Rachel was full-time in the general education classroom with supplemental aids and services.

An appeal to the Ninth Circuit was heard on August 12, 1993, and the court delivered its opinion on January 24, 1994. The circuit court affirmed the decision of the district court. The higher court stated that the school district had the burden of demonstrating that its proposed placement provided mainstreaming to the maximum extent appropriate. The circuit court adopted the district court's four-factor test in determining that the school district had not met the burden of proof that

Rachel could not be educated in the general education classroom. The court found the Hollands' position for inclusion to be more persuasive.

The school district filed a petition to have the U.S. Supreme Court review this case. The high court denied the petition, however, and did not hear the case.

Clyde K. v. Puyallup School District

In *Clyde K. v. Puyallup School District* (1994), the U.S. Court of Appeals for the Ninth Circuit applied its four-factor test to a case involving inclusion and a student with behavioral disorders. The case was especially noteworthy because it answered questions heretofore unexamined at the appellate court level.

The dispute involved Ryan K., a 15-year-old with Attention Deficit Hyperactivity Disorder (ADHD) and Tourette's syndrome. Ryan was receiving special education in the general education classroom with supplementary resource room help. His behavior, however, became increasingly disruptive. He used obscenities, was noncompliant, harassed female students with sexually explicit remarks, and physically assaulted classmates. Following two serious incidences of assaultive behavior, Ryan was suspended. When he returned, the school district had a paraprofessional observe his classroom behavior for three days. School officials met to review the IEP and concluded that Ryan's objectives could be met if he was placed in a segregated special education program called Students Temporarily Away from Regular Schools (STARS). His parents were notified of the proposed placement change. School personnel suggested that Ryan be placed in STARS while they and his parents developed a plan to reintegrate Ryan in the general education classroom. The parents initially agreed but subsequently changed their minds concerning the placement in STARS. They requested a new IEP and a due process hearing.

Ryan's parents brought their attorney to the IEP meeting to discuss Ryan's return to the general education classroom. The parents contended that the STARS program was overly restrictive and that the appropriate placement would be the general education classroom with a personal aide. During the course of discussions, the parents' attorney abruptly ended the meeting, stating that Ryan would be in the general education class the next day. According to the court, the attorney insisted that the parents leave despite pleas by school district personnel that they continue the meeting.

A due process hearing was convened. The hearing officer concluded that the school district had complied with the requirements of the IDEA. The parents appealed to the district court, which, after reviewing the record of the administrative hearing and hearing additional testimony, affirmed the decision of the hearing officer. The parents then appealed to the U.S. Court of Appeals for the Ninth Circuit.

In its ruling, the circuit court applied the four-factor test it had established in *Rachel H.* The first factor considers the academic benefits of the general education classroom. The court noted that Ryan was not receiving academic benefits from the general education classroom and that testing had actually indicated academic regression. The court also noted that the school district had made efforts to provide supplementary aids and services to accommodate Ryan in the general education classroom (e.g., staff training about Ryan's disabilities, special education support in a resource room, and the involvement of a behavioral specialist). Because of the severity of Ryan's behavioral problems, the court did not believe that the presence of a personal aide would have made a meaningful difference.

The nonacademic benefits of the general education class setting are the second factor in the *Rachel H.* test. The court stated that testimony indicated that Ryan was a social isolate and seemed to benefit little from modeling. The court believed, therefore, that the nonacademic benefits of the general education class setting were minimal.

The third factor—the negative effects the student's presence had on the teacher and peers—was considered the most important by the court. Noting that Ryan's aggressive behavior, sexually explicit remarks, and profanity had an overwhelming negative effect on the teachers and peers, the court stated that the school had a statutory duty to ensure that all students with disabilities receive an appropriate education. This duty, however, did not require that schools ignore the student's behavioral problems. According to the court, schools have an obligation to ensure that all students are educated in safe environments:

> Disruptive behavior that significantly impairs the education of other students strongly suggests a mainstream placement is no longer appropriate. While school officials have a statutory duty to ensure that disabled students receive an appropriate education, they are not required to sit on their hands when a disabled student's behavioral problems prevent him and those around him from learning. (p. 1402)

In its ruling, the Ninth Circuit court held that the STARS program was the LRE. The court also stated that the slow and tedious working of the court system made it a poor arena in which to resolve disputes regarding a student's education. The judgment of the district court was thus affirmed.

In an interesting and highly unusual move, the circuit court, in a footnote to the decision, criticized the attorney for the plaintiffs for "hardball tactics" and counterproductive dealings with the school district, which destroyed potential channels for constructive dialogue. The court noted that because of the litigation, Ryan spent 2 years in a self-contained placement that was originally intended to be a short-term interim placement, and that "Ryan's experience offers a poignant reminder that everyone's interests are better served when parents and school officials resolve their differences through cooperation and compromise rather than litigation" (p. 1402).

The Fourth Circuit's Three-Part Test

On July 8, 1997, the U.S. Court of Appeals for the Fourth Circuit handed down its decision in *Hartmann v. Loudoun County Board of Education*. Mark Hartmann was an 11-year-old child with autism. His family lived in Loudoun County, Virginia, where he attended Ashburn Elementary School. Based on Mark's previous IEP, school officials decided to place him in a general education classroom. To facilitate his educational progress, school officials hired a full-time aide, provided specialized training for his teacher and aide, provided 3 hours per week of instruction with a special education teacher (who also served as a consultant to Mark's teacher and aide), and provided 5 hours per week of speech therapy. Additionally, the entire staff at

Ashburn Elementary received inservice training on autism and inclusion. The IEP team also included the supervisor of the Loudoun County program for children with autism to provide assistance in managing Mark's behavior. Finally, the IEP team received assistance from two consultants.

Despite the measures taken, the IEP team determined that Mark was making no academic or behavioral progress in the general education setting. Moreover, his behavior problems were extremely disruptive in class. Because of his aggression toward others (e.g., kicking, biting, punching), five families asked to have their children transferred to another classroom. The IEP team proposed that Mark be moved to a program for children with autism in a regular elementary school. Mark would receive his academic instruction and speech therapy in the special class and attend a general education classroom for art, music, physical education, library, and recess. The parents disagreed with the IEP, asserting that it violated the mainstreaming provision of the IDEA. The school district initiated a due process hearing. The due process hearing officer upheld the school district's IEP, and the state review officer affirmed the decision. The Hartmanns then challenged the hearing officer's decision in federal district court. The district court reversed the due process decision, specifically rejecting the administrative findings and ruling that the school had not taken appropriate steps to include Mark in the general education classroom. The school district filed an appeal with the U.S. Court of Appeals for the Fourth Circuit.

Finding that the IDEA's mainstreaming provision established a presumption, not an inflexible mandate, the circuit court reversed the district court's ruling. The circuit court also admonished the district court for substituting its own judgment for that of educators. Additionally, the court reaffirmed a previous ruling that held that mainstreaming is not required when (1) a student with a disability would not receive educational benefit from mainstreaming in a general education class; (2) any marginal benefit from mainstreaming would be significantly outweighed by benefits that could feasibly be obtained only in a separate instructional setting; or (3) the student is a disruptive force in the general education classroom. Finally, the circuit court stated that the LRE provision of the IDEA only created a presumption, and the presumption reflected congressional judgment that receipt of social benefits is a subordinate goal to receiving educational benefit.

Summary of Judicial Standards of Review

Although a number of LRE cases have been heard by the U.S. Courts of Appeals, there exist only four acknowledged tests for determining placement in the LRE. These tests, or judicial standards of review, are the *Roncker* portability test, the *Daniel* two-part test, the *Rachel H.* four-factor test, and the Fourth Circuit's three-part test. Of these tests, the *Daniel* test has proven the most persuasive, subsequently being adopted by the U.S. Courts of Appeals for the Third and Eleventh Circuits. These standards are important because they provide lower courts in the circuit with guidance in ruling on similar cases. They are also instructive to school districts because they indicate the relevant factors that courts will examine in LRE cases. Table 12.1 lists the standards of review and the states in which they are con-

Table 12.1
Judicial Standards of Review in LRE Cases

Roncker Portability Test	*Daniel* Two-Part Test	*Rachel H.* Four-Factor Test	Fourth Circuit's Three-Part Test
Kentucky	Alabama	Alaska	Maryland
Michigan	Delaware	Arizona	North Carolina
Ohio	Georgia	California	South Carolina
Tennessee	Florida	Hawaii	Virginia
	Louisiana	Idaho	West Virginia
	Mississippi	Montana	
	New Jersey	Nevada	
	Pennsylvania	Oregon	
	Texas	Washington	

trolling authority. Figure 12.5 represents a multifactor decision-making model based on these three standards of review.

The Burden of Proof

The question of which party bears the burden of proof in litigation has often been an area of conflict. Burden of proof refers to when parties, in taking a particular position, have to prove the correctness of their position to the satisfaction of a court. Decisions in three circuits—the First Circuit in *Roland M. v. Concord School Committee* (1990), the D.C. Circuit in *Kerham v. McKenzie* (1988), and the Ninth Circuit in *Clyde K. v. Puyallup* (1994)—have held that the burden of proof rests with the party challenging the decision of the administrative agency. In *Clyde K.,* the court stated that because the IDEA does not contain language to the contrary, the burden of proof is placed on the parties challenging the ruling. Consequently, the parties that file a complaint with a court bear the burden of proving their case. The court in *Oberti v. Board of Education* (1993), however, stated that because of congressional preference for the integration of students with disabilities, the burden of proof should be placed on schools that have decided to educate a particular child in a segregated setting. The *Oberti* court stated that

> when IDEA's mainstreaming requirement is specifically at issue, it is appropriate to place the burden of proving compliance with the IDEA on the school. Indeed, the Act's strong presumption in favor of mainstreaming, 20 U.S.C. § 1422 (5) (B), would be turned on its head if parents had to prove that their child was worthy of being included, rather than the school district having to justify a decision to exclude the child from the regular classroom. (p. 1219)

Figure 12.5
Determination of the Least Restrictive Environment

School district decisions should be based on formative data collected throughout the LRE process.

1. Has the school taken steps to maintain the child in the general education classroom?
   - What supplementary aids and services were used?
   - What interventions were attempted?
   - How many interventions were attempted?
2. Benefits of placement in general education with supplementary aids and services versus special education.
   - Academic benefits
   - Nonacademic benefits (e.g., social, communication)
3. Effects on the education of other students.
   - If the student is disruptive, is the education of other students adversely effected?
   - Does the student require an inordinate amount of attention from the teacher, thereby adversely affecting the education of others?
4. If a student is being educated in a setting other than the general education classroom, are there integrated experiences with nondisabled peers to the maximum extent appropriate?
   - In what academic settings is the student integrated with nondisabled peers?
   - In what nonacademic settings is the child integrated with nondisabled peers?
5. Is the entire continuum of alternative services available from which to choose an appropriate placement?

From "Least Restrictive Environment, Inclusion, and Students with Disabilities: A Legal Analysis" by M.L. Yell, 1995, *Journal of Special Education, 28*(4), 389–404. Copyright 1995 by PRO-ED, Inc. Adapted by permission.

The parent was challenging the decision of the administrative agencies in *Oberti,* and would have borne the burden of proof in accordance with the *Roland, Kerham,* and *Clyde K.* decisions; however, the *Oberti* court placed the burden of proof on the school district. The Ninth Circuit court, in *Clyde K.,* specifically rejected the Third Circuit's ruling on burden of proof in *Oberti,* stating that the fact that a statute favors the rights of a certain group does not mean that the group is entitled to procedural advantage. Given the dicta and holdings in the above court decisions, however, it is reasonable to assume that school districts' actions will be closely scrutinized when they place students with disabilities in more restrictive settings within the continuum of placements.

Standards for Determining the LRE

Individualized Determination

The IEP team determines the least restrictive appropriate setting. The IDEA, its regulations, and comments to these regulations make it clear that the IEP team can only make this decision by examining students' needs and determining their goals based on this assessment. Federal regulations state that "the overriding rule . . . is that placement decisions must be made on an individual basis" (IDEA Regulations, 34 C.F.R. § 300.552, comment). In 1991, OSERS interpreted the LRE mandate as requiring that "children with disabilities should be educated with nondisabled children to the maximum extent appropriate; however, the determination of whether to place a child with disabilities in an integrated setting must be made on a case-by-case basis" (*Stutler & McCoy,* 1991, p. 308).

Because of the individualized nature of the LRE placement, there are no simple rules to guide IEP teams in making placement decisions. The legislation and litigation do, however, provide guidance regarding the decision-making process. Clearly, there are certain actions that are never "appropriate," such as developing blanket policies regarding LRE decisions. For example, schools must never refuse to place particular categories of students with disabilities in general education classes; neither should they refuse more restrictive placements when required.

The decisions in *Greer v. Rome City School District* (1991) and *Oberti v. Board of Education* (1993) are particularly instructive, as the courts delineated the inappropriate actions by the school districts that resulted in the districts' losses in these cases. Perhaps the most important reason for these losses was the courts' unwillingness to accept assertions of appropriateness of restrictive settings without proof by school districts as to the inappropriateness of the general education classroom (Yell, 1995). In both *Greer* and *Oberti,* the school districts did not have data from direct experience to indicate that the general education class placement was not appropriate. For example, in *Oberti* the plaintiff was a student who exhibited significant behavior problems in the general education classroom. Although the school district's special education director testified that the school had attempted to keep the student in the general education classroom through various procedures, the IEP did not contain a behavioral plan. In *Greer,* the court ruled against the school district because (a) the IEP team failed to consider the full continuum of placements in determining the LRE; (b) the school made no attempt to assist the student to remain in the mainstream setting; and (c) the school district developed the IEP prior to the IEP meeting and did not clearly inform the Greers of the full range of services that may have been required to maintain their child in the general education classroom. Conversely, in the *Daniel, Hartmann,* and *Clyde K.* decisions, in which the school districts prevailed, school officials had attempted and documented a number of efforts to maintain the students in the general education classroom.

Benefits to the Student

The *Greer* court noted "several factors that a school district may consider in determining whether education in the regular classroom may be achieved satisfactorily" (p. 697). First, the school may compare the educational benefits of the general education classroom (with supplementary aids and services) with those received in the special education classroom. This comparison should include both academic and nonacademic (e.g., language, role-modeling) activities. If the school determines that the self-contained setting will provide "significantly" greater benefits and that in the general education classroom the student will fall behind peers in the self-contained class, the general education environment may not be appropriate.

Effects on Peers

School personnel may consider the effect the presence of a student with disabilities in a general education classroom would have on the education of other students in that classroom. A student who disrupts the education of others due to behavior problems or because of needing constant teacher attention may not be appropriately placed in a general education classroom. In weighing this factor, however, the school is cautioned by both the *Oberti* and *Greer* courts of their obligation to first consider the use of supplementary aids and services to accommodate a student.

The decision in *Clyde K.* further confirmed the legitimacy of considering the rights of other students in determining placement. In this case, a crucial factor in the school district's restrictive placement's being upheld was the use of supplementary aids and services. Similarly, school districts also prevailed in the removal of disruptive students in *MR v. Lincolnwood Board of Education* (1994) and *VanderMalle v. Ambach* (1987).

Appropriate Education

The IDEA requires that schools provide a FAPE for all students with disabilities. The law also requires that to the maximum extent appropriate, students with disabilities should be educated with students without disabilities. When an appropriate education is not possible in the general education classroom, the FAPE and LRE provisions seem to be in conflict. This apparent conflict has provoked much controversy and confusion (Dubow, 1989). The FAPE and LRE requirements do not actually conflict; however, both are important elements in the special education decision-making process (McColl, 1992).

Legislation and litigation regarding LRE and FAPE indicate that the school's primary obligation is to provide the student with disabilities with a FAPE. The LRE principle, although very important, is secondary (Champagne, 1993; Osborne, 1993; Tucker & Goldstein, 1992). The language of the law reinforces this by requiring that students with disabilities be educated in the LRE to the maximum extent appropriate, and by further requiring that schools have a continuum of alternative placements. In determining placement, the IEP team balances FAPE with the preference for educating students with disabilities with their peers in the general education classroom. The team selects the most integrated setting that is compatible with the delivery of an appropriate education. That setting is the LRE.

The IDEA appears unambiguous regarding LRE: The IEP team is to determine the setting with the greatest degree of integration in which an appropriate education is available. In practice, however, this requirement has proven to be difficult to apply (Champagne, 1993; Huefner, 1994; Osborne, 1993).

Integration

The IDEA clearly requires the maximum amount of integration that is appropriate given a student's needs. The LRE mandate was a clear expression of congressional preference for educating students with disabilities in the general education classroom when appropriate. As Champagne (1993) asserts, the IDEA requires the maximum integration that will "work" for a student. An appropriate interpretation of the LRE cases is that students with disabilities belong in integrated settings and that schools must make good faith efforts to make this possible.

The Use of Supplementary Aids and Services

According to the *Oberti* court, a key to meeting the LRE mandate is a school's proper use of supplementary aids and services. School districts must make good faith efforts to maintain students in a general education class placement, and the provision of various supplementary aids and services is a means by which schools can maintain students with disabilities in these settings. Supplementary aids and services may include prereferral interventions, consultation, behavior management plans, paraprofessionals, itinerant teachers, and resource rooms. According to the court in *Daniel,* schools are required to provide supplementary aids and services and to modify the general education classroom when they mainstream students with disabilities. If such efforts are not made, schools will be in violation of the IDEA. Furthermore, if the school has made these efforts, lower courts must examine whether the efforts are sufficient, because the IDEA

> does not permit [schools] to make mere token gestures to accommodate [students with disabilities], its requirement for modifying and supplementing regular education is broad. . . . Although broad, the requirement is not limitless. . . . [Schools] need not provide every conceivable aid or service to assist a child. . . . Furthermore, the [IDEA] does not require regulate education instructors to devote all or most of their time to one [student with disabilities] or modify the curriculum beyond recognition. (p. 1048)

The question of the limit of supplementary aids and services that must be attempted or considered by the school remains undecided. In the *Daniel* decision, the court determined that the school district had fulfilled its requirements under the law, whereas the courts' rulings in the *Greer* and *Oberti* cases held that the school districts had not. In the *Oberti* case, the court believed that the school district had made negligible efforts to include the student, Rafael Oberti, in a general education classroom by mainstreaming him without a curriculum plan, behavior management plan, or special support to the teacher. The *Greer* court found that the school district failed to consider the full range of supplementary aids and services (including a resource room and itinerant instruction) that might have assisted the student, Christy Greer, in the mainstream placement. The court acknowledged that testimony by officials indicated that the school district had considered supplementary aids and services; however, this consideration was not reflected in the minutes of the IEP meeting or in the IEP itself. Neither had the school district made efforts to modify the mainstream curriculum to accommodate Christy.

The courts' direction regarding the importance of school districts' providing supplementary aids and services to place and maintain students in LREs is clear. Whether the school district needs to actually *attempt* a general education class placement with supplementary aids and services or is merely obligated to *consider* these services is, however, uncertain. Noting that the dicta in *Greer* and *Oberti* state that school districts must show that they have "considered" a range of supplementary aids and services, Huefner (1994) argues that school administrators may need to show that such considerations were made prior to concluding that an education in the general education classroom was not appropriate. Likewise, Maloney (1994) advises schools against failing to attempt general education classroom placements with adequate supplementary aids and services. Clearly, when there is a reasonable likelihood that a student can receive an appropriate education in the general education classroom with the use of supplementary aids and services, then the general education placement must be attempted (Gorn, 1996). When the general education classroom is clearly inappropriate for a student, however, it is not required that a student be placed in the general education classroom to fail prior to being moved to a more appropriate, restrictive placement (*Poolaw v. Bishop*, 1995).

A Model for Determining LRE

Notwithstanding the courts' guidance in making LRE decisions, placement teams find that determining the educational placement that constitutes the most appropriate and least restrictive setting for students with disabilities is tremendously difficult (Huefner, 1994). Champagne (1993) argues persuasively that school districts should adopt a sequential model in making placements decisions. The sequential model is an organized way of applying the LRE requirement to whatever facts a particular student's situation requires. Additionally, Champagne has tested the model against the various LRE cases. (Figure 12.6 depicts the sequential model.)

In Champagne's model, after the initial eligibility decision is made, the IEP team determines what constitutes an appropriate education for a student. Following this decision, the team determines where the education will be provided; that is, the nature of needed special education services (e.g., IEP goals and objectives) is decided before turning to placement issues. Thus the model preserves the "core statutory imperative" that placements are based on the student's educational needs.

Figure 12.6
Champagne's Sequential Model

Step 1: Make initial eligibility decision.

Step 2: Define what constitutes appropriate educational services.

Step 3: Ask whether these appropriate educational services can be delivered in the general education classroom in its current form. If yes, that is the primary placement; if no, go to step 4.

Step 4: Ask whether these appropriate educational services can be delivered in the general education classroom if it is modified through the addition of supplementary aids and services. If yes, that is the primary placement; if no, go to step 5.

Step 5: Move along the continuum of alternative placement one step at a time, from the least restrictive setting to more restrictive ones. At each step, ask whether the services called for in the IEP can be delivered there in its current form. If yes, that is the primary placement; if no, go to step 6.

Step 6: Ask whether the services called for in the IEP can be delivered in the slightly more restrictive settings if they are modified through the use of supplementary aids and services. If yes, that is the primary placement; if no, repeat step 5 for the placement on the continuum that is slightly more restrictive, and then, if necessary, go to step 6 for that setting.
(In this manner, the placement team moves along the continuum of alternative placements, one step at a time, repeating steps 5 and 6 until a yes answer is obtained.)

Step 7: In the context of the primary placement chosen, ask if there are additional opportunities for integration for some portion of the student's school day. If yes, design a split placement.

From "Decisions in Sequence: How to Make Placements in the Least Restrictive Environment" by J.F. Champagne, 1993, *EdLaw Briefing Paper, 9 & 10,* 1–16. Adapted with permission from EDLAW, Inc., P.O. Box 81-7327, Hollywood, FL 33081-0327.

Next, educational placements are examined not only as they exist, but also as they might be modified. Supplementary aids and services, therefore, are given primary consideration.

Each educational placement along the continuum of alternative placements is then considered one placement at a time. Moreover, the placements are considered in a particular sequence, namely, from least restrictive to most restrictive.

Finally, even after the primary placement has been tentatively determined, the placement team must consider all additional opportunities for integration. This includes integration during nonacademic periods. In cases where a student's primary placement is in a more restrictive setting, a split placement (one in which settings of different degrees of integration are used for different parts of a student's day) is selected.

Summary

The LRE mandate of the IDEA sets forth a clear congressional preference for integrating students with disabilities in general education classrooms. The LRE mandate has two specific components: First, students with disabilities must be educated along with students without disabilities to the maximum extent appropriate; second, students with disabilities should be removed from integrated settings only when the nature or severity of the disability is such that an appropriate education with the use of supplementary aids and services cannot be achieved satisfactorily in the general education setting. Recognizing that at times an integrated setting would not provide an appropriate education and thus a more restrictive setting may be necessary, IDEA regulations include a continuum of alternative placement options that vary in the degree of restrictiveness. The purpose of the continuum is to make appropriate educational placements available to students based on their individual needs. Recent decisions have indicated that the courts are unwilling to accept at face value a school district's assertions that student can not be educated in less restrictive settings. Schools will bear the burden of proof, therefore, when they choose more restrictive settings for students with disabilities.

For Further Information

Bartlett, L. D. (1993). Mainstreaming: On the road to clarification. *Education Law Reporter, 76,* 17–25.

Champagne, J. F. (1993). Decisions in sequence: How to make placements in the least restrictive environment. *EdLaw Briefing Paper, 9 & 10,* 1–16.

Huefner, D. S. (1994). The mainstreaming cases: Tensions and trends for school administrators. *Educational Administration Quarterly, 30,* 27–55.

Lewis, T. J., Chard, D., & Scott, T. M. (1994). Full inclusion and the education of children and youth with emotional and behavioral disorders. *Behavioral Disorders, 19,* 277–293.

Osborne, A. G., & DiMattia, P. (1994). The IDEA's least restrictive environment mandate: Legal implications. *Exceptional Children, 61,* 6–14.

Osborne, A. G., & DiMattia, P. (1994). Counterpoint: IDEA's LRE mandate: Another look. *Exceptional Children, 61,* 582–584.

Yell, M. L. (1994). The LRE cases: Judicial activism or judicial restraint? *Exceptional Children, 61,* 578–581.

Yell, M. L. (1995). Least restrictive environment, inclusion, and students with disabilities: A legal analysis. *Journal of Special Education, 28,* 389–404.

Yell, M. L. (1995). *Clyde K. and Sheila K. v. Puyallup School District:* The courts, inclusion, and students with behavioral disorders. *Behavioral Disorders, 20,* 179–189.

References

Americans with Disabilities Act of 1990, 42 U.S.C. 12101 *et seq.*

Barnett v. Fairfax, 17 EHLR 350 (4th Cir. 1991).

Bartlett, L. D. (1993). Mainstreaming: On the road to clarification. *Education Law Reporter, 76,* 17–25.

Board of Education of the Hendrick Hudson School District v. Rowley, 458 U.S. 176 (1982).

Brown v. Board of Education, 347 U.S. 483 (1954).

Carter v. Florence County School District, 950 F.2d 156 (4th Cir. 1991).

Champagne, J. F. (1993). Decisions in sequence: How to make placements in the least restrictive environment. *EdLaw Briefing Paper, 9 & 10,* 1–16.

Clyde K. v. Puyallup School District, 35 F.3d 1396 (9th Cir. 1994).

Cordero v. Pennsylvania, 19 IDELR 623 (M.D. Pa. 1993).

Daniel R.R. v. State Board of Education, 874 F.2d 1036 (5th Cir. 1989).

Dubow, S. (1989). Into the turbulent mainstream: A legal perspective on the weight to be given to the least restrictive environment in placement decisions for deaf children. *Journal of Law and Education, 18,* 215–228.

Education for All Handicapped Children Act of 1975, 20 U.S.C. § 1401 *et seq.*

Education of the Handicapped Amendments of 1974, Pub. L. No. 93-380, 88 Stat. 580.

Flour Bluff Independent School District v. Katherine M., 24 IDELR 673 (5th Cir. 1996).

Frost, Letter to, 19 IDELR 594 (OSERS 1991).

Goodling, Letter to, 18 IDELR 213 (OSERS 1991).

Gorn, S. (1996). *What do I do when . . . The answer book on special education law.* Horsham, PA: LRP Publications.

Greer v. Rome City School District, 950 F.2d 688 (11th Cir. 1991).

Hairston v. Drosick, 423 F. Supp. 180 (S.D. W.V. 1976).

Hartmann v. Loudoun County Board of Education (4th Cir. 1997). Available at http://www.law.emory .edu/4circuit/july97/962809.p.html.

Hudson v. Bloomfield Hills School District, 23 IDELR 612 (E.D. Mich 1995).

Huefner, D. S. (1994). The mainstreaming cases: Tensions and trends for school administrators. *Educational Administration Quarterly, 30,* 27–55.

Individuals with Disabilities Education Act of 1990, 20 U.S.C. § 1401 *et seq.*

Individuals with Disabilities Education Act Regulations, 34 C.F.R. § 300 *et seq.*

Kerham v. McKenzie, 862 F.2d 884 (D.C. Cir. 1988).

Lachman v. Illinois Board of Education, 852 F.2d 290 (7th Cir. 1988).

Maloney, M. (1994, May). *Full inclusion: Heaven or hell?* Paper presented at the National Institute on Legal Issues of Educating Individuals with Disabilities, San Francisco, CA.

McColl, A. (1992). Placement in the least restrictive environment for children with disabilities. *School Law Bulletin, 26,* 13–21.

MR v. Lincolnwood Board of Education, 20 IDELR 1323 (N.D. Ill. 1994).

Murray v. Montrose County School District, 22 IDELR 558 (10th Cir. 1995).

Oberti v. Board of Education of the Borough of Clementon School District, 995 F.2d 1204 (3rd Cir. 1993).

Osborne, A. G. (1993). The IDEA's least restrictive environment mandate: Implications for public policy. *Education Law Reporter, 74,* 369–380.

Poolaw v. Bishop, 23 IDELR 407 (9th Cir. 1995).

Roland M. v. Concord School Committee, 910 F.2d 983 (1st Cir. 1990).

Roncker v. Walter, 700 F.2d 1058 (6th Cir. 1983).

Sacramento City Unified School District Board of Education v. Holland, 786 F. Supp. 874 (E.D. Col. 1992).

Sacramento City Unified School District Board of Education v. Rachel H., 14 F.3d 1398 (9th Cir. 1994).

Schuldt v. Mankato ISD, 937 F.2d 1357 (8th Cir. 1991).

Section 504 Regulations, 34 C.F.R. § 104 *et seq.*

Sheldon v. Tucker, 364 U.S. 479 (1960).

Stafford, R. (1978). Education for the handicapped: A senator's perspective. *Vermont Law Review, 3,* 71–76.

Stutler and McCoy, Letter to, 18 IDELR 307 (OSERS 1991).

Tucker, B. P., & Goldstein, B. A. (1992). *Legal rights of persons with disabilities: An analysis of public law.* Horsham, PA: LRP Publications.

Turnbull, H. R. (1993). *Free appropriate public education: The law and children with disabilities* (4th ed.). Denver: Love Publishing Company.

Urban v. Jefferson County School District R-1, 21 IDELR 985 (D. Col. 1994).

VanderMalle v. Ambach, 667 F. Supp. 1015 (S.D.N.Y. 1987).

Yell, M. L. (1995). Least restrictive environment, inclusion, and students with disabilities: Analysis and commentary. *Journal of Special Education, 28,* 389–404.

Zirkel, P. (1994). *Section 504 and the schools.* Horsham, PA: LRP Publications.

CHAPTER THIRTEEN

Procedural Safeguards

The history of liberty has largely been the history of the observance of procedural safeguards.

Justice Felix Frankfurter, *McNabb v. U.S.* (1943, p. 347)

The due process clause of the Fifth and Fourteenth Amendments to the U.S. Constitution asserts that no state may deprive any person "of life, liberty, or property, without due process of law." In the American legal system, persons have two types of due process rights: procedural and substantive. According to Shrybman (1982), procedural safeguards are rules of law that govern the means by which individuals can maintain their substantive rights. In special education, procedural safeguards guide the method by which school officials make decisions regarding the education of students, and substantive due process rights are those personal rights that school officials may not abridge (Valente, 1994).

In writing the Individuals with Disabilities Education Act (IDEA), Congress created explicit procedural safeguards to be afforded students with disabilities and their parents. These safeguards were expanded in the IDEA Amendments of 1997. The purpose of these procedural safeguards is to ensure that parents of children with disabilities are meaningfully involved in their children's education (*Christopher P. v. Marcus*, 1990). According to the U.S. Supreme Court, Congress established the elaborate system of safeguards to "guarantee parents both an opportunity for meaningful input into all decisions affecting their child's education and the right to seek review of any decisions they think inappropriate" (*Honig v. Doe*, 1988, p. 598). In *Board of Education of the Hendrick Hudson School District v. Rowley* (1982), the high court stated that Congress placed as great an emphasis on school districts' compliance with the procedural safeguards as it did on their compliance with the substantive aspects of the IDEA.

The IDEA procedural safeguards include (a) notice and consent requirements; (b) examination of relevant records; (c) procedures to protect the rights of a student when parents are unavailable; (d) the independent educational evaluation; (e) voluntary meditation; and (f) the due process hearing. Additionally, parents may challenge the actions of a school district before a state educational agency (SEA) and may eventually file suit in state or federal court.

Section 504 of the Rehabilitation Act also contains procedural safeguards to protect the rights of persons with disabilities. These are not, however, as detailed and specific as those contained in the IDEA. These procedural safeguards include notice requirements, the opportunity for parents to examine all relevant records with regard to their child's education, and parents' right to request an impartial hearing to review evaluation and placement decisions made by student services teams. According to Section 504 regulations, the procedural requirements of the law may be met through compliance with IDEA regulations (Section 504 Regulations, 34 C.F.R. § 104.36).

Finally, parents challenging the special education services provided by a school may use the procedures set forth in the Education Department General Administrative Regulations (EDGAR; 34 C.F.R. §§ 76.651–76.662). EDGAR requires states to establish procedures to resolve complaints regarding a school district's possible violation of a federal law (EDGAR, 34 C.F.R. § 76.780). Under this law, therefore, parents may resolve complaints that a school district has violated the IDEA. Moreover, parents may exercise the EDGAR procedures as an alternative to the IDEA due process option (OSEP Memorandum 94-16, 1994). In a policy letter, the Office of Special Education Programs (OSEP) stated that the EDGAR procedures for resolving complaints may be preferable to the IDEA due process hearing because they are less costly and are more efficient for resolving disputes (OSEP Memorandum 94-16, 1994).

Procedural Rights of Parents

Identification of Parents

Procedural safeguards must be extended to the parents of students with disabilities under both the IDEA and Section 504. The identification of parents, therefore, is an important requirement under both laws. The biological parents or adoptive parents who reside with a child are considered parents for purposes of the IDEA. Additionally, other adults may also be considered parents under the IDEA. Regulations to the IDEA define a parent as "a parent, a guardian, a person acting as a parent of the child, or a surrogate parent" who has been appointed following the procedures of the law. "The term does not include the state if the child is a ward of the state" (IDEA Regulations, 34 C.F.R. § 300.13). Regulations further "include persons acting in place of the parent, such as a grandmother or stepparent with whom the child lives, as well as persons who are legally responsible for a child's welfare" (IDEA Regulations, 34 C.F.R. § 300.13, note). Gorn (1996) contends that there are two routes to parental eligibility under the law: living with the child in a parental role, or having legal responsibility for a child who resides elsewhere.

Because of the IDEA's encouragement of parental involvement, it seems likely that noncustodial parents should also be allowed to participate in the development of their child's special education program (Gorn, 1996). The IDEA neither compels a school district to include a noncustodial parent in special education planning nor prohibits the inclusion of that parent. The decision to include noncustodial parents in the decision-making process, therefore, is seemingly left to the school district. Gorn (1996) suggests that the involvement of noncustodial parents in the special education process is best resolved by agreement between the parents.

The IDEA does not address situations where parents of a student are divorced and live apart and one agrees with an individualized education plan (IEP) but the other disagrees. Greismann (1997) asserts that in such situations school districts should conclude the IEP process and proceed with implementing the IEP. According to Greismann, "[IDEA] regulations do not require both parents to be in agreement and if one parent believes the IEP is appropriate, that arguably satisfies the parental consent provision of the [IDEA]" (p. 3). The parent in disagreement with the IEP, however, should be notified of the IDEA due process rights.

In *Lower Moreland Township School District* (1992), a hearing officer in Pennsylvania ruled that a father who shared legal custody, but not physical custody, had the right to challenge an IEP agreed to by the mother, who had both legal and physical custody of their child. In this case, the father had been involved in educational planning until he objected to the school's proposed special education program. The school then asserted that he was not a "parent" under the IDEA. The hearing officer disagreed, ruling that the father had the right to participate under a court order that granted him legal custody of the child. The hearing officer, aware of the potential problems that such a ruling could cause school districts, stated that not every noncustodial parent could veto special education decisions, thereby burdening school districts with the difficult task of securing approval of special education decisions from absent, and possibly uninterested, parents. The hearing officer, nevertheless, recognized the right of the noncustodial father, who had been involved in previous education decisions, to make good faith objections to the proposed program.

Questions regarding the role of foster parents in the special education decision-making process remain unsettled (Guernsey & Klare, 1993). The role of foster parents is not addressed in the IDEA. The term "person acting as a parent of the child" does not include foster parents (Baker, 1993). Neither does the IDEA require that a state recognize a foster parent as a "parent." A state, however, may allow a foster parent to act as a parent for purposes of the IDEA if (a) a foster parent is legally responsible for a foster child's welfare and (b) the natural parents' authority to make educational decisions has been relinquished (Gorn, 1996). The primary question concerns when a foster parent becomes a parent under federal or state law. If a foster parent becomes a parent under the law, a surrogate parent need not be appointed to represent the student. The crucial determinant may be whether the foster care placement is permanent. OSEP has not established guidelines as to the length of time that a foster care relationship must exist to be considered permanent, but it has asserted that a state policy that considered foster placements in excess of 6 months to be long-term, and therefore permanent, had to be followed (Hargan, 1990). There are no guidelines regarding the appointment of foster parents who do not meet the standards of permanent parents as surrogate parents for a child. Decisions regarding the use of foster parents as "parents" under the IDEA should be made on a case-by-case basis.

Surrogate Parents

The IDEA requires that parents be central participants in the special education decision-making process. If the child does not have a parent, the parent cannot be found, or the child is a ward of the state,* the IDEA requires that a surrogate parent be appointed (IDEA Regulations, 34 C.F.R. § 300.514). The surrogate parent is appointed to safeguard the educational rights of the child with disabilities by acting as an advocate for the child (Shrybman, 1982). Because a surrogate parent is considered a "parent" under the IDEA, he or she has all the rights, responsibilities, and procedural safeguards of a natural parent under the IDEA (Gorn, 1996). The surrogate parent must have no conflicts of interest, must have the requisite knowledge and skills to ensure that the child is adequately represented, and may not be an employee of the school or be involved in the education or care of the child (IDEA Regulations, 34 C.F.R. § 300.514 (c) (d)).

If the parents' whereabouts are known but they do not make themselves available, there is no need to appoint a surrogate parent, even if the child is in a foster placement (Hargan, 1990). Under the IDEA, the appointment of surrogate parents does not terminate parental rights, nor do the surrogate parents act as replacements for parents in other matters.

The public agency responsible for the surrogate parent must have procedures for determining whether a student needs a surrogate parent and for assigning the surrogate parent. Regulations to the IDEA require that school districts determine the need for surrogate parents when the natural parents have not been located "after reasonable efforts" (IDEA Regulations, 34 C.F.R. § 300.514(a) (2)). What constitutes a reasonable effort, however, is not clear. A federal district court found that a school district had made reasonable efforts to locate parents when it made repeated telephone calls and sent letters to the child's residence and the parents' last known address (*Jesu D. v. Lucas County Children Services Board,* 1985).

If the parents can be located but seem to have no interest in their child's educational program or refuse to participate in the special education process, the IDEA does not empower school districts to appoint surrogate parents (Perryman, 1987). Neither can a school district appoint a surrogate parent to represent the interests of the child or obtain an injunction to prohibit parents from participating in the process, even if the parents act in bad faith or attempt to "sabotage" the process (*Board of Education of Northfield High School District, 225 v. Roy H. and Lynn H.,* 1995).

---

*A child is a ward of the state when the state has assumed legal responsibility to make decisions regarding the child (Shrybman, 1982).

General Procedural Requirements

Notice Requirements

Both the IDEA and Section 504 require that schools notify parents at various stages in the special education process regarding their substantive and procedural rights. Notification means that the school must inform the parent of any actions proposed by the school district. The IDEA requires that written notice be provided to parents prior to the school's proposing to initiate or change the identification, evaluation, educational placement, or provision of a FAPE to the child, or prior to the school's refusing to make such changes (IDEA Regulations, 34 C.F.R. § 300.504–300.505). The purpose of notifying parents is to provide them with information to protect their rights and the rights of their child, to allow them to make informed decisions, and to enable them to fully participate in the special education process (Osborne, 1995). Notice must be provided to parents after an appropriate decision has been reached concerning identification, evaluation, or placement. Furthermore, notice must be given in a reasonable amount of time prior to the implementation of the decision (Helmuth, 1990). Because a school district's failure to provide notification is a very serious matter, school districts often use various methods to document that the required notices have been sent (Shrybman, 1982). The IDEA, however, does not require that school districts have parents acknowledge the receipt of a notice in writing.

The notice must be written so that it is understandable to the general public. Sending parents a copy of the pertinent statutes and regulations is not an appropriate form of notice (*Max M. v. Thompson,* 1984). Moreover, the notice must provide enough information for parents to understand what the school district is proposing or why a particular option was chosen. Figure 13.1 contains the IDEA's specific requirements regarding the content of the notice (IDEA Regulations, 34 C.F.R. § 300.504–300.505).

Section 504 also requires schools to notify parents prior to taking any action regarding the identification, evaluation, or educational placement of a child with a disability (Section 504 Regulations, 34 C.F.R. § 104.36). Compliance with the IDEA's notice requirements is one method by which the requirements of Section 504 may be satisfied.

Consent Requirements

The IDEA requires parental consent prior to the initial evaluation and placement of a student in special education (IDEA Regulations, 34 C.F.R. § 300.504(b) (1)). Before consent is obtained, a school district must inform parents of relevant information regarding the evaluation or placement. When a school obtains consent, it is given permission by the parents to carry out the action proposed in the notice. Once a student is initially placed in a special education program, the IDEA does not require that parental consent be obtained for subsequent evaluations or for changes in the student's special education program. In these situations, however, the school must

Figure 13.1
The IDEA's Content of Notice Requirements

1. A full explanation of all procedural safeguards.
2. A description of the action proposed or refused by the school:
   - An explanation of why the action is being taken.
   - A description of any options considered.
   - Reasons why those options were rejected.
3. A description of each evaluation procedure the school used to make its decision.
4. A description of any other factors that were relevant to the school's decision.
5. The notice must be:
   - Written in language understandable to the general public.
   - Provided in the parent's native language or mode of communication unless it is clearly not feasible to do so.
6. If the language or mode of communication is not written, the school shall ensure that:
   - The notice is translated orally or by other means to the parents in their native language or mode of communication.
   - The parent understands the content of the notice.
   - There is written evidence that these requirements have been met.

provide notice of intent to evaluate or change placement, and must follow the requirements for changing the IEP (IDEA Regulations, 34 C.F.R. § 300.504, note 1). Moreover, consent is recommended, even though it is not legally required (Shrybman, 1982). States may have more stringent consent requirements, but they must not have the effect of excluding a child from special education (IDEA Regulations, 34 C.F.R. § 300.504(d)).

When obtaining consent, the school must ensure that the parents understand and agree to the proposal in writing (IDEA Regulations, 34 C.F.R. § 300.500(a)(3)). To be valid, consent must be given voluntarily by parents who have sufficient information to make an informed decision and have the capacity to give consent. Figure 13.2 contains the IDEA's specific requirements regarding consent and the content of the consent notice (IDEA Regulations, 34 C.F.R. § 300.504–300.505).

Parents must understand that the granting of consent is voluntary and may be revoked at any time (IDEA Regulations, 34 C.F.R. § 300.500(a) (3)). The right of revocation is somewhat limited because the opportunity to revoke consent is only available while the activity for which consent was given is taking place. For example, if consent is given for an evaluation, the time in which consent can be revoked ends when the evaluation is completed (Williams, 1991). When given in a timely manner, a revocation of consent has the same effect as an initial refusal to consent. According

Figure 13.2
The IDEA's Consent Procedures

1. Parental consent must be obtained before:
   - Preplacement evaluation.
   - Initial placement in special education.
   - Reevaluation (unless the LEA can demonstrate that it took measures to secure parental consent but was unsuccessful).
2. Procedures when parents refuse consent:
   - School may continue to pursue evaluation or placement by using the mediation or due process hearing procedures.
   - State law governs the actions of LEA if state requires consent prior to evaluation or placement.

to OSEP, when consent is withdrawn, members of the school staffing team should determine if they agree with the revocation. If they do not, they should continue providing appropriate educational services and pursue formal means to resolve the dispute, such as requesting a due process hearing (Grant, 1991; Williams, 1991).

Similar and equally troublesome situations may arise when parents refuse to grant consent for what the school staffing team believes are needed special education services. For example, a school's multidisciplinary team may believe that a student needs special education services and request consent for an initial evaluation, but the parents refuse to give consent. The regulations to the IDEA, which are intended not to conflict with existing state laws, require that state law must be followed (IDEA Regulations, 34 C.F.R. § 504(C)). If, for example, the state requires that a court order be obtained to override refusal to consent, the school must obtain a court order. If state law does not address the issue of refusal for consent, the school may request a due process hearing and attempt to obtain a decision to allow the proposed action. If this action is taken, the parents must be notified.

Even in the face of a parental refusal to consent or withdrawal of consent, school districts are not absolved of their responsibility, under the IDEA and Section 504, to provide needed special education services. Gorn (1996) argues that school districts faced with such situations should not take the path of least resistance and accede to the refusal if they believe special education is necessary. This is because a district, if sued for compensatory services, could probably not raise removal of needed services in response to parents' request as defense against a claim under the IDEA.

Section 504 contains no specific consent requirements. The Office of Civil Rights (OCR), however, has found evaluations (*Sachem N.Y. Central School District,* 1987) and placements made without parental consent (*Powhatten, KS Unified School District No. 150,* 1979) to be violations of Section 504.

Opportunity to Examine Records

Both the IDEA and Section 504 contain regulations regarding parental access to student records. The IDEA contains very specific requirements concerning parental access rights (IDEA regulations, 34 C.F.R. § 300.562–300.567). Regulations state that

> the parents of a child with a disability shall be afforded . . . an opportunity to inspect and review all educational records with respect to—
> (a) The identification, evaluation, and educational placement of the child, and
> (b) The provision of FAPE to the child. (IDEA Regulations, 34 C.F.R. § 300.502)

Schools must permit parents to inspect and review all educational records collected, maintained, and used by the school concerning the student's special education (IDEA Regulations, 34 C.F.R. § 300.562). When parents make a request to review educational records, they must be allowed to do so without unnecessary delay. Additionally, requests to inspect records must be granted prior to any meeting regarding the student's IEP or a due process hearing. The length of time between the parents' request to the school and the inspection or review of the records cannot exceed 45 days (IDEA Regulations, 34 C.F.R. § 300.562(a)). Figure 13.3 contains specific inspection and review rights granted to parents under the IDEA (IDEA Regulations, 34 C.F.R. § 300.562(b)).

Figure 13.3
Parents' Inspection and Review Rights

- Schools shall permit parents to inspect and review any educational records relating to their child.
- The school must comply with the request without unnecessary delay and before any meeting regarding the child's education (45 days or less).
- The school must respond to reasonable requests for explanations and interpretations of records.
- Parents can request that the school provide copies of the records if failure to provide these copies would prevent the parents from exercising their rights.
- Parents can have a representative inspect and review the records.
- Schools must assume that parents have the right to inspect records unless they have been advised that the parents do not have the right under the applicable state laws.
- Schools must keep a record of parties obtaining access to educational records, including name of the party, date, and purpose.
- On request, schools shall provide parents with a list of types and locations of educational records used by the school.
- Parents who believe that information in the records is inaccurate or misleading may request that the school amend the information. If the school refuses to amend the records, the parents must be informed of their right to a hearing.

The IDEA's confidentiality of information requirements direct schools to keep a record of parties obtaining access to the student records. The records maintained must include the name of the party obtaining access, the date access was given, and the purpose for which the records were used (IDEA Regulations, 34 C.F.R. § 300.563). This requirement, however, does not extend to parental access.

Section 504 contains a general requirement regarding parental access. The regulations state that the school

> shall establish and implement, with respect to actions regarding the identification, evaluation, or educational placement of persons who, because of a handicap, need or are believed to need special instruction or related services, a system of procedural safeguards that includes notice, the opportunity for the parents or guardian of the person to examine relevant records. (Section 504 Regulations, 34 C.F.R. § 104.36)

Independent Educational Evaluation

The IDEA's procedural safeguards include the right of parents to obtain an independent educational evaluation (IEE) of their child (IDEA regulations, 34 C.F.R. § 300.503). Under certain circumstances, the school may be required to provide this evaluation at public expense. (For elaborations on IEEs see Chapter 11.)

An IEE is an "evaluation conducted by a qualified examiner who is not employed by the public agency responsible for the education of the child" (IDEA Regulations, 34 C.F.R. § 300.503(3) (i)). If the parents disagree with the school's evaluation, they may request an IEE at public expense. If, however, school personnel believe the evaluation to be appropriate, they may request a due process hearing. If the hearing officer determines that the school's evaluation was appropriate, the parents retain the right to an IEE, but not at public expense (IDEA Regulations, 34 C.F.R. § 300.503(b)). Section 504 does not address public funding of IEEs (Guernsey & Klare, 1993).

When parents obtain an evaluation at their own expense, school personnel must consider it in the special education decision-making process (IDEA Regulations, 34 C.F.R. § 300.503(c)). The IEE may also be presented as evidence at an impartial due process hearing (IDEA Regulations, 34 C.F.R. § 300.503(c) (2)).

Parents have received reimbursement for IEEs when schools have violated procedural safeguards (*Akers v. Bolton*, 1981), when parents have taken unilateral actions that were later determined necessary (*Anderson v. Thompson*, 1981), and when the IEE was later used to determine placement (*Hoover Schrum Ill. School District No. 157*, 1980). The U.S. Court of Appeals for the Fourth Circuit has held that only one IEE at public expense is required (*Hudson v. Wilson*, 1987). A due process hearing officer may also request that an IEE be performed at public expense (IDEA Regulations, 34 C.F.R. § 300.503(d)). Specific requirements of school districts regarding IEEs are listed in Figure 13.4.

Figure 13.4
Individual Educational Evaluations

- The parents of a child with disabilities have the right to obtain one IEE of the child at public expense.
- On request, schools shall provide to parents information about where an IEE may be obtained.
- Parents have the right to an IEE at public expense if they disagree with the school's evaluation.
- The school may initiate a hearing to show that its evaluation was appropriate. If the final decision is in favor of the school, the parents still have the right to an IEE, but not at public expense.
- If parents obtain an IEE at private expense, the results of the evaluation must be considered by the school.
- If a hearing officer requests an IEE, the cost must be borne by the school.

Mediation

The IDEA Amendments of 1997 added voluntary mediation requirements to the procedural safeguards. Prior to the amendments, most states had already adopted some form of mediation. The federal standard, however, provided for greater uniformity among the states and furnished a model for the states that had not yet implemented mediation.

Mediation is a dispute-resolution and collaborative problem-solving process in which a trained impartial party facilitates a negotiation process between parties who have reached an impasse (Dobbs, Primm, & Primm, 1991; Goldberg & Huefner, 1995). The role of the mediator is to facilitate discussion, encourage open exchange of information, assist the involved parties in understanding each other's viewpoints, and help the parties to reach mutually agreeable solutions. The mediator has no authority to impose solutions on either party. In mediation sessions, the focus is on the negotiated resolution of the conflict rather than factual presentations, witnesses, or formal rules of evidence (Goldberg & Huefner, 1995). Mediation is an intervening step that may be used prior to conducting a formal due process hearing (Gorn, 1996).

When a mediation session is conducted, a neutral third party helps the parents and the school arrive at their own solution to the disagreement. Mediation is structured, but it is less formal and adversarial than due process hearings or court proceedings. Additional advantages of mediation are that it is less time-consuming, costs less, allows for greater discussion of the issues, and helps to maintain a workable relationship between schools and parents (Dobbs et al., 1991; Primm, 1990). Dobbs, Primm, and Primm (1993) reported that a questionnaire given to parents and school personnel following special education mediation sessions revealed that 90% of the parents and 99% of the teachers who had been involved in the mediation would recommend the process to others to help resolve disputes.

Under the 1997 amendments, states are required to offer mediation as a voluntary option for parents and local educational agencies (LEAs) to resolve disputes. The law clearly specifies, however, that mediation cannot be used to delay or deny parents' right to an impartial due process hearing. If parents choose not to use mediation, the amendments allow LEAs and SEAs to establish procedures to require parents to meet with a disinterested third party who would encourage and explain the benefits of mediation to them. Such meetings must be held at a time and place convenient to the parents.

Because states had been successful in using mediation systems that both allowed and disallowed attorneys at mediation sessions, Congress left to the states decisions regarding the attendance of attorneys at mediation. Procedurally, SEAs are required to maintain a list of qualified mediators. When an LEA and parents go to mediation, both the parents and the school officials should be involved in selecting a mutually agreed upon mediator from the list. The mediator must be impartial, so employees of the involved LEAs or persons with personal or professional conflicts of interest are not allowed to mediate. Furthermore, the mediator is supposed to be experienced, trained, and knowledgeable about the law. Mediators do not have to be attorneys. When mediation is used, the states will bear the costs.

Mediation agreements are to be put in writing. Furthermore, the discussions held at mediation sessions are confidential and cannot be used as evidence in subsequent due process hearings or civil actions. Parties in the mediation process may be required to sign a confidentiality pledge prior to the commencement of mediation.

The Due Process Hearing

According to the U.S. Court of Appeals for the Fourth Circuit, the IDEA contains a bill of rights for parents wishing to contest a school's special education decisions regarding their child (*Stemple v. Board of Education,* 1980). The sine qua non of the IDEA's procedural safeguards is the due process hearing. The purpose of the due process hearing is to allow an impartial third party, the due process hearing officer, to hear both sides of a dispute, examine the issues, and settle the dispute (Anderson, Chitwood, & Hayden, 1990). Congress deliberately chose an adversarial system for resolving disputes, believing it was the best way to ensure that both parents and school officials would receive an equal opportunity to present their case (Goldberg & Huefner, 1995).

Section 504 also requires an impartial hearing to resolve disputes arising over a child's education. The Section 504 hearing requirements are general, while those in the IDEA are very specific.

Parents may request a due process hearing to contest a school's identification, evaluation, educational placement, or provision of FAPE (IDEA Regulations, 34 C.F.R. § 506(a)), or to question the information in their child's educational records*

---

*Disputes over educational records are subject to hearings under EDGAR rather than the due process hearing rules of the IDEA (EDGAR Regulations, 34 C.F.R. § 99.22).

(IDEA Regulations, 34 C.F.R. § 568). The due process hearing may also be used to seek resolution of procedural violations if the violations adversely affect a student's education (Guernsey & Klare, 1993). In addition to parents, students who have reached the age of majority can also request hearings. Schools may also seek due process hearings (IDEA Regulations, 34 C.F.R. § 506(a)); this may occur when parents refuse consent to an evaluation or placement (Guernsey & Klare, 1993).

The IDEA leaves the choice of the agency that conducts due process hearings to individual states (IDEA Regulations, 34 C.F.R. § 506(b)). Usually the state will assign the conduct of hearings to the SEA, an intermediate educational agency, or the LEA (i.e., the local school district). The agency responsible for the hearing is required to inform the parents of any free or low-cost legal and other relevant services if requested to do so by the parents (IDEA Regulations, 34 C.F.R. § 506(c)). The hearing must be conducted at a time and place that is convenient to the parents (IDEA Regulations, 34 C.F.R. § 300.512(d)).

States also have the option of adopting a one-tier or two-tier hearing procedure. In a one-tier system, the initial level of review is conducted by the SEA. Judicial review of the SEA's decision is immediately available in a state or federal court. In a two-tier system, the initial review is usually conducted by the LEA, and an appeal of the hearing officer's decision is made to the SEA for an intermediate administrative review. Following a decision at the second tier, a civil action can be filed in a state or federal court (Katsiyannis & Kale, 1991). In a survey of state practices in due process hearings, Katsiyannis and Kale (1991) found that 24 states and the District of Columbia used a one-tier system, while 26 states had a two-tier system.

State laws or regulations direct the method by which due process hearings are requested. If the due process hearing is conducted by the school district, the request normally goes through the district. Guernsey and Klare (1993) suggest that the request be made to the superintendent of schools, with a copy going to the director of special education. The nature of the disagreement and the names of the parties involved should be included in the request. The U.S. Court of Appeals for the Ninth Circuit has ruled that due process hearings may be requested by parents even if their child has not been formally accepted into special education (*Hacienda La Puente Unified School District v. Honig*, 1992). Also, parents can request a due process hearing even if their child is not attending public school, but the reason that the child is not in the public school must be related to the public school's failure to provide a FAPE (*S-1 v. Turlington*, 1981).

The Impartial Hearing Officer

The integrity of the due process hearing is maintained by ensuring that the hearing officer is impartial. The officer must have no involvement with the child, the parent, or the school system. Regulations to the IDEA state that

    (a) A hearing may not be conducted:
    (1) By a person who is an employee of a public agency which is involved in the education or care of the child, or
    (2) By any person having a personal or professional interest which would conflict with his or her objectivity in the hearing. (IDEA Regulations, 34 C.F.R. § 300.507(a) (1), (2)).

Potential hearing officers are not considered employees of the public agency if they are paid by the school only for the hearing and for no other reason. No guidelines for the training and evaluation of hearing officers are provided in the IDEA. Neither are qualifications of hearing officers furnished in the federal law or regulations.

School districts must maintain a list of persons who may serve as due process hearing officers. If parents request a copy of the list, it must be provided by the school district. Although parents are given no right to participate in the selection of the hearing officer, they can challenge the selection of the officer. The majority of these challenges involve the impartiality of hearing officers (Guernsey & Klare, 1993). Challenges to the impartiality of a hearing officer must be made during the due process hearing or subsequent administrative or judicial reviews (*Colin K. v. Schmidt*, 1983).

The Role of the Hearing Officer

When a dispute concerning a student's special education reaches the due process hearing level, the authority to decide the issue passes from the parents and the school to the hearing officer (Shrybman, 1982). The primary duties of the hearing officer are to inform the parties of their rights during the hearing, allow all parties the opportunity to present their cases, conduct the hearing in a fair, orderly, and impartial manner, and render a decision in accordance with the law. According to the U.S. Supreme Court,

> the role of the [hearing officer] . . . is functionally comparable to that of a judge. . . . More importantly, the process of agency adjudication is currently structured so as to assure that the hearing examiner exercises his independent judgment on the evidence before him, free from pressures by the parties or other officials within the agency. (*Butz v. Economou*, 1978, p. 513)

Although the role of the hearing officer may be comparable to that of a judge, the hearing officer's authority to grant particular remedies is less extensive (Guernsey & Klare, 1993). A hearing officer may order an IEE, reimbursement of educational expenses, or compensatory education, but he or she may not award attorneys' fees. Neither does the hearing officer have any authority over outside agencies. OSEP has stated that the hearing officer may order specific placements (Eig, 1980), but OCR has held that hearing officers can only accept or reject a school's proposed placement (*District of Columbia Public Schools*, 1981). Guernsey and Klare (1993) assert that the better view is that the hearing officer is not limited to accepting or rejecting placements proposed by the school, but may consider placements sought by the parents.

The hearing officer must render a decision no later than 45 days after the request for the hearing. A copy of the decision must be mailed to each of the parties. The decision of the hearing officer is final unless it is appealed.

Hearing officers cannot be held liable for actions taken in their official capacity. The U.S. Supreme Court, in *Butz v. Economou* (1978), held that hearing officers, like judges, have immunity from damages when fulfilling their duties as hearing officers. The high court held that "persons . . . in performing their adjudicatory functions . . . are entitled to absolute immunity for their judicial acts. Those who complain of error in such proceedings must seek agency or judicial review" (p. 514).

Hearing officers may, however, be sued for damages resulting from actions taken in their individual capacities. If hearing officers take actions that they know, or should have known, are violations of the constitutional rights of the student, or if they take actions with malicious intent to deprive a student of his or her rights, they may be held liable for damages (Shrybman, 1982). The Supreme Court had ruled that hearing officers cannot be held liable for monetary damages if there were reasonable grounds for their actions and if they acted in good faith (*Schever v. Rhodes,* 1974), or if they merely made mistakes in judgment (*Butz v. Economou,* 1978).

Hearing Rights

The IDEA contains a set of procedural rights that must be afforded all parties in a due process hearing (IDEA Regulations, 34 C.F.R. § 300.508). These rights are listed in Figure 13.5.

Both parties in the hearing have the right to be represented by counsel if they desire. Additionally, schools must inform the parents of free or low-cost legal services if the parents request the information. The school's obligation, however, does not extend to obtaining these services for the parents or paying for them (Shrybman, 1982).

The parents have the exclusive right to open the hearing to the public. The school does not have the right to open the hearing (IDEA Regulations, 34 C.F.R. § 508(c)), nor can the school compel the attendance of the student (IDEA Regulations, 34 C.F.R. § 508(b)).

Figure 13.5
Due Process Hearing Rights

1. Any party to a hearing has the right to:
   - Be accompanied and advised by counsel and by individuals with special knowledge or training with respect to special education.
   - Present evidence and confront, cross-examine, and compel the attendance of witnesses.
   - Prohibit the introduction of any evidence at the hearing that has not been disclosed to that party at least five days prior to the hearing.
   - Obtain a written or electronic verbatim record of the hearing.
   - Obtain written findings of fact and decisions.
2. Parents involved in the hearing have the right to:
   - Have the child who is the subject of the hearing present.
   - Require the LEA to provide an electronic verbatim record of the hearing.
   - Require the LEA to provide electronic findings of fact and decision.
   - Open the hearing to the public.

Either party in a hearing has the right to appeal the hearing officer's decision. In a two-tier state, the party files an appeal with the appropriate agency. Following review of the hearing officer's decision, the aggrieved party may file a civil action in state or federal court. In a one-tier state, the aggrieved party may file a civil action in state or federal court immediately following the decision in the due process hearing.

The Stay-Put Provision

Unless the school and parents agree otherwise, when a request for a hearing is made the IDEA's "stay-put" provision is invoked. According to this provision,

> During the pendency of any administrative or judicial proceeding regarding a complaint, unless the public agency and the parents of the child agree otherwise, the child involved in the complaint must remain in his or her present educational placement. (IDEA Regulations, 34 C.F.R. § 300.513)

The U.S. Supreme Court, in *Honig v. Doe* (1988), stated that the stay-put provision prevents schools from unilaterally moving students from placement to placement. Essentially, the stay-put provision acts as a automatic preliminary injunction pending a resolution of a due process hearing or judicial action. The objective of the stay-put provision is to maintain stability and continuity for the student until the dispute is resolved (Gorn, 1996). The stay-put provision can be suspended during the pendency of a review, however, by an agreement between the schools and the parents regarding placement.

A comment to the regulation states that although the student's placement may not be changed, the school may use its normal procedures for dealing with students who are endangering themselves or others (IDEA Regulations, 34 C.F.R. § 300.513, Note). There is, however, no "dangerous exception" which allows the school to suspend the stay-put rule (*Honig v. Doe,* 1988).

The IDEA Amendments of 1997 allow school officials to abrogate the stay-put amendment when a student with a disability brings a weapon to school or a school function or uses or sells illegal drugs. In such situations an administrator may immediately remove the student to an interim alternative setting for up to 45 days. If a due process hearing is requested, the stay-put placement becomes the current setting. During the pendency of the proceedings, therefore, the student remains in the interim alternative setting. (For elaborations on the discipline of students with disabilities see Chapter 15.)

The U.S. Court of Appeals for the District of Columbia ruled that the stay-put provision applies during due process hearings, during state administrative reviews, and at the trial court level but does not apply to the appellate level (*Anderson v. District of Columbia,* 1989). According to the court, a school is not required to maintain the current educational placement if an appeal goes to the appellate court.

If students are not in special education and the hearing concerns their eligibility to receive special education services, they must remain in the general education placement until the dispute is resolved. Similarly, if students are in special education and the dispute concerns a change of placement, they must remain in the placement where they were when the request was made. If the dispute involves initial admission to public school, students must be placed in the public school program until the dispute is resolved.*

The Conduct of the Hearing

The purpose of the due process hearing is to provide a legally constituted forum in which the contending parties have an opportunity to present their cases to an impartial hearing officer. From the perspective of a hearing officer, the purpose of the hearing is to give the parties an opportunity to present the information necessary for an informed ruling to be made.

Although the conduct of hearings varies among hearing officers, usually hearings are conducted in a professional manner but with a more informal atmosphere than a trial court. There should be a structure to the hearing so that everyone clearly understands his or her role and participates fully. Shrybman (1982) warns that hearing officers must be in control of the proceedings and not allow any participants to abuse the process. Proceedings that erupt into acrimonious exchanges will accomplish little.

Either party in a hearing has the right to a written record of the hearing. Parents may, at their option, require an electronic record of the hearing. In such situations, court reporters must be used. In addition to meeting the legal mandate, the verbatim record is essential for hearing officers in writing their decision and, if the decision is appealed, for review of the hearing decision. According to Shrybman (1982), if no verbatim record is available, the case must be reheard.

The hearing room should be arranged in a manner that is conducive to the orderly presentation of evidence and testimony (Shrybman, 1982). The arrangement should allow all participants to see and hear each other clearly. Often hearing rooms are set up like a trial court, with the hearing officer in a central position and the respective parties on the sides. Figure 13.6 illustrates a possible hearing room arrangement.

The hearing officer will typically open the hearing with a call to order and an introductory statement. This statement should include the introduction of the hearing officer and the case, a statement of legal authority for the hearing, an explanation of the purpose of the hearing and the role of the hearing officer, an acknowledgment of persons present, an explanation of the rights of the parties in the hearing, and instructions on appropriate decorum and the structure and the procedures to be followed during the hearing (Ginn, Carruth, & McCarthy, 1988; Hamway, 1994; Shrybman, 1982).

Shrybman (1982) suggests a format to which hearings should adhere. The hearing should begin with preliminary matters such as questions, objections, or requests from participants. Following the preliminaries, representatives of each party should present a brief opening statement outlining their positions. During the opening statement, evidence is not presented. When opening statements have been completed, the evidence is presented. The formal rules of evidence that are used in courts do not

---

*The U.S. Department of Education has stated that if a student transfers into a school district within a state with an existing IEP, this is not to be treated as an initial admission and the school should continue to implement the existing IEP (Campbell, 1989).

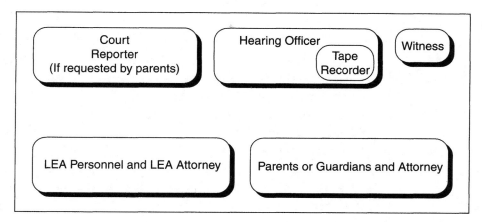

Figure 13.6
Due Process Hearing Room Arrangement

apply to administrative hearings. Relevancy and reliability should be the rules for introducing evidence in the hearing (Guernsey & Klare, 1993). Because the school district is legally responsible for the student's placement and special education program, and bears the burden of proof as to the appropriateness of the education, the school system should present its case first. Shrybman (1982) asserts that "it is the responsibility of the public schools to provide a [child with disabilities] with a free appropriate public education so they must always stand ready to prove that their conduct on behalf of the student meets this fundamental legal requirement" (p. 325). During the presentation, the school will present documents and testimony to support its position. The parents or their counsel, if they have one, may cross-examine the school district's witnesses after their testimony. After the school's presentation, the parents present their case. The school's counsel may cross-examine the parents' witnesses at this time. After both sides have completed their initial presentations and offered their witnesses and evidence, they should have the opportunity to cross-examine witnesses again and present additional evidence. Finally, both parties conclude with a closing statement that summarizes their positions.

Following the presentations and concluding statements, the hearing officer should close the hearing. This may be done by briefly stating when the decision will be available, telling how transcripts can be obtained, explaining the appeal procedures, and stating that the hearing is adjourned. Figure 13.7 outlines this format for the due process hearing.

Appeals

In states with a two-tiered process, the decision of the hearing officer can be appealed to the SEA. In an appeal, the agency will review the entire hearing record, ensure that procedures were followed, seek additional evidence if necessary, allow additional

Figure 13.7
Possible Format for a Due Process Hearing

1. Opening statements of the hearing officer:
   - Introduction of the officer and the case
   - Statement of legal authority for the hearing
   - Explanation of the purpose for the hearing
   - Explanation of the hearing officer's role
   - Introduction of persons present
   - Inform parties of due process rights
   - Instructions of decorum, structure, and procedures of the hearing
2. Order of presentation during the hearing:
   - Preliminary matters
   - Opening statements
   - Public school presentation
   - Parents' presentation
   - Repeat cross-examination and present additional evidence
   - Closing statements
3. Closing the hearing:
   - Explanation of the issuance of the decision
   - Explanation of appeal procedures
   - Thanking the participants and closing the hearing

arguments at its discretion, and make an independent decision (IDEA Regulations, 34 C.F.R. § 300.510). If additional evidence is heard at the state review, the protections available to parties in the original due process hearing are available at the review (e.g., disclosure of evidence 5 days prior to the hearing, the right to cross-examine witnesses).

The appeal is usually made to the office of special education of the state's department of education. The IDEA contains no timeline in which an appeal must be made, although individual states may address the issue (Guernsey & Klare, 1993). A written copy of the findings must be sent to both parties within 30 days of the date of the appeal to the state. Unless appealed, this decision is final and binding on all parties. Either party may appeal the SEA's decision and may file a civil action in a state or federal court (IDEA Regulations, 34 C.F.R. § 300.511).

In a one-tier state, the civil action may be filed following the due process hearing. In a two-tier state, the civil action usually cannot be filed until all the administrative options have been exhausted; that is, both the due process hearing and the

SEA hearing must have been completed before an action may be filed in state or federal court. An exception to the exhaustion rule may exist if administrative hearings would be futile or inadequate (*Honig v. Doe,* 1988). Although the time-consuming nature of a hearing is not, by itself, a basis for overturning the exhaustion rule (*Cox v. Jenkins,* 1989), situations such as the agency's failure to properly implement administrative appeal measures may provide such a basis.

The court will usually not rehear the case, nor will it focus on the entire case. Rather, the court will review the record to determine the presence of serious error of law at the hearing level. Courts, following a review of pertinent materials, can affirm the decision of the lower authority, modify the decision of the lower authority, reverse the decision of the lower authority, or remand all or part of the lower authority's decision. To remand means that the court will order the lower authority to conduct further proceedings in accordance with the court's instructions (Weber, 1992).

A party in a due process hearing may also file a civil action if the other party fails to follow the decision of the hearing officer. In this case, the purpose of the civil action is to have the decision enforced. Enforcement actions are usually brought by parents against schools. Schools, however, have little legal leverage to force parents to comply with a decision (Shrybman, 1982).

Alternatives to the Due Process Hearing

Criticisms have been leveled at the system of procedural safeguards, especially due process hearings, as being too expensive, time-consuming, adversarial, and emotionally draining for all parties involved (Goldberg & Huefner, 1995; Maloney, 1993; Zirkel, 1994). The hearings rarely solve problems and soothe anger, but instead often alienate and sustain antagonism and undermine cooperation (Beekman, 1993; Goldberg & Huefner, 1995). Parents also tend to view the due process system as unfair (Goldberg & Kuriloff, 1991). Finally, both sides have the right to be represented by attorneys (although it is not required), and the presence of attorneys may contribute to the adversarial nature of the proceedings (Shrybman, 1982). In a 1994 case from the U.S. Court of Appeals for the Ninth Circuit, the court upbraided an attorney for the use of "hardball tactics" in dealing with a school (*Clyde K. v. Puyallup School District*). The court also noted that the interests of schools, parents, and students would be more effectively served by compromise and cooperation rather than through adversarial positioning.

In the IDEA Amendments of 1997, Congress required states to adopt voluntary mediation systems to alleviate the overly adversarial nature of the dispute-resolution process. Mediation had been suggested by a number of legal scholars as an alternative to the due process hearing (Dobbs et al., 1991; Goldberg & Huefner, 1995; Goldberg & Kuriloff, 1991; Zirkel, 1994).

Zirkel (1994) asserts that the current system of special education due process hearings serves the best interests of neither the school nor the child. He suggests a five-part solution to the problems inherent in the hearing process. First, the due process hearing should be the final stage for most special education disputes. The hearing officer's decision should be binding on both parties. Judicial review would only be available for an occasional case that presents an important legal issue. This suggestion would require an amendment to the IDEA to delete the option of a second tier. The single tier would be at the state level to remove the possible influence of the school district's paying the hearing officer. The selection, training, and payment of hearing officers would become the responsibility of an independent state agency. Zirkel's second suggestion is that because the due process hearing would escalate in importance under the first suggestion, regulations would specify that hearing officers must have expertise in special education. Third, the conduct of due process hearings would be changed to a problem-solving model rather than an adversarial model. To reinforce the less adversarial model, the fourth suggestion is that attorneys' fees would be limited to the judicial stage. School districts could not be represented by counsel at the hearing unless the parents chose to be represented by counsel. This suggestion would require amending the attorneys' fees provision of the IDEA. Finally, hearings in routine cases should be limited to one full day. Zirkel believes that by using this model the due process hearing would become a faster and less expensive problem-solving process.

School District Responsibilities

Guernsey and Klare (1993) found that the available evidence indicates that success in the due process hearing is critical to the ultimate outcome of the case. They further cite evidence that most decisions by due process hearing officers are upheld on review and that the vast majority of cases never go to court. It is critical to all parties, therefore, that the best possible case be made at this level.

Schools must prepare seriously when approaching a due process hearing. The results of the initial hearing are critical because appeals will often be based solely on the transcripts of the initial hearing (Reusch, 1993). If schools do not succeed in making their case at this level, they probably will not succeed on appeal (Zirkel, 1994).

Maloney (1993) listed "seven deadly sins" that frequently lead to due process hearings. Schools should attempt to avoid these errors. More often than not, these errors will also lead to losses in hearings or court and possible liability.

The most common errors committed by schools leading to hearings, and the first "deadly sin," are procedural violations. According to Mattison (1994), a district's failure to meet the IDEA's procedural protections are adequate grounds, in and of themselves, for finding that the school district has failed to provide a FAPE. A number of courts have ruled that procedural violations can subject a school district to liability for damages, compensatory education, or tuition reimbursement (*Burr v. Ambach,* 1988; *Evans v. Douglas County School District No. 17,* 1988; *McKenzie v. Smith,* 1985; *Salley v. St. Tammany Parish School Board,* 1993; *W.G. v. Target Range School District No. 23,* 1992). However, minor procedural violations that do not deprive the student of a FAPE probably will not result in a due process hearing or a lost case (Maloney, 1994; Mattison, 1993). The procedural violations most likely to lead to due process hearings are (a) insufficient notice of proposal or refusal to change placement; (b) failure to obtain consent; (c) denial of an IEE; (d) incomplete or insufficient IEPs (especially regarding transition services, graduation, and the provision of assistive technology); (e) improper or insufficient evaluations; (f) substantially or procedurally deficient IEP committees; (g) unilateral change of placement; (h) restricted opportunity to examine student records; (i) improper suspension or expulsion; and (j) failure to implement or issue due process hearing orders.

The second violation likely to lead to due process hearings, and an error Maloney describes as the "kiss of death," is telling parents that a particular service or program is appropriate for their child but that the school district cannot afford it. Schools cannot deny appropriate services based on cost considerations.

The third error is rigidity (e.g., "We haven't done it in the past and we won't do it now"). Blanket statements that exclude the consideration of certain programs or services are clearly illegal. Rigidity on the part of schools (e.g., refusal to consider the provision of extended school services, to evaluate children with attention deficit disorders, or to provide certain related services) has led to many due process hearings and court cases.

The fourth error is giving in to parental demands when the demands will not provide the child with a FAPE. Because the right to a FAPE belongs to the child and not the parents, school districts must attempt to provide what they believe to be appropriate services, even if it requires requesting a due process hearing (Maloney 1993).

The fifth error is acting on the basis of principle rather than reason. Schools should not act out of frustration or to prove a point. An example of this type of error was provided in *Rapid City School District v. Vahle* (1990). The school district determined that the services of an occupational therapist (OT) were necessary to provide a FAPE; however, the amount of services provided by the district was not sufficient to meet the student's needs. The parents purchased the services of an OT. The district then agreed that more services were necessary and agreed to provide them. The district refused, however, to reimburse the parents for the $861 they had paid for the OT services. The parents prevailed in federal court. The district's bill for attorneys' fees was over $30,000.

Sixth is the problem of burden of proof—the responsibility of proving a case. Although the IDEA does not address the issue, most hearing officers require school districts to assume the burden of proof in hearings (Maloney, 1993). Schools must assume that in a due process hearing they have the responsibility of proving that they have provided the child with a FAPE.

Finally, the failure to act promptly to secure services recommended by the IEP team often leads to due process hearings. Procrastination may also lead to the school's being held liable for compensatory services.

It is, therefore, an important school responsibility to ensure that the procedural safeguards in the IDEA are followed. Figure 13.8 presents a list of procedural safeguards.

Figure 13.8
Procedural Safeguards

1. The school shall:
   - Provide written notice to the parents when the school is proposing or refusing to initiate or change the identification, evaluation, or placement of the child or the provision of a FAPE to the child.
   - Afford the parents of children with disabilities the opportunity to inspect and review all educational records regarding the identification, evaluation, or placement of the child or the provision of a FAPE to the child.
   - Obtain parental consent before conducting a preplacement evaluation and initial placement of the child in special education.
2. Except for the initial evaluation and placement, the school may not require consent as a condition of any benefit to the parents of the child.

Summary

In the IDEA, Congress created substantive and procedural rights for students with disabilities. The substantive rights include the FAPE guaranteed to each student in special education. The procedural rights, referred to in the IDEA as procedural safeguards, are meant to ensure that schools follow proper procedures in planning and delivering a FAPE to students with disabilities. The procedural safeguards require involvement of both parents and professionals in the special education decision-making process.

The procedural safeguards consist of seven components: notice requirements, consent requirements, the opportunity to examine records, procedures to protect the rights of the child when the parents are unavailable, the independent educational evaluation, voluntary mediation, and the due process hearing. The heart of the procedural safeguards is the due process hearing. When there is a disagreement over identification, evaluation, placement, or any matters pertaining to a FAPE, parents may request a due process hearing. The purpose of the hearing is to resolve differences by presenting information to an impartial due process hearing officer. The task of the hearing officer is to make a final decision regarding the settlement of the disagreement. Either party can appeal the decision.

The due process hearing procedure has been the subject of much criticism. The process is time-consuming, expensive, and emotionally difficult, and tends to create an adversarial relationship between the parents and the school. In an attempt to alleviate the adversarial nature of many disputes between parents and school districts, the IDEA Amendments of 1997 required states to offer parents voluntary mediation.

For Further Information

Anderson, W., Chitwood, S., & Hayden, D. (1990). *Negotiating the special education maze: A guide for parents and teachers* (2nd ed.). Alexandria, VA: Woodbine House.

Dobbs, R. F., Primm, E. B., & Primm, B. (1991). Mediation: A common sense approach for resolving conflicts in special education. *Focus on Exceptional Children, 24,* 1–11.

Goldberg, S. S., & Huefner, D. S. (1995). Dispute resolution in special education: An introduction to litigative alternatives. *Education Law Reporter, 99,* 703–803.

Katsiyannis, A., & Kale, K. (1991). State practices in due process hearings: Considerations for better practice. *Remedial and Special Education, 12,* 54–58.

Osborne, A. G. (1995). Procedural due process rights for parents under the IDEA. *Preventing School Failure, 39,* 22–26.

Shrybman, J. A. (1982). *Due process in special education.* Rockville, MD: Aspen.

Zirkel, P. A. (1994). Over-due process revisions for the Individuals with Disabilities Education Act. *Montana Law Review, 55,* 403–414.

References

Akers v. Bolton, 531 F. Supp. 300 (D. Kan. 1981).

Anderson, W., Chitwood, S., & Hayden, D. (1990). *Negotiating the special education maze: A guide for parents and teachers* (2nd ed.). Alexandria, VA: Woodbine House.

Anderson v. District of Columbia, 877 F.2d 1018 (D.C. Cir. 1989).

Anderson v. Thompson, 658 F. Supp. 1205 (7th Cir., 1981).

Baker, Letter to, 20 IDELR 1169 (OSEP 1993).

Beekman, L. E. (1993). Making due process hearings more efficient and effective (aka How to run a hearing—and get away with it!). In *Proceedings of the 14th National Institute on Legal Issues of Educating Individuals with Disabilities.* Horsham, PA: LRP Publications.

Board of Education of the Hendrick Hudson School District v. Rowley, 458 U.S. 176 (1982).

Board of Education of Northfield High School District, 225 v. Roy H. and Lynn H., 21 IDELR 1171 (N.D. Ill, 1995).

Burr v. Ambach, 863 F.2d 1071 (2nd Cir. 1988).

Butz v. Economou, 438 U.S. 478 (1978).

Campbell Inquiry, 211 EHLR 265 (OSEP 1989).

Christopher P. v. Marcus, 16 EHLR 1346 (2nd Cir. 1990).

Clyde K. v. Puyallup School District, 35 F.3d 1396 (9th Cir. 1994).

Colin K. v. Schmidt, 715 F.2d 1 (1st Cir. 1983).

Cox v. Jenkins, 878 F.2d 414 (D.C. Cir. 1989).

District of Columbia Public Schools, 257 EHLR 208 (OCR 1981).

Dobbs, R. F., Primm, E. B., & Primm, B. (1991). Mediation: A common sense approach for resolving conflicts in special education. *Focus on Exceptional Children, 24,* 1–11.

Dobbs, R. F., Primm, E. B., & Primm, B. (1993). Mediation. In *Proceedings of the 14th National Institute on Legal Issues of Educating Individuals with Disabilities.* Horsham, PA: LRP Publications.

Education Department General Administration Regulations (EDGAR), 34 C.F.R. § 99.22.

Eig Inquiry, 211 EHLR 174 (OSEP 1980).

Evans v. Douglas County School District No. 17, 17 IDELR 559 (8th Cir. 1988).

Ginn, M., Carruth, E., & McCarthy, G. (1988). *South Carolina handbook for hearing officers.* Columbia: South Carolina Department of Education.

Goldberg, S. S., & Huefner, D. S. (1995). Dispute resolution in special education: An introduction to litigative alternatives. *Education Law Reporter, 99,* 703–803.

Goldberg, S. S., & Kuriloff, P. J. (1991). Evaluating the fairness of special education hearings. *Exceptional Children, 57,* 546–555.

Gorn, S. (1996). *What do I do when . . . The answer book on special education law.* Horsham, PA: LRP Publications.

Grant, Letter to, 17 EHLR 1184 (OSEP 1991).

Greismann, Z. (1997, February 23). Question and answer. *The Special Educator, 12* (14), 3.

Guernsey, T. F., & Klare, K. (1993). *Special education law.* Durham, NC: Carolina Academic Press.

Hacienda La Puente Unified School District v. Honig, 976 F.2d 487 (9th Cir. 1992).

Hamway, T. J. (1994). Presenting expert testimony in due process hearings: A guide to courtroom survival. In *Proceedings of the 15th National Institute on Legal Issues of Educating Individuals with Disabilities.* Horsham, PA: LRP Publications.

Hargan Inquiry, 16 EHLR 738 (OSEP 1990).

Helmuth Inquiry, 16 EHLR 550 (OSEP, 1990).

Honig v. Doe, 479 U.S. 1084 (1988).

Hoover Schrum, Ill. School District No. 157, 257 EHLR 136 (OCR 1980).

Hudson v. Wilson, 828 F.2d 1059 (4th Cir. 1987).

Individuals with Disabilities Education Act (IDEA), 20 U.S.C. § 1400 *et seq.*

Individuals with Disabilities Education Act Amendments of 1997, Pub. L. No. 105–17, 105th Cong., 1st sess.

Individuals with Disabilities Education Act Regulations, 34 C.F.R. § 300.533 *et seq.*

Jesu D. v. Lucas County Children Services Board, 1984–85, EHLR 556;484 (N.D. Ohio, 1985).

Katsiyannis, A., & Kale, K. (1991). State practices in due process hearings: Considerations for better practice. *Remedial and Special Education, 12,* 54–58.

Lower Moreland Township School District, 18 IDELR 1160 (SEA Pa. 1992).

Maloney, M. H. (1993). The seven deadly sins: Common mistakes which can lead to due process hearings. In *Proceedings of the 14th National Institute on Legal Issues of Educating Individuals with Disabilities.* Horsham, PA: LRP Publications.

Mattison, D. A. (1994). An overview in the development of procedural safeguards. In *Proceedings of the 15th National Institute on Legal Issues of Educating Individuals with Disabilities.* Horsham, PA: LRP Publications.

Max M. v. Thompson, 592 F. Supp. 1450 (1984).

McKenzie v. Smith, 771 F.2d 1527 (D.C. Cir. 1985).

McNabb v. U.S., 318 U.S. 332 (1943).

Osborne, A. G. (1995). Procedural due process rights for parents under the IDEA. *Preventing School Failure, 39,* 22–26.

OSEP Memorandum 94-16, 21 IDELR 85 (OSEP, 1994).

Perryman, Letter to, EHLR 211:438 (OSEP 1987).

Powhatten, KS Unified School District No. 150, 257 EHLR 32 (OCR 1979).

Primm, E. B. (1990). Mediation: A comment under Part B; common sense for Part H. *Early Childhood Report, 1* (6), 4–6.

Rapid City School District v. Vahle, 733 F. Supp. 1364 (D.S.D. 1990).

Reusch, G. M. (1993). Special education disputes: Practical issues facing school board attorneys. In *Proceedings of the 14th National Institute on Legal Issues of Educating Individuals with Disabilities.* Horsham, PA: LRP Publications.

S-1 v. Turlington, 635 F.2d 342 (5th Cir. 1981).

Sachem N.Y. Central School District, 352 EHLR 462 (OCR 1987).

Salley v. St. Tammany Parish School Board, 20 IDELR 520 (E.D. La. 1993).

Schever v. Rhodes, 416 U.S. 232 (1974).

Section 504 of the Rehabilitation Act of 1973 Regulations, 34 C.F.R. § 104.36.

Shrybman, J. A. (1982). *Due process in special education.* Rockville, MD: Aspen.

Stemple v. Board of Education, 623 F.2d 893 (4th Cir. 1980).

Valente, R. (1994). *Law in the schools* (3rd ed.). Upper Saddle River, NJ: Merrill/Prentice Hall.

W.G. v. Board of Trustees of Target Range School District No. 23, 960 F.2d 1479 (9th Cir. 1992).

Weber, M. (1992). *Special education law and litigation treatise.* Horsham, PA: LRP Publications.

Williams, Letter to, 18 IDELR 534 (OSEP 1991).

Zirkel, P. A. (1994). Over-due process revisions for the Individuals with Disabilities Education Act. *Montana Law Review, 55,* 403–414.

CHAPTER FOURTEEN

Remedies

Public education authorities who want to avoid reimbursing parents for the private education of a disabled child can do one of two things: give the child a free appropriate public education in a public setting, or place the child in an appropriate private setting of the state's choice. This is the IDEA's mandate, and school officials who conform to it need not worry.

Justice Sandra Day O'Connor, *Florence County School District Four v. Carter* (1993, p. 366)

Both the Individuals with Disabilities Education Act (IDEA) and Section 504 of the Rehabilitation Act of 1973 set forth the due process hearing as the principal mechanism for resolving disputes between schools and the parents of children with disabilities. The parties seeking review of a special education decision in a due process hearing typically want a determination of the relative responsibilities of the school system and the parents for the delivery of educational services to the child (Gorn, 1996; Guernsey & Klare, 1993). For example, a parent may believe that the school district is not providing an appropriate education and want different services provided, or the school district may be seeking a hearing officer's determination as to whether it is providing appropriate services under the IDEA or Section 504.

In such situations, either the school personnel or the parents may seek remedies through the due process hearing. The party that is "aggrieved" by the hearing officer's decision (i.e., the losing party) may choose to exercise its right to file a suit in state or federal court (IDEA Regulations, 34 C.F.R. § 300.511). The party that prevails at the hearing cannot file a civil action (*Paula P.B. v. New Hampshire Department of Education,* 1991).

The right to appeal to state or federal court usually begins when the final due process hearing decision is received. A civil action may then be brought either by the school or by the parents. In most situations, administrative remedies (e.g., due process hearing, state review) must be exhausted prior to filing in state or federal court. This rule, however, can be abrogated if exhaustion of administrative procedures would be futile or if irreparable harm would result during the pendency of the procedures.

When a suit is filed, usually the court will defer to the facts as determined during the due process or administrative hearing, although the court may also hear additional evidence at the request of either party. The IDEA authorizes courts to provide relief (i.e., redress or assistance) to the prevailing party. According to the language of the IDEA,

> the court shall receive the records of the administrative proceedings, shall hear additional evidence at the request of a party, and basing its decision on the preponderance of the evidence, shall grant such relief as the court determines is appropriate. (IDEA, 20 U.S.C. § 1415 (e)(2))

The statute, however, does not clarify what exactly "appropriate relief" might entail. Determination of what constitutes appropriate relief, therefore, has been left to the discretion of the courts. The types of relief provided by courts to redress violations of the law are referred to as remedies (Black, Nolan, & Nolan-Haley, 1990). Early interpretations of appropriate relief in special education cases were narrowly drawn; that is, relief was usually limited to ordering that a school refrain from a particular practice (e.g., expelling students with disabilities) or add a service to a student's educational program (e.g., provide extended school year services). Additionally, the courts often required the parties to arrive at a cooperative agreement regarding the matter (Dagley, 1995). In recent years, however, the courts have expanded the definition of appropriate relief.

Similarly, remedies are available for violations of Section 504. These violations are set forth in Section 505 of the Rehabilitation Act (29 U.S.C. § 795a). Because the withholding of federal funds for violations of Section 504 does not assist the victim of discrimination, Congress and the courts have expanded the remedies available for violation of Section 504.

The purpose of this chapter is to examine remedies or types of relief that may be awarded by courts under the IDEA and Section 504. This chapter will examine five types of remedies: injunctive relief, tuition reimbursement, compensatory education, attorneys' fees, and punitive damages. Prior to a discussion of these remedies, a brief explanation of sovereign immunity is in order.

Sovereign Immunity

In 1990, Congress passed the Education of the Handicapped Amendments (IDEA, 20 U.S.C. § 1403).* One of the results of the law was to allow parties to sue states, as well as school districts, under the IDEA. In effect, the law overturned the doctrine of

---

*P.L. 101-476 renamed the law the Individuals with Disabilities Education Act (IDEA).

sovereign immunity in actions brought under the IDEA. Sovereign immunity refers to the immunity of the states against damage suits. Under this doctrine, lawsuits against a governmental entity or its officials are prohibited. In *Dellmuth v. Muth* (1989), the U.S. Supreme Court ruled that while school districts could be sued under the IDEA, states were immune from liability regarding suits under the law by the Eleventh Amendment (see the Appendix). The case involved a student with a learning disability and emotional problems attending school in a Pennsylvania school district. The student's father requested a due process hearing to challenge the school's individualized education plan (IEP). The father also enrolled his son in a private school for students with learning disabilities. The hearing officer determined that the IEP was inappropriate. Subsequently, the IEP was rewritten and determined to be appropriate. While the lengthy hearing was under way, the father also filed a suit against the school district in federal district court. The court ruled against the school district, holding that the father was entitled to reimbursement for the private school tuition. The court further held that the state and school district were both liable. The IDEA, according to the court, had nullified the state's Eleventh Amendment immunity from damage suits. An appeal was filed with the U.S. Court of Appeals for the Third Circuit, which affirmed the lower court's ruling. The decision was then appealed to the U.S. Supreme Court.

In its ruling, the Supreme Court reversed the lower courts' rulings, noting that a congressional act does not abrogate sovereign immunity unless it specifically does so within the language of the act. Because the IDEA did not specifically mention state immunity from lawsuits, states were immune from suits for liability. The parents could not collect reimbursement from the state. The decision only involved state immunity, so the parents' ability to seek reimbursement from the school district was not affected. This decision was overturned by Congress in P.L. 101-476, the Education of the Handicapped Amendments of 1990. The law, as amended, specifically required that "states shall not be immune under the 11th Amendment to the Constitution of the United States from suit in Federal court for violation of this Act" (IDEA, 20 U.S.C. § 1403 (a)). This amendment, therefore, allows parties to sue states, as well as schools, for violations of the IDEA.

Injunctive Relief

An injunction is a judicial remedy awarded for the purpose of requiring a party to refrain from or discontinue a certain action. An injunction is a preventive measure that guards against a similar action being committed in the future. Injunctions are not remedies for past injustices. For example, if parents believed that their child was not receiving an appropriate education and a court granted an injunction, typically the injunction might compel the school district to provide the education that the court deemed appropriate. Injunctive relief is available under both the IDEA and Section 504.

Two major types of injunctions are preliminary and permanent injunctions. Preliminary injunctions, which are temporary, are issued prior to a trial. To be granted a preliminary injunction, the plaintiffs (i.e., the party bringing the lawsuit) must convince the court that harm may result if the injunction is not issued. Plaintiffs must also show that there is a substantial likelihood that in a trial they would succeed in obtaining a permanent injunction, which is the second type of injunction. A permanent injunction is awarded when a court, after hearing the case, is convinced that such an injunction is required to prevent harm. The party seeking the injunction bears the burden of proof.

Mills v. Board of Education of the District of Columbia (1972) is an example of a court decision that granted a permanent injunction. (See Chapter 4 for elaborations of the *Mills* decision.) The case involved a lawsuit brought on behalf of seven children with disabilities. The school district had excluded the children from all District of Columbia public schools. The court issued an injunction that prohibited the school district from excluding students with disabilities from schools or denying them an education.

Schools may also seek injunctions in the courts. In *Honig v. Doe* (1988), the U.S. Supreme Court affirmed the ruling of the lower courts against a school district for unilaterally excluding two students in special education from school pending the outcome of an administrative hearing. The school district had argued that the stay-put provision of the IDEA* contained an exception for students that present a danger to others. (See Chapter 15 for elaborations on the stay-put provision.) The court disagreed but did comment that schools had the option of seeking an injunction from a court to have a dangerous child prohibited from attending school. The court also gave lower courts guidance in granting such injunctions. Courts may grant injunctions when schools prove that maintaining a student in a current placement is substantially likely to result in injury to the student, to staff, or to other students.

The U.S. Court of Appeals for the Eighth Circuit, in *Light v. Parkway School District* (1994), gave schools guidance in seeking an injunction for dangerous and disruptive student behavior. The circuit court developed a two-part test for obtaining an injunction. The court ruled that schools must first prove that a child is substantially likely to cause injury. Second, the school must show that all reasonable steps have been undertaken to reduce the risk that the student would cause injury.

When school officials attempt to obtain an injunction, they must convince the court that they will likely succeed on the merits of the case in trial (Mattison & Hakola, 1992). Furthermore, the district must persuade the court that without the injunction the school or students will suffer harm, that the harm to the student removed from school by the injunction does not outweigh the harm caused to the school district, and that the injunction is in the public interest.

---

*The stay-put provision requires that during any administrative hearing or judicial proceeding, the student shall remain in the then-current placement during the pendency of the hearing unless the parents and school agree otherwise. Typically the current placement is the student's placement at the time the dispute arose.

Tuition Reimbursement

Tuition reimbursement is typically an award to compensate parents for the costs of a unilateral placement of their child in a private school when the school has failed to provide an appropriate education. Tuition reimbursement is not a monetary award in the traditional sense, but rather is viewed by the courts as the school district's reimbursing the parents for the education that should have been provided in the first place. The appropriate education that the parents had to obtain, therefore, is provided at no cost to the parent.

The U.S. Supreme Court examined the question of tuition reimbursement under the IDEA in *Burlington School Committee of the Town of Burlington v. Department of Education of Massachusetts* (1985; hereafter *Burlington*). In *Florence County School District Four v. Carter* (1993; hereafter *Carter*), the high court clarified further questions regarding tuition reimbursement. In the *Burlington* case, the high court ruled on a unilateral change of placement made by the parents of a child with learning disabilities. In *Carter,* the Court considered a unilateral placement in a school that was not approved by the state. In both instances, prior to the Supreme Court's ruling the lower courts were split as to whether tuition reimbursement was available and if it was only available when the parents placed their child in an approved school.

Burlington School Committee v. Department of Education

Burlington involved a school district's education of a third grader, Michael Panico, who had learning disabilities and emotional problems. Michael's father became dissatisfied with his son's lack of progress and obtained an independent evaluation of the boy. The evaluation indicated that Michael should be placed in a private school for students with learning disabilities. When the Burlington school district offered placement in a highly structured class within the district, Michael's father withdrew him from the school and placed him at a state-approved facility in Massachusetts. Following a hearing, the state board of appeals found that the public school placement was inappropriate. The hearing officer ordered the school board to fund the private school placement and to reimburse the parents for expenses they had incurred.

The school district filed a lawsuit in a federal district court. While the case was being heard, the school district agreed to fund the cost of the private school education, though it refused to reimburse the parents. The court, determining that the proposed public school placement was appropriate, ruled in favor of the school district.

Michael's father appealed the decision. The U.S. Court of Appeals for the First Circuit reversed the ruling of the lower court. The appeals court ruled that the IDEA did not bar reimbursement when the parents of a child with disabilities had to unilaterally change the child's placement, if the court found that the parent's action was appropriate. Reimbursement was not available, however, when the school district had proposed and could implement an appropriate placement. The school district filed an appeal with the U.S. Supreme Court. The school district argued that the parents had violated the stay-put rule, which required that students remain in their current placement during the review process.

In unanimously affirming the ruling of the appeals court, the high court stated that parents who unilaterally place their children with disabilities in a private school setting are entitled to reimbursement for tuition and living expenses if a court finds that the school had proposed an inappropriate IEP. If the school's proposed placement, however, was found to be appropriate, the school would not have to reimburse the parents. Justice Rehnquist, writing for the majority, noted that the IDEA gave the courts broad discretion in granting relief. The majority opinion also stated that to deny reimbursement, when appropriate, would be to deny the parent meaningful input in the development of an appropriate education and would lessen the importance of the procedural safeguards. Rehnquist asserted that the decision requiring reimbursement did not constitute a damage award, but rather "required the [school district] to belatedly pay expenses that it should have paid all along and would have been borne in the first instance had it developed a proper IEP" (*Burlington*, pp. 370–371).

The high court also commented that if the school's placement was found to be appropriate, parents were not entitled to reimbursement. Parents who unilaterally change their child's placement, therefore, do so at their own risk.

In noting that the IDEA conferred broad discretion, the high court was saying that courts, in ordering appropriate relief, have a great deal of leeway. As the *Burlington* decision indicates, this discretion clearly includes the power to award tuition reimbursement. Parents are not required to bear the costs of providing an appropriate education for their children with disabilities (Mattison & Hakola, 1992).

Chief Justice Rehnquist negated the possibility of school districts' using the stay-put provision as a defense against unilateral placements made by parents. Rehnquist noted that if the stay-put provision was read in such a way as to prohibit parents from making unilateral placements, parents would be forced to either (a) leave their child in what may be an inappropriate placement or (b) obtain an appropriate education only by sacrificing any claim for reimbursement. The majority opinion stated that "the [IDEA] was intended to give handicapped children both an appropriate education and a free one; it should not be interpreted to defeat one or the other of these objectives" (*Burlington*, p. 372).

The Supreme Court also recognized that related expenses, in addition to tuition, may also be awarded to parents. Subsequent decisions have held that such expenses may include the following: cost of transportation and costs incurred during transportation (*Taylor v. Board of Education*, 1986); lost earnings by parents for time expended related to protecting their child's rights, and interest on tuition loans (*Board of Education of the County of Cabell v. Dienelt*, 1988); costs of residential placement (*Babb v. Knox County School System*, 1992); expenses for related services (*Rapid City School District v. Vahle*, 1990); reimbursement for psychotherapy (*Max M. v. Illinois State Board of Education*, 1986); and insurance reimbursement when the parents had financed the tuition with their insurance (*Shook v. Gaston County Board of Education*, 1989).

Following the *Burlington* decision, a number of issues regarding tuition reimbursement were litigated. A primary issue involved reimbursement for parents who unilaterally placed their child in an unapproved school—that is, one that had not been approved by the state educational agency (SEA). Lower courts were split on this issue. The Supreme Court put this controversy to rest in *Carter.*

Florence County School District Four v. Carter

Shannon Carter was a high school student in Florence County School District Four in Florence, South Carolina. Educational evaluations, done privately and by the school district, indicated that she had a learning disability and Attention Deficit Disorder (ADD). Her parents requested that Shannon be placed in a self-contained classroom in a neighboring school district. Because the Florence school district had no self-contained setting, it proposed that Shannon receive instruction from a special education teacher in a resource room. The parents refused the placement and requested a due process hearing. They continued to press for placement in a neighboring school district's self-contained classroom or placement at Trident Academy, a private school in Charleston, South Carolina. The hearing officer decided in favor of the school district. The Carters took Shannon out of the public school and placed her at Trident Academy. The Carters also appealed the hearing officer's decision to the state reviewing officer. The reviewing officer upheld the original decision. The Carters filed suit in the federal district court.

After hearing the evidence from court-appointed evaluators, the district court held that the school district's program was "wholly inadequate" and directed the school district to reimburse the Carters for expenses incurred at Trident Academy. The school district appealed the decision to the U.S. Court of Appeals for the Fourth Circuit. The circuit court ruled that even though Trident Academy was not on the state's list of approved special education schools, the school had to reimburse the Carters for tuition at Trident Academy. The school district appealed to the U.S. Supreme Court.

The Supreme Court requested that the solicitor general's office of the Department of Justice file a brief outlining the government's position. The Department of Justice filed a brief recommending that the Fourth Circuit court's decision be upheld (Wright, 1994). Seventeen states filed amicus curiae (friend of the court) briefs supporting the school district. The high court affirmed the circuit court's decision in ruling that the school district had to reimburse the parents for placement in the school, even though it was not on the SEA's approved list. The high court stated that limiting parental reimbursement to state-approved schools would be contrary to the IDEA when the school district had not complied with the law. Furthermore, the Court determined that applying state standards to parental placements would be fundamentally unfair in situations where parents have to find a private school that offers an appropriate education.

In *Carter,* the Supreme Court held that parents could be reimbursed for the use of unapproved personnel and schools for services obtained when school districts failed in their duty to offer an appropriate education for students with disabilities under Part B of the IDEA. The U.S. Court of Appeals for the Second Circuit, in *Still v. Debuono* (1996), ruled that the principles announced in *Carter* were equally applicable to Part H of the IDEA. Although Part H imposes a requirement that early intervention services are provided by qualified personnel, privately obtained services that were provided by unapproved personnel are reimbursable.

Compensatory Education

Compensatory educational services are designed to remedy the progress lost by students with disabilities because they were previously denied a free appropriate public education (FAPE) (Tucker & Goldstein, 1992). The award of compensatory education is the award of additional educational services, above and beyond the educational services normally due a student under state law (Gorn, 1996). Typically, compensatory education extends a student's eligibility for educational services beyond age 21 as compensation for inappropriate educational services (Mattison & Hakola, 1992). According to Gorn (1996), when students currently attending school are awarded compensatory education, it may take the form of extended-day programs, extended school year services, summer school, tutoring, compensatory related services (e.g., occupational or physical therapy), or future compensatory education (i.e., provision of educational services after the student turns 21). Following the *Burlington* decision, the issue of compensatory education received a great deal of attention in the courts. Even though the early decisions tended to rule that compensatory education was not available, the majority of recent decisions have ruled that compensatory educational services are remedies available in the IDEA (Zirkel, 1991, 1995).

Compensatory Awards Under the IDEA

An example of judicial thinking regarding compensatory education was delivered by the U.S. Court of Appeals for the Eighth Circuit in *Meiner v. Missouri* (1986). The appeals court ruled in favor of an award of compensatory education, explaining that

> Like the retroactive reimbursement in *Burlington*, imposing liability for compensatory educational services on the defendants "merely requires [them] to belatedly pay expenses that [they] should have paid all along." Here, as in *Burlington*, recovery is necessary to the child's right to a free appropriate public education. We are confident that Congress did not intend the child's entitlement to a free education to turn upon her parent's ability to front its costs. (p. 753)

In a policy letter, the Office of Special Education Programs (OSEP) stated a similar position on compensatory education: "In certain instances, compensatory education may be the only means through which children who are forced to remain in an inappropriate placement, due to their parents' financial inability to pay for an appropriate placement, would receive FAPE" (Murray, 1992, p. 496). OSEP further stated that compensatory education could be awarded by hearing officers or SEAs. Courts have also reached similar conclusions regarding a hearing officer's ability to award compensatory education (*Murphy v. Timberlane Regional School District*, 1993).

Compensatory education may be ordered if it is determined that a school district did not provide an appropriate education. Such a violation could involve programming or procedural violations (Mattison & Hakola, 1992). Additionally, compensatory education awards may take the form of either extending the student's eligibility beyond age 21 or providing summer programming (Murray, 1992). Zirkel (1995) asserts that compensatory education may also extend to educational services beyond the regular school day.

Zirkel (1995) refers to compensatory educational services as the "coin of the realm" (p. 483) in relief cases arising under the IDEA. This is because tuition reimbursement represents an up-front risk that many parents cannot afford; also, unlike attorneys' fees awards, parents need not resort to litigation to receive an enforceable award of compensatory education. A due process hearing officer and the SEA may grant awards of compensatory educational services.

Compensatory Awards Under Section 504

Courts have also held that compensatory awards are available under Section 504. In *Meiner v. Missouri* (1986), the U.S. Court of Appeals for the Eighth Circuit held that a full array of remedies, including damages, was available to plaintiffs succeeding in actions under Section 504. Other courts have also awarded compensatory damages under the law (*Fitzgerald v. Green Valley Education Agency,* 1984; *Gelman v. Department of Education,* 1982). Some courts, however, have held that compensatory damages are not available unless intentional discrimination can be shown (*Marvin H. v. Austin Independent School District,* 1983; *Sabo v. O'Bannon,* 1984). The U.S. Supreme Court, in *Alexander v. Choate* (1985), held that Section 504 may be violated regardless of the intent of the party that committed the discrimination. This ruling appears to indicate that remedies, including compensatory awards, may be granted absent discriminatory intent.

Attorneys' Fees

Because the IDEA contained no provision for reimbursement of attorneys' fees, parties prevailing in suits against school districts prior to 1984 often sought reimbursement through other means. Reimbursement of attorneys' fees was usually sought through Section 505 of the Rehabilitation Act of 1973 or Section 1988 of the Civil Rights Attorney's Fees Award Act, both of which allowed courts to grant reimbursement of attorneys' fees to prevailing parties. In 1984, however, this practice was halted by the U.S. Supreme Court in *Smith v. Robinson* (1984; hereafter *Smith*).

Smith v. Robinson

In *Smith,* the parents of a child with cerebral palsy prevailed in their claim against a school district that had discontinued their child's special education program. The parents sued successfully for attorneys' fees under Section 505 of the Rehabilitation

Act in federal district court. On appeal, however, the attorneys' fee award was overturned. The appellate court ruled that attorneys' fees were not available under the IDEA. The parents appealed to the U.S. Supreme Court. In a 5–4 ruling, the high court affirmed the ruling of the appeals court. In the majority opinion, Justice Blackmun stated that Congress had intended that the IDEA be the exclusive remedy for protecting the rights of students with disabilities. This law, therefore, was the only avenue by which special education actions could be pursued. Because the law contained no provisions for attorneys' fees, none were available. In another special education decision handed down on the same day as *Smith, Irving Independent School District v. Tatro* (1984), the parents were denied attorneys' fees even though they prevailed in their action.

Justice Brennan, in a dissenting opinion, asserted that the majority had misconstrued and frustrated congressional intent in their ruling. He stated that Congress would have to revisit the matter so that the parents of children who must sue for their rights under the law can be recompensed if they prevail.

The Handicapped Children's Protection Act

Congress did revisit the law, and in 1986 passed the Handicapped Children's Protection Act (HCPA). The HCPA amended the IDEA to allow the provision of attorneys' fees to parties prevailing in special education lawsuits (HCPA, 20 U.S.C. § 1415). The HCPA consisted of three major parts: (a) authorization of the courts to award reasonable attorneys' fees to parents of a child with disabilities when they prevail in a lawsuit under the IDEA; (b) clarification of the effect of the IDEA on other laws; and (c) retroactive application of the HCPA (Yell & Espin, 1990). The HCPA effectively overturned *Smith*.

The major purpose of the HCPA was to allow parents to recover attorneys' fees in successful actions under the IDEA without having to use other laws to sue. The HCPA provided that

> In any action or proceeding brought under [the HCPA], the court, in its discretion, may award reasonable attorneys' fees as part of the costs to the parents or guardian of a [child with disabilities] who is the prevailing party. (IDEA, 20 U.S.C. § 1415(e)(4)(B)(1990))

Issues in the Award of Attorneys' Fees

The law, however, contained several stipulations regarding the reimbursement of these fees. A major proviso in the law was that parents could collect attorneys' fees only if they were the prevailing party. If parents did not prevail on a major point of their suit, therefore, they were not entitled to attorneys' fees. Subsequent cases have held that for plaintiffs to prevail they must succeed on any significant issue in their action (*Angela L. v. Pasadena Independent School District No. 2*, 1990; *Burr v. Sobol*, 1990; *Mitten v. Muscogee County School District*, 1989). That is, for parties to prevail it is not necessary that they were successful in obtaining all relief or even the primary relief sought, but merely that they succeeded on some significant issue

(Tucker & Goldstein, 1992). Findings of bad faith or unjustified conduct on the part of school officials are not required in the awarding of fees (*Mitten v. Muscogee County School District*, 1989).

In many cases brought to trial, school districts have made good faith efforts to provide services to students with disabilities, but parents and the schools have not been able to agree regarding the specific services required. In such cases, the determination of the prevailing party is decidedly more difficult for the courts (Dagley, 1994). In these instances, the courts have often turned to the U.S. Supreme Court's ruling in *Hensley v. Eckerhart* (1983; hereafter *Hensley*) for guidance. In *Hensley*, the Court defined a significant relief standard as relief on any significant issue that achieved some of the benefits the party sought in bringing the suit. Relief on a significant issue would result in that party's prevailing, and thus being awarded attorneys' fees. In a later ruling by the high court in *Texas State Teachers Association v. Garland Independent School District* (1989), the *Hensley* standard was further clarified. According to the Court's decision, parties are considered to have prevailed when they succeed on a significant issue they raise. It is not necessary that the plaintiff prevail on the most significant issue or on the majority of issues raised. Furthermore, to be eligible for an award of attorneys' fees, the plaintiff must be able to point to the resolution of the dispute which changes the legal relationship between the parties.

The courts have also awarded attorneys' fees for work done in administrative hearings (e.g., due process hearings). Furthermore, courts have awarded fees for time spent working prior to a due process hearing (*Angela L. v. Pasadena Independent School District*, 1990; *Counsel v. Dow*, 1988; *Duane M. v. New Orleans Parish School Board*, 1988). Courts have also awarded attorneys' fees in cases that have been settled prior to the administrative hearing (*Barlow-Gresham Union High School District No. 2 v. Mitchell*, 1991; *Shelly C. v. Venus Independent School District*, 1989).

The HCPA addresses the calculation of fee awards as follows:

> For the purpose of [the HCPA], fees awarded shall be based on rates prevailing in the community in which the action or proceeding arose for the kind and quality of services furnished. No bonus or multiplier may be used in calculating the fees. (IDEA, 20 U.S.C. § 1415 (e)(4)(C) (1990))

In addition to the costs of litigating the case, attorneys' fees may include fees of expert witnesses, costs of tests and evaluations, time spent in monitoring and enforcing a judgment, travel time, secretarial tasks, and the work of paraprofessionals (e.g., paralegals, law clerks).

The law prohibits the awarding of attorneys' fees in cases where parents have rejected a properly made settlement offer if they ultimately obtained essentially the same relief as originally offered. The HCPA also permits courts to reduce attorneys' fees if they find that the parents or attorneys have unreasonably protracted the final resolution of the matter or if the fees unreasonably exceed the prevailing community rates. This provision of the law, which has been termed the vexatious litigant provision, provides schools with protection against parents and attorneys who become overly adversarial to the point of working to protract proceedings and undermine efforts at settlement (Dagley, 1994).

The HCPA also reversed the Court's ruling in *Smith* regarding the exclusivity of the IDEA in lawsuits. The high court had ruled that there was no option to sue school districts under Section 505 or Section 1988 because the IDEA was the exclusive remedy. The HCPA overturned this part of the decision, stating that nothing in the law should be construed as restricting or limiting the rights of parents to sue under another statute.

Finally, the law made the attorneys' fees provision retroactive to cases pending on or brought after the date of *Smith* but before the passage of the HCPA. The effect of this clause was to allow plaintiffs to sue for attorneys' fees if they had been denied fees because of the *Smith* ruling.

The IDEA Amendments of 1997

The 1997 amendments retained the HCPA's provisions regarding attorneys' fees and added a few qualifications. These provisions served to limit the situations in which attorneys could seek reimbursement from school districts. Attorneys' fees may be reduced in situations where the attorney representing the parents failed to provide the local educational agency with information regarding the specific nature of the dispute. The amendments also require that parents notify school officials in a timely manner about the problem and any proposed solutions. Additionally, because Congress believed that the IEP process should be devoted to considering students' needs and planning for their education rather than being used as an adversarial forum, the IDEA amendments specifically exclude the payment of attorneys' fees for attorneys' participation in the IEP process. The only exception is when the IEP meeting is ordered in an administrative or court proceeding. Similarly, attorneys' fees are not available for mediation sessions prior to the filing of a due process action.

The amendments also specifically adopted the *Hensley* standard for determining the amount of any attorneys' fees award. That is, in determining awards courts are required to assess the degree to which the plaintiff prevailed on significant issues (Senate Report, 1997).

Attorneys' Fees Under the Rehabilitation Act of 1973

Section 505 of the Rehabilitation Act states that "the court, in its discretion, may allow the prevailing party . . . a reasonable attorney's fee as part of the costs" (Section 504 of the Rehabilitation Act, 29 U.S.C. § 794(a)(2)(b)). Plaintiffs must satisfy a two-part test to be awarded attorneys' fees under Section 505 (Tucker & Goldstein, 1992). First, a court must determine if the plaintiffs achieved their goals in bringing the suit. The court, in making this determination, compares the relief the plaintiff originally requested with the relief obtained. As with the IDEA, the plaintiff need only succeed on some part of the original claim. Second, the court must determine whether the relief was obtained from the defendant as a result of the plaintiff's suit or if it was granted as a "gratuitous act" on the part of the defendant (*Greater Los Angeles Council on Deafness (GLAD) v. Community Television of Southern California*, 1987; hereafter *GLAD*). There must be a relationship between the award and the plaintiff's suit.

Following the determination that the plaintiff is to be awarded attorneys' fees under Section 505, the court must determine the amount of the award. The court in *GLAD* determined fees by multiplying the number of hours worked by a reasonable hourly rate. The determination, unlike the method described in the HCPA, may then increase the fee by a multiplier. The multiplier is arrived at by determining the complexity of the case, the degree of the plaintiff's success, and other factors.

Punitive Damages

Punitive damage awards, which are monetary awards in excess of actual damages, are intended to serve as punishment and recompense for a legal wrong. There has been an extensive amount of litigation as to whether courts can order the award of punitive damages in special education cases brought under the IDEA. The majority of these cases have held that these damages are not available (*Colin K. v. Schmidt*, 1983; *Hall v. Knott County Board of Education*, 1991; *Meiner v. Missouri*, 1986; *Heidemann v. Rother*, 1996; *Hoekstra v. Independent School District No. 283*, 1996).

In *Anderson v. Thompson* (1981), the U.S. Court of Appeals for the Seventh Circuit held that punitive damages were unavailable under the IDEA. In this influential ruling, the court stated that although there was no basis for awarding damages in the law's legislative history, damages might be available in exceptional circumstances. Such circumstances might include the school district's acting in bad faith in failing to comply with the IDEA (*Anderson v. Thompson*) or intentional violation of a student's right to a FAPE (*Taylor v. Honig*, 1992).

Recently, some legal developments have indicated that school districts can be held liable for punitive damages for violations of the IDEA (Guernsey & Klare, 1993; Mattison & Hakola, 1992). The first major development was the HCPA. In overturning the U.S. Supreme Court's decision in *Smith,* Congress restored parents' right to sue school districts under other laws besides the IDEA. According to the statutory language, "Nothing in this chapter shall be construed to restrict or limit the rights, procedures, and remedies available under the Constitution, Title V of the Rehabilitation Act of 1973, or other federal statutes" (IDEA, 20 U.S.C. § 1415(e)(3)(f) (1994)). A number of observers have noted that because of the HCPA, Section 1983 of the Civil Rights Act (Civil Rights Act, 42 U.S.C. § 1983) may now be used by attorneys in special education lawsuits, although this is not specifically mentioned in the statute (Guernsey & Klare, 1993; Mattison & Hakola, 1992).

Section 1983

In their review of legislative history of the HCPA, Mattison and Hakola (1992) maintain that Congress clearly sought to restore plaintiffs' ability to use Section 1983 of the Civil Rights Act in special education lawsuits. The primary significance of Section

1983 to plaintiffs in special education lawsuits is the availability of monetary damages under the law. Section 1983 was derived from the Civil Rights Act of 1871. The basic purpose of this law, commonly referred to as the Ku Klux Klan Act, was to protect freed slaves from denial of their federal rights by state and local governments (Mattison & Hakola, 1992; Sorenson, 1992). This was accomplished by providing a legal action for damages and injunctive relief. In the last few decades, courts have extended the protections of Section 1983 to any person whose rights under the U.S. Constitution or federal statutes are violated by a governmental entity or official. Thus, persons can sue for violations of their federal rights.

Whether Section 1983 claims can be based on violations of the IDEA, however, has not been clearly answered by the courts. Although courts have recognized that Section 1983 is now available to plaintiffs as a result of the HCPA, the results of cases in which plaintiffs have used Section 1983 based on violations of the IDEA have been mixed. Some courts have concluded that plaintiffs can seek monetary damages based on violations of the IDEA (*Hiller v. Board of Education of the Brunswick Central School District,* 1988), while others have ruled that a Section 1983 violation cannot be based solely on violations of the IDEA (*Barnett v. Fairfax County School Board,* 1991). *Jackson v. Franklin County School Board* (1986) also recognized that suit could be brought under both the IDEA and Section 1983, thereby leading to awards of monetary damages.

In *Doe v. Withers* (1993) a jury assessed monetary damages against a teacher under Section 1983. In this case, a history teacher had refused to comply with the requirement on an IEP that tests be read orally to a student with learning disabilities. The teacher was aware of the requirement and deliberately ignored it. As a result of the teacher's action, the student failed the history course. The following semester, the history teacher was replaced by a substitute teacher. The substitute implemented oral reading of tests, and the student's grades improved dramatically. The parents brought an action under Section 1983 against the school district and the history teacher. A jury found in favor of the parents and awarded them damages against the history teacher in the amount of $5,000 in compensatory damages and $10,000 in punitive damages.

W.B. v. Matula

In an indication that monetary damages may be available, the U.S. Court of Appeals for the Third Circuit ruled that a lawsuit seeking punitive damages under the IDEA, Section 504, and Section 1983 against a school district and several educators was permissible. *W.B. v. Matula* (1995) reversed a decision by a federal district court granting summary judgment (i.e., a preverdict rendered by a court in response to a motion by a plaintiff or defendant) for the school district of Mansfield Township, New Jersey, regarding a question of damages because of a failure on the part of a school district to properly evaluate and educate a student with a disability. The circuit court remanded the case to the district court for a trial on the damages claim. The case involved a first-grade boy with behavioral problems and Attention Deficit

Hyperactivity Disorder (ADHD). The student's parents wanted an evaluation, which the school district initially declined to conduct. When the district conducted an evaluation a year after first being requested to do so, it found that the student did have ADHD but did not qualify for special education. The school district, however, found the boy eligible for services under Section 504 but failed to provide the necessary services. An independent evaluation determined that the boy had Tourette's syndrome, severe obsessive-compulsive disorder, and ADHD. Several due process hearings were held and the district reclassified the student, implemented an IEP, and paid $14,000 to settle all the disputes with the parents. Following an administrative hearing in late 1994, the district was further ordered to pay for a private school placement for the student. The boy's parents sued in federal district court against nine school officials (including the school principal and two general education teachers). The case eventually was appealed to the circuit court, which, in dicta, rejected the school district's argument that damages were unavailable in a Section 1983 action premised on an IDEA violation. According to the court, when the IDEA was amended in 1986, Congress specifically allowed IDEA violations to be redressed by Section 504 and Section 1983 actions. The Third Circuit court's decision was widely seen as a strong indication that lawsuits seeking monetary damages for violations of the IDEA and Section 504 were available. Rather than going back to trial on the damages action, the school district agreed to an out-of-court settlement. The district paid a total of $245,000, including a $125,000 cash payment to the family in addition to court costs and attorneys' fees.

In *Whitehead v. School Board of Hillsborough County* (1996), a federal district court agreed with the Third Circuit that compensatory and punitive damages were available under Section 504. The court disagreed regarding the IDEA, however, stating that relief under the law was generally limited to reimbursement that compensated parents for the cost of services that the school should have provided.

Section 1403 of the IDEA

A second development that indicates that monetary damages may be available was Section 1403 of the 1990 amendments to the IDEA, which overturned the U.S. Supreme Court's ruling in *Dellmuth v. Muth* (1989). This section of the 1990 amendments indicated that

> In a suit against a State for a violation of this act, remedies (including remedies both at law and in equity) are available for such a violation to the same extent as such remedies are available for such a violation in the suit against any public entity other than a state. (IDEA, 20 U.S.C. § 1403(B))

This language is significant in its recognition that remedies both at law and in equity are available under the IDEA. The phrase "remedies at law" generally includes monetary damages. Thus, a number of legal scholars have inferred that Congress has recognized that monetary damages are within the scope of appropriate relief (Guernsey & Klare, 1993; Mattison & Hakola, 1992; Tucker & Goldstein, 1992).

Franklin v. Gwinett County Public Schools

An important development occurred in the U.S. Supreme Court's ruling in *Franklin v. Gwinett County Public Schools* (1992; hereafter *Franklin*), even though the case did not involve special education. In *Franklin,* a high school student was repeatedly sexually abused and harassed by a teacher. The student brought suit against the school and the teacher under Title IX of the Education Amendments of 1972. Subsequently, the teacher resigned and charges against him were dropped. A federal district court then dismissed the suit against the school, ruling that Title IX did not allow an award of damages. The U.S. Court of Appeals for the Eleventh Circuit affirmed the district court's decision. On appeal, the U.S. Supreme Court reversed the lower courts' rulings, holding that monetary damages were available under Title IX, even though not specifically mentioned in the law. The Court stated:

> The general rule, therefore, is that absent clear direction to the contrary by Congress, the federal courts have the power to award any appropriate relief in a cognizable cause of action brought pursuant to a federal statute. (p. 1035)

Because the language of the IDEA does not prohibit monetary awards, it seems that they may be available in accordance with the high court's ruling in *Franklin.*

Hoekstra v. Independent School District No. 283

The U.S. Court of Appeals for the Eighth Circuit, in *Hoekstra v. Independent School District No. 283* (1996), refused to award parents punitive damages as a remedy in a case involving a district's delay in providing compensatory educational services for a student in special education. The court held that punitive damages were not available as a remedy under the IDEA. In an earlier decision, the Eighth Circuit court also held that punitive damages were not available under the IDEA (*Heidemann v. Rother,* 1996).

Punitive Damages and Section 504

Neither is the issue of punitive damages under Section 504 settled. While some courts have awarded damages under Section 504 (*Hurry v. Jones,* 1983), others have not (*Martin v. Cardinal Glennon Memorial Hospital for Children,* 1984). The court in *Tanberg v. Weld County Sheriff* (1992) held that punitive damages were available in cases involving intentional discrimination. Similarly, a district court in Minnesota ruled that punitive damages were available under Section 504 when violations were due to bad faith or gross misjudgments (*Brantley v. Independent School District,* 1996). In *Hoekstra v. Independent School District No. 283* (1996), the U.S. Court of Appeals for the Eighth Circuit ruled that monetary damages were available under both Section 504 and the Americans with Disabilities Act (ADA) if the violations were made in bad faith. The U.S. Court of Appeals for the Sixth Circuit, however, held that punitive damages are not available in cases of discrimination under Section 504 (*Moreno v. Consolidated Rail Corporation,* 1996).

Summary of Punitive Damages

The majority of courts have not granted punitive damages under the IDEA, although a few courts have indicated that such damages may be available. Some courts have found punitive damages available for violations of Section 504 or the ADA in cases involving bad faith or gross misjudgment. Courts are usually loath to open the public coffers to punitive damages unless Congress clearly makes such a remedy available under the law (Tucker & Goldstein, 1992). Congress has not expressly made punitive damages an available remedy under the IDEA. At present, the generally accepted view is that punitive damages are not available under the IDEA, although the issue is not settled.

Summary

In special education, not only are parents involved in the process of designing an appropriate education for their child, but they may also serve as the stimulus for forcing school districts to comply with the laws. When parents or school districts go to court, they often seek to determine the responsibilities for the delivery of educational services. Typically the parents, believing that the school district's IEP will not offer an appropriate education, will seek to have different services provided. If a court finds that a school district has committed statutory or procedural violations under either the IDEA or Section 504, it may award some form of relief to redress these violations. Such awards are usually in the form of injunctive relief, tuition reimbursement, and attorneys' fees. Increasingly, courts are awarding compensatory educational services. The majority of courts have generally not granted punitive damages under the IDEA, although a few have indicated that such damages may be available. Some courts have found punitive damages available for violations of Section 504 in cases involving bad faith.

School districts need not act in bad faith to be directed to provide relief. Intentional violations, however, may lead to courts' ordering larger awards to plaintiffs. Minor or inconsequential violations will not lead to relief; however, violations that result in the provision of an inappropriate education or result in discrimination based on a disability will lead to relief. The best defense to prevent such awards is in providing an appropriate education.

For Further Information

Dagley, D. L. (1994). Prevailing under the HCPA. *Education Law Reporter, 90,* 547–560.

Dagley, D. L. (1995). Enforcing compliance with IDEA: Dispute resolution and appropriate relief. *Preventing School Failure, 39*(2), 27–32.

Mattison, D. A., & Hakola, S. R. (1992). *The availability of damages and equitable remedies under the IDEA, Section 504, and 42 U.S.C. Section 1983.* Horsham, PA: LRP Publications.

Sorenson, G. P. (1992). School district liability for federal civil rights violations under Section 1983. *Education Law Reporter, 76,* 313–330.

Yell, M. L., & Espin, C. A. (1990). The Handicapped Children's Protection Act of 1986: Time to pay the piper? *Exceptional Children, 56,* 396–407.

Zirkel, P. A. (1995). The remedy of compensatory education under the IDEA. *Education Law Reporter, 95,* 483–488.

References

Alexander v. Choate, 469 U.S. 287 (1985).

Americans with Disabilities Act of 1990, 42 U.S.C.A. § 12101 *et seq.*

Anderson v. Thompson, 658 F.2d 1205 (7th Cir. 1981).

Angela L. v. Pasadena Independent School District, 918 F.2d 1188 (5th Cir. 1990).

Babb v. Knox County School System, 965 F.2d 104 (6th Cir. 1992).

Barlow-Gresham Union High School District No. 2 v. Mitchell, 940 F.2d 1280 (9th Cir. 1991).

Barnett v. Fairfax County School Board, 927 F.2d 146 (4th Cir. 1991).

Black, H. C., Nolan, J. R., & Nolan-Haley, J. M. (1990). *Black's law dictionary* (6th ed.). St. Paul, MN: West Publishing Company.

Board of Education of County of Cabell v. Dienelt, 843 F.2d 813 (4th Cir. 1988).

Brantley v. Independent School District No. 625, 24 IDELR 696 (D. Minn. 1996).

Burlington School Committee of the Town of Burlington v. Department of Education of Massachusetts, 471 U.S. 359 (1985).

Burr v. Sobol, 888 F.2d 258 (2nd Cir. 1990).

Civil Rights Act (Section 1983), 42 U.S.C. § 1983.

Civil Rights Attorney's Fees Award Act (Section 1988), 42 U.S.C. § 1988.

Colin K. v. Schmidt, 715 F.2d 1 (1st Cir. 1983).

Counsel v. Dow, 849 F.2d 731 (2nd Cir. 1988).

Dagley, D. L. (1994). Prevailing under the HCPA. *Education Law Reporter, 90,* 547–560.

Dagley, D. L. (1995). Enforcing compliance with IDEA: Dispute resolution and appropriate relief. *Preventing School Failure, 39* (2), 27–32.

Dellmuth v. Muth, 491 U.S. 223 (1989).

Doe v. Withers, 20 IDELR 442 (W.Va. Cir. Ct. 1993).

Duane M. v. New Orleans Parish School Board, 861 F.2d. 115 (5th Cir. 1988).

Fitzgerald v. Green Valley Education Agency, 589 F. Supp. 1130 (S.D. Iowa 1984).

Florence County School District Four v. Carter, 114 S.Ct. 361 (1993).

Franklin v. Gwinett County Public Schools, 112 S.Ct. 1028 (1992).

Gelman v. Department of Education, 544 F. Supp. 651 (D. Colo. 1982).

Gorn, S. (1996). *What do I do when . . . The answer book on special education law.* Horsham, PA: LRP Publications.

Greater Los Angeles Council on Deafness (GLAD) v. Community Television of Southern California, 813 F.2d 217 (9th Cir. 1987).

Guernsey, T. F., & Klare, K. (1993). *Special education law.* Durham, NC: Carolina Academic Press.

Hall v. Knott County Board of Education, 941 F.2d 402 (6th Cir. 1991).

Handicapped Children's Protection Act of 1986, 20 U.S.C. § 1415.

Heidemann v. Rother, 84 F.3d 1021 (8th Cir. 1996).

Hensley v. Eckerhart, 461 U.S. 424 (1983).

Hiller v. Board of Education of the Brunswick Central School District, 687 F. Supp. 735 (N.D.N.Y. 1988).

Hoekstra v. Independent School District No. 283, 25 IDELR 136 (8th Cir. 1996).

Honig v. Doe, 484 U.S. 305 (1988).

Hurry v. Jones, 560 F. Supp. 500 (D.R.I. 1983).

Individuals with Disabilities Education Act (IDEA), 20 U.S.C. § 1400 *et seq.*

Individuals with Disabilities Education Act Regulations, 34 C.F.R. § 300.1 *et seq.*

Irving Independent School District v. Tatro, 468 U.S. 883 (1984).

Jackson v. Franklin County School Board, 806 F.2d 623 (5th Cir. 1986).

Light v. Parkway School District, 21 IDELR 933 (8th Cir. 1994).

Martin v. Cardinal Glennon Memorial Hospital for Children, 599 F. Supp. 284 (E.D. Mo. 1984).

Marvin H. v. Austin Independent School District, 714 F.2d 1348 (5th Cir. 1983).

Mattison, D. A., & Hakola, S. R. (1992). *The availability of damages and equitable remedies under the IDEA, Section 504, and 42 U.S.C. Section 1983.* Horsham, PA: LRP Publications.

Max M. v. Illinois State Board of Education, 629 F. Supp. 1504 (N.D. Ill. 1986).

Meiner v. Missouri, 673 F.2d 969 (8th Cir. 1986).

Mills v. Board of Education of the District of Columbia, 348 F. Supp. 866 (D.C. 1972).

Mitten v. Muscogee County School District, 877 F.2d 932 (11th Cir. 1989).

Moreno v. Consolidated Rail Corporation, 25 IDELR 7 (6th Cir. 1996).

Murphy v. Timberlane Regional School District, 819 F. Supp. 1127 (D.N.H. 1993).

Murray, Letter to, 19 IDELR 496 (OSEP, 1992).

Paula P. B. v. New Hampshire Department of Education, 17 EHLR 897 (D.N.H. 1991).

Rapid City School District v. Vahle, 922 F.2d 476 (8th Cir. 1990).

Sabo v. O'Bannon, 586 F. Supp. 1132 (E.D. Pa. 1984).

Section 504 of the Rehabilitation Act of 1973, 29 U.S.C. §§ 706(8), 794, 794a.

Section 505 of the Rehabilitation Act of 1973, 29 U.S.C. § 795a.

Senate Report of the Individuals with Disabilities Act Amendments of 1997, available at wais. access.gpo.gov.

Shelly C. v. Venus Independent School District, 878 F.2d 862 (5th Cir. 1989).

Shook v. Gaston County Board of Education, 882 F.2d 119 (4th Cir. 1989).

Smith v. Robinson, 468 U.S. 992 (1984).

Sorenson, G.P. (1992). School district liability for federal civil rights violations under Section 1983. *Education Law Reporter, 76,* 313–330.

Still v. Debuono, 25 IDELR 32 (2nd Cir. 1996).

Tanberg v. Weld County Sheriff, 787 F. Supp. 970 (D. Colo. 1992).

Taylor v. Board of Education, 649 F. Supp. 1253 (N.D.N.Y. 1986).

Taylor v. Honig, 19 IDELR 472 (9th Cir. 1992).

Texas State Teachers Association v. Garland Independent School District, 489 U.S. 782 (1989).

Tucker, B. P., & Goldstein, B. A. (1992). *Legal rights of persons with disabilities: An analysis of federal law.* Horsham, PA: LRP Publications.

W.B. v. Matula, 67 F.3d 484 (3rd Cir. 1995).

Whitehead v. School Board of Hillsborough County, 932 F. Supp. 1393 (M.D. Fla. 1996).

Wright, P. W. (1994). Shannon Carter: The untold story. In *Proceedings of the 15th National Institute on Legal Issues of Educating Students with Disabilities.* Horsham, PA: LRP Publications.

Yell, M. L., & Espin, C. A. (1990). The Handicapped Children's Protection Act of 1986: Time to pay the piper? *Exceptional Children, 56,* 396–407.

Zirkel, P. A. (1991). Compensatory educational services in special education cases. *Education Law Reporter, 67,* 881–887.

Zirkel, P. A. (1995). The remedy of compensatory education under the IDEA. *Education Law Reporter, 95,* 483–488.

CHAPTER FIFTEEN

Disciplining Students with Disabilities

Handicapped children are neither immune from a school's disciplinary process nor are they entitled to participate in programs when their behavior impairs the education of other children . . . school authorities can take swift disciplinary measures . . . against disruptive handicapped students.

Judge Daly, *Stuart v. Nappi* (1978, p. 1244)

The use of disciplinary procedures with students with disabilities has proven to be a very controversial and confusing issue. Although the Individuals with Disabilities Education Act (IDEA), Section 504 of the Rehabilitation Act of 1973, and regulations implementing these laws are quite detailed, until recently there were no specific federal guidelines regarding the discipline of students with disabilities (Hartwig & Reusch, 1994). The lack of statutory or regulatory guidance resulted in uncertainty among school administrators and teachers regarding appropriate disciplinary procedures. A number of judicial decisions, however, have addressed this issue, and these decisions have led to the formation of a body of case law. Generally, the case law indicated that disciplinary actions against students with disabilities were subject to different rules and limitations than those applicable to students without disabilities (Tucker, Goldstein, & Sorenson, 1993). Maloney (1994) argued that because of these different rules, administrators, teachers, and school board members needed to acknowledge that a dual standard of discipline existed between students with and without disabilities. She further contended that for administrators to claim that all students were treated equally in terms of discipline and, thus, that there is no dual disciplinary standard would not be convincing to a court, because students with disabilities do, in fact, have special protections against certain types of disciplinary procedures.

In the IDEA Amendments of 1997, the subject of disciplining students with disabilities was finally addressed in federal legislation. In the process of drafting these amendments, Congress heard testimony regarding the difficulties school administrators and teachers faced when having to discipline students with disabilities. To ameliorate these problems, Congress added a section to the IDEA that specifically addresses discipline issues. In doing so, Congress sought to strike a balance between school officials' duty to ensure that schools are safe and conducive to learning, and their continuing obligation to ensure that students with disabilities receive a free appropriate public education.

The purpose of this chapter is to examine the discipline of students with disabilities. The chapter begins with a discussion of the right of schools to regulate the behavior of all students. An examination of the obligations of schools in disciplinary matters will be followed by a review of the use of disciplinary procedures specifically with students protected by the IDEA and Section 504. It is important to note that many of these issues may also be addressed by state law.

Discipline in the Schools

To operate efficiently and effectively, schools must have rules that regulate student conduct. If students violate reasonable school rules, they should be held accountable. Student accountability to rules usually implies that violators will be subject to disciplinary sanctions. Courts have recognized the importance of student management and have granted latitude to teachers to exercise this control through the use of discipline.

The courts' recognition of the importance of school authority over student behavior originates from the English common-law concept of in loco parentis (i.e., in place of the parent). According to this concept, parents acquiesce in the control over their children when they are placed in the charge of school personnel (Alexander & Alexander, 1984, 1992). The principal and the teacher have the authority not only to teach, but to guide, correct, and discipline the child to accomplish educational objectives. In loco parentis does not mean that the teacher stands fully in the place of parents in controlling their child during the school day, but that school officials, acting in concert with appropriate laws and regulations, have a duty to maintain an orderly and effective learning environment through reasonable and prudent control of students. Although the concept does not have the importance it once did, it is nevertheless an active legal concept that helps to define the school–student relationship. In relation to the use of disciplinary procedures, the doctrine implies that teachers have the duty to see that school order is maintained by requiring students to obey reasonable rules and commands and to respect the rights of others.

Due Process Protections

All students, with and without disabilities, have rights in disciplinary matters based on the due process clause of the Fifth and Fourteenth Amendments to the U.S. Constitution (see Appendix). In practice, however, the due process protections afforded students are limited by the state's interest in maintaining order and discipline in the schools. The courts, therefore, have had to strike a balance between student rights and the needs and interests of the schools.

The two general areas of due process rights afforded students are procedural and substantive. In terms of discipline, procedural due process involves the fairness of methods and procedures used by the schools; substantive due process refers to the protection of student rights from violation by school officials and involves the reasonableness of the disciplinary processes (Valente, 1994). School authorities, however, are vested with broad authority for establishing rules and procedures to maintain order and discipline. Unless a student can show that he or she was deprived of a liberty or property interest, there is no student right to due process. According to a federal district court in Tennessee, "teachers should be free to impose minor forms of classroom discipline, such as admonishing students, requiring special assignments, restricting activities, and denying certain privileges, without being subjected to strictures of due process" (*Dickens v. Johnson County Board of Education,* 1987, p. 157).

Procedural Due Process: The Right to Fair Procedures

The importance of education to a student's future requires that disciplinary actions that result in the student's being deprived of an education (e.g., suspension, expulsion) be subjected to the standards of due process. The purpose of due process procedures is to ensure that official decisions are made in a fair manner. Due process procedures in school settings do not require the full range of protections afforded to persons in formal court trials, such as representation by counsel and cross-examination of witnesses (Sorenson, 1993). The procedures do, however, include the basic protections such as notice, hearing, and impartiality.

Due process protections, which must be afforded to all students, were outlined by the U.S. Supreme Court in *Goss v. Lopez* (1975; hereafter *Goss*). The case involved whether nine high school students who had been suspended from school without a hearing had been denied due process of law under the Fourteenth Amendment. The Supreme Court ruled that the students had the right to at least minimal due process protections in cases of suspension. The high court stated that, "Having chosen to extend the right to an education . . . [the state] may not withdraw the right on grounds of misconduct absent fundamentally fair procedures to determine whether the misconduct had occurred" (p. 574). The Court, noting the broad authority of the schools to prescribe and enforce standards of behavior, held that states are constrained to recognize a student's entitlement to a public education as a property interest that is protected by the Fourteenth Amendment. Because education is protected, it may not be taken away without adhering to the due process procedures required by the amendment. The school had argued that a 10-day suspension was only a minor and temporary interference with the students' education; the high court disagreed, stating that a 10-day suspension was not de minimus (i.e., trivial or minor) but was a "serious event in the life of the suspended child" (p. 576). The imposition of the 10-day suspension, therefore, must include "the fundamental requisite of due process of law . . . the opportunity to be heard" (*Grannis v. Ordean*, 1914, p. 388).

The opportunity to be heard, when applied to the school setting, involves the right to notice and hearing. The right to notice and hearing requires that students are presented with the charges against them and have an opportunity to state their case (Yudof, Kirp, & Levin, 1992). The due process protections to be afforded to students will not shield them from properly imposed suspensions, but they will protect them from an unfair or mistaken exclusion. The Court in *Goss* recognized the necessity of order and discipline and the need for immediate and effective action, stating that suspension is a "necessary tool to maintain order . . . [and] a valuable educational device" (p. 572). Although the prospect of imposing cumbersome hearing requirements on every suspension case was a concern, the Court felt that schools should not have the power to act unilaterally, free of notice and hearing requirements. The Court held that when students are suspended for a period of 10 days or less, therefore, the school must give them oral or written notice of the charges, an explanation of the reasons for the suspension, and an opportunity to present their side of the story.

The requirement does not imply that there will be a delay between the time notice is given and the time of a student's hearing. The disciplinarian could informally discuss the misconduct with students immediately after the behavior occurs and give them an opportunity to present their version of the facts. In such situations, notice and hearing would precede the disciplinary action. If, however, the behavior posed a danger to students or teachers or a threat to disrupt the academic process, a student could be immediately removed and the notice and hearing could follow as soon as possible. In this event, notice of disciplinary hearings should follow within 24 hours and the hearing be held within 72 hours. The basic due process protections prescribed by the high court in *Goss* applied solely to short suspension of 10 days or less. Longer suspensions or expulsions, according to the Court, require more extensive and formal due process procedures. Figure 15.1 lists the due process protections that must be afforded to students in short- and long-term suspensions.

Substantive Due Process: The Right to Reasonableness

Courts have given schools great authority in promulgating rules governing student behavior. The power to establish rules and regulations, however, is not absolute, for these regulations may not violate constitutional principles. Generally, this requires that the regulation of student behavior be reasonable. To be reasonable, rules must have a rationale and a school-related purpose, and the school must employ reasonable means to achieve compliance with the rule. Schools may not prohibit or punish conduct that has no adverse effect on public education. Neither may they employ disciplinary penalties or restraints that are unnecessary or excessive for the achievement of proper school purposes (Hartwig & Reusch, 1994). Reasonableness essentially means that procedures must be rational and fair and not excessive or unsuitable for the educational setting.

Figure 15.1
Due Process Protections for All Students

Short-Term Suspension (may be a formal or informal meeting)

- Written or oral notice of charges
- Opportunity to respond to charges

Long-Term Suspension and Expulsion (must be a formal meeting)

- Written notice specifying charges
- Notice of evidence, witnesses, and substance of testimony
- Hearing (advance notice of time, place, and procedures)
- Right to confront witnesses and present their own witnesses
- A written or taped record of the proceedings
- Right of appeal

Brief in-school sanctions do not require a due process hearing

Dangerous students may be immediately removed

Rules must be sufficiently clear and specific to allow students to distinguish permissible from proscribed behavior. School rules that are too vague or general may result in the violation of students' rights. Appropriate school rules are specific and definitive; they provide students with information regarding behavioral expectations.

A federal district court in Indiana addressed the issue of the reasonableness of a school's use of discipline in *Cole v. Greenfield-Central Community Schools* (1986). The plaintiff, Christopher Bruce Cole, an elementary student, exhibited management and adjustment problems and was diagnosed as emotionally disturbed under Indiana state law. The school had attempted, and documented, numerous positive and negative procedures in efforts to control and modify Christopher's behavior. Included in the disciplinary procedures were timeout, response cost, and corporal punishment. The plaintiff sued the school, contending that in using these procedures the school had violated his civil rights.

The court recognized that although Christopher had a disability covered by the IDEA, he was not immune from the school's disciplinary procedures. The court held that the validity of the plaintiff's claim, therefore, rested on the "reasonableness" of the disciplinary procedures used by the school in attempting to manage Christopher's behavior. To determine reasonableness, the court analyzed four elements: (a) Did the teacher have the authority under state and local laws to discipline the student? (b) Was the rule violated within the scope of the educational function? (c) Was the rule violator the one who was disciplined? and (d) Was the discipline in proportion to the gravity of the offense? Finding that all four elements of reasonableness were satisfied, the court held for the school district.

Search and Seizure

Stating that students do not "shed their Constitutional rights . . . at the schoolhouse gate," the U.S. Supreme Court held that "school officials do not possess absolute authority over their students . . . students in school as well as out of school are 'persons' under the Constitution . . . possessed of fundamental [constitutional] rights" (*Tinker v. Des Moines Independent Community School,* 1969, p. 511). These rights include freedom of expression, bodily security, and privacy. If these rights are regulated, school officials must be able to justify the regulations.

Another category of student rights is the right to be free of unreasonable searches. Student searches have assumed increasing importance in recent years due to the introduction of drugs and other contraband into public schools and the increasing levels of violence. The Fourth Amendment to the Constitution prohibits unreasonable searches of persons. This amendment protects student privacy rights and must be respected by school officials. The frequency of student searches and locker searches by school officials without warrants has led to litigation decrying this practice as an invasion of students' constitutional rights. Application of the Fourth Amendment to the schools has also caused a great deal of disagreement among the lower courts.

Searches of Students and Student Property

New Jersey v. T.L.O.

Recognizing the division among the courts, the U.S. Supreme Court, in *New Jersey v. T.L.O.* (1985; hereafter *T.L.O.*), addressed warrantless searches in the schools. The case involved a teacher in a New Jersey high school who discovered two students smoking in the school lavatory. The students were taken to the principal's office. One student, called T.L.O. by the court, denied smoking. The vice principal took T.L.O.'s purse to examine it for cigarettes. In addition to the cigarettes, the purse also contained cigarette rolling papers, a pipe, a small amount of marijuana, a substantial amount of money, and two letters implicating her in marijuana dealing. The principal notified T.L.O.'s parents and the police. Delinquency charges were brought against T.L.O. in juvenile court. Based on this evidence, a juvenile court in New Jersey declared T.L.O. delinquent. T.L.O.'s lawyer defended her by asserting that the search was improper under the Fourth Amendment and that the evidence was inadmissible. The case went to the New Jersey Supreme Court, which reversed the decision and ordered the evidence obtained during the school's search suppressed on the grounds that the warrantless search was unconstitutional.

The case was eventually heard by the U.S. Supreme Court. The high court ruled that the Fourth Amendment applied to school personnel. However, the Court also noted the need to balance the need to conduct a search against a student's legitimate expectation of privacy. Noting that a student's privacy interest must be weighed against the need of administrators and teachers to maintain order and discipline in schools, the U.S. Supreme Court reversed the New Jersey Supreme Court, stating that the fourth amendment applies to searches conducted by school authorities, but the special needs of the school environment require assessment of such searches against a standard less exacting than probable cause . . . [C]ourts have . . . upheld warrantless searches by school authorities provided that they are supported by a reasonable suspicion that the search will uncover evidence of school disciplinary rules or a violation of the law. (p. 333)

The *T.L.O.* decision affirmed the constitutional protection of students against searches. The court, however, granted a great deal of latitude to schools by holding them to the standard of *reasonable suspicion,* a standard less exacting than the standard of *probable cause* (the standard required of police before a warrant can be obtained). Reasonable suspicion, nonetheless, does place some degree of restraint on school personnel. There must be reasonable grounds to lead school authorities to believe a search is necessary, and the search must be related to the original suspicion. Situations that justify a reasonable suspicion include information from student informers, police tips, anonymous tips and phone calls, and unusual student conduct. The intrusiveness of the search is also a relevant factor.

The high court stated that school personnel did not need a search warrant before searching a student or his or her property. The Court also developed a two-part test for determining whether a school search is valid. First, the search must be justified at inception; that is, the search must be based on reasonable suspicion that exists prior to the search. Second, the reason for conducting the search must be related to the violation of the law or the school rules. The scope of the search, therefore, must be reasonably related to the circumstances leading to the search. Finding that the school had satisfied both parts of the test, the high court overturned the New Jersey Supreme Court's ruling that evidence collected against T.L.O. during the school search was inadmissible.

Court decisions have also recognized situations in which searches and seizures in school environments do not give rise to Fourth Amendment concerns as long as the search meets the two-part T.L.O. test. These situations include (a) searches to which a student voluntarily consents; (b) searches of material left in view of the school authorities; (c) emergency searches to prevent injury or property damage; (d) searches by police authorities that are incidental to arrests; (e) searches of automobiles on school property; (f) searches of students' desks; (g) searches of students' personal belongings (e.g., book bags, briefcases, purses); and (h) searches of lost property (Dise, Iyer, & Noorman, 1996).

Cornfield v. Consolidated High School District No. 230

In a decision by the U.S. Court of Appeals for the Seventh Circuit, *Cornfield v. Consolidated High School District No. 230* (1993), a high school student classified as seriously emotionally disturbed (SED) brought a suit alleging that a strip search conducted by the teacher and dean was a violation of his constitutional rights. Suspecting that the student was hiding drugs, the dean phoned the student's mother, who refused to consent to a search of the boy. The teacher and dean then escorted the student to the boys' locker room, where they conducted a strip search and physically inspected his clothing. No drugs were found. The student sued the school district, the teacher, and the dean. The district court ruled in favor of the defendants.

On appeal, the circuit court affirmed the decision of the district court, stating that the strip search met the Fourth Amendment standard of reasonableness for searches conducted by school officials. The court noted that prior drug-related incidents involving the student, combined with the personal observations of the teacher and aide, created a reasonable suspicion that the student was concealing drugs. According to Maloney (1993), this ruling indicates that students, with or without disabilities, who are actively using or dealing drugs are subjected to the same search procedures. Because of the highly intrusive nature of these types of student searches, they should only be used as a last resort, should employ the least intrusive means, and should be based on reasonable suspicion (Miller & Ahrbecker, 1995). When strip searches are necessary, they should be conducted by persons of the same sex as the student, in a private area, and in the presence of school personnel also of the same sex as the student.

Thomas v. Carthage School District

Finally, the U.S. Court of Appeals for the Eighth Circuit, in *Thomas v. Carthage School District* (1996), ruled that the exclusionary rule does not apply in school settings. The exclusionary rule is a judicially created rule that bars the admission of unlawfully seized evidence in criminal trials. The case involved a student who was expelled from school after school officials found crack cocaine in his possession during a random search for weapons. A federal district court had awarded the student $10,000 in damages for wrongful expulsion because the school had violated the student's Fourth Amendment rights. The circuit court reversed the lower court, holding that the exclusionary rule does not apply to school disciplinary matters.

According to the court, school officials are not law enforcement agents, and students have reduced expectations of privacy at school. The court saw the societal costs of applying the exclusionary rule in schools as unacceptably high. The court's opinion gave the example of a school unable to expel a student who confessed to killing another student if the school failed to inform the student of his or her Miranda rights. The court also held that individual suspicion is not required to conduct minimally intrusive searches of students.

Locker Searches

In *O'Connor v. Ortega* (1987), the U.S. Supreme Court upheld searches of government-supplied offices, desks, and file cabinets based on reasonable suspicion. Courts, using this decision as precedent, have upheld school officials' searches of student lockers, whether targeted or random, based on reasonable suspicion (*In the Interest of Isaiah B.*, 1993, hereafter *Isaiah B.*; *People v. Overton,* 1969). Searches by school authorities may also extend to students' cars and locked briefcases (*State of Washington v. Slattery,* 1990), as well as objects, such as backpacks, in which contraband may be hidden (*People v. Dilworth,* 1996). The use of metal detectors to search students even though there is no suspicion or consent to a search is permitted (*Illinois v. Pruitt*, 1996). The use of random searches has also been determined to be constitutionally permissible (McKinney, 1994).

In *Isaiah B.*, the Wisconsin Supreme Court ruled that a student did not have reasonable expectations of privacy in his school locker. The court based its decision largely on the existence of a school policy regarding student lockers. According to the school policy,

> School lockers are the property of Milwaukee Public Schools. At no time does the Milwaukee School District relinquish its exclusive control of lockers provided for the convenience of students. Periodic general inspections of lockers may be conducted by school authorities for any reason at any time, without notice, without student consent, and without a search warrant. (*Isaiah B.*, p.; 639, n. 1)

Miller and Ahrbecker (1995) suggest that schools develop—unless they are prohibited from doing so by state law—policies regarding locker searches, such as the Milwaukee Public Schools' policy, that notify students and parents that there is no reasonable expectation of privacy in a student locker and that both random and targeted searches of the locker may be conducted without student or parental consent. Bjorklun (1994) likewise concludes that random locker searches may be conducted without individualized suspicion. Figure 15.2 lists procedural suggestions for conducting searches of students and their property.

Figure 15.2
Legally Sound Searches

1. Draft a public policy regarding searches and seizures:
   - Describe circumstances that will lead to searches of property.
   - State that lockers are the property of the school and not students'.
   - Describe circumstances that will lead to student searches.
   - Specify when police will be notified regarding searches.
   - Notify public regarding district policy (e.g., parent manual).
2. Officials must have reasonable suspicion to search a student.
3. The scope of the search must be reasonable in relation to the age of the student and the circumstances.
4. Require that strip searches be conducted only when school officials possess reliable information and as a last resort.
5. Strip searches should be conducted by at least two officials of the same gender as the student.
6. Random searches should only be conducted when school officials possess reliable information.
7. Document student searches and seizures.

The Dual Disciplinary Standard

Administrators and teachers face a different set of rules and limitations in using disciplinary procedures with students with disabilities who are protected by the IDEA or Section 504 (Maloney, 1994; Tucker et al., 1993). This dual standard only exists, however, when disciplinary procedures may result in a change of placement. The determination of what constitutes a change of placement is, therefore, critical under both the IDEA and Section 504. Under the IDEA, changes of placement cannot be made without following the procedural requirements of the law. A procedural requirement that often comes into play in disciplinary changes of placement is the stay-put provision of the IDEA.

The Stay-Put Provision

When parents disagree with a change in placement proposed by a school district, the IDEA's stay-put provision prohibits the district from unilaterally changing placement. This provision states that "during the pendency of any proceedings . . . unless the [school] and the parents . . . otherwise agree, the child shall remain in the then current placement of such child" (IDEA, 20 U.S.C. § 1415(e)(3)). The purpose of the stay-put provision is to continue students in their current placement (i.e., their placement before the dispute arose) until the dispute is resolved. The stay-put provision effectively operates to limit the actions of the school district (Tucker et al., 1993). The court in *Zvi D. v. Ambach* (1982) stated that the stay-put procedures operated as an automatic preliminary injunction because a request for a hearing automatically requires that schools maintain a student's placement. It is only permissible to move a student during the pendency of a hearing when the parents and school agree on an interim change of placement.

The IDEA Amendments of 1997 significantly altered the stay-put rule. First, the amendments allow school officials to unilaterally change the placement of students with disabilities who bring weapons to school or a school function or who knowingly possess, use, or sell illegal drugs in a school building. Officials may move such a student to an interim alternative educational setting (IAES) for no more than 45 school days. If a parent objects to this placement change and requests a due process hearing, the stay-put rule would normally function to keep a student in the previous placement during the hearing. With the new language in 1997, the stay-put placement now becomes the IAES; that is, a student will remain in that setting during the pendency of the hearing. If a student is placed in an IAES and school personnel propose to change the student's placement or do not return the student to the original placement at the end of the 45-day period, however, the student must be returned to the placement prior to the interim setting during the pendency of any future proceeding.

If school personnel maintain that a student with disabilities is dangerous to other students if he or she remains in the current placement, the school district may request an expedited hearing to challenge the continued placement. The hearing officer may change a student's placement to an interim alternative setting for 45 school days if school officials convince the hearing officer that the student, in the current placement, is very likely to injure him- or herself or others. In making this decision, the hearing officer will consider whether the school has made reasonable efforts to minimize the risk of harm in the student's current placement and if the current placement enables the student to continue to participate in the general education curriculum.

Section 504, unlike the IDEA, does not contain any references to a stay-put provision. The Office of Civil Rights (OCR) has held, however, that the law contains an implicit stay-put provision and that schools should not change a student's placement during the pendency of a hearing (Zirkel, 1995).

Long-Term Suspension and Expulsion

Long-term suspension and expulsion qualify as a change of placement. A federal district court in Connecticut held that expulsion was a unilateral change of placement that was inconsistent with the IDEA (*Stuart v. Nappi,* 1978). Because expelling a student with disabilities would result in a placement change, the procedural safeguards of the IDEA would automatically be triggered. The U.S. Courts of Appeals for the Fourth Circuit, in *Prince William County School Board v. Malone* (1985); for the Fifth Circuit, in *S-1 v. Turlington* (1981); for the Sixth Circuit, in *Kaelin v. Grubbs* (1982); and for the Ninth Circuit in, *Doe v. Maher* (1986), reached similar conclusions. Not all courts, however, have agreed with this interpretation. The U.S. Court of Appeals for the Eleventh Circuit, in *Victoria L. v. District School Board* (1984), held that a school district could—unilaterally, if necessary—transfer a dangerous student to a more restrictive setting. The question was settled in 1988, when the U.S. Supreme Court issued a ruling in *Honig v. Doe.*

Honig v. Doe

Honig v. Doe (1988; hereafter *Honig*) involved the proposed expulsion of two students with emotional disabilities from the San Francisco public school system. Both students, following separate behavior incidents, had been suspended from school and recommended for expulsion. In accordance with California law, the suspensions were continued indefinitely while the expulsion proceedings were being held. Attorneys for the students filed a joint lawsuit in federal district court. The district court issued an injunction that prevented the school district from suspending any student with disabilities for misbehavior causally related to the student's disability. The school district appealed. The U.S. Court of Appeals for the Ninth Circuit, in *Doe v. Maher* (1986), held that expulsion is a change in placement, triggering the procedural safeguards of the law. The California superintendent of public instruction, Bill Honig, filed a petition of certiorari with the U.S. Supreme Court. One of the issues raised on appeal concerned the stay-put provision. Honig contended that the circuit court's interpretation of the rule—that no student with a disability could be excluded from school during the pendency of the administrative review regardless of the danger presented by the student—was untenable. A literal reading of this provision, according to Honig, would require schools to return potentially violent and dangerous students to the classroom, a situation Congress could not have intended.

Ruling in *Honig*

On January 20, 1988, the U.S. Supreme Court issued a ruling in the case renamed *Honig v. Doe*. Justice Brennan, writing for the majority, rejected Honig's argument that Congress did not intend to deny schools the authority to remove dangerous and disruptive students from the school environment. Stating that Congress had intended to strip schools of their unilateral authority to exclude students with disabilities from school, the high court declined to read a dangerousness exception into the law. The Court ruled that during the pendency of any review meetings, the student must remain in the then-current placement unless school officials and parents agree otherwise. Expulsion, the Court held, constituted a change in placement.

The Court noted that this decision regarding the stay-put provision did not leave educators "hamstrung." While the ruling would not allow a school to change a student's placement during proceedings, it did not preclude the use of a school's normal disciplinary procedures for dealing with students with disabilities. Such normal procedures included timeouts, the use of study carrels, detention, restriction of privileges, and suspension for up to 10 days. These procedures would allow the prompt removal of dangerous students. During the 10-day period, school officials could initiate an individualized education program (IEP) meeting and "seek to persuade the child's parents to agree to an interim placement" (*Honig*, p. 605). If a student was truly "dangerous" and the parents refused to agree to a change, school officials, according to the high court, could immediately seek the aid of the courts. When seeking the aid of the courts, the burden of proof would rest upon the school to demonstrate that going through the IDEA's procedural mechanisms (i.e., due process hearing) would be futile and that in the current placement the student was "substantially likely" to present a danger to others. The stay-put provision, therefore, does not preempt the authority of the courts from granting an injunction to temporarily remove the student from the school. In effect, the court did read a dangerousness exemption into the stay-put rule; however, this determination could only be made by a judge and not by school officials.

Unanswered Questions

Although the *Honig* decision ruled on some important issues, it also left many questions unanswered (Bartlett, 1989; Huefner, 1991; Sorenson, 1993; Tucker & Goldstein, 1992; Yell, 1989). Some of the unresolved issues involve changes in placement, the causal connection between the misbehavior and the disability (i.e., the manifestation determination), the provision of educational services during suspension, and appropriate forms of discipline. Post-*Honig* rulings have helped to clarify these issues. Also, many of these questions were answered in the IDEA Amendments of 1997. Figure 15.3 lists differences in the disciplinary standards used for students with disabilities in accordance with *Honig,* post-*Honig* rulings, and the IDEA amendments.

Figure 15.3
Dual Disciplinary Standard

- Suspensions over 10 days are not allowed.
- Long-term suspension or expulsion for disability-related misbehavior is not allowed.
- Educational services must continue in the event of proper long-term suspension or expulsion.
- Proper forum for disciplinary decisions is the IEP team (decisions must not be made unilaterally).

Change in Placement

The case law clearly indicates that schools may not unilaterally change the placement of a student with disabilities. If the school proposes a change in placement, and the proposal is contested by the student's parents, the stay-put provision comes into play and the student cannot be removed from the then-current educational placement. The only exception is when a student brings a weapon to school or uses, possesses, or sells illegal drugs. In such situations, school officials may immediately and unilaterally move a student to an interim alternative educational setting.

The determination of what constitutes a change of placement is important to understanding the limits of discipline under the IDEA and Section 504 (Tucker & Goldstein, 1992). Minor changes in the student's educational program that do not involve a change in the general nature of the program do not constitute a change in placement. For example, in *Concerned Parents and Citizens for Continuing Education at Malcolm X v. The New York City Board of Education* (1980) a circuit court held that a change in the location of the program, in and of itself, did not constitute a change of placement.

A change in the educational program that substantially or significantly affects the delivery of education to a student constitutes a change in placement and is not permissible. *Honig* established that any suspension of more than 10 days constitutes a change. The 10-day rule became the federal norm with the IDEA Amendments of 1997. Indefinite suspensions or expulsions in excess of 10 days, therefore, constitute a change in placement. In a 1988 memorandum, OCR issued a policy statement indicating that a series of suspensions cumulatively totaling more than 10 days would constitute a change of placement if the result was a pattern of exclusions that effectively changed a student's placement. The Office of Special Education Programs (OSEP) of the U.S. Department of Education issued a statement regarding short-term suspensions that adopted the OCR interpretation of short-term suspensions and change of placement (OSEP Memorandum 95-16, 1995). A 1989 OCR memorandum clarified the factors to consider in determining whether a series of suspensions would constitute a pattern of exclusions; these factors include the length of each suspension, the proximity of the suspensions to each other, and the total amount of time the student is excluded from school.

The Legal Status of Disciplinary Procedures

In *Honig,* the U.S. Supreme Court ruled that typical disciplinary procedures—those that are often used for establishing school discipline, such as restriction of privileges, detention, and removal of students to study carrels—may be used with students with disabilities. Such disciplinary procedures do not change placement and are generally not restricted by the courts. A significant restriction exists, however, against certain types of discipline that may result in a unilateral change in placement. To clarify which disciplinary practices are legal and which are not, disciplinary procedures may be placed into one of three categories: permitted, controlled, and prohibited (Yell, Cline, & Bradley, 1995; Yell & Peterson, 1995). See Table 15.1 for a list of interventions the courts have addressed.

Permitted Procedures

Permitted disciplinary procedures include those practices that are part of a school district's disciplinary plan and that are commonly used with all students. These procedures are unobtrusive and do not result in a change of placement or the denial of

Table 15.1
Legal Status of Disciplinary Procedures

Permitted	Controlled	Prohibited
Contingent observation	Bus suspension (if student isn't in school it counts as part of 10 days)	Corporal punishment
Detention	Change of placement (adhere to IDEA safeguards)	Expulsion (unless no relationship exists between misconduct and disability)
Emergency procedures	In-school suspension	Long-term suspension (unless no relationship exists between misconduct and disability)
Exclusionary timeout	Out-of-school suspension	
Reprimands	Seclusion/Isolation timeout	
Response cost		
Restricting privileges		
Temporary delay of meals		
Warnings		

the right to a free appropriate public education (FAPE). Such procedures include verbal reprimands, warnings, contingent observation (a form of timeout where the student is briefly removed to a location where he or she can observe but not participate in an activity), exclusionary timeout, response cost (the removal of points or privileges when a student misbehaves), detention, and the temporary delay or withdrawal of goods, services, or activities (e.g., recess, lunch). As long as these procedures do not interfere significantly with the student's IEP goals and are not applied in a discriminatory manner, they are permitted. In general, if the disciplining of a student with disabilities does not result in a change of placement, the methods of discipline available to schools are the same for all students (Guernsey & Klare, 1993). In the case of emergency situations, procedures such as physical restraint or immediate suspension are permissible.

There is no legal restriction on involving the police if a law has been violated (Maloney, 1994). The IDEA Amendments of 1997 specifically addressed the issue of police involvement and students with disabilities. The law clarified that nothing prohibits school officials from reporting a crime by students with disabilities to the police. Moreover, law enforcement officials and judicial authorities may exercise their responsibilities with regard to such reports. Schools that report crimes should ensure that all copies of special education and disciplinary records are forwarded to the appropriate authorities.

School officials may unilaterally use emergency suspensions from school. In such situations, a student may be removed immediately from the school environment. Emergency suspensions may not exceed 10 school days. Officials may also move a student to an interim alternative educational setting for a period not to exceed 10 days.

Controlled Procedures

Controlled procedures are those interventions that the courts have held to be permissible as long as they are used appropriately. The difficulty with these practices is that if they are used in an inappropriate manner, they can result in interference with IEP goals or objectives or in a unilateral change in placement. Controlled procedures include disciplinary techniques such as seclusion/isolation timeout, in-school suspension, and out-of-school suspension.

Seclusion/Isolation Timeout

Timeout is a disciplinary procedure frequently used by teachers of students with disabilities. Timeout generally involves placing a student in a less reinforcing environment for a period of time following inappropriate behavior. A type of timeout that should be classified as a controlled procedure is seclusion/isolation timeout (Yell, 1994). In this type of timeout the student, contingent on misbehavior, is required to leave the classroom and enter a separate timeout room for a brief duration of time. Two federal court cases considered the legality of seclusion/isolation timeout.

In *Dickens v. Johnson County Board of Education* (1987), a federal district court ruled that the use of timeout with the plaintiff, Ronnie Dickens, was only a de minimus (trivial or minor) interference with the student's education. The use of timeout did not, therefore, violate the plaintiff's right to an education. While extremely harsh and abusive use of timeout may violate a student's rights, the court found that the legitimate and reasonable use of timeout was a particularly appropriate disciplinary procedure to use with students with disabilities because it would not deprive them of their right to an education.

Hayes v. Unified School District No. 377 (1987) involved the use of seclusion/isolation timeout with two students with behavioral disorders. The teacher used a system of written warnings to allow the students time to alter their behavior to escape timeout. If the students received three warnings, they were placed in a timeout room. The court ruled that the teacher had used timeout to ensure the safety of others, protect the educational environment from disruptive behavior, and teach the students more appropriate behavior. According to the court, the appropriate use of seclusion/isolation timeout is not prohibited by the IDEA.

OCR affirmed the use of timeout following an investigation of a complaint against a school district's use of this procedure (*Marion County (FL) School District*, 1993). The investigation revealed that the school district properly followed state and local educational policies, established a disciplinary policy that included timeout procedures for students with and without disabilities, incorporated behavior management plans into students' IEPs that included the use of timeout, and kept records on the use of timeout. Furthermore, parents were informed about the possible use of timeout and agreed to its use. Concluding that the school district was not in violation of Section 504 or the Americans with Disabilities Act, OCR stated that timeout prevented the necessity of using more restrictive measures to control behaviors. When timeout escalates to the level of punishment that infringes on a student's personal safety rights and appropriate education, however, it may be a violation of Section 504 or the IDEA (Cline, 1994). In a 1991 OCR ruling, for example, the excessive and prolonged use of timeout was ruled a violation of Section 504 (*McCracken County School District*, 1991).

In-School Suspension

In-school suspension (ISS) programs require the suspended student to serve the suspension period in the school, usually in a classroom isolated from schoolmates. During ISS, the student works on appropriate educational material provided by the teacher. Several advantages of using ISS are that (a) it avoids the possibility of the suspended student roaming the community unsupervised; (b) the student being disciplined is segregated from the general school population; and (c) the student continues to receive an education during the suspension period (Yell, 1990). In *Hayes v. Unified School District No. 377* (1987), a school district's use of ISS was challenged. The plaintiffs, who had not consented to its use, argued that ISS, which sometimes lasted as long as 5 days, constituted an illegal change of placement and a deprivation of due process. The court noted that the school had clearly specified the behaviors that would lead to ISS, thereby providing the students with adequate notice to protect themselves from being placed in ISS. The court also ruled that as long as the school continued to provide an appropriate education, ISS for 5 days did not constitute an illegal change of placement.

In a ruling regarding a school district's use of ISS, OCR determined that ISS was being used appropriately (*Chester County (TN) School District*, 1990). The complainant alleged that the district had improperly placed special education students in ISS for periods in excess of 10 days and had failed to provide adequate notice of these disciplinary actions to parents. OCR determined that the district had established formal procedures regarding their disciplinary policies (including the use of ISS), provided parents with written explanations of these procedures, and adequately informed notified parents prior to the use of ISS. OCR also stated that the ISS program, when used for 10 days or more (in this case 28 days), did not constitute a change in placement because the school district provided a program that was "comparable, in nature and quality, to the educational services regularly provided to special education students" (p. 301). The ISS instructor was a certified special education teacher, usually the number of students in ISS was less than six, and lesson plans were sent daily or weekly from the student's regular and special education teachers. OCR confirmed that the goals and objectives on the students' IEPs were followed when students were in ISS. Figure 15.4 lists the necessary components of a legally sound ISS program.

Despite the fact that ISS programs remove students with disabilities from their classrooms, the courts have not considered them either long-term suspensions, expulsions, or changes of placement as long as the programs are comparable to the educational program regularly offer to students (Gorn, 1996). Schools, however, must not use ISS as a de facto long-term suspension or expulsion. In such cases, ISS may be viewed as an illegal change of placement.

Out-of-School Suspension

Out-of-school suspension generally refers to a short-term exclusion from school for a specified period of time, accompanied by a cessation of educational services. Numerous cases have ruled on the use of out-of-school suspension with students with disabilities (*Doe v. Koger,* 1979; *Doe v. Maher,* 1986; *Honig v. Doe,* 1988; *Kaelin v. Grubbs,* 1982; *S-1 v. Turlington,* 1981; *Stuart v. Nappi,* 1978; *Victoria*

Figure 15.4
Legally Sound In-School Suspension Policies

- Have written policy informing students and parents when violation of rules may result in student being placed in ISS.
- Provide a warning to students when their behavior may lead to ISS.
- Inform parents when student is placed in ISS.
- Supervise ISS with paraprofessional or a teacher.
- Continue to provide an appropriate education (e.g., have student's teacher prepare lesson plans, provide materials).
- Document in-school suspension.

L. v. District School Board, 1984). According to the courts, expulsion and indefinite out-of-school suspensions are changes in placement and cannot be made unilaterally even in cases where students present a danger to themselves or others. Courts have stated, however, that schools can use short-term suspensions of up to 10 days. Suspension from transportation to school, unless alternative means of transportation are available, should be treated as part of the 10 days (*Mobile County (AL) School District,* 1991). Sorenson (1993) suggests that schools adopt a 10-day suspension policy. The IDEA Amendments of 1997 specifically allow school officials to suspend students with disabilities for up to 10 school days. Suspensions for longer than 10 days constitute a change of placement under the IDEA, and if a student's parents do not agree to a change in placement, the IDEA procedural safeguards must be followed.

Timeout, in-school suspension, and out-of-school suspension are permitted if used appropriately. Basic due process rights, such as notice and hearing, must be given to students prior to the use of suspension. It is important in using such procedures that schools not abuse or overuse them, as these could be interpreted as unilateral changes of placement or discriminatory by the courts.

Prohibited Procedures

Disciplinary procedures that result in a unilateral change in placement are prohibited. Thus, expulsions (i.e., the exclusion from school for an indefinite period of time) and long-term suspensions are illegal if made without following the IDEA's procedural safeguards. In many states, corporal punishment is illegal and, therefore, a prohibited procedure.

Long-Term Suspension and Expulsion

If the IEP team determines that a student's misbehavior and his or her disability are not related, long-term suspensions and expulsions are legal. However, even when no relationship is found and an expulsion is made in accordance with procedural rules, there cannot be a complete cessation of educational services. If the IEP team determines that the misbehavior and the disability are related, long-term suspensions and expulsions are not legal.

Attempts to bypass the suspension and expulsion rules have not been looked upon favorably by the courts or administrative agencies. OCR has stated that a series of suspensions cumulatively totaling more than 10 days constitutes a change of placement if the results create a pattern of exclusion (OCR Memorandum, 1988). Serial and indefinite suspensions, therefore, are prohibited. A series of five suspensions totaling 22 days over a school year was found to be a pattern of exclusions that created a significant change of placement for a student with disabilities (*Cobb County (GA) School District,* 1993). In *Big Beaver Falls Area School District v. Jackson* (1993), a Pennsylvania court ruled that a school district, in violation of the IDEA and state law, had effectively suspended a student by continually assigning her to ISS. Rather than serve the ISS, the student was allowed to leave school, which she usually did.

According to the court, the school continually assigned the ISS knowing that the student would leave school; therefore, the action amounted to a de facto expulsion in violation of the IDEA.

Corporal Punishment

One of the most controversial disciplinary procedures is corporal punishment. Courts have heard many challenges to the use of this type of disciplinary action in schools. In 1977 the U.S. Supreme Court, in *Ingraham v. Wright,* held that corporal punishment in public schools was a routine disciplinary procedure not proscribed by constitutional law. The U.S. Court of Appeals for the Fourth Circuit, in *Hall v. Tawney* (1980), stated that brutal, demeaning, or harmful corporal punishment would be a violation of a student's substantive due process rights. The court applied the standard of reasonableness in holding that corporal punishment that is reasonable is legitimate, but if is not reasonable (e.g., excessive) it is illegal.

Many states have made the use of corporal punishment illegal. Furthermore, in states where corporal punishment is not prohibited, many local school districts proscribe its use. In many schools throughout the country, therefore, corporal punishment is illegal. According to Weber (1992), even in states where corporal punishment is legal, its use might be a violation of Section 504 and the IDEA.

The Manifestation Determination

Numerous court cases regarding the discipline of students with disabilities have stressed the importance of having a group of knowledgeable persons conduct a manifestation determination or relationship test prior to disciplining a student by using long-term suspension (i.e., over 10 days) or expulsion. In fact, the importance of the manifestation determination has been universally accepted as a requirement in such instances (Sorenson, 1993). This requirement became federal law with the IDEA Amendments of 1997. If school officials contemplate disciplinary actions against a student in special education as a result of the student's possessing a weapon or using illegal drugs, or if they plan to change a student's placement, the amendments require that no later than 10 school days after the action that amounts to a change in placement (e.g., suspension in excess of 10 school days), the IEP team must conduct the manifestation determination. The manifestation determination is a determination, by the IEP team and other qualified persons, of whether a student's misbehavior is caused by, or is related to, the student's disability (Dagley, McGuire, & Evans, 1994; OSEP Memorandum 95-16, 1995; Senate Report, 1997). The manifestation hearing also involves an inquiry into the appropriateness of a student's IEP (Dagley et al., 1994; Hartwig & Reusch, 1994; Senate Report, 1997). If the determination is made either that the disability is related to the misbehavior or that the IEP is inappropriate, the student cannot be suspended for more than 10 days or expelled. The requirements regarding the manifestation determination also apply to students protected strictly by Section 504 (Dagley et al., 1994).

Forum for Conducting the Test

The proper forum for determining the relationship between misconduct and behavior is a multidisciplinary team composed of persons knowledgeable about a student and his or her disability. This decision may not be made by administrators or school officials who lack the necessary expertise to make special education placement decisions (*S-1 v. Turlington*, 1981). The IDEA Amendments of 1997 require that the team that makes this decision be the IEP team and other qualified personnel. Courts have consistently held that these decisions may not be made using normal school procedures for disciplining students without disabilities (Guernsey & Klare, 1993); that is, school boards, members of school boards, administrators acting unilaterally, or any one school representative may not make the manifestation determination (OSEP Memorandum 95-16, 1995).

If the team determines that a relationship between behavior and disability exists or that a student's IEP is not appropriate, the student may not be expelled, although school officials will still be able to initiate change-of-placement procedures. The standard specifies that if a relationship exists between a student's misbehavior and the school's failure to provide or properly implement the IEP or placement, the IEP team must conclude that the misbehavior was a manifestation of the student's disability (Senate Report, 1997). If, however, the IEP team determines that the student's misbehavior was not a manifestation of the disability and that the IEP was appropriate, the disciplinary procedures that would be applicable to students without disabilities may be used with a student who has a disability. A number of federal court decisions have reached similar conclusions (*Doe v. Koger,* 1979; *Doe v. Maher,* 1986; *Honig v. Doe,* 1988; *Kaelin v. Grubbs,* 1982; *Stuart v. Nappi,* 1978). The reasoning behind the manifestation determination is that students should not be denied special education services because of misbehavior that could be anticipated as a result of their disabilities (Dagley et al., 1994; Tucker et al., 1993).

Conducting the Manifestation Determination

Although numerous cases have referred to the manifestation determination, the courts have offered little guidance to schools regarding standards for making this determination. As Dagley, McGuire, and Evans (1994) remark, "a careful reading of court cases implicating the relationship test creates the suspicion that no one really knows how to conduct the relationship test" (p. 326). In the IDEA Amendments of 1997, Congress provided guidance to IEP teams in conducting manifestation determinations. In conducting the test, the IEP team shall consider the behavior subject to the disciplinary action and relevant information, including evaluation and diagnostic results and the student's IEP and placement.

Evaluation and Diagnostic Results

The courts and Congress have indicated that in making the manifestation determination, decisions must be based on an individualized inquiry informed by up-to-date evaluation data. Team members responsible for collected data should be qualified and knowledgeable regarding the student, the misbehavior, and the disability. Moreover, the data used to inform the decision-making process should be recent and collected from a variety of sources. Data collection procedures should include review of records of past behavioral incidences, interviews, direct observation, behavior rating scales, and standardized instruments. Finally, the team must consider any other relevant information supplied by the parents of the student.

The Student's IEP and Placement

In conducting the manifestation determination, the team should first look to the appropriateness and implementation of a student's IEP and the student's placement. Furthermore, the supplementary aids and services and any behavior strategies that were provided in the IEP must have been implemented as written. If the IEP is inappropriate or is not being implemented as written, the determination is essentially over because such problems indicate the presence of a causal relationship between the misbehavior and the disability.

Appropriate Considerations

The IEP team should attempt to answer two questions in assessing the relationship between misconduct and disability. First, did the student's disability impair the student's ability to understand the impact and consequences of the behavior subject to disciplinary action; that is, does the student understand the consequences of his or her behavior, and is he or she able to adjust accordingly when the consequences are negative, by choosing not to perform the behavior? If the team determines that a student did understand the consequences of the misbehavior and yet chose to misbehave, it is strongly indicative of no relationship between disability and misconduct.

Second, did the student's disability impair the student's ability to control the behavior subject to disciplinary action; that is, was the misbehavior solely an impulsive act, or did it require some amount of forethought or planning? Foresight or planning is also indicative of no relationship between the disability and the misconduct.

Inappropriate Considerations

Courts have clearly indicated what will not constitute proper lines of inquiry in the manifestation determination. First, the determination must be independent of a student's disability classification. The *Turlington* court noted that a causal relationship between misconduct and behavior can occur in any disability area, not just in students with behavioral disabilities; that is, the test should be conducted when suspending or expelling any student protected by the IDEA or Section 504, regardless of the student's disability classification. Second, the manifestation determination is not an inquiry into whether a student knew the difference between right and wrong. According to the Fifth Circuit court in *Turlington*, determining whether students are capable of understanding rules or regulations or right from wrong is not tantamount to determining that the student's misconduct was or was not a manifestation of the disability.

The Nature of the Relationship

An important, and unresolved, issue in conducting the manifestation determination is the nature of the relationship between the misbehavior and the disability; that is, must the relationship be direct or causal, which is a very rigorous standard, or is it sufficient that the relationship be less rigorous? Unfortunately, the courts do not agree on the degree of relationship. OCR has said that misconduct is causally related to a disability when the disability significantly impairs a student's behavioral controls (OCR Memorandum, 1988). The key determination to be made, according to Hartwig, Robertshaw, and Reusch (1991), is not whether there is a correlation between the disability and misbehavior but whether there is a cause-and-effect relationship. For example, the U.S. Court of Appeals for the Ninth Circuit, in *Doe v. Maher* (1986), stated that

> [a] handicapped child's conduct is covered by [the relationship between behavior and disability] only if the handicap significantly impairs the child's behavioral controls . . . it does not embrace conduct that bears only an attenuated relationship to the child's handicap. . . . An example . . . would be a case where a child's physical handicap results in loss of self-esteem, and the child consciously misbehaves in order to get attention. (p. 1480)

The U.S. Court of Appeals for the Fourth Circuit, in *Prince William County School Board v. Malone* (1985), however, affirmed a district court's decision that prohibited a school's expulsion of a student with learning disabilities. The school board had expelled the student for serving as a go-between in a drug transaction. The court determined that as a result of his learning disability the student had low self-esteem, which in turn resulted in his being a "ready stooge" in order to gain peer approval. The Fourth Circuit, therefore, adopted a standard for determining the relationship that is less exacting than that of the Ninth Circuit.

The Burden of Proof

If school personnel make a decision that there is no relationship between the behavior and the disability and expel a student, the burden of proof will be placed on the school district to prove that there is no relationship. Hartog-Rapp (1985) argues that if the school district is questioned regarding a decision of expulsion, it must prove that there is no causal relationship. Sorenson (1993) contends, however, that it is probable that if an appropriate group of knowledgeable persons follows appropriate procedures in conducting the manifestation determination, their decision will be upheld in the appeals process. Recent rulings by OCR (*Hopewell (VA) Public Schools,* 1994) and the Texas Department of Education (*Beaumont Independent School District,* 1994), which upheld school districts' expulsion of students with disabilities for bringing weapons to school when the IEP teams found no relationship between the behavior and disability, support this contention. In conducting the determination, it is important that teams keep thorough documentation

Figure 15.5
Manifestation Determination

- Is the IEP appropriate?
- Is the IEP being implemented as written?
- Did the disability prevent the student from understanding the impact and consequences of behavior?
- Did the disability prevent the student from controlling the behavior?

of the process. Figure 15.5 lists the questions that should be addressed in the manifestation determination.

Continuing Educational Services

Are schools required to continue educational services during long-term suspension or expulsion? The answer to this question was once the subject of controversy and disagreements among the courts. The *Honig* ruling did not address the provision of educational services during suspension or expulsion, although the *Turlington* court did in holding that

> expulsion is still a proper disciplinary tool under the [IDEA] and Section 504 when proper procedures are utilized and under proper circumstances. We cannot, however, authorize the complete cessation of educational services during an expulsion period. (p. 348)

The U.S. Court of Appeals for the Sixth Circuit, in *Kaelin v. Grubbs* (1982), followed the *Turlington* rule and did not allow the termination of educational services during suspension or expulsion. The prohibition against termination governs courts in the Fifth, Six, and Eleventh Circuits.* In *Doe v. Maher* (1986), however, the Ninth Circuit court stated that if a student is suspended and no causal relationship exists between the misbehavior and disability, the school may terminate educational services.

OSEP, which interprets the IDEA, and OCR, which interprets Section 504, have different positions on this issue. According to OSEP, if a student with disabilities is properly suspended in excess of 10 days or expelled, regardless of the causal relationship, alternative educational services must be provided (OSEP Memorandum 95-16, 1995). OCR has determined that Section 504 is not violated when a school district terminates educational services to a properly suspended or expelled student with disabilities when there is no causal relationship (OCR Memorandum, 1988). Because of the *Turlington* ruling, this OCR policy does not apply to the Fifth and Eleventh Circuits.

---

*The *Turlington* ruling was issued before the then Fifth Circuit—which consisted of Alabama, Florida, Georgia, Louisiana, Mississippi, and Texas—was split into two circuits, the Fifth and the Eleventh. The decision, therefore, is controlling in both circuits.

Virginia Department of Education v. Riley

The U.S. Court of Appeals for the Fourth Circuit, in *Virginia Department of Education v. Riley* (1996), ruled that the U.S. Department of Education (DOE) could not withhold federal funding from the Virginia Department of Education because the state refused to provide educational services to students with disabilities who were properly suspended or expelled. The DOE decided to withhold Virginia's funds under Part B of the IDEA, which amounted to approximately $60 million, until the state complied with the department's policy of continuing educational services. Virginia sued to protect the federal funding. The case was eventually appealed to the Fourth Circuit court, which, in a 2–1 ruling, upheld the position of the DOE. The case was then reheard by the full Fourth Circuit court. In an 11–2 ruling, the appeals court overturned the previous decision.

The court ruled that the U.S. DOE had no authority to condition Virginia's IDEA funding on following their disciplinary guidelines. In dicta, the court noted that when a student with disabilities was properly expelled, the district could cease providing all education services. The court held that the IDEA contained no language that conditioned a state's receipt of federal funds on the continued provision of educational services when students were expelled for misconduct unrelated to their disability. Furthermore, the court stated that the DOE's decision to withhold the IDEA funds amounted to impermissible coercion if not forbidden regulation.

The decision in *Virginia Department of Education v. Riley* indicated that if there is no relationship between misconduct and a student's disability, the student may be disciplined like any other student. Therefore, when no relationship exists between the disability and misconduct, and a student is suspended in excess of 10 days or expelled, school districts seemingly will not be required to continue educational services. This result was essentially nullified in the IDEA Amendments of 1997.

The IDEA Amendments of 1997 and Educational Services

The 1997 IDEA amendments put an end to this controversial and vexatious issue by clearly requiring that educational services be continued to properly suspended or expelled students in special education. To cease providing educational services would amount to a denial of a FAPE.

Educational Services and Short-Term Suspensions

Educational services may be discontinued, however, when short-term suspensions of 10 days or less are used (OSEP Memorandum 95-16, 1995). A federal district court, in *Eric J. v. Huntsville City Board of Education* (1995), ruled that a school district was not required to continue services to a student in special education who was suspended on a short-term basis. This case was especially significant because it was the first federal case that addressed school districts' responsibilities when suspending students in special education for 10 days or less. The court held that in such situations, school districts may cease providing educational services.

Students with Disabilities Who Present a Danger

The *Honig* decision left no doubt that schools cannot unilaterally act to expel students with disabilities, regardless of the degree of danger presented. When students with disabilities present a substantial risk of danger to themselves or others, however, schools can take actions to maintain safety and order.

Emergency Actions

School officials may take a number of actions to maintain a safe school environment. If a student with disabilities presents a risk of danger to others, school officials can legally use an emergency suspension for up to 10 days without having to make a manifestation determination. Moreover, this action can be taken immediately and unilaterally. Furthermore, officials can change a student's placement to an interim alternative educational setting for up to 10 days. During this period the IEP team may be convened to make the manifestation determination or to rewrite the IEP. Additionally, physical restraint is permitted in an emergency situation to prevent students from injuring themselves or others.

Change of Placement

The IEP team, which includes the parents, may change a student's placement to a more restrictive setting. The only placement change that must be avoided is one that is made unilaterally. If parents agree to a change (e.g., a more restrictive setting such as a homebound placement with a continuation of appropriate educational services, or a special school placement), this would be in keeping with the IDEA's procedural safeguards.

Honig Injunctions

If the parents refuse to agree to a change of placement, however, and the school is convinced that the student is truly dangerous, school officials can request an injunction or temporary restraining order (TRO) from a hearing officer to remove the student from the school environment. A TRO issued to remove a dangerous student with disabilities from school has been frequently referred to as a *Honig* injunction. When an injunction is issued, schools may use the time when a student is not in school to determine if a change of placement is needed or to conduct a manifestation determination.

Obtaining an Injunction

In *Honig,* the Supreme Court stated that in any action brought by a school district to obtain a TRO, there will be a presumption in favor of a student's current educational placement. School officials can only overcome this preference by "showing that maintaining [the] child in his or her current placement is substantially likely to result in injury either to himself or herself, or to others" (p. 606). Prior to the IDEA Amendments of 1997, *Honig* injunctions could only be granted by courts, but now such injunctions can be granted by hearing officers. School officials must convince a hearing officer that unless a student is removed from the current placement, the student is dangerous and substantially likely to injure himself or others. Additionally, school officials must prove that reasonable steps have been taken to minimize the risk of harm in the current setting; that the current IEP is appropriate; that the interim setting allows the student to participate in the general education curriculum, although in a different setting; and that the student can continue to work on the goals in the IEP. Furthermore, the school must demonstrate these factors with substantial evidence, which the IDEA defines as being beyond a preponderance of the evidence (IDEA Amendments, 1997).

The substantial evidence requirement would seem to be a difficult threshold to meet. Nevertheless, in a number of post-*Honig* rulings schools have been granted discipline-related TROs (e.g., *Binghamton City School District v. Borgna*, 1991; *Board of Education of Township High School District No. 211 v. Corral*, 1989; *Board of Education of Township No. 211 v. Linda Kurtz-Imig*, 1989; *Prince William County School Board v. Willis*, 1989; *Texas City Independent School District v. Jorstad*, 1990).

Texas Independent School District v. Jorstad

In *Texas Independent School District v. Jorstad* (1990), a school was granted a TRO after parents refused a change in placement sought by the school. The student, classified as seriously emotionally disturbed (SED), was placed in a regular classroom with an individual aide and resource room services. Following a number of serious behavioral problems in the classroom, the student's IEP team met to change the student's placement to a more restrictive setting. The student had been physically aggressive to the teacher and other students and had attempted to escape the classroom by jumping from a second-story window. All school personnel working with the student believed that he was an extreme danger to himself and others. The parents did not agree with the more restrictive placement, and neither did the boy's psychologist, who believed placement in a more restrictive would cause a regression in his social skills. The parents requested an administrative hearing. The case went before the federal district court for the Southern District of Texas.

The federal court, citing the stay-put rule, held that only under limited circumstance could a school change the placement of a student during the pendency of a due process hearing. A change of placement would only be permitted if the school could show that maintaining a student in the current placement was substantially likely to result in injury to the student or others in the environment. The court concluded that in this situation the student would not suffer any realistic harm by being placed in the more restrictive setting pending completion of the administrative hearing. Potential harm to others, however, was seen by the court as being substantial. Thus, a TRO was issued and the school district was allowed to change the student's placement.

Light v. Parkway School District

In *Light v. Parkway School District* (1994), the U.S. Court of Appeals for the Eighth Circuit established a two-part test for determining the appropriateness of removing a disruptive student with disabilities from school. In its ruling, the court interpreted the U.S. Supreme Court's decision in *Honig v. Doe.* The court delineated circumstances under which a school can seek an injunction to remove a disruptive student. The case involved a 13-year-old girl, Lauren Light, with moderate mental retardation, autism, and a history of aggressiveness toward students and staff. The student was enrolled in a self-contained classroom with full integration in art, physical education, and computer education. A full-time aide and a special education teacher were assigned to the student during the school day. Despite the presence of the aide, special education teacher, regular classroom teacher, and a consultant selected by the girl's parents, Lauren's aggressiveness escalated. The parents of other students in the class began to complain that Lauren's behavior was disrupting the educational environment and creating a dangerous situation. The IEP team met and recommended a change in placement. The girl's parents requested a due process hearing, thereby invoking the stay-put rule. Before the due process hearing was held, Lauren hit a student. She was suspended from school for 10 days.

Following the suspension, the Lights sued in federal court, contending that Lauren had been denied due process. The school district also went to court to seek an injunction to remove Lauren as a substantial risk to herself and others. The federal district court granted the injunction. The Lights appealed to the Eighth Circuit court, contending that the school had to prove that Lauren was truly dangerous before the school could remove her. They also stated that under *Honig,* the school could only remove a student who intended to injure another student.

The court, citing the records kept by the school regarding Lauren's behavior, asserted that students do not actually have to cause harm before a school may remove them; rather, students only have to be substantially *likely* to cause harm. The court pointed to the school district's record of efforts to modify Lauren's behavior as an attempt to accommodate the student. Finally, the court established a two-part test to determine the appropriateness of a student removal (see Figure 15.6 for the *Light v. Parkway* two-part test). First, the school must determine and show that the student is substantially likely to cause injury. Second, the school must show that it has done all that it reasonably can to reduce the risk of injury and to modify a student's behavior. If a school can prove these two points, it will be issued a temporary injunction to remove a student from school.

Figure 15.6
The *Light v. Parkway* Two-Part Test

Part One: Maintaining the student in the current educational placement is likely to result in injury to the student or peers (actual injury is not required).

Part Two: The school district has made reasonable attempts to minimize the risk of injury.

Weapons

A topic that has received a great deal of attention recently is the issue of school officials' authority in disciplining students with disabilities who bring weapons to school. The Gun-Free Schools Act (GFSA), which was enacted as part of the Goals 2000: Educate America Act (20 U.S.C. § 5801 *et seq.*), essentially required school districts to expel any student who brings a gun to school. According to the statutory language,

> No assistance may be provided to any local educational agency under this Act unless such agency has in effect a policy requiring the expulsion from school for a period of not less than one year of any student who is determined to have brought a weapon to school under the jurisdiction of the agency except such policy may allow the chief administering officer of the agency to modify such expulsion requirement for a student on a case-by-case basis. (Gun-Free Schools Act, 20 U.S.C.S. § 3351(a)(1))

The Gun-Free Schools Act and Students with Disabilities

A policy guidance statement issued by the U.S. Department of Education stated that the FAPE and stay-put requirements of the IDEA prohibited the automatic removal of any student with a disability for disability-related misbehavior (Gun-Free Schools Act Guidance, 1995). This position appeared to be at odds with the expulsion requirement of the GFSA. According to the statement, no conflict between the laws existed because administrators were allowed to consider discipline on a case-by-case basis; therefore, administrators could take the laws affecting students with disabilities into account. Congress sought to alter this apparent discrepancy with the Jeffords amendment to the IDEA (IDEA, 20 U.S.C. § 1415(e)(3)). This amendment allowed schools to immediately and unilaterally remove students with disabilities who bring guns to school to an interim alternative setting for up to 45 days. The primary effect of the law was to modify the stay-put provision of the IDEA. During the 45-day period, the school and parents may decide on a permanent placement. The school may also convene a team to conduct a manifestation determination. If the result of the determination is that the misbehavior was not a manifestation of the disability, a student may be expelled or receive a long-term suspension. If parents request a due process hearing to contest the placement in the interim setting or an expulsion, the school may keep the student in the alternative placement during the pendency of the hearing.

The IDEA Amendments of 1997 and Dangerous Students

The IDEA Amendments of 1997 gave school officials greater authority to discipline students in special education. The amendments expanded the provision that allowed school officials to unilaterally place students who bring firearms to school in an interim alternative setting for 45 days. The new language allowed the unilateral placement in an interim alternative setting of any student in special education who brought a weapon to school or a school function and of students using, possessing, or selling illegal drugs. Furthermore, school officials could request a hearing for the purpose of convincing a hearing officer that a student in special education was substantially likely to cause injury to him- or herself or to others. If school officials could convince the hearing officer by demonstrating with substantial evidence—which was defined as "beyond a preponderance of evidence"—that the student was a risk to himself or others and that school officials had made reasonable efforts to minimize the risk, the officer could order that the student be moved to an interim alternative educational setting.

The 1997 amendments also describe the standards that the interim alternative educational setting must meet. First, this setting must be determined by the IEP team. Although the setting is not in the school environment, the student must be able to continue to participate in the general education curriculum and continue to receive the services and modifications listed in the IEP. Moreover, the student must continue to work toward the goals and objectives of the IEP, including goals that address the behavior problems that led to the placement.

Disciplining Students Not Eligible for Special Education

Court rulings and OCR policies indicate that the procedural safeguards of Section 504 and the IDEA may protect students from disciplinary exclusions prior to a formal classification. In such situations, the crucial issue turns on whether the school district had sufficient notice to suspect that students' misconduct might be related to their disability (Senate Report, 1997; Tucker et al., 1993).

In a 1989 letter of finding, OCR determined that a school district had violated regulations when it expelled a student with Attention Deficit Hyperactivity Disorder without examining the possibility that the behavior may have been caused by the student's disability. OCR noted that despite the parents' request for a full evaluation of the child, the school district had failed to do so. In an OCR decision in 1990, a school district was found to have made an illegal change in placement when the school district had reason to believe that the student had a disability but had not classified the student (*Mineral County (NV) School District 167*).

In *Doe v. Rockingham School Board* (1987), a federal district court ruled that a student suspected of having a disability was entitled to procedural safeguards. The court held that once the school had been notified of a student's learning disability by his psychologist, the student's due process rights had to be considered in the light of the IDEA. The court further ordered the school district to provide the student with an appropriate educational program. In *M.P. v. Governing Board of the Grossmont Union School District* (1994), a federal district court in California noted that the stay-put rule of the IDEA could be misused by students without disabilities. According to the court, students without disabilities could circumvent state education laws and gain the protection of the IDEA by claiming to have disabilities.

In a memorandum, OSEP took the position that students not previously identified as eligible under the IDEA could not invoke the stay-put provision to avoid disciplinary sanctions such as expulsion (OSEP Memorandum 95-16, 1995). In situations in which a request for an evaluation or due process hearing was made following a disciplinary suspension or expulsion, school districts were not obligated to reinstate students to in-school status during the pendency of the evaluation or hearing. OSEP noted that this was because the stay-put setting in such situations would be the out-of-school placement.

Hacienda La Puente Unified School District of Los Angeles v. Honig

The U.S. Court of Appeals for the Ninth Circuit, in *Hacienda La Puente Unified School District of Los Angeles v. Honig* (1992), affirmed the ruling of a due process hearing officer overturning the school's expulsion of a student who had been determined by the school district not to be eligible for special education services. The hearing officer's decision involved a student expelled for frightening students with a starter pistol. Prior to the incident, the parents had requested a special education evaluation. After completing testing, however, the school district concluded that the student did not qualify for special education. The parents then requested a due process hearing to determine the student's eligibility for special education and to find out if the misbehavior was causally related to the disability. The hearing officer determined that the student was SED. Furthermore, the hearing officer held that the student's actions were a manifestation of his disability and that the school district had wrongly denied the student the procedural protections of the IDEA in expelling him. The school district was ordered to reinstate the student.

The district filed suit in district court challenging the hearing officer's ruling. District officials contended that it was necessary for a student to be identified as having a disability before procedural safeguards of the IDEA could be invoked. Because the student was found by the district not to have a disability, the district believed that the hearing officer lacked jurisdiction to consider the parents' complaint.

After the case was removed from state court, the federal district court held for the parents and dismissed the school district's complaint. School district officials appealed to the U.S. Court of Appeals for the Ninth Circuit. The court of appeals affirmed the district court's opinion, holding that the hearing officer could hold hearings on such issues. However, the ruling avoided the question of whether the stay-put provision prohibited expulsion of students not diagnosed as having disabilities. The court stated that the IDEA and accompanying federal regulations

> make plain that, even though not previously identified as disabled, the student's alleged disability may be raised in an IDEA administrative due process hearing. . . . [A] contrary result would frustrate the core purpose of the IDEA, which is to prevent schools from indiscriminately excluding disabled students from educational opportunities. . . . [I]f we found issues concerning the detection of disabilities to be outside the scope of IDEA "due process hearings," school districts could easily circumvent the statute's strictures by refusing to identify students as disabled. . . . [A]ll disabled students, whether or not possessing "previously identified exceptional needs" are entitled to the procedural protections afforded under the IDEA. (pp. 492–494)

Rodiriecus L. v. Waukegan School District

In an important ruling, the U.S. Court of Appeals for the Seventh Circuit upheld the OSEP position regarding students' avoiding discipline by invoking the procedural protections of the IDEA. In *Rodiriecus L.v. Waukegan School District* (1996), the circuit court held that a student in general education could not avoid expulsion by claiming protection under the IDEA unless school district officials knew or reasonably should have known that the student had a disability. The court held that

> If the stay-put provision is automatically applied to every student who files an application for special education, then an avenue will be open for disruptive, nondisabled students to forestall any attempts at routine discipline by simply requesting a disability evaluation and demanding to "stay-put," thus disrupting the educational goals of an already over-burdened . . . public school system. . . . However . . . there may arise circumstances where a truly disabled child, who has not as yet been identified by the school . . . or has been misidentified, is improperly denied appropriate public education. In those situations, the stay-put provision is necessary to keep the student in school until a hearing officer has resolved the dispute. (p. 562)

In this case, the court believed that the school district had no reason to suspect that the student had a disability, even though he had a poor academic record and a history of disciplinary contacts. That the student may have had a disability had never been suggested until he was recommended for expulsion.

Additionally, the Seventh Circuit court offered guidance to other courts in determining if school officials should have known that a student had a disability and was, therefore, entitled to the procedural protections of the IDEA. Courts should weigh the following four factors in making such decisions: (a) the likelihood that the student will succeed on the merits of his or her claim; (b) the irreparability of the harm to the student if the stay-put provision is not invoked; (c) whether the harm to the student outweighs the harm to the district; and (d) the public interest. Furthermore, students must show that they reasonably would have been found eligible for special education through the IDEA's administrative procedures.

IDEA Amendments of 1997 and Students Not Yet Eligible

The IDEA Amendments of 1997 also addressed the issue of disciplining students not yet eligible under the IDEA. According to the statutory language, students may only assert protection under the IDEA if school district personnel had knowledge that the student had a disability before the behavior that precipitated the disciplinary sanctions occurred. School district personnel will be determined to have had prior knowledge of a student's disability if the parents of the child had expressed in writing to appropriate school personnel that the student needed special education, if a student's behavior or performance demonstrated the need for special education services, or if the parents or teacher had requested an evaluation or expressed concern to the appropriate personnel. If school personnel did not know, or should not reasonably have known, prior to taking the disciplinary actions, that the student had a disability, the student will be subject to the same rules and sanctions applied to students without disabilities. If the parents request an evaluation during the period in which the student is being disciplined, the evaluation must be conducted in an expeditious manner. Students not currently considered to have disabilities may, in fact, be protected by the IDEA and Section 504. Therefore, if a student is suspected of having a disability, if evidence exists of a disability, or if parents have alerted the school to a possible disability, it would be prudent for school officials to have the student evaluated prior to using long-term suspension or expulsion. The evaluation should address eligibility under both the IDEA and Section 504.

School District Responsibilities

From the body of case law on discipline, as well as the IDEA Amendments of 1997, a number of important school district responsibilities can be extrapolated. These responsibilities are listed in Figure 15.7.

Formulate and Disseminate Discipline Policies and Procedures

School districts should develop policies and procedures for ensuring that schools maintain safe and orderly environments where teachers can teach and students can learn. Procedures for disciplining students in order to maintain safety and order, to reduce misbehavior, and to teach appropriate behavior are essential. Such policies must contain clearly delineated behavioral expectations of students, as well as the consequences for not conforming to these expectations. If the consequences include suspension and expulsion, all students are entitled to basic due process rights before exclusion occurs. For suspensions of 10 days or less, students must be afforded oral or written notice of the charges and the opportunity to respond to these charges. For suspensions in excess of 10 days, in addition to a notice and hearing, students must be provided with the opportunity for a more formal hearing process. When students present a danger to themselves or others, they can be removed from the school immediately, with notice and hearing to follow. When students violate the law, the legal authorities should be informed (Maloney, 1994).

Schools should also develop policies regarding search and seizure of students and property. Such policies should include statements addressing the diminished right of student privacy in school lockers and on school property.

It is extremely important that school administrators, teachers, and other personnel understand the district's disciplinary policies and procedures. Steps should also be taken to ensure that parents have access to, and understand, information in the school district's discipline policy. Methods to ensure parental access include mailing discipline policy brochures to district parents and having teachers explain the procedures in parent–teacher conferences.

Recognize the Dual Disciplinary Standard

Courts have repeatedly held that students with disabilities are not immune from a school's normal disciplinary procedures. Students with disabilities, however, have special protections against any procedures that result in a unilateral change of placement.

Figure 15.7
School District Responsibilities

1. Formulate and disseminate discipline policies and procedures. Ensure that parents have access to and understanding of the school district policies.

   • *Expectations for student conduct.* Should include statements regarding student property and the diminished right of student privacy in regards to lockers and school property.

   • *Rules and consequences.* Delineate inappropriate student behavior and conduct through school rules. Specify consequences for violating school rules.

   • *Due process rights.* If students are suspended for 10 days or less, notify students of charges and give them an opportunity to respond. If suspended over 10 days or expelled, notification, opportunity to respond, and more formalized hearing procedures are required.

2. Recognize the dual disciplinary standard.

   • *IDEA students.* Suspension of change of placement for 10 days is allowed. No long-term suspension or expulsion is allowed unless the behavior is unrelated to the disability (can only be determined in a manifestation hearing). No cessation of educational services. If a student brings a weapon or uses or sells drugs, he or she may be placed in an IAES for up to 45 days.

   • *Section 504 students.* Suspension of change of placement for 10 days is allowed. No long-term suspension or expulsion is allowed unless the behavior is unrelated to the disability (can only be determined in a manifestation hearing). Cessation of educational services is allowed (check state guidelines).

3. Include a behavior intervention plan in students' IEPs or Section 504 accommodation plans. The plan should be based on a functional assessment, including positive procedures and consequences. Delineate consequences that may be used (e.g., in-school suspension, timeout) and a crisis intervention plan.

4. Document behavioral incidences. In situations involving problem behavior, document disciplinary actions taken in writing. Notify school administrators and parents.

5. Evaluate the effectiveness of disciplinary procedures and interventions.

Expulsions and long-term or indefinite suspensions are changes in placement and cannot be made without following the procedural safeguards of the IDEA or Section 504. If a school decides to use long-term suspension or expulsion, the IEP team must meet to determine the relationship between the behavior and the student's disability. A school district cannot expel a student on the basis of misbehavior caused by the disability.

Because of these additional protections, it is crucial that school officials know which students are classified as having disabilities under the IDEA and Section 504. A disciplinary meeting may involve many issues and concerns. The two issues, however, that must be resolved in the meeting concern the appropriateness of the IEP and the manifestation determination (Cline, 1994). Figure 15.8 summarizes the requirements in disciplining students with disabilities.

Figure 15.8
Discipline of Students with Disabilities Under the IDEA Amendments of 1997

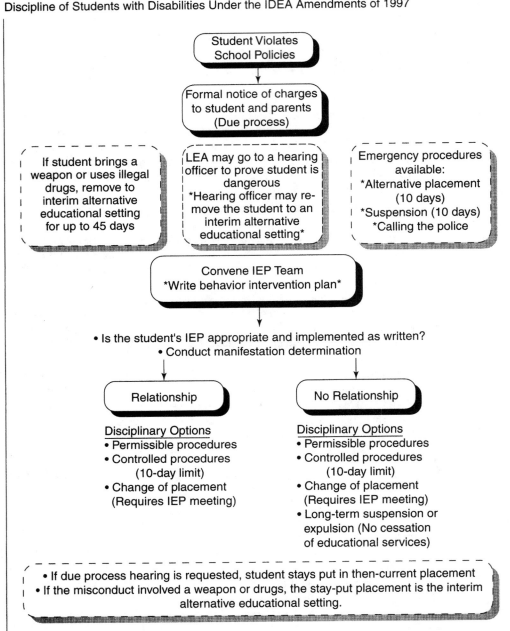

Include Behavior Intervention Plans in IEPs or Accommodation Plans

Students with disabilities who have a tendency to misbehave must have behavior goals and objectives and a disciplinary plan included in their IEP (Hartwig et al., 1991; Senate Report, 1997). This requirement, which applies to all students in special education regardless of their disability category, was included in the IDEA Amendments of 1997. The plan must be based on a functional behavioral assessment and should include strategies, including proactive positive behavioral interventions and supports, to address the behavior problems. Additionally, because these elements would be discussed at an IEP meeting, the plan would have an increased probability of success because of parental support and participation. The intervention plan would also be less likely to be legally challenged and more likely to meet legal muster if challenged.

The discipline plan for each student should delineate expected behaviors, inappropriate behaviors, and positive and negative consequences for the behaviors (Hartwig & Reusch, 1994). The disciplinary process that will be followed, including intervention techniques, should be outlined in the plan. The plan should also include procedures for dealing with a behavioral crisis. A sample behavior intervention plan is represented in Figure 15.9.

Behavior intervention plans must be based on legitimate disciplinary procedures. To ensure that procedures are used reasonably, schools should use disciplinary methods in accordance with the principle of hierarchical application. According to Braaten, Simpson, Rosell, and Reilly (1988), this principle requires that school officials use more intrusive disciplinary procedures (e.g., in-school suspension) only after less intrusive procedures (e.g., warnings and reprimands) have failed.

Document Disciplinary Actions Taken and Evaluate Their Effectiveness

Maloney (1994) contends that in the law, "if it isn't written down, it didn't happen" (p. 4). In disciplining students with disabilities, therefore, it is crucial to keep written records of all discussions and of all disciplinary actions taken. An examination of court cases and administrative rulings in disciplinary matters indicates that in many instances, decisions turned on the quality of the school's records. For example, in *Cole v. Greenfield-Central Community Schools (1986),* Dickens v. Johnson County Board of Education (1987), and *Hayes v. Unified School District No. 377* (1987), the thoroughness of the schools' record keeping played a significant part in the court's decisions in favor of the schools. In *Oberti v. Board of Education of the Borough of Clementon School District* (1993), the court decided against the school district, partly because no behavior intervention plan to improve the student's behavior in the regular classroom was included in the IEP. Although the school district maintained that it did have a behavior intervention plan, because it was not written down it did not exist in the eyes of the court.

Figure 15.9
A Sample Behavior Intervention Plan

Behavior Intervention Plan

Student: _____   Date of Meeting: _____

Teacher: _____   Administrator:_____

Teacher: _____   _____

Parents: _____   _____

Others: _____   _____

Problem behaviors:

Antecedents of problem behaviors:

Positive procedures to redirect behaviors:

Intervention plan (reinforcers and consequences):

Procedures to teach positive replacement behaviors:

Methods of evaluation:

Criteria for success:

Records on emergency disciplinary actions are also important. Such records should contain an adequate description of the incident and disciplinary action taken, as well as the signatures of witnesses present. Figure 15.10 is an example of a behavior incident report.

Finally, it is important that teachers evaluate the effectiveness of disciplinary procedures used. There are a number of reasons for collecting data on an ongoing basis. To make decisions about whether an intervention is reducing target behaviors, teachers need data collected during the course of the intervention. If formative data are not collected, teachers will not know with certainty if a given procedure is actually achieving the desired results. Teachers are accountable to supervisors and parents, and data collection is useful for accountability purposes. From a legal standpoint, it is imperative that teachers collect such data. Anecdotal information is not readily accepted by courts, but data-based decisions certainly would be viewed much more favorably.

Summary

Specific guidelines regarding the discipline of students with disabilities were not written into federal law (e.g., the IDEA, Section 504) until the IDEA Amendments of 1997. Prior to that time, school districts had to operate on guidelines extrapolated from the decisions of administrative agencies (e.g., OSEP, OCR) and case law.

Students with disabilities are not immune from a school's disciplinary procedure. Schools may use procedures such as reprimands, detention, restriction of privileges, response cost, in-school suspension (if the student's education is continued), and out-of-school suspensions (10 days or less) as long as the procedures are not abused or applied in a discriminatory manner. Disciplinary procedures that effectively change a student's placement are, however, not legal if not done in accordance with the procedural safeguards afforded students with disabilities by the IDEA and Section 504. Such procedures include suspension (if over 10 days) and expulsion.

When determining whether or not to use a long-term suspension or expulsion, the school must convene the student's IEP team and other qualified personnel to determine the relationship between the student's misbehavior and the disability. If there is a relationship, the student cannot be expelled. If the team determines that no relationship exists, the student may be expelled. Even when an expulsion follows a determination of no relationship and is done in accordance with procedural safeguards, there cannot be a complete cessation of educational services.

A school district cannot unilaterally exclude a student with disabilities from school, regardless of the degree of danger or disruption. School districts may go to court, however, to obtain a temporary restraining order to have the student removed from school. The school will bear the burden of proof when attempting to get a TRO. In situations where students with disabilities bring weapons to school or they use, possess, or sell illegal drugs, school officials may unilaterally remove them to an interim alternative setting for 45 school days. During this time the IEP team should meet to consider the appropriate actions.

Figure 15.10
A Sample Behavior Incident Report

Behavior Incident Report

Student: _____   Date: _____

Teacher: _____   Time: _____

Observed behavior prior to the incident:

Description of incident:

Parents notified: Yes   No

Description of positive approaches to correct behavior:

Did behavior endanger the safety of students or disrupt the learning environment? If yes, how?

Intervention(s) used:
☐ Warning
☐ Response cost
☐ Exclusion timeout
☐ Isolation/seclusion timeout
☐ Overcorrection
☐ Physical restraint
☐ In-school suspension
☐ Out-of-school suspension
☐ Other

Reasons for the choice of intervention:

Results of Intervention:

Remarks:

Signatures

Teacher: _____   Witness: _____

Principal: _____   Parents: _____

Disciplining students with disabilities is a complex issue. In addition to observing the due process rights that protect all students, administrators and teachers have to be aware of the additional safeguards afforded students with disabilities by the IDEA and Section 504. In using disciplinary procedures with students with disabilities, educators should be aware of state and local policies regarding discipline, develop and inform parents of school discipline policies, and continuously evaluate the effectiveness of disciplinary procedures. When disciplinary procedures are used, proper documentation is critical. Teachers must collect formative data to determine if the procedures are having the desired effect on student behavior. Finally, disciplinary procedures should be used reasonably and for legitimate educational purposes; they must not compromise a student's FAPE or be applied in a discriminatory manner.

For Further Information

Bartlett, L. (1989). Disciplining handicapped students: Legal issues in light of *Honig v. Doe*. *Exceptional Children, 55,* 357–366.

Bjorklun, E. C. (1994). School locker searches and the Fourth Amendment. *Education Law Reporter, 92,* 1065–1071.

Cline, D. (1994). *Fundamentals of special education law: Emphasis on discipline.* (Available from the Behavioral Institute for Children and Adolescents, 1153 Benton Way, Arden Hills, MN 55112-3753)

Dagley, D. L., McGuire, M. D., Evans, C. W. (1994). The relationship test in the discipline of disabled students. *Education Law Reporter, 88,* 13–31.

Dies, J. H., Iyer, C. S., & Noorman, J. J. (1996). *Searches of students, lockers, and automobiles.* Detroit: Educational Risk, Inc.

Hartwig, E. P., & Reusch, G. M. (1994). *Discipline in the schools.* Horsham, PA: LRP Publications.

Hartwig, E. P., Robertshaw, C. S., & Reusch, G. M. (1991). Disciplining children with disabilities: Balancing procedural expectations and positive educational practice. In *Individuals with disabilities education law report, special report #8.* Horsham, PA: LRP Publications.

McKinney, J. P. (1994). The Fourth Amendment and the public schools: Reasonable suspicion in the 1990's. *Education Law Reporter, 91,* 455–463.

Sorenson, G. (1993). Update on legal issues in special education discipline. *Education Law Reporter, 81,* 399–411.

Yell, M. L., Cline, D., & Bradley, R. (1995). Disciplining students with emotional and behavioral disorders: A legal update. *Education and Treatment of Children, 18,* 299–308.

References

Alexander, K., & Alexander, M. D. (1984). *The law of schools, students, and teachers in a nutshell.* St. Paul, MN: West Publishing Company.

Alexander, K., & Alexander, M. D. (1992). *American public school law* (3rd ed.). St. Paul, MN: West Publishing Company.

Bartlett, L. (1989). Disciplining handicapped students: Legal issues in light of *Honig v. Doe*. *Exceptional Children, 55,* 357–366.

Beaumont Independent School District, 21 IDELR 261 (SEA TX, 1994).

Big Beaver Falls Area School District v. Jackson, 624 A.2d 806 (Pa. Cmwlth. 1993).

Binghamton City School District v. Borgna, 1991 W. L. 29985 (N.D.N.Y. 1991).

Bjorklun, E. C. (1994). School locker searches and the Fourth Amendment. *Education Law Reporter, 92,* 1065–1071.

Board of Education of Township High School District No. 211 v. Corral, 441 EHLR Dec. 390 (N.D. Ill. 1989).

Board of Education of Township No. 211 v. Linda Kurtz-Imig, 16 EHLR Dec. 17 (N.D. Ill. 1989).

Braaten, S., Simpson, R., Rosell, J., & Reilly, T. (1988). Using punishment with exceptional children: A dilemma for educators. *Teaching Exceptional Children, 20,* 79–81.

Chester County (TN) School District, 17 EHLR 301 (OCR, 1990).

Cline, D. (1994). *Fundamentals of special education law: Emphasis on discipline.* Arden Hills, MN: Behavioral Institute for Children and Adolescents.

Cobb County (GA) School District, 20 IDELR 1171 (OCR, 1993).

Cole v. Greenfield-Central Community Schools, 657 F. Supp. 56 (S.D. Ind. 1986).

Concerned Parents and Citizens for Continuing Education at Malcolm X v. The New York City Board of Education, 629 F.2d 751 (2nd Cir. 1980).

Cornfield v. Consolidated High School District No. 230, 991 F.2d 1316 (7th Cir. 1993).

Dagley, D. L., McGuire, M. D., Evans, C. W. (1994). The relationship test in the discipline of disabled students. *Education Law Reporter, 88,* 13–31.

Dickens v. Johnson County Board of Education, 661 F. Supp. 155 (E.D. Tenn. 1987).

Dise, J. H., Iyer, C. S., & Noorman, J. J. (1996). *Searches of students, lockers, and automobiles.* Detroit: Educational Risk, Inc.

Doe v. Koger, 480 F. Supp. 225 (N.D. Ind. 1979).

Doe v. Maher, 793 F.2d 1470 (9th Cir. 1986).

Doe v. Rockingham School Board, 658 F. Supp. 403 (W.D. Va. 1987).

Eric J. v. Huntsville City Board of Education, 22 IDELR 858 (N.D. Ala. 1995).

Goals 2000: Educate America Act, 20 U.S.C.S. § 5801 *et seq.*

Gorn, S. (1996). *What do I do when: The answer book on special education law.* Horsham, PA: LRP Publications.

Goss v. Lopez, 419 U.S. 565 (1975).

Grannis v. Ordean, 234 U.S. 383 (1914).

Guernsey, T. F., & Klare, K. (1993). *Special education law.* Durham, NC: Carolina Academic Press.

Gun-Free Schools Act, 20 U.S.C. § 1415(e) (3).

Gun-Free Schools Act Guidance. (1995, January 20). United States Department of Education, Office of Elementary and Secondary Education, Assistant Secretary, Thomas W. Payzant. Washington, DC: Author

Hacienda La Puente Unified School District of Los Angeles v. Honig, 976 F.2d 487 (9th Cir. 1992).

Hall v. Tawney, 621 F.2d 607 (4th Cir. 1980).

Hartog-Rapp, F. (1985). The legal standards for determining the relationship between a child's handicapping condition and misconduct charged in a school disciplinary proceeding. *Southern Illinois University Law Journal, 2,* 243–262.

Hartwig, E. P., & Reusch, G. M. (1994). *Discipline in the schools.* Horsham, PA: LRP Publications.

Hartwig, E. P., Robertshaw, C. S., & Reusch, G. M. (1991). Disciplining children with disabilities: Balancing procedural expectations and positive educational practice. In *Individuals with disabilities education law report, special report #8.* Horsham, PA: LRP Publications.

Hayes v. Unified School District No. 377, 669 F. Supp. 1519 (D. Kan. 1987).

Honig v. Doe, 479 U.S. 1084 (1988).

Hopewell (VA) Public Schools, 21 IDELR 189 (OCR, 1994).

Huefner, D. S. (1991). Another view of the suspension and expulsion cases. *Exceptional Children, 57,* 360–393.

Illinois v. Pruitt, 64 USLW 2575 (Ill. App. 1996).

Individuals with Disabilities Education Act (IDEA), 20 U.S.A. § 1400 *et seq.*

Individuals with Disabilities Education Act Amendments of 1997, Pub. L. No. 105–17, 105th Cong., 1st sess.

Ingraham v. Wright, 430 U.S. 651 (1977).

In the Interests of Isaiah B., 500 N.W. 2d 637 (Wis. 1993).

Kaelin v. Grubbs, 682 F.2d 595 (6th Cir. 1982).

Light v. Parkway School District, 21 IDELR 933 (8th Cir. 1994).

M. P. v. Governing Board of the Grossmont Union School District, 21 IDELR 639 (S.D. Cal. 1994).

Maloney, M. (1993). Strip search for drugs did not violate student rights. *The Special Educator, 9*(3), 42.

Maloney, M. (1994). How to avoid the discipline trap, *The Special Educator,* Winter Index, 1–4.

Marion County (FL) School District, 20 IDELR 634 (OCR, 1993).

McCracken County School District, 18 IDELR 482 (OCR, 1991).

McKinney, J. P. (1994). The Fourth Amendment and the public schools: Reasonable suspicion in the 1990's. *Education Law Reporter, 91,* 455–463.

Miller, M. B., & Ahrbecker, W. C. (1995). *Legal issues and school violence.* Paper presented at Violence in the Schools, a conference of LRP Publications, Arlington, VA.

Mineral County (NV) School District 167, 16 EHLR 668 (OCR 1990).

Mobile County (AL) School District, 18 IDELR 70 (OCR 1991).

New Jersey v. T.L.O., 469 U.S. 325, 105 S.Ct. 733 (1985).

Oberti v. Board of Education of the Borough of Clementon School District, 995 F.2d 1204 (3rd Cir. 1993).

O'Connor v. Ortega, 480 U.S. 709 (1987).

OCR Letter of Finding, EHLR 307:06 (OCR 1988).

OCR Letter of Finding, EHLR 353:205 (OCR 1989).

OCR Memorandum, EHLR 307:05 (OCR 1988).

OCR Memorandum, 16 EHLR 491 n. 3 (OCR 1989).

OSEP Memorandum 95–16, 22 IDELR 531 (OSEP 1995).

People v. Dilworth, 661 N.E.2d 310 (Ill. 1996).

People v. Overton, 249 N.E.2d 366 (NY 1969).

Prince William County School Board v. Malone, 762 F.2d 1210 (4th Cir. 1985).

Prince William County School Board v. Willis, 16 EHLR 1109 (VA Cir. Ct., 1989).

Rodiriecus L. v. Waukegan School District, 24 IDELR 563 (7th Cir. 1996).

S-1 v. Turlington, 635 F.2d 342 (5th Cir. 1981).

Section 504 of the Rehabilitation Act of 1973, 29 U.S.C. § 794 *et seq.*

Senate Report of the Individuals with Disabilities Act Amendments of 1997, available at wais. access.gpo.gov.

Sorenson, G. (1993). Update on legal issues in special education discipline. *Education Law Reporter, 81,* 399–411.

State of Washington v. Slattery, 787 P.2d 932 (Div. 1 1990).

Stuart v. Nappi, 443 F. Supp. 1235 (D. Conn. 1978).

Texas City Independent School District v. Jorstad, 752 F. Supp. 231 (S.D. Tex. 1990).

Thomas v. Carthage School District, 87 F.3d 979 (8th Cir. 1996).

Tinker v. Des Moines Independent Community School, 393 U.S. 1058 (1969).

Tucker, B. P., & Goldstein, B. A. (1992). *Legal rights of persons with disabilities: An analysis of federal law.* Horsham, PA: LRP Publications.

Tucker, B. P., Goldstein, B. A., & Sorenson, G. (1993). *The educational rights of children with disabilities: Analysis, decisions, and commentary.* Horsham, PA: LRP Publications.

Valente, R. (1994). *Law in the schools* (3rd ed.). Upper Saddle River, NJ: Merrill/Prentice Hall.

Victoria L. v. District School Board, 741 F.2d 369 (11th Cir. 1984).

Virginia Department of Education v. Riley, 25 IDELR 309 (4th Cir. 1996).

Weber, M. (1992). *Special education law and litigation treatise.* Horsham, PA: LRP Publications.

Yell, M. L. (1989). *Honig v. Doe:* The suspension and expulsion of handicapped students. *Exceptional Children, 56,* 60–69.

Yell, M. L. (1990). The use of corporal punishment, suspension, expulsion, and timeout with behaviorally disordered students in public schools: Legal considerations. *Behavioral Disorders, 15,* 100–109.

Yell, M. L. (1994). Timeout and students with behavior disorders: A legal analysis. *Education and Treatment of Children, 17,* 293–301.

Yell, M. L., Cline, D., & Bradley, R. (1995). Disciplining students with emotional and behavioral disorders: A legal update. *Education and Treatment of Children, 18,* 299–308.

Yell, M. L., & Peterson, R. L. (1995). Disciplining students with disabilities and those at risk for school failure: Legal issues. *Preventing School Failure, 39*(2), 39–44.

Yudof, M. G., Kirp, D. L., & Levin, B. (1992). *Educational policy and the law* (3rd ed.). St. Paul, MN: West Publishing Company.

Zirkel, Letter to, 22 IDELR 667 (OCR 1995).

Zvi D. v. Ambach, 694 F.2d 904 (1982).

CHAPTER SIXTEEN

Additional Issues

The [IDEA] does not define appropriate education but leaves to the courts and the hearing officers the responsibility of giving [it] content.

Chief Justice William Rehnquist, *Board of Education of the Hendrick Hudson Central School District v. Rowley* (1982, p. 187)

Special education was born in the arena of advocacy, litigation, and legislation. Previous chapters have delineated a number of highly regulated and litigated issues. There have been a number of other issues in special education, however, that have only recently begun receiving attention in the courts. The purpose of this chapter is to review some of these issues. First, issues regarding the accessibility and confidentiality of student records will be briefly reviewed. Next, two areas of increasing importance in special education—public schools' responsibility for students with disabilities attending private schools, and special education students in sectarian or church-related schools—will be examined. Finally, the topic of teachers' legal liability for student injury will be discussed.

Issue #1: Student Records

Prior to 1974, it was common for schools to deny parental access to educational records. Granting access was time-consuming and costly, and often was seen as a negative because it increased a school's potential liability by opening up these records to public scrutiny. Additionally, students' educational records, although denied to parents, were often made available to third parties without regard to student confidentiality (Thomas & Russo, 1995).

In 1974, Congress enacted the Family Educational Rights and Privacy Act to address concerns regarding the confidentiality and accessibility of student records. The law, also known as the Buckley Amendment, was introduced by Senator James Buckley of New York.

Family Educational Rights and Privacy Act

The Family Educational Rights and Privacy Act (FERPA) applies to all students attending institutions receiving federal financial assistance and requires that these institutions adhere to the following requirements: (a) school districts must establish written policies regarding student records and inform parents of their rights under FERPA annually; (b) parents are guaranteed access to their children's educational records; (c) parents have the right to challenge the accuracy of the records; (d) disclosure of these records to third parties without parental consent is prohibited; and (e) parents may file complaints under FERPA regarding a school's failure to comply with the law. Figure 16.1 lists school district responsibilities under FERPA.

FERPA's Coverage

FERPA covers all records, files, documents, and other materials that contain personally identifiable information directly related to a student that are maintained by the educational agency or by a person acting for that agency. Records that are not covered by the FERPA disclosure rules include (a) those records made by educational personnel who are in sole possession of the maker and are not accessible or revealed to other persons except substitutes (e.g., personal notes made by a child's

Figure 16.1
School District Responsibilities Under FERPA

1. Establish written policies regarding student records:

   - *Records covered.* Any information compiled by the school that is directly related to a student is included.
   - *Parental accessibility.* Parents have the right to be informed about, inspect, and review the educational records of their children.
   - *Confidentiality.* The written consent of the parent is needed before a school can disclose personally identifiable information from the educational record of a student.
   - *Challenging records.* If parents believe that the school record is inaccurate, misleading, or violates privacy rights, they may request that the school amend it.

2. Annually inform parents of all current students of their rights under FERPA.

3. Establish complaint procedures.

4. Establish procedures for destruction of records.

Parents must be notified of school district policies and procedures teacher, a school psychologist's interview records); and (b) records of the law enforcement unit of an educational agency (e.g., a school's police liaison officer) that are maintained solely for law enforcement purposes. Additionally, schools need not obtain parental consent when records are made available to correctional facilities (*Alexander v. Boyd*, 1995), school attorneys, or special education service providers (*Marshfield School District*, 1995), or when disclosure of information is related to child find activities under the Individuals with Disabilities Act (IDEA) (Schipp, 1995). A school district's release of confidential information to a family doctor without parental permission, however, was ruled a violation of FERPA (*Irvine Unified School District*, 1995).

Accessibility Rights

Parents and eligible students over 18 years of age have the right to see, inspect, reproduce, and challenge the accuracy of educational records. These rights extend to custodial and noncustodial parents unless a court order is issued denying the noncustodial parent access rights. Additionally, schools must explain and interpret records to parents if they ask school officials to do so.

School officials must comply promptly with parental requests to inspect educational records. The response must be made "in a reasonable time frame"—within 45 days of the parent's request.

Amending Records

If parents believe educational records are misleading or incorrect, they may request that the school amend the records. The school may deny the parents' request. The parents may contest this refusal, however, in a due process hearing. The task of the hearing officer in this situation is to determine whether the information in the file is accurate and appropriate. If the officer determines that the information is not accurate or does not belong in the file, it must be removed from the file immediately. If the hearing officer determines that the files are accurate and appropriate, the school does not need to amend the records. The parents, however, may attach a statement regarding their objection to the educational record. This statement must be kept in the student's records.

Confidentiality of Information

Third-party access to educational records is permitted only if the parents provide written consent. The exceptions to these confidentiality provisions include (a) school personnel with legitimate educational interests; (b) officials representing schools to which the student has applied; (c) persons responsible for determining eligibility for financial aid; (d) judicial orders for release; and (e) in emergency situations, persons who act to protect the health and safety of the student. Additionally, FERPA allows a school to use and make public directory information including the name and address of a student, if the school gives parents prior notice of the type of information to be released and gives them adequate time to respond if they disagree. The content of directory information is left to school districts. Courts have held that the directory information provision of the law is the one significant exception to FERPA's confidentiality requirements (Johnson, 1993).

Destruction of Records

Finally, when the local educational agency (LEA) no longer needs the records, it must notify the parents. The parents may request copies of the file or may request that the records be destroyed. If destruction is requested, the LEA may retain a permanent record of the student's name, address, telephone number, grades, attendance, grade level, and the last year of school the student completed.

Enforcement of FERPA

Schools receiving federal financial assistance are in violation of FERPA when they deny parents their rights to inspect and review records or if third parties that are not exempt from FERPA's requirements are allowed to view records without parental permission. If a school district does not take steps to voluntarily remedy the violation, the Department of Education may terminate federal aid to the district. Under FERPA, however, there is no private right of action; that is, a person cannot sue a school under the law (Johnson, 1993; Mawdsley, 1996). If a FERPA violation occurs with a student also covered by the IDEA, the parent may, following exhaustion of due process remedies, initiate a lawsuit under the latter law.

FERPA and the IDEA

The IDEA contains all of the components of FERPA, and both laws apply to the educational records of students with disabilities. The IDEA requires that state and local educational agencies formulate policies that are consistent with FERPA regarding the educational records of students with disabilities. Furthermore, school districts must inform parents of students with disabilities of district policies on educational record access, confidentiality, and maintenance and destruction of records, as well as explain to parents their rights regarding their children's records.

Additionally, the IDEA requires that school districts assign a qualified person at each school to protect the confidentiality of all personally identifiable educational records. Persons who have access to these records must be trained in the policies and procedures of the state as well as the requirements of FERPA. The school must also keep a record of persons obtaining access to educational records. The information that must be collected for the access records includes the name of the party reading the records, the date of access, and the purpose.

Issue #2: Providing Special Education Services in Private Schools

The IDEA guarantees a free appropriate public education (FAPE) to eligible students with disabilities. A question that has vexed special educators—and one that has no clear answer in the IDEA—concerns the extent of the public schools' responsibilities to students with disabilities whose parents enroll them in private schools. Do these students have the same right to special education and related services under the IDEA as do students attending public school? According to the IDEA Amendments of 1997, children with disabilities attending private schools are entitled to a proportionate amount of IDEA funds. Moreover, these funds may be provided to students on the premises of the private schools, including parochial schools, to the extent consistent with existing law. The IDEA unquestionably extends some benefits to private school students with disabilities; however, the extent of these benefits is unclear.

Private School Students and Private Schools

Regulations to the IDEA define "private school students with disabilities" as "children with disabilities enrolled by their parents in private schools or facilities" (IDEA Regulations, 34 C.F.R. § 300.450). Although private schools or facilities are not specifically defined, the Office of Special Education Programs (OSEP) has indicated that the definition is to be determined by state law (Williams, 1992). If a state defines home schooling as a private school, these children will also be included under state law (Mehfoud, 1994). Private schools are typically understood to encompass schools of either a nonsectarian (not church-related) or sectarian (church-related) nature that are not publicly financed.

Private School Placements Made by Public Schools

Regulations to the IDEA indicate that local public school districts placing students with disabilities in private schools must provide special education and related services to these students (IDEA Regulations, 34 C.F.R. §§ 300.401–300.402). The public school's responsibility is to "initiate and conduct meetings to develop, review, and revise an individualized education program for the child" (IDEA Regulations, 34 C.F.R. § 300.348). Furthermore, case law clearly indicates that if a school district fails to provide an appropriate education to a student with disabilities, and the parents unilaterally place the child in a private school to receive an appropriate education, the school has to reimburse the parents for private school placement (*Burlington School Committee v. Department of Education*, 1985).

Private School Placements Made by Parents

The more difficult issue arises when students for whom the school district would normally have been obligated to provide a special education are directly placed in a private school by their parents. That is, when parents choose a private school placement rather than the public school (and the special education services that the public school would have provided), does the public school still have an obligation to provide these services? Clearly, in such situations the public school will not be liable for the private school placement if the public school's program is found appropriate and the private school's program inappropriate. The public school, however, still retains some obligations to the privately placed student derived from its duty under the

IDEA to provide access to a FAPE to students with disabilities residing within the school district. Regulations to the IDEA regarding students with disabilities not referred or placed in the private schools by the public school district require that "each [school district] shall provide special education and related services designed to meet the needs of private school children with disabilities residing in the jurisdiction of the agency" (IDEA regulations, 34 C.F.R. § 300.452(a)). While on its face the regulation seems clear, in reality it has not proven to be so. According to the IDEA Amendments of 1997, if a school district does not offer an appropriate education, a court or hearing officer may require the district to reimburse the parents for the cost of enrollment. Reimbursement can be withheld or reversed, however, if the parents do not inform school officials that they have a concern with the individualized education plan (IEP) and that they were seeking private placement and reimbursement.

Mehfoud (1994) reports that many school districts choose to offer special education services to private school students; however, these services are usually offered in the public school setting. According to an OSEP policy letter (1991), in such situations the transportation of the private school student to the public school may be required under the IDEA (*Felter v. Cape Girardeau School District,* 1993). School districts may also choose to provide the services at the private school. In these instances, however, public money cannot be expended to benefit the private school (Education Department General Administrative Regulations, 34 C.F.R. § 76.658(a)). For example, educational equipment may only be used for students served under the IDEA when this equipment is put in the private school to provide special education and related services to a student.

Public School Responsibilities Under the IDEA

Public schools have certain obligations to private school students with disabilities that are identical to those obligations they have to public school students. For example, public schools must include all students residing in the district in child find efforts, including those in private schools and facilities. Additionally, school districts have an obligation to evaluate these children for special education and related services. When public schools determine that a child in a private school is eligible for special education, an IEP must be developed that provides for a FAPE. If parents and the school disagree as to the appropriateness of the IEP, the parents may request an impartial due process hearing.

Parents may choose to reject the public school district's FAPE and continue their child's education in the private school setting. In such situations, the public schools are obligated to make FAPE available to these students if they return to the public school, and then to provide them with a genuine opportunity for equitable participation in special education programs (Mentink, 1991).

At this point the public school districts' obligations for private and public school students with disabilities diverge and become decidedly less clear. OSEP, however, has taken a specific position on the issue. According to OSEP, once an IEP has been developed that provides a FAPE for the privately placed student, IDEA regulations require the school only to make special education services available (IDEA Regulations, 34 C.F.R. § 300.403(a)). There is no obligation on the part of public school districts to actually provide a FAPE to parent-placed private school students when a FAPE is available through the public school (Mehfoud, 1994). As OSEP has declared, the benefits to which private school students are entitled are limited (Aschenbrenner, 1979; Wing, 1986). Although the FAPE must be offered, students with disabilities enrolled by their parents in a private school are not entitled to a FAPE or to have the cost of the entire placement paid for by the public agency (Wing, 1986). In 1993, OSEP again affirmed that parent-placed students with disabilities did not have an individual entitlement to services under Part B (of the IDEA); therefore, school districts were not required to provide those students with all of the services under Part B to which they would be entitled if they were served in a public placement (Schmidt 1993).

According to the IDEA Amendments of 1997, school districts are not required to pay for private schooling if a FAPE has been made available to a student. However, if a hearing officer or court later determines that the school had not made a FAPE available to a student, the officer or judge may order the school to reimburse the parents for tuition and expenses. In such situations, the critical consideration is whether the special education offered by the school was appropriate to the student's needs.

Additionally, the amendments require that parents must give schools notice about their concerns 10 days prior to transferring their child to a private school. If parents do not adhere to this requirement, hearing officers and courts may reduce or deny reimbursement for unilateral private school placement. Moreover, if the parents act in an unreasonable manner, reimbursement may also be withheld or reduced. The amendments also specify that special education and related services may be provided to students with disabilities on the premises of private and parochial schools to the extent consistent with the law.

Public School Responsibilities Under EDGAR

Regulations to the IDEA (IDEA Regulations, 34 C.F.R. § 300.451) cite the Education Department General Administrative Regulations (EDGAR; 34 C.F.R. §§ 76.651–76.662) regarding the obligations of public schools to privately placed students. EDGAR requires that private school students must be given a "genuine opportunity for equitable participation" (EDGAR, 34 C.F.R. § 76.651(a)(1)). To fulfill these obligations, a public school district must consult with representatives from the private schools (e.g., administrators, teachers). Furthermore, EDGAR indicates that private school students must receive benefits comparable to those provided to students in public schools. The regulations, however, do not include a directive to provide a FAPE to privately placed students when a FAPE is available in a public school.

Litigation

The issue of public schools' responsibility to students with disabilities in private schools is currently the subject of much litigation, but it has yet to be resolved judicially. In fact, the decisions are so mixed that a school district's obligation to parent-enrolled private school students with disabilities depends largely on which judicial circuit the school is in. A number of court decisions have held that there is no individual entitlement to special education for private school students when the public school makes these services available at the public school site. An equal number, however, have ruled that the IDEA rights of private school students are mandatory and that the obligations of public schools are considerable. The split among the lower courts regarding this issue greatly increases the likelihood that the U.S. Supreme Court will settle the issue. The following section will examine these circuit court decisions.

Work v. McKenzie (1987; hereafter *Work*), *Barnett v. Fairfax County School Board* (1991; hereafter *Barnett*), and *Dreher v. Amphitheater Unified School District* (1992; hereafter *Dreher*) affirmed OSEP's opinion that privately placed students have no entitlement to Part B services under the IDEA. In *Work*, the court ruled that by making a special education available in the public schools to a private school student, the McKenzie School Board had satisfied its obligations under the IDEA. Furthermore, the court ruled that the public school district had no obligation to provide transportation to and from a private school for a student with disabilities. In *Barnett*, the U.S. Court of Appeals for the Fourth Circuit held that a school board was not required to offer duplicate special education and related services at a private school site. Finally, in *Dreher*, the court denied reimbursement for speech therapy services at a private school because the services had been made available at a public school. These decisions seem to indicate that public schools can satisfy the requirement to provide special education services to students in private schools by making them available at the public school.

Goodall v. Stafford County School Board

In *Goodall v. Stafford County School Board* (1991; hereafter *Goodall*), the U.S. Court of Appeals for the Fourth Circuit found that a public school had fulfilled its obligations under the IDEA by making services available in the public school, even though services were not available at the parochial school the plaintiff's son attended. Matthew Goodall attended a parochial school. Because he was profoundly deaf, his parents requested an interpreter. The Stafford County School Board offered Matthew the services of the interpreter at the public school but not at the parochial school. Matthew's parents contended this offer was meaningless because Matthew did not attend the public school. The circuit court disagreed, ruling that the school board had met its obligations under the IDEA by making the services available. According to the court, the availability of the interpreter was made meaningless, not by a violation of state or federal law by the school board, but by the parents' educational decision to remove their child from the public school. The court ruled that "by offering [the student] the services of a cued speech interpreter at [the public school] the [district] is in full compliance with the requirements of the IDEA" (*Goodall*, p. 749). The Goodalls' arguments regarding violation of the free exercise and establishment clauses of the First Amendment were also rejected by the circuit court.

The *Goodall* decision strongly supported OSEP's policy regarding special education services and private school students. This ruling is law in the Fourth Circuit, which is comprised of Maryland, North Carolina, South Carolina, Virginia, and West Virginia.

Tribble v. Montgomery County Board of Education

In *Tribble v. Montgomery County Board of Education* (1992), the court ruled that children placed in private schools by their parents must be provided with the related services needed to meet their individual needs. The court further asserted that public schools must deliver a FAPE to each eligible student in a private school. The decision, however, was vacated (i.e., set aside) by agreement of the parties in the suit. The ruling, therefore, has no precedential value. It is instructive, however, as the first in a series of decisions that appeared to enlarge the IDEA entitlement to private school students.

K.R. v. Anderson Community School Corporation

K.R. v. Anderson Community School Corporation (1995; hereafter *KR*) involved a 7-year-old parochial school student with multiple and severe disabilities. She had attended a public school, but her parents removed her and enrolled her in a parochial school. While she was in the public school, an IEP was developed that provided K.R. with speech, occupational, and physical therapy as well as an instructional aide. Following K.R.'s enrollment in the parochial school, she continued to receive the speech, occupational, and physical therapy at the public school site. K.R.'s parents also asked the public school district to provide a full-time instructional aide. The public school refused and informed the child's parents that the special education and related services would only be offered in the public school. The parents then requested a due process hearing. The hearing officer concluded that the public school was not required to provide the instructional aide. In an appeal to the federal district court, the parents argued that, according to the IDEA and the EDGAR comparable benefits requirement, the public school district was required to provide a full-time instructional aide. The district court agreed with the parents in ruling that the school district must supply the instructional aide in the private school. The district court also specifically rejected the Fourth Circuit's ruling in *Goodall,* stating that if it were to follow that decision, its ruling would be contrary to the language of EDGAR. The school district appealed to the U.S. Court of Appeals for the Seventh Circuit.

The U.S. Department of Education (DOE) submitted a brief to the Seventh Circuit urging the court to overturn the decision in *KR.* The DOE's position was that the ruling in *KR* misinterpreted the regulations that require states to make services available to parent-enrolled private school students (IDEA Regulations, 34 C.F.R. §§ 450–452). Furthermore, the IDEA only requires that provisions be made for the participation of private school students in special education programs (IDEA, 20 U.S.C. § 1413(a) (4) (A)) and does not require the state to offer a FAPE to all children with disabilities *in* private schools.

In a decision that strongly affirmed the position of the DOE, the Seventh Circuit court reversed the district court's ruling in *KR.* Stating that the lower court had misinterpreted the IDEA, the circuit court held that public schools need only to offer private school students a genuine opportunity for equitable participation. The court also interpreted the IDEA as requiring a lesser entitlement to students with disabilities when parents opt out of the public school system and place their children in private schools. The court viewed the public school's willingness to continue to provide the student with the special education services in the public school, as well as the school's provision of related services, as evidence that the public school was meeting its obligations under the IDEA. The court noted, however, that if a public school fails to or refuses to provide any special education services to students with disabilities in private schools, especially those that can be provided at a neutral or public school site, such practices would constitute evidence that the public school was not meeting its obligations under the IDEA.

The *KR* decision was supportive of OSEP's position. This ruling is law in the states of Illinois, Indiana, and Wisconsin. The decision has been appealed to the U.S. Supreme Court. The high court returned the case to the Seventh Circuit court for review in the light of the IDEA Amendments of 1997.

Russman v. Sobol

In *Russman v. Sobol* (1996; hereafter *Russman*), the U.S. Court of Appeals for the Second Circuit ruled that a school board had violated the IDEA by refusing to provide the services of a consulting teacher and a teacher aide to a student with a disability on the premises of the student's parochial school. In this case, the parents of an adolescent girl with mental retardation sought an inclusive placement. The girl's IEP also called for the services of a consultant teacher and a teaching aide. When the parents requested that the services of the aide be provided on-site at a parochial school, the district refused. Following a due process hearing, a federal district court ruled that the establishment clause did not bar the public school's provision of the teacher and aide to the parochial school. (The case was then called *Russman v. Watervliet*). In ruling on an appeal of the decision, the circuit court stated that school districts have greater discretion in providing special education services to private school students than they do with public school students. Nevertheless, the court held that the rights of private school students to special education and related services under the IDEA were more consistent with mandatory entitlements than with discretionary authority. The court essentially held that the IDEA requires that public schools provide special education services. School officials may not choose whether they will provide these services. In *Russman,* therefore, the school district was required to provide the teaching aide to the student.

The *Russman* court disagreed with the *KR* decision and the OSEP position on special education services provided to private school students. The court did not, however, view the entitlements to special education services to private and public school services as equal. For example, when determining the extent of services for private school students, schools may limit the services if the costs are excessive when compared to the costs of providing special education services to public school students. The *Russman* court held that

> The IDEA requires the necessary services be provided to disabled private school students according to their needs rather than the name of the school . . . such services must be comparable in quality, scope, and opportunity for participation to those offered public school students. (p. 1056)

This decision is law in the states of Connecticut, New York, and Vermont. The *Russman* decision was appealed to the U.S. Supreme Court. The high court, however, returned the case to the lower court to review in the light of the IDEA Amendments of 1997.

Cefalu v. East Baton Rouge Parish School Board

In *Cefalu v. East Baton Rouge Parish School Board* (1996; hereafter *Cefalu*), a district court in Louisiana ruled that the IDEA required a public school to provide a sign language interpreter to a student with a hearing impairment at his parochial school. The school had refused the Cefalus' request, but had offered to provide the services at the public school. The court held that because an interpreter provides constant assistance in the classroom, potential benefits would be meaningless if they were not available in the private school.

The school district appealed to the U.S. Court of Appeals for the Fifth Circuit. The circuit court recognized that the IDEA does not mandate that services be provided to private school students with disabilities on the private school premises; nevertheless, a school's refusal to provide services may deny students their rights to equitable participation under the IDEA. School officials may also consider funding in making decisions regarding private school services because private school students have no right to a greater share of benefits and funds than do public school students.

The Fifth Circuit court developed a three-part test for lower courts to use in determining whether a school district is required to provide special education and related services to parent-placed private school students on the premises of the private school. In the first part of the test, the private school student must convince the court of a genuine need for on-site services. The burden of proof is clearly on the student to prove need; the school is not directly involved in part one. If the student proves a genuine need, the court moves to part two of the test. The school district must either provide the service or have a justifiable reason for refusing to do so. If the district presents a valid case for not providing the service, the student is entitled, in part three of the test, to prove that the district's position violates the IDEA. The ruling is law in the Fifth Circuit, which is comprised of Louisiana, Mississippi, and Texas.

The circuit court remanded the case to the lower court to apply this test and to determine whether the school district had to provide the interpreter at the private school. Before the district court could rehear the case, however, the Fifth Circuit court agreed to a rehearing.

The circuit court reversed its original position in the light of the IDEA Amendments of 1997. The school district, according to the court, was not required to provide the student's sign language interpreter at the parochial school. Once a school district offers a FAPE, the district is under no further obligation to parent-placed private school students with disabilities. Because the East Baton Rouge Parish School District had offered a FAPE, it was not required to provide the student with the requested services.

Fowler v. Unified School District

In *Fowler v. Unified School District* (1996; hereafter *Fowler*), the U.S. Court of Appeals for the Tenth Circuit became the fifth circuit court to rule on the issue of private school services. The case involved an appeal of a judgment by a federal district court in Montana. The district court ordered a school district to provide one-on-one interpretive services at a parochial school. The school district had developed an IEP and offered related services either in the public school, in an after-school program, or in locations in the public school and the after-school program. The parents rejected all three options, seeking instead to have these services offered at the parochial school. The court held that the IDEA required the school district to provide these services in a private school unless there was no reasonable way to do so. The decision was appealed to the U.S. Court of Appeals for the Tenth Circuit. The ruling in the case is controlling authority in Colorado, Kansas, New Mexico, Oklahoma, Utah, and Wyoming. The circuit court affirmed the ruling of the district court, ordering a school district to provide one-on-one interpretive services to a student with disabilities at his private school. Additionally, the circuit court held that the school district had to pay for the services in an amount up to what would be expended if the student were in a public school. The school district was not required to exceed that cost. Cost, therefore, is a relevant factor in providing services in private schools. The *Fowler* decision, like *Russman,* views the rights of students with disabilities in private schools to a FAPE as an entitlement.

The decision of the circuit court was appealed to the U.S. Supreme Court. The high court returned the case to the lower court to review in the light of the IDEA Amendments of 1997.

School District Responsibilities to Private School Students

Clearly, public schools are obligated to include parent-enrolled private school students in the child find process. If the school suspects the existence of a disability, it is obligated to evaluate the private school student. If the student is found to have a disability covered by the IDEA, the school is required to write an IEP that provides a FAPE.

Mehfoud (1994) states that a beginning point for public schools in meeting their obligations to private school students with disabilities is to consult with representatives of the private school. The purpose of the consultation is to determine which students will be provided services, as well as to gather information about those students. OSEP has indicated that the state or local educational agency is responsible for determining the private school representative, although the IDEA contains no guidelines as to whom this representative must be (Cernosia, 1994). Mehfoud suggests that public schools send annual letters to private schools advising them of services available and requesting notification regarding the presence of students with disabilities in the private schools (Know Your Obligations, 1995). Also, the public school should determine the nature and location of services that will be provided. The school district may not have to provide the same special education and related services in a private school that it would have had to provide students if they were placed in a public school. The district must, however, offer comparable special education and related services. At present, it seems that if the public school offers special education services on-site at the parochial school, at a neutral site, or at the public school, thereby giving the private school student with disabilities a genuine opportunity to participate, the public school will have met its responsibilities under the IDEA. The split in the circuit courts, however, makes unclear what constitutes a genuine opportunity to participate and benefit.

The nature of the public school's obligation to actually provide these services remains undecided. The position of the DOE is that public schools are required only to make these services available to the child. Three circuit courts—the Fourth, in *Goodall*, the Fifth, in *Cefalu*, and the Seventh, in *KR*—agree with this position. The Second Circuit, in *Russman*, and the Tenth Circuit, in *Fowler*, however, ruled that the IDEA requires an equal entitlements approach. Moreover, it is a virtual certainty that the U.S. Supreme Court will soon have to bring order to this issue because of the split among the circuit courts regarding public schools' responsibility to students in private schools. The different requirements of the various circuit court decisions are listed in Table 16.1.

Table 16.1
Circuit Court Rulings on Special Education in Private Schools

	Russman	Goodall	Cefalu	KR	Fowler
Circuit	Second Circuit	Fourth Circuit	Fifth Circuit	Seventh Circuit	Tenth Circuit
	Connecticut, New York, Vermont	Maryland, North Carolina, South Carolina, Virginia, West Virginia	Louisiana, Mississippi, Texas	Illinois, Indiana, Wisconsin	Colorado, Kansas, New Mexico, Oklahoma, Utah, Wyoming
Ruling	Responsibilities of public schools to students in public and private schools are comparable, although not necessarily equal.	Public schools are required to provide private school students with disabilities with a FAPE. Once a FAPE has been offered, the school district has no further obligation to parent-placed private school students.	Public schools are required to provide private school students with disabilities with a FAPE. Once a FAPE has been offered, the school district has no further obligation to parent-placed private school students.	Responsibilities of public schools to students in public and private schools are not comparable. Students in private schools have no entitlement to the full range of special education services.	Responsibilities of public schools to students in public and private schools are comparable. Public schools are not required to exceed costs of services provided to students in public school.

Summary of the IDEA and Private Schools

If public school officials place a student in a private school, the public school is responsible for writing, reviewing, and revising the IEP unless the private school assumes this responsibility. In the latter case, the public school must have a district representative at IEP meetings. If parents unilaterally enroll their children in private schools, the public school district's responsibilities include (a) identification; (b) evaluation; (c) writing the IEP; and (d) offering the special education services. Gorn (1996) asserts that schools should continue the IEP process even after the student is enrolled in the private school. Continuing the process demonstrates the school's interest in the student's education as well as its willingness to provide an appropriate education if the student returns to the public school. The extent of school districts' responsibility to provide a special education to students with disabilities placed by their parents in private schools seems to have been largely settled by the IDEA Amendments of 1997. According to the amendments, a school district is not required to pay for private schooling if the district had made a FAPE available to the student. The court in *Cefalu,* which was the first circuit court decision made after the passage of the IDEA amendments, ruled that once a FAPE has been offered, the school district has no further obligation to the parent-placed private school student. If a hearing officer or a judge determines that a school did not offer a FAPE, however, reimbursement for tuition and expenses may be ordered.

Issue #3: The IDEA and the Establishment Clause

An additional level of legal complexity exists when the private school in question is sectarian or church-sponsored. Sectarian schools are also referred to as parochial schools. The primary legal question involves the extent to which the Constitution permits the use of public funds for services to students with disabilities who are attending parochial schools (Linden, 1995). The constitutional concern is that special education services, when made available in parochial schools, may be construed as state aid to parochial schools and, thus, violate the First Amendment. The First Amendment requires that governmental relations with religions be guided by two fundamental principles: the government cannot make a law establishing a religion, nor can it deny the free exercise of any religion (see the Appendix). This amendment contains two separate elements regarding the government and religion. The first, referred to as the establishment clause, was summarized by Justice Black in *Everson v. Board of Education* (1947):

> Neither a state nor the Federal Government can set up a church. Neither can pass laws which aid one religion, aid all religion, or prefer one religion over another. . . . No tax in any amount, large or small, can be levied to support any religious activities or institutions . . . to teach or practice religion. (p. 15)

The second element, the free exercise clause, constrains state governments and the federal government from intruding upon an individual's religious beliefs and practices. Educational practices involving church/state issues primarily concern the establishment clause.

The exact meaning of the establishment clause has been the subject of much debate. The U.S. Supreme Court has recognized only two instances in which education becomes intertwined with the establishment clause. The first involves religious activities within the public schools (e.g., school prayer), and the second concerns public aid to sectarian schools (e.g., providing educational materials). Special education services, when provided in parochial school, involve the latter.

Everson v. Board of Education

The U.S. Supreme Court first addressed the question of state aid to a parochial school in *Everson v. Board of Education* (1947; hereafter *Everson*). The case involved a New Jersey statute that authorized the state to reimburse the parents of public and parochial school children for bus fares paid for the purpose of transporting their children to and from school. The statute was challenged on the grounds that it violated the First Amendment by providing state support to church-sponsored schools. In the majority opinion, Justice Black wrote a lengthy historical analysis of the establishment clause. Black cited Thomas Jefferson's writings regarding the establishment clause as being intended to erect a "wall of separation between church and state." Based on this analysis, Black concluded that the primary concept underlying the establishment clause was the principle of neutrality. The establishment clause "requires the state to be neutral in its relations with groups of religious believers and nonbelievers, it does not require the state to be their adversary" (*Everson*, p. 18). The high court held that the New Jersey statute did not violate the establishment clause because the bus fares were paid directly to the parents, regardless of whether or not their children attended a church-sponsored school, thereby not breaching the "wall" between church and state. In fact, the Court stated that to deny parents of children attending parochial schools the reimbursement would be tantamount to denying children their rights based on their parents' religious convictions.

Under the *Everson* neutrality test, the question of special education aid to parochial school students would probably have passed constitutional muster because the IDEA requires that special education services be provided to all students with disabilities whether they attend public, private, or parochial schools (Guernsey & Klare, 1993; Linden, 1995). The high court, however, has analyzed cases involving state aid to students in parochial schools not according to whether these services should be provided, but rather according to how those benefits can be provided so as not to violate the establishment clause.

The EDGAR requirements mirror the *Everson* standard in setting forth limitations on the use of public education funds at sectarian schools. According to the EDGAR requirements, the use of funds for religion is prohibited, and

> (a) No State or subgrantee may use its grant or subgrant to pay for any of the following:
> (1) Religious worship, instruction, or proselytization
> (2) Equipment or supplies to be used for any activities specified. (EDGAR, 34 C.F.R. § 76.532(a))

Lemon v. Kurtzman

In *Lemon v. Kurtzman* (1971), the U.S. Supreme Court devised a test to determine the validity of laws that may violate the establishment clause. The test consisted of a three-part analysis. To be judged permissible, federal or state laws must (a) have a secular purpose; (b) have a primary effect that neither advances nor inhibits religion; and (c) avoid excessive government entanglement with religion (see Figure 16.2). The test was used to rule on the constitutional validly of programs in both Rhode Island and Pennsylvania. The program in Rhode Island authorized salary supplements for teachers of secular subjects in nonpublic schools. In reality, the program benefited only 250 teachers in Catholic schools in the state. The Pennsylvania statute authorized the reimbursement of private schools for teacher salaries, texts, and instructional materials in secular subjects. The majority of the schools that received the reimbursement were parochial schools. In both instances the laws were ruled unconstitutional because they would result in excessive church-state entanglement due to the necessary administration and surveillance they would require.

The Supreme Court subsequently applied the *Lemon* test to a number of programs that provided state aid or assistance to parochial schools. The Court has struck down direct monetary reimbursement to parochial schools for state-mandated educational expenditures such as testing (*Levitt v. Committee for Public Education,* 1973) and maintenance of school facilities (*Committee for Public Education v. Nyquist,* 1973). Additionally, the purchase or loan of instructional materials or equipment to parochial schools and the provision of guidance counseling and remedial and accelerated instruction in parochial schools were found to be violations of the *Lemon* test (*Meek v. Pittenger,* 1975).

A common fault of many of these state statutes was the lack of control of state monies once they were given to the parochial schools. If the state could not guarantee that the money was used only for sectarian purposes, it was in violation of the second prong of the *Lemon* test because the monies could possibly be used to advance a religion. The test created a problem in instances where the state set up monitoring systems to ensure that state monies would not be used for religious purposes. In such situations, the third part of the *Lemon* test, prohibiting excessive entanglement of church and state, would be violated.

Because special education and related services under the IDEA are provided directly to the student, not the parochial school, it would seem less likely that the pro-

Figure 16.2
The *Lemon* Test

1. Does the policy or practice have a secular purpose?
2. Is the primary effect of the policy or practice one that neither advances nor inhibits religion?
3. Does the policy or practice avoid excessive entanglement with religion?

vision of these services would violate the establishment clause. Two Supreme Court decisions from 1985, however, seemed to counter this notion.

Grand Rapids School District v. Ball

The high court's decision in *Grand Rapids School District v. Ball* (1985; hereafter *Grand Rapids*) involved a program to enrich the curriculum of private schools through the provision of supplementary classes conducted by state-paid teachers. The classes were held in rooms in private schools that were leased for these classes. Parochial schools were required to remove all religious symbols from the classrooms and post signs on the classroom doors noting that the rooms were public school classrooms. The Supreme Court found that these programs violated the establishment clause because the sectarian atmosphere might influence the state-paid teachers to indoctrinate the students at public expense. The Court also stated that the symbolic union of the state and the parochial school might convey a message of state support for religion and noted that the programs were actually subsidizing parochial schools by freeing up the resources they would normally spend on the teaching of the secular classes for religious purposes.

Aguilar v. Felton

Aguilar v. Felton (1985; hereafter *Aguilar*) concerned the implementation of Title I of the Elementary and Secondary Education Act of 1965. Title I provides federal funds to assist schools to provide remedial instruction for educationally deprived children from low-income families. *Aguilar* involved the implementation of these programs in New York. The state was offering Title I services in parochial schools in clearly designated classrooms. As in *Grand Rapids,* the classrooms were devoid of all religious materials. New York had also instituted a surveillance system for monitoring the Title I classes to keep them free of religious content. The high court held that the Title I program violated the establishment clause because the monitoring system resulted in an excessive entanglement of church and state.

The decisions in *Grand Rapids* and *Aguilar* seem to portend possible violations of the establishment clause when special education and related services are provided on-site to students with disabilities in parochial schools. Justice O'Connor's dissent in *Aguilar* was an indication of a new direction the Court may be headed regarding the establishment clause. O'Connor examined the decision and specifically questioned the value of the *Lemon* test. Her dissent viewed educational services less as a form of aid to parochial schools and more as a general government program designed to benefit all children without reference to religion (Linden, 1995). This has been called the child benefit theory. According to this theory, if a governmental practice is neutral toward religion, the program or activity will pass constitutional muster if it benefits a child's general welfare, even if it aids the sectarian function of the parochial school (McKinney, 1993).

Opinions in a few decisions in the early 1990s indicated that a majority of the Supreme Court justices shared Justice O'Connor's view or held similar views. In an important development, the Court agreed to reexamine its decision in *Aguilar* (renamed *Agostini v. Felton*). On June 23, 1997, the high court handed down a decision in *Agostini v. Felton*.

Zobrest v. Catalina Foothills School District

The Supreme Court, in *Zobrest v. Catalina Foothills School District* (1993; hereafter *Zobrest*), ruled that there is no general prohibition against providing services at parochial schools. The case involved a deaf student, James Zobrest, who received special education and related services while attending a public middle school. He was mainstreamed with resource room services and was provided with a sign language interpreter in his classes. When he reached high school age, his parents unilaterally enrolled him in a Catholic high school. While in the parochial high school, James received speech therapy in a public school classroom. James's parents requested that the public school provide the services of the interpreter in the parochial school. The public school board declined to provide the services, although it indicated that these services would be provided if James were still in the public school. The Zobrests filed a suit in federal district court, seeking to have the services of the interpreter be provided by the public school. The court held that the provision of the interpreter violated the establishment clause of the First Amendment. The decision was upheld on appeal to the U.S. Court of Appeals for the Ninth Circuit. The Zobrests appealed to the U.S. Supreme Court, which chose to hear the case. In a 5 to 4 decision, the high court reversed the decision of the lower courts and ruled in favor of the Zobrests. The Court ruled that the public financing of James's sign language interpreter did not conflict with the establishment clause of the Constitution.

The Court developed a three-part test to determine whether a program of governmental services would survive an establishment clause challenge (see Figure 16.3). First, the services must be provided in a neutral manner, without regard to religion; that is, the services provided must provide assistance to a student without regard to the religious nature of the school. Second, the services cannot be provided at the sectarian school as a result of legislative choice but rather as a result of private choice of the person using the services. A student, therefore must be placed in the parochial school because of parental choice and not from the choice of school district

Figure 16.3
The *Zobrest* Three-Part Test

1. Services to the parochial school student must be provided in a religiously neutral manner.
2. Services can only be provided when the placement in the parochial school is the result of parental choice.
3. IDEA funds must not find their way into the parochial school's coffers.

officials. Finally, the funds traceable to the government must not find their way into the sectarian school's coffers. The funds must not provide direct assistance to the parochial school, although indirect aid may be difficult to avoid.

The Establishment Clause and the IDEA

Chief Justice Rehnquist, writing for the majority in *Zobrest,* noted that the IDEA conferred benefits on the student and that these benefits were neutral; that is, the public funds were distributed to an eligible child without regard to the nature of the school the child attended. Also, the public school funds did not go directly to the parochial school, so no public assistance was provided to the parochial school. The student, not the school, was the primary beneficiary of the public school's funds. The Court held that the establishment clause does not bar religious organizations from participating in publicly sponsored welfare programs that neutrally provide benefits to a broad class of citizens defined without reference to religion. Neither does the establishment clause create an absolute bar to placing a public employee at a sectarian school. Because an interpreter for James Zobrest would do no more than accurately interpret the material presented to the student's class, the interpreter would neither add to nor subtract from the sectarian environment of the school.

The high court held that the IDEA is a program distributing benefits neutrally to students with disabilities without regard to the religious or secular nature of the school they attend. Neither does the law encourage religion, because it creates no incentive for parents to select a sectarian school. Finally, the IDEA funds only benefit sectarian schools indirectly, at best. In providing IDEA funds, the government is not subsidizing costs that the sectarian school would otherwise have assumed in educating its students.

The Court also noted that the duties of the sign language interpreter were considerably different from the duties of a teacher or counselor. Because the role of the interpreter was to relay instructional content, the provision of the interpreter was not prohibited by the establishment clause.

The Court did not answer whether the IDEA requires or permits public schools to provide interpreters on-site in parochial schools. Rather, the Court dealt exclusively with the establishment clause issue. The holding of the high court in *Zobrest* was a narrow one. The Court simply stated that certain services, which can only be provided on-site, may be provided without violating the First Amendment. In this decision the Court seemed firmly to adopt the child benefit theory.

Post-*Zobrest* Cases

The *Zobrest* court, in dicta, indicated that the services of a teacher or guidance counselor may be prohibited by the establishment clause. Following *Zobrest,* the issue facing the courts involved questions of what on-site services could be provided by personnel other than interpreters.

A decision in the U.S. Court of Appeals for the Second Circuit provided some direction regarding the scope of services that were not barred by the establishment clause. In *Russman,* a school district had written an IEP for an 11-year-old girl with moderate mental disabilities. The IEP called for an inclusive placement with the services of a consultant teacher and a teacher's aide. The girl was subsequently placed in a parochial school, where the parents demanded that she receive the services called for in the IEP. The parents won a judgment at the district court level, and the school district appealed. The Second Circuit court affirmed the lower court's decision, holding that the special education services sought by the parents (i.e., the services of a consultant teacher and the teacher's aide) were limited to core academic subjects and were permissible under the First Amendment. The court held that the purpose of the consultant and the aide, like the sign language interpreter in *Zobrest,* was to make material intelligible to the student, not to advance a religious viewpoint.

In a policy letter following the *Zobrest* decision, OSEP wrote that the provision of a personal computer for in-school use by a student with disabilities attending a sectarian school was not prohibited by the establishment clause (Moore, 1993). According to OSEP,

> Part B funds [may be used] to purchase a computer if the personal computer, like the sign language interpreter at issue in *Zobrest,* is provided to overcome the child's disability by enhancing his ability to communicate, not for religious worship, instruction, or proselytization. (p. 1213)

Board of Education of Kiryas Joel Village School District v. Grumet

In 1994, the U.S. Supreme Court issued a ruling in *Board of Education of Kiryas Joel Village School District v. Grumet* (hereafter *Kiryas Joel*). Kiryas Joel is a village in New York comprised of about 8,500 Satmar Hasidim. Members of this Orthodox Jewish sect speak Yiddish and choose to remove themselves from certain aspects of modern society (e.g., they wear traditional religious clothes and do not watch television). Children generally attend sex-segregated parochial schools. In the mid-1980s, the local public school district began to provide special education services for the children with disabilities from Kiryas Joel in an annex to their religious school. In 1985, however, the public school suspended this practice after the Supreme Court's decisions in *Aguilar* and *Grand Rapids.* The Satmar children who needed special education services were forced to attend public schools in order to continue to receive these services. Within a short period of time, most of the children were withdrawn from these services because of the trauma the children suffered from attending the public schools. The village elders sought help from the New York legislature. The legislature created a public school district in Kiryas Joel. The district consisted of one school, which served the children with disabilities from the village. The school was secular, no religious classes were included in the curriculum, boys and girls were educated together, and there were no religious symbols in the school. The New York State School Boards Association claimed that the state-sponsored special school district violated the establishment clause of the Constitution. The association prevailed in the lower courts. An appeal was filed with the U.S. Supreme Court, which agreed to hear the case.

In a 6 to 3 decision, the high court ruled that the establishment of the special school district in Kiryas Joel was unconstitutional. The Court issued a narrow ruling (i.e., a ruling on a fine point of law) based on the principle of government neutrality toward religion (Schimmel, 1994). The greatest significance of *Kiryas Joel,* however, was in the concurring and dissenting opinions issued by the justices. These opinions indicated possible directions the Court may take in future establishment cases. A majority of the justices seemed to believe that *Aguilar* was wrongly decided and that it should be overturned. Schimmel (1994) asserted that if the Court overruled *Aguilar,* it would be a victory for those advocating greater government accommodation for religion and a lower wall of separation between church and state.

Agostini v. Felton

In a 5 to 4 ruling in *Agostini v. Felton* (1997), the U.S. Supreme Court reversed *Aguilar.* The petitioners emphasized the costs of complying with the decision and the assertions of five of the high court justices that *Aguilar* should be reconsidered because it was no longer good law. According to the Court's opinion, written by Justice O'Connor, federally funded programs that provide supplemental, remedial instruction to disadvantaged students on-site in parochial schools are valid under the establishment clause when such instruction contains safeguards such as those of the New York program (i.e., sending a school supervisor into the parochial schools on unannounced monthly visits). The Court also noted that the portion of the decision in *Grand Rapids* that addressed a similar program in Grand Rapids, Michigan, was also invalid. The opinion was based on the Court's more recent decisions regarding this issue. These cases had served to undermine the assumptions of *Aguilar* and *Grand Rapids.* The majority opinion stated that placing full-time government employees on parochial school campuses did not, as a matter of law, have the effect of advancing religion through indoctrination. The Court did not believe that the mere presence of public employees in parochial schools would inevitably inculcate religion or that their presence would constitute a symbolic union between government and religion. Neither would the presence of public school teachers in parochial schools illegally support religion. The teachers would benefit the students, not the parochial school.

Clearly, the decision allows public school districts to use public money to provide services on-site in parochial schools. Nevertheless, the decision does not create a new entitlement for parochial school students. Essentially, the Court ruled that there is no First Amendment problem when public schools send teachers into parochial schools.

Summary of the IDEA and Parochial Schools

Conclusions regarding the IDEA and the church–state issue must be considered tentative at best. School districts have a significant obligation to children with disabilities in parochial schools. Public school districts must identify all children with disabilities living in the district's attendance area, including those attending parochial schools, and must offer special education and related services to eligible parochial school students. The primary question that remains unanswered is how the students should be served. The Supreme Court's decision in *Zobrest* indicates that school districts may provide supportive services to students with disabilities in parochial schools. This decision does not indicate, however, that districts are allowed to provide all types of services on-site at parochial schools (e.g., counseling or direct teaching). The U.S. Supreme Court's decision in *Agostini* seems to enlarge the *Zobrest* decision to other types of supportive services.

Neither does *Zobrest* or *Agostini* indicate that public schools are required to provide special education and related services to parochial school students; they merely indicate that certain services may be offered on-site at parochial schools without violating the establishment clause. Post-*Zobrest* decisions, such as *Russman*, expanded the types of related services that may be provided in private schools without violating the establishment clause.

Regarding the actual services that should be extended by public schools to parochial school students, the standard is whether the student with disabilities is provided with a genuine opportunity for meaningful participation. As was the case in *KR* and *Goodall,* the public school may discharge its responsibilities by making an appropriate education, consisting of special education and related services, available at a neutral or public school site. The IDEA Amendments of 1997 seem to confirm this position. The amendments do allow public schools to provide special education services on the premises of parochial schools to the extent consistent with the law.

Issue #4: Liability for Student Injury

In the past few years, there has been a substantial increase in the number of lawsuits filed on behalf of students with disabilities injured while at school. These suits are usually filed against the schools and school personnel (Pitasky, 1995). Typically these cases involve injuries, either physical or emotional, that occur either accidentally or intentionally. Often these suits involve tort claims of negligence.

Tort Laws

Tort laws are laws that offer remedies to individuals harmed by the unreasonable actions of others. Tort claims usually involve state law and are based on the legal premise that individuals are liable for the consequences of their conduct if it results in injury to others (McCarthy & Cambron-McCabe, 1992). Tort claims involve civil suits, which are actions brought to protect an individual's private rights. Civil suits are different from criminal prosecution. Criminal prosecutions are actions brought by the state to redress violations of the law. There are two major categories of torts typically seen in education-related cases: intentional torts and negligence.

Intentional Torts

Intentional torts are usually committed when a person attempts or intends to do harm. For intent to exist, the individual must know with reasonable certainty that injury will be the result of the act (Alexander & Alexander, 1992). A common type of intentional tort is assault. Assault refers to an overt attempt to physically injure a person or to create a feeling of fear and apprehension of injury. No actual physical contact need take place for an assault to occur. Battery, on the other hand, is an intentional tort that results from physical contact. For example, if a person picks up a chair and threatens to hit another person, assault has occurred; if the person then actually hits the second person, battery has occurred. Both assault and battery can occur if a person threatens another, causing apprehension and fear, and then actually strikes the other, resulting in actual injury. According to Alexander and Alexander (1992), teachers accused of assault and battery are typically given considerable leeway by the courts. This is because assault and battery cases often result from attempts to discipline a child, usually by some manner of corporal punishment, and courts are generally reluctant to interfere with a teacher's authority to discipline students (Alexander & Alexander, 1992; McCarthy & Cambron-McCabe, 1992; Valente, 1994).

Courts have found teachers guilty of assault and battery, however, when a teacher's discipline has been cruel, brutal, excessive, or administered with malice, anger, or intent to injure. In determining if a teacher's discipline constitutes excessive and unreasonable punishment, courts will often examine the age of the student; the instrument, if any, used to administer the discipline; the extent of the discipline; the nature and gravity of the student's offense; the history of the student's previous conduct; and the temper and conduct of the teacher. For example, a teacher in Louisiana was sued and lost a case for assault and battery for picking up a student, slamming him against bleachers, and then dropping the student to the floor, breaking his arm (*Frank v. New Orleans Parish School Board,* 1967). In Connecticut, a student was awarded damages when a teacher slammed the student against a chalkboard and then a wall, breaking the student's clavicle (*Sansone v. Bechtel,* 1980). Clearly, teachers may be held personally liable for injuries that occur to students because of teachers' behavior. The legal principles that apply to teachers whose behavior causes injury are the same principles that apply to all citizens (Fischer, Schimmel, & Kelly, 1994).

A small body of case law also indicates that school districts and school officials may be liable for damages in cases alleging teacher abuse of students. In *C.M. v. Southeast Delco School District* (1993), the Federal District Court for the Eastern District of Pennsylvania ruled that a student could proceed with a suit for damages against a school district and school officials because of injuries incurred as a result of alleged abuse perpetrated by a special education teacher. The abuse in this case included verbal harassment, (e.g., name-calling, ridiculing, profanity), physical abuse (e.g., slapping, hitting, grabbing and slamming into a locker, spraying with water and Lysol), and sexual abuse. The court ruled that the state had an affirmative duty to protect people from its own employees. Furthermore, the court stated that this was particularly true of teachers, because they are in positions of great sensitivity and responsibility. Later that year, the same court heard another damage claim against the same school district and teacher for sexual, physical, and verbal abuse. In *K.L. v. Southeast Delco School District* (1993), the court reiterated that the student had an appropriate claim for damages based on the school district's actions or inaction which resulted in injuries to the student. Again the court noted that school districts and school officials have a heightened duty to supervise and monitor teachers. Pitasky (1995) posited that these cases, although legally binding only in their districts, have created a potential for damages to be imposed on school districts and school officials for liability claims against teachers and other school personnel.

Teachers have also won assault and damage suits against students. A Wisconsin court awarded a teacher compensatory and punitive damages for a battery case he brought against a student who physically attacked and injured him as he brought the student to the principal's office for a rule violation (*Anello v. Savignac*, 1983). An Oregon court assessed damages against a student who struck and injured his teacher for not allowing him to leave the classroom during class period (*Garret v. Olson*, 1984).

Negligence

The second type of tort seen most frequently in education-related cases is negligence. The difference between negligence and an intentional tort is that in negligence the acts leading to injury are neither expected nor intended (Alexander & Alexander, 1992). Negligence arises in instances where conduct falls below an acceptable standard of care, thereby resulting in injury. For negligence to occur, an injury must have been avoidable by the exercise of reasonable care. The ability to foresee injury or harm is an important factor in determining negligence. Unforeseeable accidents that could not have been prevented by reasonable care do not constitute negligence.

There are four elements that must be present for negligence to occur:

1. The teacher must have a duty to protect another from unreasonable risks.
2. The teacher must have failed in that duty by failing to exercise a reasonable standard of care.
3. There must be a causal connection between the breach of the duty to care and the resulting injury.
4. There must be an actual physical or mental injury resulting from the negligence.

In a court all four elements must be proven before a court will award damages for negligence (Freedman, 1995; McCarthy & Cambron-McCabe, 1992).

Duty to Protect.   The first element, the duty to protect, is clearly part of a teacher's responsibilities. Teachers have a duty to anticipate foreseeable dangers and take necessary precautions to protect students in their care from such dangers (McCarthy & Cambron-McCabe, 1992). Specifically, teachers' duties include adequate supervision, maintenance of equipment and facilities, and heightened supervision of high-risk activities. In the majority cases of negligence against teachers, the duty to protect is easily proven (Fischer et al., 1994). Clearly, this duty applies to activities during the school day; however, courts have also held that this duty may extend beyond regular school hours and away from school grounds (e.g., after-school activities, summer activities, field trips, bus rides).

Failure to Exercise a Reasonable Standard of Care.   The second element occurs when teachers fail to exercise a reasonable standard of care in their duties to students. If a teacher fails to exercise reasonable care to protect students from injury, then the teacher is negligent. In negligence cases, courts will gauge a teacher's conduct on how a "reasonable" teacher in a similar situation might have acted (Alexander & Alexander, 1992). The degree of care exercised by a "reasonable" teacher is determined by factors such as (a) the training and experience of the teacher in charge; (b) the student's age; (c) the environment in which the injury occurred; (d) the type of instructional activity; (e) the presence or absence of the supervising teacher; and (f) a student's disability, if one exists (Mawdsley, 1993; McCarthy & Cambron-McCabe, 1992). For example, a primary-grade student will require closer supervision than a secondary student; a physical education class in a gymnasium or an industrial arts class in a school woodshop will require closer supervision than a reading class in the school library; and a student with a mental disability will require closer supervision than a student with average intelligence. In *Foster v. Houston General* (1981), a student with a moderate mental disability was struck and fatally injured when she darted into traffic while being escorted, along with nine other students from her special education class, to a park three blocks from the school. The court held that the teacher had failed to select the safest route to the park and to maintain the close supervisory duties required in this situation. The court also found that the general level of care required for all students becomes greater when the student body is composed of students with mental retardation. The court also stated that the standard of care was heightened because the children were being taken off the school campus. A number of cases have held that the student's IEP, disability, and unique needs are all relevant factors in determining the level of supervision that is reasonable (Daggett, 1995). Additionally, school officials may be liable for damage claims resulting from a failure to supervise a student with a disability when that student injures another student. In *Cohen v. School District* (1992), a federal district court ruled that a liability claim could go forward when a behaviorally disordered student with known violent tendencies was placed in a general education classroom without adequate supervision and subsequently attacked and injured another student.

Proximate Cause.   The third element that must be proven in a negligence case is a connection between the breach of duty by the teacher (element two) and the subsequent injury to the student (element four). This element, referred to as proximate cause, often hinges on the concept of foreseeability; that is, was the student's injury something that could have been anticipated by a teacher? If the injury could have been foreseen and prevented by a teacher if a reasonable standard of care had been exercised, a logical connection and, therefore, negligence may exist. This logical connection is referred to as proximate cause. To answer questions regarding proximate cause, courts will ask, "Was the injury a natural and probable cause of the wrongful act (i.e., failure to supervise), and ought [it] to have been foreseen in light of the attendant circumstances?" (*Scott v. Greenville*, 1965). Negligence claims will not be successful if the accident could not have been foreseen. In *Sheehan v. St. Peter's Catholic School* (1971), a teacher was supervising a group of students at recess when some of the students began throwing rocks. The rock throwing had continued for almost 10 minutes when a student was struck in the eye and injured. The court found the supervising teacher liable for negligence because a reasonable teacher would have anticipated or foreseen potential harm arising from the incident and stopped it. In a Wyoming case, *Fagan v. Summers* (1978), a teacher's aide was determined not to be the proximate cause of a playground-related injury that occurred during her supervision. Immediately after the aide walked by a group of students, one child threw rock which was deflected and hit another child. The court concluded that the injury was unforeseen and could not have been prevented even with the aide's providing adequate supervision.

Actual Injury.   The final element that must be proven in negligence cases is that there was an actual physical or mental injury. Even in instances where there is negligence, damage suits will not be successful unless there is provable injury.

Teachers' Defenses Against Liability

If it can be shown that a student contributed to the injury, the teacher may use a defense of contributory negligence. If the court finds that contributory negligence was present, the teacher will not be held liable. With younger students (i.e., under age 6), it is difficult to prove contributory negligence because the tort laws in many states hold that young children are incapable of contributory negligence. In these instances, therefore, students can collect damages even if they did contribute to the injury. If students are between the ages of 7 and 14, unless it can be shown that they are quite intelligent and mature, contributory negligence is difficult to prove.

With older students, assumption of risk can also be used as a defense against negligence claims. Assumption of risk has been recognized as a defense against claims of liability in activities such as competitive sports (Fischer et al., 1994). If a student is mature enough to recognize the dangers of certain activities and still volunteers to participate, the student assumes a certain amount of risk. For example, in *Kluka v. Livingston Parish Board* (1983), an 11th-grade student challenged his basketball coach to a wrestling match. The student was injured during the match and subsequently sued the coach for damages. The student testified that he had not contributed to the injury because he had not known he could be injured wrestling. The court found the teacher not liable for damages, stating that there were some risks that everyone must appreciate. As is the case with contributory negligence, it is unlikely that young and less mature students would be found by a court to assume the risk in activities, since they are often seen as not able to understand or appreciate the consequences of high-risk activities.

Finally, it is often assumed that teachers and schools can release themselves from damages by having parents sign waivers or releases. This is untrue, because parents cannot waive their children's claims for damages (Fischer et al., 1994; Freedman, 1995; McCarthy & Cambron-McCabe, 1992). Teachers always have a duty to their students to supervise them to prevent foreseeable injury. Parental releases, waivers, and permission slips do not relieve teacher or school of liability if they fail to appropriately discharge their duties. According to Fischer, Schimmel, and Kelly (1994), such waivers may be useful for public relations purposes, but they will not relieve teachers or school officials of possible liability for negligence.

School District Responsibilities Regarding Student Care and Supervision

Schools, school officials, and teachers may have a heightened standard of care for students with disabilities (Mawdsley, 1993). School districts should take actions to make certain that administrators, special education and regular education teachers, and other personnel are aware of their care and supervisory duties under the law (Daggett, 1995; Freedman, 1995; Mawdsley, 1993). (These responsibilities are listed in Figure 16.4). The following are suggestions to assist administrators and teachers in meeting these responsibilities:

- School districts should develop policies regarding standards of care and supervision. These policies should be in writing. Because this area of law changes rapidly, legal developments should be monitored and school policies should be updated when necessary. Additionally, tort laws vary by state, so it is extremely important that school district officials understand tort laws in their states prior to developing policies.

- Special education and regular education teachers, as well as administrators and other staff, should be trained in their responsibilities under the law. Training may be important in convincing a court that a school district acted with care and good faith.

- The IEP team should address potential safety risks and plan for them when appropriate. The IEP should include actions that will be taken to minimize these risks. The listing of precautionary procedures in the IEP provides convincing evidence that a school district has made an effort to prevent student injury. If, on other hand, procedures listed in the IEP are not followed and an injury results, the school's negligence can more easily be proven (Daggett, 1995).

Figure 16.4
Avoiding Liability for Student Injury

- Develop written school district policies regarding care and supervision of students.
- Train administrators, teachers, paraprofessionals, and other staff in responsibilities for care and supervision of students.
- Have the IEP team address potential safety risks for students with disabilities.

For Further Information

FERPA:

Johnson, T. P. (1993). Managing student records: The courts and the Family Educational Rights and Privacy Act of 1974. *Education Law Reporter, 79,* 1–16.

Mawdsley, R. D. (1996). Litigation involving FERPA. *Education Law Reporter, 110,* 897–914.

Providing special education services in private schools:

Mehfoud, K. S. (1994). *Special education services for private school students.* Horsham, PA: LRP Publications.

Providing special education services in parochial schools:

Linden, M. A. (1995). Special educational services and parochial schools: Constitutional constraints and other policy considerations. *Journal of Law and Education, 24,* 345–375.

Teacher liability:

Mawdsley, R. D. (1993). Supervisory standard of care for students with disabilities. *Education Law Reporter, 80,* 779–791.

Pitasky, V. M. (1995). *Liability for injury to special education students.* Horsham, PA: LRP Publications.

References

Agostini v. Felton, 65 LW 4524 (Supreme Court, June 24, 1997).

Aguilar v. Felton, 473 U.S. 402 (1985).

Alexander, K., & Alexander, M. D. (1992). *American public school law.* St. Paul, MN: West Publishing Company.

Alexander v. Boyd, 22 IDELR 139 (D.S.C. 1995).

Anello v. Savignac, 342 N.W. 2d 440 (Wis. Ct. App. 1983).

Aschenbrenner, Letter to, EHLR 211:110 (1979).

Barnett v. Fairfax County School Board, 927 F.2d 146 (4th Cir. 1991).

Board of Education of the Hendrick Hudson School District v. Rowley, 458 U.S. 176 (1982).

Board of Education of Kiryas Joel Village School District v. Grumet, 114 S.Ct. 2481 (1994).

Burlington School Committee v. Department of Education, 471 U.S. 359 (1985).

C.M. v. Southeast Delco School District, 19 IDELR 1084 (E.D. Pa. 1993).

Cefalu v. East Baton Rouge Parish School Board, 25 IDELR 142 (5th Cir. 1996).

Cernosia, Letter to, 22 IDELR 365 (OSEP 1994).

Cohen v. School District, 18 IDELR 911 (1992).

Committee for Public Education v. Nyquist, 413 U.S. 756 (1973).

Daggett, L. M. (April, 1995). *Reasonable schools and special students: Tort liability of school districts and employees for injuries to, or caused by, students with disabilities.* Paper presented at the International Conference of the Council for Exceptional Children, Indianapolis, IN.

Dreher v. Amphitheater Unified School District, 19 IDELR 315 (D.C. AZ, 1992).

Education Department General Administrative Regulations (EDGAR), 34 C.F.R. §§ 76.651–76.662.

Everson v. Board of Education, 330 U.S. 1 (1947).

Fagan v. Summers, 498 P.2 457 1227 (1978).

Family Educational Rights and Privacy Act (FERPA), 20 U.S.C. § 1232 *et seq.*

Felter v. Cape Girardeau School District, 810 F. Supp. 1062 (E.D. Mo., 1993).

Fischer, L., Schimmel, D., & Kelly, C. (1994). *Teachers and the law* (3rd ed.). White Plains, NY: Longman.

Foster v. Houston General, 407 So.2d 758 (1981).

Fowler v. Unified School District, 25 IDELR 348 (10th Cir. 1996).

Frank v. New Orleans Parish School Board, 195 So. 2d 451 (La. Ct. App. 1967).

Freedman, M. (August, 1995). *Substance and shadows: Potential liability of schools and school personnel in special education cases.* Paper presented at the Seventh Utah Institute on Special Education Law and Practice, Salt Lake City, UT.

Garret v. Olson, 691 P. 2d 123 (Or. Ct. App. 1984).

Goodall v. Stafford County School Board, 930 F.2d 363 (4th Cir. 1991).

Gorn, S. (1996). *What do I do when . . . The answer book on special education law.* Horsham, PA: LRP Publications.

Grand Rapids School District v. Ball, 473 U.S. 373 (1985).

Guernsey, T. F., & Klare, K. (1993). *Special education law.* Durham, NC: Carolina Academic Press.

Individuals with Disabilities Education Act (IDEA), 20 U.S.C. § 1401 *et seq.*

Individuals with Disabilities Education Act Amendments of 1997, Pub. L. No. 105–17, 105th Cong., 1st sess.

Individuals with Disabilities Education Act Regulations, 34 C.F.R. § 300.1 *et seq.*

Irvine Unified School District, 23 IDELR 911 (FPCO, 1995).

Johnson, T. P. (1993). Managing student records: The courts and the Family Educational Rights and Privacy Act of 1974. *Education Law Reporter, 79,* 1–16.

K.L. v. Southeast Delco School District, 20 IDELR 244 (E.D. Pa. 1993).

K.R. v. Anderson Community School Corporation, 887 F. Supp. 1217 (S.D. IND. 1995), *aff'd,* 81 F.3d 673 (7th Cir. 1996).

Kluka v. Livingston Parish Board, 433 So.2d 213 (1983).

Know your obligations to serve private school students. (1995, August 8). *The Special Educator, 11*(2), 5.

Lemon v. Kurtzman, 403 U.S. 602 (1971).

Levitt v. Committee for Public Education, 413 U.S. 472 (1973).

Linden, M. A. (1995). Special educational services and parochial schools: Constitutional constraints and other policy considerations. *Journal of Law and Education, 24,* 345–375.

Marshfield School District, 23 IDELR 198 (SEA ME 1995).

Mawdsley, R. D. (1993). Supervisory standard of care for students with disabilities. *Education Law Reporter, 80,* 779–791.

Mawdsley, R. D. (1996). Litigation involving FERPA. *Education Law Reporter, 110,* 897–914.

McCarthy, M. M., & Cambron-McCabe, N. H. (1992). *Public school law: Teachers' and students' rights* (3rd ed.). Boston: Allyn & Bacon.

McKinney, J. R. (1993). Special education and the establishment clause in the wake of *Zobrest:* Back to the future. *Education Law Reporter, 85,* 587–599.

Meek v. Pittenger, 421 U.S. 349 (1975).

Mehfoud, K. S. (1994). *Special education services for private school students.* Horsham, PA: LRP Publications.

Mentink, Letter to, 18 IDELR 276 (OSERS, 1991).

Moore, Letter to, 20 IDELR 1213 (OSEP 1993).

OSEP Policy letter, 17 IDELR 1117 (OSEP 1991).

Pitasky, V. M. (1995). *Liability for injury to special education students.* Horsham, PA: LRP Publications.

Russman v. Sobol, 22 IDELR 1028 (N.D.N.Y. 1995), *aff'd,* 85 F.3d 1050 (2nd Cir. 1996).

Sansone v. Bechtel, 429 A.2d 820 (Conn. 1980).

Schimmel, D. (1994). *Kiryas Joel Village School District v. Grumet:* The establishment clause controversy continues. *Education Law Reporter, 94,* 685–697.

Schipp, Letter to, 23 IDELR 442 (OSEP 1995).

Schmidt, Letter to, 20 IDELR 1224 (OSERS 1993).

Scott v. Greenville, 48 S.E. 2d 324 (1965).

Sheehan v. St. Peter's Catholic School, 188 N.W. 2d 868 (Minn. 1971).

Thomas, S. B., & Russo, C. J. (1995). *Special education law: Issues and implications for the 90's.* Topeka, KS: National Organization on Legal Problems in Education.

Tribble v. Montgomery County Board of Education 19 IDELR 102 (1992).

Valente, W. D. (1994). *Law in the schools* (3rd ed.). Upper Saddle River, NJ: Merrill/Prentice Hall.

Williams, Letter to, 18 IDELR 742 (OSEP, 1992).

Wing, Letter to, EHLR 211:414 (OSEP 1986).

Work v. McKenzie, 661 F. Supp. 225 (D.D.C. 1987).

Zobrest v. Catalina Foothills School District, 113 S.Ct. 2462 (1993).

Relevant Sections of
the U.S. Constitution

* * *

Preamble

We the people of the United States, in order to form a more perfect union, establish justice, insure domestic tranquillity, provide for the common defense, promote the general welfare, and secure the blessings of liberty to ourselves and our posterity, do ordain and establish this Constitution for the United States of America.

* * *

Article 1

Section VIII. [1] The Congress shall have power to lay and collect taxes, duties, imposts and excises, to pay the debts and provide for the common defence and general welfare of the United States. . .

* * *

Article III

Section I. The judicial power of the United States shall be vested in one Supreme Court, and in such inferior courts as the Congress may from time to time ordain and establish. . .

* * *

Article VI

[2] This Constitution, and the laws of the United States which shall be made in pursuance thereof . . . shall be the supreme law of the land; and the judges in every State shall be bound thereby, anything in the Constitution or laws of any State to the contrary notwithstanding.

* * *

Amendment I

Congress shall make no law respecting an establishment of religion, or prohibiting the free exercise thereof; or abridging the freedom of speech or of the press; or the right of the people peaceably to assemble, and to petition the Government for a redress of grievances.

* * *

Amendment IV

The right of the people to be secure in their persons, houses, papers, and effects, against unreasonable searches and seizures, shall not be violated, and no warrants shall issue but upon probable cause, supported by oath or affirmation, and particularly describing the place to be searched, and the persons or things to be seized.

* * *

Amendment V

No person shall be . . . compelled in any criminal case to be a witness against himself, nor be deprived of life, liberty or property, without due process of law; nor shall private property be taken for public use without just compensation.

* * *

Amendment X

The powers not delegated to the United States by the Constitution, nor prohibited by it to the States, are reserved to the States respectively, or to the people.

* * *

Amendment XI

The judicial power of the United States shall not be construed to extend to any suit in law or equity, commended or prosecuted against one of the United States by citizens of another State . . .

* * *

Amendment XIV

Section I. All persons born or naturalized in the United States, and subject to the jurisdiction thereof, are citizens of the United States and of the State wherein they reside. No State shall make or enforce any law which shall abridge the privileges or immunities of citizens of the United States; nor shall any state deprive any person of life, liberty or property, without due process of law; nor deny to any person within its jurisdiction the equal protection of the laws.

GLOSSARY

ADA   Americans with Disabilities Act.

Affirm   When a higher court upholds the opinion of a lower court in an appeal.

Amicus curiae   "Friend of the court." A person (or organization) who is allowed to appear in court or file arguments with the court even though he or she is not a party to the suit.

Appeal   A request to a higher court requesting a review of the decision of a lower court to correct mistakes or an improper ruling.

Appellate court   A court that has jurisdiction to review decisions by lower courts but which does not have the power to hear a case initially.

Case law   Law developed by courts (also called common law).

Certiorari   A request to a higher court to review a decision of a lower court. The request can be refused.

C.F.R.   *Code of Federal Regulations.*

Civil case   All lawsuits other than criminal proceedings. Usually brought by one person against another, and usually involves monetary damages.

Class action   A lawsuit brought by a person on behalf of all persons in similar situations. To bring such a suit, the person must meet certain statutory criteria.

Consent decree.   An agreement by the parties in a lawsuit, sanctioned by the court, that settles the matter.

Defendant   The person a legal action is brought against. At the appeals stage this person is the appellee.

De minimus   Trivial or unimportant matter.

Dicta   The part of an opinion in which the court discusses the reasoning behind the court's ruling. It is not binding. The singular is *dictum.*

DOE   Department of Education.

Due process   A phrase introduced in the Fifth Amendment to the Constitution. Although the phrase does not have a fixed meaning, it generally refers to an established course for judicial proceedings or other governmental activities designed to safeguard the legal rights of individuals.

EAHCA   Education for All Handicapped Children Act (renamed the Individuals with Disabilities Education Act in 1990).

En banc   "In the bench." When a full panel of judges hears a case.

Et al.   The term means "and others." When it appears in the opinion it signifies that unnamed parties went before the court.

Et seq.   The term means "and following." It is used in a legal citation to indicate the sections that follow the cited section.

F.2d   *Federal Reporter, Second Series.* The reporter contains selected rulings of the U.S. Courts of Appeals. Published by West Publishing Company.

F.3d   *Federal Reporter, Third Series.* The reporter contains selected rulings of the U.S. Courts of Appeals. Published by West Publishing Company.

FAPE   Free appropriate public education.

FERPA   Family Educational Rights and Privacy Act.

F. Supp.   *The Federal Supplement.* The supplement contains selected decisions of federal district courts. Published by West Publishing Company.

Guardian ad litem   A guardian appointed by the court to represent a minor.

HCPA   Handicapped Children's Protection Act.

Holding   The part of a judicial opinion in which the law is applied to the facts of the case. The ruling.

IDEA   Individuals with Disabilities Education Act.

Informed consent   When a person agrees to let an action take place. The decision must be based on a full disclosure of the relevant facts.

Injunction   A court order requiring a person or entity to do something or refrain from taking a particular action.

In re   "In the matter of." This prefix is often used in a case in which a child is involved.

LEA   Local educational agency (i.e., local school district).

LRE   Least restrictive environment.

Manifestation determination   An inquiry into whether a student's misbehavior was related to his or her disability. If there is a relationship, the student cannot be suspended for over 10 days or expelled. If there is no relationship, however, the student may be disciplined in the same manner as a student without disabilities, including long-term suspension or expulsion.

Negligence   Failure to exercise a reasonable degree of care that a person would normally exercise under similar circumstances.

OCR   Office of Civil Rights.

Opinion   Judges' statement of a decision reached in a case. It consists of the dicta and the ruling.

OSEP   Office of Special Education Programs.

OSERS   Office of Special Education and Rehabilitative Services.

Petitioner   A person who initiates a judicial proceeding and requests that relief be granted.

P.L. 94-142   The number of the Education of All Handicapped Children Act of 1975. It means the bill was a public law, the 142nd bill passed by the 94th Congress.

Plaintiff   A person who initiates a lawsuit.

Precedent   A court decision that gives direction to lower courts on how to decide similar questions of law in cases with similar facts.

Procedural rights   Rules that guarantee procedural fairness. The exact nature of procedural rights varies according to context.

Remand   To send back. A higher court may send back a ruling to a lower court with directions from the higher court.

Respondent   A person who responds to a lawsuit.

SEA   State educational agency.

Sectarian   Church-related.

Section 504   Section 504 of the Rehabilitation Act of 1973.

Sine qua non   An indispensable part or condition.

Stare decisis   "To stand by that which was decided." Similar to precedent.

Substantive rights   Generally refers to the rights and duties of parties. The exact nature of substantive rights varies according to context.

Tort   A civil wrong done by one person to another.

U.S.C.   *United States Code.*

Vacate   When a higher court overturns or sets aside the opinion of a lower court in an appeal.

INDEX
OF CASES

AUTHOR
INDEX

SUBJECT INDEX